# Prescribing Ovid

Heerkens aged sixty-six, perhaps holding a volume of Ovid.
*Source*: Augustus Christiaan Hauck and Friedrich Ludwig Hauck, *Dr. Gerhardus Nicolaas Heerkens*, oil on canvas, 1792. Courtesy of the Groninger Museum.

# Prescribing Ovid

## The Latin Works and Networks of the Enlightened Dr Heerkens

Yasmin Haskell

BLOOMSBURY
LONDON • NEW DELHI • NEW YORK • SYDNEY

**Bloomsbury Academic**
An imprint of Bloomsbury Publishing Plc

| | |
|---|---|
| 50 Bedford Square | 1385 Broadway |
| London | New York |
| WC1B 3DP | NY 10018 |
| UK | USA |

www.bloomsbury.com

**Bloomsbury is a registered trade mark of Bloomsbury Publishing Plc**

First published 2013
Paperback edition first published 2014

© Yasmin Haskell, 2013

Yasmin Haskell has asserted her right under the Copyright, Designs and Patents Act, 1988, to be identified as Author of this work.

All rights reserved. No part of this publication may be reproduced or transmitted in any form or by any means, electronic or mechanical, including photocopying, recording, or any information storage or retrieval system, without prior permission in writing from the publishers.

No responsibility for loss caused to any individual or organization acting on or refraining from action as a result of the material in this publication can be accepted by Bloomsbury or the author.

**British Library Cataloguing-in-Publication Data**
A catalogue record for this book is available from the British Library.

ISBN: HB:   978-0-7156-3723-4
        PB:   978-1-4725-8750-3

**Library of Congress Cataloging-in-Publication Data**
Haskell, Yasmin Annabel.
Prescribing Ovid : the Latin works and networks of the enlightened
Dr Heerkens / Yasmin Haskell.
pages. cm.
Includes bibliographical references and index.
ISBN 978-0-7156-3723-4 (hardcover)
1. Heerkens, Gerard Nicolaas, 1726-1801. 2. Latin literature, Medieval and modern–History and criticism. I. Title.
PA8524.H34Z68 2013
871'.04--dc23
2012043450

Typeset by Newgen Imaging Systems Pvt Ltd, Chennai, India

*For my mother, and in loving memory of my father*

# Contents

List of Figures ix

Acknowledgements xi

Introduction: Cultivating the Two Apollos 1
1 Finding His Feet: Six or Five? 33
2 Stepping Out: Healing the Republic of Letters 71
3 Tomi Calling: Letters to/from Italy 105
4 Writing Home: Lessons from Italy 129
5 Patriots in Portraits: From National to Natural History 155
6 Inscriptions and Prescriptions: The Art of Healing in Long and Short 199
Conclusion: Notes from the Margins 227

Appendix: Published Works of Gerard Nicolaas Heerkens 239
Bibliography 247
Index 260

# List of Figures

Heerkens aged sixty-six, perhaps holding a volume of Ovid     ii
Figure 1.1 The Dutch poetess, Clara Feyoena van Sytzama     34
Figure 2.1 Heerkens discussing the causes for Ovid's exile     96
Figure 3.1 Cornelius Valerius Vonck     106
Figure 3.2 Elegy to Cardinal Angelo Maria Querini     113
Figure 5.1 *Alauda* – The Lark     183
Figure 5.2 Heerkens's epitaph for the trusty dog he adopted in Italy     198

# Acknowledgements

It is a pleasure to acknowledge the many colleagues and friends who have contributed their ideas and advice to this book, beginning with my research associates in the Australian Research Council Discovery project, 'Mapping the Latin Enlightenment': Jan Waszink, Maurizio Campanelli and Agata Pincelli. In particular, Jan Waszink identified important collections of manuscript letters in Leiden and The Hague and was most spectacularly successful in tracking down a distant relative of our author, Mrs H. C. J. Canter Cremers-Kappeijne v.d. Copello of Rotterdam, who kindly provided access to copies of some of the lost correspondence consulted by Heerkens's nineteenth-century biographer. Gerda Huisman at the University Library of Groningen was a miracle of helpfulness and bibliographical revelations. I also thank the rare books librarians and archivists of Leiden University Library, the Museum Meermanno-Westreenianum, the Biblioteca Queriniana, the Regionaal Archief Alkmaar, the Houghton library at Harvard University and bookseller, Thierry Bodin, for supplying copies of or allowing us to photograph manuscript sources.

I was very fortunate to enjoy visiting research fellowships at All Souls and Christ Church colleges, Oxford, in 2009 and 2011. I have spoken on Heerkens to audiences in Uppsala, Naples, Oxford, Cambridge, Paris, Brisbane, Perth, Sydney and Zagreb, and warmly thank for their kind invitations: Hans Helander; Siegfried Zielinski and the 'Variantology' group; Richard Yeo; Peter Holbrook, Peter Cryle and the Centre for the History of European Discourses; Anna Clark and Matthew Leigh of the Oxford Philological Society; Philip Ford and many old friends in the Cambridge Society for Neo-Latin Studies; Koen Vermeir and Karine Chemla at the Centre national de recherche scientifique; Terence Cave, Olivia Smith and Karin Kukkonnen of the Balzan Research Project at St John's College, Oxford; Neven Jovanović and the Philosophy Faculty at the University of Zagreb; and the Australian Research Council Network for Early European Research.

Some parts of this book appear in different shapes and lengths as 'A Dutch doctor's observations on the health of scholars, young and old: Gerard Nicolaas Heerkens's *De valetudine litteratorum* (Leiden, 1749; Rheims, 1749; Groningen, 1790)', in Maria Berggren and Christer Henriksén (eds), *Miraculum eruditionis: Neo-Latin Studies in Honour of Hans Helander* (Uppsala: Uppsala Universitet, 2007), pp. 151–65; 'Latin Poet-Doctors of the Eighteenth Century: The German Lucretius (Johann Ernst Hebenstreit) versus the Dutch Ovid (Gerard Nicolaas Heerkens)', *Intellectual History Review* 18 (2008), pp. 91–101; 'Finding his way home? The Groningener physician Gerard Nicolaas Heerkens and the road back from Rome', in *De Oudheid in de Achttiende Eeuw/Classical Antiquity in the Eighteenth Century* (Utrecht: Uitgave Werkgroep 18e Eeuw, 2012), pp. 139–45; and 'Physician, heal thyself! Emotions and the Health of the Learned in Samuel Auguste André David Tissot (1728–1797) and Gerard Nicolaas Heerkens (1728–1801)', in Henry Martyn Lloyd (ed.), 'The Discourse of Sensibility: The Knowing Body in the Enlightenment', Special Issue of *Studies in History and Philosophy of Science* (forthcoming).

For assistance with translations and bibliography, for the solving of puzzles big and small, as well as for all kinds of practical and moral support, my sincere thanks go to Pam Bond, Paola Bertucci, Susan Broomhall, Nicholas Cronk, Jane Davidson, Antonella Deledda, K. D. Fischer, Philip Ford, Allison Goudie, Susan Griffiths, Philip Hardie, Sarah Hay, Brett Hirsch, Manfred Horstmanshof, Danijela Kambasković-Sawers, Martyn Lloyd, Walther Ludwig, Elena Lugli, Ian Maclean, Philippa Maddern, Noel Malcolm, Jenna and Philip Mead, David Money, Krister Östlund, Tim Pitman, Harry de Raad, Lex Raat, Claudia Rapp, Juanita Ruys, Dirk Sacré, Stéphane Schmitt, Geoffrey Shellam, Richard Small, Jacob Soll, Giovanni Tarantino, Jacques Tersteeg, Corinna Vermeulen, Jos van Heel, Dirk van Miert, Zweder von Martels, Brenda Walker and Anne Vila.

Deborah Blake, who originally commissioned this book for Duckworth, has been encouraging and accommodating for more years than she probably bargained for. My colleague, Lesley O'Brien, whipped an un-house-trained typescript into line at the last minute with her hallmark patience and precision.

My mother, Janetta, first guided me through Worp's entertaining Dutch biography of Heerkens over a hot Perth Christmas in 2006. We had fun reading about our author's consistently nifty footwork in avoiding the matrimonial dressing gown (*kamerjapon*)! This book is dedicated to her, and to the memory of my father, John, in celebration of their fiftieth wedding anniversary last year.

# Introduction: Cultivating the Two Apollos

## Touring the Latin Enlightenment

To compose one's life in Latin verse, to make one's *living* out of Latin verse, might seem an unlikely ambition for an eighteenth-century Dutch gentleman who wanted to be thought smart and contemporary. The subject of this book, Groningen physician Gerard Nicolaas Heerkens, not only accomplished that doubly dubious feat, but it was precisely his flair for Latin verse that facilitated his entry into some of the most élite literary and scientific circles of the day, including those of the notoriously Latinophobic *philosophes*. Understanding how and why the well-travelled Heerkens contrived to live as a cosmopolitan Latin humanist between (climatically, at least) gloomy Groningen and the big smoke of Voltaire's Paris, coming and going, and commenting on his comings and goings in the guise of a worldly Frisian[1] Ovid, is the first aim of this book. In the process I hope to reveal some of the contours of a relatively unexplored intellectual landscape of the late seventeenth and eighteenth centuries, which we shall call the 'Latin Enlightenment'. Far from being a contradiction in terms, the Latin Enlightenment, I suggest, has a legitimate and urgent claim to join the assorted national, radical, moderate, religious and now even 'super', Enlightenments jostling for the attention of intellectual and literary historians of the long eighteenth century.[2]

---

[1] The province of Groningen was part of Frisia until the eighth century, and Heerkens regularly adopts the 'Frisian' tag to describe his native land.

[2] For example Roy Porter and Mikuláš Teich, *The Enlightenment in National Context* (Cambridge: Cambridge University Press, 1981); Jonathan I. Israel, *Radical Enlightenment: Philosophy and the Making of Modernity 1650–1750* (Oxford: Oxford University Press, 2002) and idem, *Enlightenment Contested: Philosophy, Modernity, and the Emancipation of Man 1670–1752* (Oxford: Oxford University Press, 2006); John Robertson, *The Case for the Enlightenment: Scotland and Naples 1680–*

Of course, it has not gone unnoticed by intellectual historians that Latin maintained part of its traditional empire in scholarship and the sciences well into the eighteenth century, even if the Latin used in university dissertations and scientific writing did not always evince the highest aspirations to stylistic elegance.[3] On the other hand, 'humanist' Latin was by no means the exclusive preserve of unengaged, belletristic writers. Philosophers, theologians, jurists and political writers of all persuasions cultivated a classicizing, if not literary, Latin throughout the early modern period. One group that continued to exploit and to some extent define themselves by it was that of learned physicians.[4] Viewed from the perspective of, say, a Johannes Cuspinianus (1473–1529) or a Johannes Sambucus (1531–84), Heerkens's dual commitment first to medicine and (Latin) poetry, then to history and archaeology, does not in fact appear that novel. He may be seen as bringing up the tail of a respectable line of physician–scholar–historian poets reaching back to the late Renaissance.[5] But Heerkens's Latin was also a quite distinctive flower. Derived from Italian Renaissance stocks, propagated in the rich soil of late baroque German Jesuit humanism, it was crossed with the vigorous chromatic strains of Dutch religious and political classics from Erasmus through Hugo Grotius and

---

*1760* (Cambridge: Cambridge University Press, 2003); David Sorkin, *The Religious Enlightenment: Protestants, Jews, and Catholics from London to Vienna* (Princeton: Princeton University Press, 2008); Franco Venturi, *Settecento Riformatore. III, La prima crisi dell'Antico Regime (1768-1776)* (Turin: Einaudi, 1979); Daniel Edelstein's digital archive 'The Super-Enlightenment', Stanford University Libraries, <http://collections.stanford.edu/supere/>; Ulrich L. Lehner and Michael Printy (eds), *A Companion to the Catholic Enlightenment in Europe* (Leiden: Brill, 2010).

[3] Isabelle Pantin, 'Latin et langues vernaculaires dans la littérature scientifique européenne au début de l'époque moderne (1550-1635)', in R. Chartier and P. Corsi (eds), *Sciences et langues en Europe* (Paris: E.H.E.S.S., 1996), pp. 43-58; idem, 'The Role of Translations in European Scientific Exchanges (XVIth-XVIIth centuries)', in Peter Burke and Ronnie Hsia (eds), *Cultural Translation in Early Modern Europe* (Cambridge: Cambridge University Press, 2007), pp. 163-79; Peter Burke, *Languages and Communities in Early Modern Europe* (Cambridge: Cambridge University Press, 2004); Peter Burke, 'Translations into Latin in Early Modern Europe', in Burke and Hsia (eds), *Cultural Translation*, pp. 65-80; Emmanuel Bury (ed.), *Tous vos gens à Latin: Le latin, langue savante, langue mondaine (XIVe-XVIIe siècles)* (Geneva: Droz, 2005); Hans Helander, *Neo-latin Literature in Sweden in the Period 1620-1720: Stylistics, Vocabulary & Chracteristic Ideas* (Uppsala: Uppsala Universitet, 2004); Claudia Stancati, '"Mais j'en écrirai en latin" Latin as an "Epilanguage" in Descartes' Philosophy', in Pascale Hummel (ed.), *Epilanguages: Beyond Idioms and Languages* (Paris: Philologicum, 2009), pp. 52-69.

[4] K.-D. Fischer, 'Medici poetae de sanitate conservanda', *Vox Latina* 42 (fasc. 94) (1988), pp. 472-85; Dirk Sacré, 'An Imitator of Fracastorius's *Syphilis*: Gadso Coopmans (1746-1810) and his *Varis*', *Humanistica Lovaniensia* 45 (1996), pp. 520-38; Philip Ford, 'Claude Quillet's *Callipaedia* (1655): Eugenics Treatise or Pregnancy Manual?', in Yasmin Haskell and Philip Hardie (eds), *Poets and Teachers: Latin Didactic Poetry and the Didactic Authority of Latin Poet from the Renaissance to the Present* (Bari: Levante Editori, 1999), pp. 125-39; Yasmin Haskell and Susan Broomhall (eds), 'Humanism and Medicine in the Early Modern Era', special issue of *Intellectual History Review* 18.1 (2008).

[5] Nancy G. Siraisi, *History, Medicine, and the Traditions of Renaissance Learning* (Ann Arbor: University of Michigan Press, 2007); cf. Gianna Pomata and Nancy Siraisi (eds), *Historia: Empiricism and Erudition in Early Modern Europe* (Massachussets: MIT Press, 2005).

Justus Lipsius; and it was fertilized by the Latin writing of eighteenth-century Italy, which was experiencing an efflorescence that has not been adequately appreciated by modern scholars.[6] Suffice it to say that Heerkens's Latin was *organic*, not merely a convenient tool for dispassionate scientific communication. We shall see, moreover, that it had a culturally healing significance, and to that end was consciously employed by him for the preservation and perpetuation of traditional (not necessarily defunct...) literary and scientific discourses.

Perhaps Heerkens's best claim to be noticed by the historian of the Enlightenment, however, lies in his having played the role of unsuspected Latin Boswell to the stars. Observing from behind the scenes our affable, apparently innocuous, Dutch mole reports in delicious detail, in verse and prose, on his conversations with French and Italian men of letters and science – academicians, physicians, priests and politicians – conversations about religion, philosophy, medicine and, not least, the 'Latin question'. Over the course of half a century he sends periodic despatches from the frontline on the battle between Latin and French for European cultural domination. Towards the end of his life, cutting a pitiful and even paranoid figure in a place (Groningen) and a time (Batavian revolution) more than a little hostile to his internationalist pretensions, Heerkens is reduced to fighting a rear-guard action, proclaiming the United Provinces the last bastion of Latin humanism against the onslaught of the French language, the latter now so polluted with Parisian neologisms that even provincial Frenchmen can no longer understand it.[7] But when he was in his prime, mid-century, it is less

---

[6] As Maurizio Campanelli has shown in a recent series of articles, many Italians of this period considered Latin to be a more important national language than the Tuscan dialect, and believed that they were living in a new Renaissance: 'Settecento Latino I', *L'Ellisse. Studi storici di letteratura italiana* 2 (2007), pp. 99–133; idem, 'Settecento Latino II', *L'Ellisse. Studi storici di letteratura italiana* 3 (2008), pp. 85–110; and idem, 'Dal Colosseo alla Fontana di Trevi, da Piranesi a Winckelmann: una satira sull'architettura nella Roma del 1763', *Atti e Memorie dell'Arcadia*, n.s. 1 (forthcoming). In 1791, a defender of Italian, Galeani Napione, wrote that Latin had no need of apologies – namely the many that had appeared since d'Alembert's attacks, since 'we can be proud that our century will be considered by right-minded posterity as the most fortunate age of Latin since the Renaissance'. Galeani Napione is quoted by Giulio Natali, *Il Settecento*, 2 vols, 6th edn (Milan, 1964), I, p. 472.

[7] In the preface to the second edition of his *Empedocles sive Physicorum epigrammatum libri septem* (a collection of epigrams on health) (Groningen, 1798), Heerkens commends his Latin work to the most cultivated Jacobus van der Steege, senator in Groningen: 'It comes out at a time which is indeed most hostile to Latin literature, but among a people which has been most devoted to this literature from the time of Erasmus. Has any other nation, enclosed within such narrow borders, established five Academies for this language? They all seem to have been losing heart now for some years, it's true; while no work from any of them appeared for ten years, note that Jacob Henry Hoeufft's Muse has been published to great applause twice in the past three years. And within that triennium the much desiderated Anthology of Grotius, a huge work, requiring a considerable outlay, has been published for the learned world. Let's not forget the Muses of [Jan Adam] Nodell and [Henri Collet] d'Escury which have recently shown themselves to the light on the Meuse. Accordingly, then, the hope of the Latin language rests in the

clear that Heerkens's choice of Latin signalled resigned allegiance with beleaguered 'ancients' against ascendant 'moderns', or with social and religious conservatives against more secular and progressive voices in politics and culture. Through his twenties and thirties, when he was dining out on Latin verse in Paris and Padua, Heerkens could be forgiven for believing that he was riding the crest of a new wave of modern Latinity, a wave that promised to bring him fame, fortune and even more famous friends.[8]

But where did Heerkens and members of his wider Latin-writing networks sit in relation to the major intellectual trends of the day? A desultory reading of the *philosophes* – above all, d'Alembert – would suggest that 'Latin Enlightenment' is, indeed, a contradiction in terms; that Latin literature was a fast-fading footnote by the middle of the eighteenth century. In his preface to the *Encyclopédie*, d'Alembert conceded the usefulness of Latin as a scientific language but – prematurely, if not mischievously – declared its use to be in general decline.[9] This was of course not a new view in France. Seventeenth-century style-setter Nicolas Boileau-Despréaux, though a partisan and imitator of the *anciens*, had expressed contempt for modern Latin poetry in his letters to Brosette.[10] One of the subsidiary aims of the present book is to provide an aperçu on a more nuanced topography

poets of our people alone' ('Tempore quidem prodit, scriptis Latinis iniquissimo, inter gentem tamen, ab Erasmi aevo his literis deditam maxime. Tamque arctis inclusa finibus ecqua gentium quinque huic linguae fundavit Academias? Eae quidem omnes jam ab aliquot annis videntur despondere: nullumque illae dum a bilustri jam tempore Latinum ostentant luci antecessoris cujusdam sui opusculum, vide Musam Jacobi Henrici Hoeuftii bis jam se à triennio cum plausu ostendisse. Intraque triennium Hieronymus Boschius Amstelodamensis, desideratissimam Grotii Anthologiam, grande, et sumptu indigens opus, docto ostendit orbi. Quin et ad Mosam recens Nodellii et Descurii adolescentis Musae luci se obtulere. Solis proinde nostratium poetis spes de Latina superest lingua', p. i).

[8] This, I suspect, in spite of his intermittent complaints even then about the challenges faced by Latin letters in France, for example in his poem on the health of the learned *De valetudine litteratorum* (1749) (see Chapter 2), and in *De officio medici* (Groningen, 1752), his poem on the duties of the doctor (see Chapter 6), and in the verse letter to Jean-Jacques le Franc accompanying it. Cf. the dedicatory poem to Heerkens's revised satires (*Marii Curilli Groningensis Satyrae* (Groningen, 1758)), to Brescian physician, Count Francesco Roncalli Parolino (1692–1763).

[9] Cf. his dissertation, 'Sur l'harmonie des langues, et en particulier sur celle qu'on croit sentir dans les langues mortes; et a cette occasion sur la latinité des modernes' ('On the harmony of languages, and in particular on that which one is believed to hear in the dead languages, and on this occasion, on modern Latinity'): 'Mais autant il serait à souhaiter qu'on n'écrivît jamais des ouvrage de goût que dans sa propre langue, autant il serait utile ques les ouvrages de science, comme de géométrie, de physique, de médecine, d'érudition même, ne fussent écrits qu'en langue latine, c'est-à-dire dans une langue qu'il n'est pas necessaire en ces cas-là de parler élégamment, mais qui est familière à presque soient placés. C'est un voeu que nous avons fait il y a long-temps, mais que nous n'espérons pas de voir réaliser' (*Œuvres de d'Alembert*, 5 vols (Paris, 1821-2), IV (1822), p. 25).

[10] For example in his letter to Brossette of 6 October 1701. Some neo-Latin poets aspired or dared to translate Boileau's works into Latin, for example François Gacon, discussed by Christopher Allen in 'Boileau's *Art poétique* Latinized', in Yasmin Haskell and Juanita Feros Ruys (eds), *Latinity and Alterity in the Early Modern Period* (Tempe, AZ: ACMRS, 2010), pp. 79–96.

of eighteenth-century intellectual and cultural life by illuminating its Latin dimension. We reserve judgement on whether Latin writers either routinely resisted or even blindly echoed 'mainstream' Enlightenment views. Sometimes, it would seem, they were simply carrying on their own, discrete, conversations. If nothing else, Heerkens's accounts of his travels in the German-speaking lands, in France and in Italy, of his meetings with scholars and scientists, physicians and antiquarians, priests and politicians, provide us with an excellent opportunity to calibrate different attitudes to what constituted knowledge in this period. What was it necessary to know, in which contexts, and how did one demonstrate what one knew to the people that mattered? Our exploration of Heerkens's Latin circles and conversations vis-à-vis those he conducted in French and Dutch may thus serve as a case study in the linguistic dimension to eighteenth-century knowledge production across different regional, professional, religio- and intellectual–political settings.

Gerard Nicolaas Heerkens was a cosmopolitan Latin-using intellectual keen to distinguish himself both as a man of the latest science *and* culture, both as a sensitive student of historical, *and* a critical observer of modern, manners. As such, he does not sit comfortably under the exclusive rubrics of crusty *érudit* or dilettante *bel esprit*. In addition to many books of elegiac verses on medicine and natural history, Heerkens wrote satires of contemporary French and Dutch literary life, poetic portraits of historical kings and present-day notables, and speculated in verse and prose on ancient monuments and manuscripts. But while these elements crystallize to some extent around the typical and traditional interests of the late Renaissance humanist physician,[11] the nature, range and regularity of Heerkens's literary outputs, in this period at least, beg the question of his primary vocation. Is he a medical 'professional' doing Latin poetry on the side, or a poet who finds his feet, as it were, in learned medicine? And for whom is he writing? These questions can only begin to be answered once we have become better acquainted with Heerkens's Latin works and networks. In what follows I furnish a makeshift scaffold of the life around which these works and networks were almost compulsively constructed – and vice versa.

---

[11] See Pomata and Siraisi (eds), *Historia: Empiricism and Erudition*, esp. Introduction; and Siraisi, *History, Medicine*, passim.

## A Dutch Ovid is born, and a father frets

In Kleinemeer, a small peat colony near Sappemeer in the province of Groningen, in the remote Protestant north of the Netherlands, a Catholic boy learned to love the Muses from his father, Eppo Johannes Ignatius Heerkens.[12] Young Gerard Nicolaas's literary talents were nurtured by the Jesuits of Meppen, in Westphalia, for whom he maintained a lifelong affection. It was from Meppen, however, that he fled the rigours of the Jesuit philosophy curriculum for the paternal home and library, to be reunited, all too briefly, with his beloved Catullus and Ovid.[13] Eppo was determined to see his eldest son graduate into a profitable profession, but, when Gerard Nicolaas made no progress in the law after a year at the University of Groningen, the old man relented, or, at least, did not now stand in the way of our author's long-cherished dream of studying medicine.[14] Under the pseudonym 'Curillus', the teenaged Heerkens made his sensational poetic debut in Groningen as a satirist, flagrantly mocking members of the local literary establishment. A full-scale pamphlet war erupted (discussed in Chapter 1), and the young rebel, with three years of law and two of medicine under his belt, had to hightail it to Leiden.[15] As Rina Knoeff has recently reminded us, the town of Leiden held other attractions than the academic. In addition to the university's anatomy theatre, botanical garden, greenhouse, natural history and anatomical collections 'it had excellent facilities for extracurricular activities such as theatre visits, pub crawls, horse riding and boating. Unlike most other universities, the University of Leiden welcomed students of all religious affiliations and it was praised for its "great liberty, the freedom of

---

[12] Gerard Nicolaas Heerkens was born on 8 July 1726. The following sketch of his life is compiled from his published works and letters, from nineteenth-century biographical dictionaries and from J. A. Worp, 'Gerard Nicolaas Heerkens', *Groningsche Volksalmanak voor het jaar 1899* (1898), pp. 1–51. Worp's engaging little biography is rather desultorily documented, however; some of the events he relates were presumably gleaned from lost correspondence once in the possession of Mr E. J. M. I. Canter Cremers in Heerenveen.

[13] See the autobiographical elegy to Cardinal Angelo Maria Querini prefaced to the poem *De officio medici*, pp. 3–16.

[14] It seems that Heerkens persevered in his legal studies for some time after this, and in the preface to the 1790 edition of the *De valetudine literatorum* we learn that he was frequenting the Palais de Justice in Paris during his year there (see below, p. 8).

[15] He later reflects, with nice understatement, that 'my father had seen that I was industrious enough, and equally in both disciplines, but he had a fear about the Muses – he himself had endeared them to me – because some songs published by me had received so little favour' (preface to *Empedocles* (1798), p. ii).

[16] Rina Knoeff, 'Herman Boerhaave at Leiden: *Communis Europae praeceptor*', in Ole Peter Grell, Andrew Cunningham and Jon Arrizabalaga (eds), *Centres of Medical Excellence? Medical Travel*

thinking, speaking and believing".[16] It was during his Leiden university days, at any rate, that Heerkens discovered a mellower way of combining his twin vocations for poetry and medicine (in spite of a prohibition by his father on further versification). Leiden professor of medicine and botany, Adriaan van Royen (1704–79), a correspondent of Linnaeus, had composed several books of elegiac Latin poetry on medical topics. Heerkens's friends encouraged him to follow suit, and his first volume of medical epigrams, *Xenia Physico-Medica*, was published by Elie Luzac in the spring of 1748. In his preface to Groningen philosophy professor and mentor, Nicolaus Engelhard (1696–1765), Heerkens apologizes that he has been absent from Pindus since coming to Leiden; he has, however, composed these Hippocratic verses on the sly ('furtim'), and ventures that they cannot be held against him as they are not detrimental to his medical studies.[17] Even so, Heerkens reveals in a later work that he felt obliged to have his elderly Leiden boon companion, Hamilton, a 'Scot', write to his father and vouch for the fact that he was still in the good books of the local professors.[18]

In the late summer of 1748 our young Groningener travelled to Paris for the first time, to continue his studies under the celebrated medical professors Jean Astruc (1684–1766) and Antoine Ferrein (1693–1769). A charming letter to his parents in Dutch records his first impressions of the metropolis, the price of wine and silk stockings, and the impressive acquaintances he was already beginning to notch up.[19] In the preface to the second edition of his three-book didactic poem, *De valetudine literatorum* ('On the Health of Learned Men', Groningen, 1790), Heerkens confesses that he found Paris rather noisy and overwhelming at first.

---

*and Education in Europe: 1500–1789* (Aldershot: Ashgate, 2010), pp. 269–86, at p. 270, following G. D. J. Schotel, *De Academie te Leiden in de 16e, 17e en 18e Eeuw* (Haarlem, 1875), p. 272. Cf. John C. Powers, 'Herman Boerhaave and the Pedagogical Reform of Eighteenth-Century Chemistry' (unpublished PhD thesis, Indiana University, 2001), p. 46.

[17] The Wolffian Engelhard, a Swiss, was professor of philosophy and mathematics at Groningen. He had originally suggested to Heerkens that he translate Louis Racine's French didactic poem on 'Religion' into Latin. His obliging protégé gave up after two books when he learned that a new edition of that poem was about to hit the Paris presses (*Xenia*, pp. 3–4). Heerkens published an elegiac eulogy for Engelhard in *Journal des sçavans* (August 1765), pp. 262–4. On the latter's philosophical views, see Paul Schuurman, 'Nicolaus Engelhard's Wolffianism (1732)', in Schuurman (ed.), *Ideas, Mental Faculties, and Method: The Logic of Ideas of Descartes and Locke and Its Reception in the Dutch Republic, 1630–1750* (Leiden: Brill, 2004), pp. 110–28; Michiel R. Wielema, 'Nicolaus Engelhard (1696–1765). De Leibniz-Wolffiaanse metafysica in Groningen', in H. Krop, J. A. van Ruler and A. J. Vanderjagt (eds), *Zeer kundige professoren: beoefening van de filosofie in Groningen van 1614 tot 1996* (Hilversum: Verloren, 1997), pp. 149–61.

[18] Thus at *Empedocles* (1798), p. iv. Heerkens is probably referring to the Irishman, Ezechial Hamilton, as suggested by Worp, p. 9. Cf. Esther Myers, 'Irish Students in the Netherlands', *Archivum Hibernicum* 59 (2005), pp. 66–78, at p. 76.

[19] Manuscript letter held in the Rijksarchief in Overijssel, Zwolle (Familie Heerkens: Inv. #1493/64).

The Austrian Netherlands was occupied at the time by the French and our Dutch tourist was frequently stopped for questioning. His anxiety levels had already been raised by the uncouth French soldiers who shared his coach from Brussels. Soon enough, though, the reticent international student began to frequent the Palais de Justice by day, the Comédie française by night, and a local café, the Procope, where he observed and gradually became acquainted with several learned and influential men. Among the cultural celebrities with whom Heerkens came into contact at this time were tragedian and royal censor, Prosper Jolyot de Crébillon (1674–1762); comedy-writer, Alexis Piron (1689–1773); epigrammatist, statesman and later cardinal, François-Joachim de Pierre de Bernis (1715–94); and religious poets Jean-Jacques le Franc, Marquis de Pompignan (1709–84)[20] and Louis Racine (1692–1763), son of the more famous playwright.[21] The dashing abbé and professor of physics, Jean-Antoine Nollet (1700–70), showed him around town and secured him many useful introductions.[22] During his first year in Paris he also regularly visited the elderly abbé d'Olivet, Pierre-Joseph Thouillier (1682–1768), an *académicien* and former Jesuit and teacher of Voltaire.

Heerkens's most stellar Parisian conquest was, undoubtedly, Voltaire himself. In preparation for his first audience with the great man the conscientious postulant attended nine performances of the *Semiramis*, then playing almost continuously at the Comédie française, eventually committing a long passage of it to heart.[23] On the day, we are told, Heerkens won Voltaire over by reciting from recent Dutch translations of the latter's poetry, flattering the Frenchman with imputed connoisseurship of his exotic language. More surprisingly,

---

[20] Elevated to the Academie française in 1760, but effectively blackballed in Paris thereafter for having churlishly attacked the Encyclopedists in his acceptance speech.
[21] With Racine, Heerkens entered into an extensive correspondence. In the collection of Mr Canter Cremers, Worp counted 46 letters from Racine running from 3 February 1749 through to 1 May 1758. Cf. *Cahiers Raciniens* 21 (1969), pp. 78–9, notice of sale by Sotheby and Co., 8 November 1966, where the complete set of 47 letters is advertised. In this correspondence, of some 150 pages, Racine is said to have discussed his own and Heerkens's literary works. Unfortunately the collection has been dispersed. I have only only had access to the three letters held in the University of Groningen library (dated 8 September 1750, 1 October 1750 and 15 November 1750), one in Harvard's Houghton Library (8 March 1750), and one now in private hands, a copy of which was kindly made available to me by Thierry Bodin of 'Les Autographes', Paris (dated 1 May 1758).
[22] On Nollet's travels in Italy in 1749, see Paola Bertucci, *Viaggio nel paese delle meraviglie: scienza e curiosità nell'Italia del Settecento* ('A Journey in Wonderland. Science and Curiosity in Eighteenth-Century Italy') (Turin: Bollati Boringhieri, 2007).
[23] Heerkens had sent ahead the commendatory letter written him by Willem van Haren (*De valetudine literatorum* (1790), p. 11 of unnumbered preface), poet of a pompous, lyrical epic, *Leonidas*, which nevertheless shamed the Dutch Republic into despatching troops to defend Maria Theresa in the War of the Austrian Succession. Van Haren had been praised by Voltaire as 'Démosthène au Conseil et Pindare au Parnasse'. For the correspondence of Heerkens with Willem and Onno van Haren, see H. E. Moltzer (ed.), '*Hareniana*', *brieven van W. en O. Z. Van Haren* (Groningen: J. B. Wolters, 1876).

perhaps, it seems that Voltaire himself solicited and approved his young visitor's opinions on the contemporary pronunciation of *Latin*.[24] Heerkens was charmed, and was to remain an affectionate supporter of his grand old friend for years to come – even if Louis Racine chided his naïve reverence for 'votre cher Voltaire'.

After arriving in Paris, Heerkens tells us that he was forced by straitened financial circumstances to disobey his father, who had strenuously reiterated his prohibition on Latin versifying after the Groningen fiasco. There are, to be sure, shades of Ovidian self-fashioning here, but Eppo's interdict was probably real enough. Heerkens's letters of introduction had failed to open the desired doors in Paris, and he reasoned that his father would not, surely, object if he used his literary talents to gain admission to the city's leading scientific circles. A Latin elegy composed in honour of his former Jesuit teachers in Westphalia, published soon after his arrival, seems to have hit the mark.[25] At Fontenelle's house, Heerkens was encouraged by Pierre de Bernis to improvise some verses on their host's cold feet – a topic on which two distinguished physicians in attendance had hastened to offer their respective learned opinions.[26] The assembled company was astounded at the young Dutchman's impromptu poetic efforts – all except Monsieur d'Alembert, implacable enemy of modern Latin verse.[27] Three months after his arrival in Paris, moreover, a highly laudatory review in the Jesuit *Journal de Trévoux* of some of his juvenile compositions emboldened the adolescent poet.[28] In his old age Heerkens reflects wistfully on those heady Parisian days, on his prodigious youthful productivity: 'It is no

---

[24] Surprising even to Heerkens, who had initially despaired of meeting Voltaire because of his rumoured aversion to contemporary Latin poetry.

[25] A fair copy, if not autograph, of this poem, 'Frisii Poetae Elegia de adventu suo in Galliam', is held in the Rijksarchief in Overijssel, Zwolle (Familie Heerkens: Inv. #1493/75), with an approbation and permission to print signed in Paris by Crebillon and Berrijer (?) on 12 and 15 October 1748 respectively. In the preface to *Empedocles* (1798), Heerkens writes that d'Alembert had 'whispered to many' guests at one of Fontenelle's soirees that this poem had been 'dictated to me by the Jesuits' (p. vi).

[26] The story is told in the prefaces to the second editions of the *De valetudine literatorum* (1790) and *Empedocles* (1798). The latter retelling is more elaborate: it seems that Heerkens's French patrons were encouraging him to continue in the genre of medical epigram, but he intermitted this work, he says, because he had already embarked on his long didactic poem on the health of learned men (pp. vi–vii).

[27] The cultivation of humanistic Latin by modern *literary* writers was, according to d'Alembert in the Preliminary Discourse to the *Encyclopédie*, 'ridiculous'. (I thank Hans Helander for bringing this passage to my attention some years ago.) D'Alembert's most concerted attack, however, is contained in his 'Sur l'harmonie des langues, et en particulier sur celle qu'on croit sentir dans les langues mortes; et a cette occasion, sur la latinité des modernes' (*Œuvres de d'Alembert*, IV, pt 1, pp. 11–28). Cf. (*inter alia*) his article 'Collège' in the third volume of the *Encyclopédie*. D'Alembert was far from immune to the charms of Latin literature and published a translation of Tacitus in 1758.

[28] Preface to *De valetudine literatorum* (1790), p. x. The review to which Heerkens refers (December 1788, pp. 2815–17) begins: 'Il y a ici un jeune Poëte de Groningue, nommé M, Heerkens, d'un

wonder that these praises bestowed from so many quarters made me persevere in my enterprise!' Within a year he had composed more than 3,000 verses, most of which, presumably, were destined for his long didactic poem on the health of the learned.[29] As we shall see in Chapter 2, however, less than a tenth of that poem would find its way into print when Heerkens returned to his homeland the following year, graduating *en route* in Reims.[30]

## Romeward bound

It was a slightly disgruntled Doctor Heerkens who returned to Groningen mid-century. A satire comparing the *mores* of the Parisians and 'Friesians' (in fact, the Groningeners) published semi-anonymously in 1750 cannot have endeared him much to his countrymen.[31] It began with an arch dig at the weather, comparing the joyful Ulysses arriving back home after his trials by sea, and Jason with the golden fleece, to the Dutch 'sailor returning from the dusky Indes, who rejoices as he catches sight, from port, of the Capitol of the Batavians, and the roofs and homes which clouds protect from every enemy'.[32] To judge from his correspondence around this time with Nijmegen friend and publishing entrepreneur, Cornelis Walraven Vonck (1724–68), our cosmopolitan Catholic

caractére tres-aimable, & d'un zèle singulier pour les Muses Latines'. What the older poet does not care to remember is that the journalist commends him for exhorting his compatriots to extend an olive branch to their French conquerors, revealing that Heerkens was subsequently the object of a vitriolic Philippic impugning his patriotism; and that he was obliged to sing a toadying song to the Stadtholder to make amends. The poem which occasioned this furore (not mentioned in the *Journal de Trévoux* article) was the *Elegia ad Magistratum Groninganum ut restituantur Academiae Professores* ('Elegy to the municipal authority of Groningen, that the vacant university Chairs should be refilled', Van Alphen Collection, Groningen University Library, #1012). (The collection is available digitally via subscription at 'The Early Modern Pamphlets Online', <http://tempo.idcpublishers.info/>.)

[29] Preface to *De valetudine literatorum* (1790), p. ix.

[30] Heerkens points out in his preface that Reims was a prestigious venue for the conferral of medical degrees. Laurence Brockliss tells a slightly different story. Gaining one's doctorate from the University of Paris was almost impossibly time-consuming and expensive. Instead, students 'went off to Reims, which offered three different doctorates – one that required effort for someone who wanted to practise in the city, another for those who did not and that could be obtained in a couple of days, and a third, a 'quicky', for non-natives who merely wanted a piece of paper to impress their clients when they returned home' (Brockliss, 'Medical Education and Centres of Excellence in Eighteenth-Century Europe: Towards an Identification', in Grell, Cunningham and Arrizabalaga (eds), *Centres of Medical Excellence?*, pp. 17–46, at pp. 33–4). Presumably Heerkens took the third option.

[31] This was, after all, the first thing he had published in Groningen since the literary quarrel only four years earlier. See below, Conclusion, p. 235.

[32] 'Gestiit exactis erroribus acer Ulisses, / Gestiit Aesonides, et capto vellere laetus / Exsiliit, fuscis ut nauta reversus ab Indis / Dum videt e portu Batavum Capitolia, quaeque / Tecta domusque *omni nebulae tueantur ab hoste*' (p. 5, my emphasis). But in a verse letter from Venice to patrician Groningener, and soldier-turned-farmer, Bernard van Sijzen, Heerkens is almost nostalgic for that

the United Provinces? In 1757 he accepted from Groningen publishing entrepreneur, Jacob Sipkes, the post of editor of two local newspapers, the daily *Opregte Groninger Courant* and the monthly *De Groninger Patriot*.[39] In this role he succeeded another learned physician, Nathaniel Remkes, who shared the publisher's Orange sympathies against a background of inveterate privilege, if not abuse of power, by the local, oligarchical 'regents'. But it seems that the well-travelled and -connected new editor exploited these publications less as party-political soap-boxes than as podia from which to preach international, especially French, high culture to his benighted countrymen – 'amo modestum vulgus et instruo' ('I love the humble mob and teach them') as the *Patriot*'s new motto announced. Less altruistically, as he confessed in a letter to Vonck, he was also in need of gainful employment. It is not surprising, perhaps, that Heerkens was relieved of his duties within a year.[40] In his Dutch-language journalism, at least, he seems to have worn his political opinions lightly. In later years he kept company with 'Patriots' Van der Cappellen tot den Pol (1741–84) and Jacob van der Steege (1756–1812) and wrote harshly about the Nassau dynasty in his *Icones*.[41] That said, if Heerkens did lean towards the fomenters of the Batavian revolution in the 1780s, he can hardly be deemed to have been anti-Nassau in 1747, when he sang an 'Elegy to the Prince of Orange' (Groningen, 1747) on the occasion of Willem IV's being made 'perpetual dictator of the Republic of

---

[39] See C. Hoitsema, *De Drukkersgeslachten Sipkes-Hoitsema en de Groninger Courant* (Groningen, 1953), pp. 104–6; B. P. Tammeling, 'Jacob Sipkes, De Groninger Courant en de Nouvellist', in his *De Krant Bekeken. De Geschiedenis van de Dagbladen in Groningen en Drenthe* (Groningen: Noorden, 1988), pp. 19–27. Tammeling writes that Heerkens was not as politically engaged as his predecessor, and while he commanded excellent sources in his articles for the *Patriot* he did not take a clear position. He aimed, moreover, too high for the 'middle-class' reader: 'Heerkens, die in Parijs in de bekendste literaire kringen had vertoefd en daar o.m. Voltaire en Racine had leren kennen, greep met zijn ongetwijfeld niveau hebbende artikelen te hoog voor de gemiddelde lezer' (p. 25).
[40] In a letter to Vonck of April 1758 (?) he complains: 'Nothing but my wretched work has prevented me from replying to your dear letters in a timely fashion. You know I am flat-out writing public news ('nova publica'), the falsehoods of rumour, and I have been appointed storyteller to the mob – I who used to sing proudly, a poet, for you and the Muses! If you and the Graces could see how much paper I have filled in ten months, you and the Graces would be horrified, excellent Vonck! So far, so far have I retreated from Parnassus – but to be honest I wasn't very happy there in recent years, and like those who are tired of life, I was dead. I needed to find a job which smiled on me, one that would remove me from the ungrateful Muses so that I could earn a crust.' But in an October letter Heerkens would rejoice: 'I have freed myself, excellent Vonck, from those chains to the rock, caught up in which I did not think of the Muses, of loves, or of any other pleasures. No more do I gawp after fame's clashing cymbals that I may instruct the unteachable mob!'
[41] For a review of trends in modern historiography on the Dutch 'Patriots' of the later eighteenth century (opponents of the Stadtholder who fought, among other things, for access to political power by non-Calvinists), see Wyger R. E. Velema, *Republicans: Essays on Eighteenth-Century Dutch Political Thought* (Leiden: Brill, 2007), especially chap. 6, 'Revolution, Counterrevolution and the Stadtholderate, 1780–1795', pp. 115–38, and chap. 8, 'Contemporary Reactions to Patriot Political Discourse', pp. 159–77.

the Belgae';[42] nor in 1748, when he published a 20-page *Panegyris, de laudibus Gulielmi principis Arausii ... Reipublicae Belgii gubernatoris* ('Panegyric on the Praises of William, Prince of Orange ... Governor of the Belgic Republic')[43] and an 'Elegy on Two Comets Celebrating the Coming of Peace', both published by pro-Orange bookseller, Elie Luzac;[44] and not even in 1765, when he dedicated the first two books of his *Notabilia* to the incoming Stadtholder, Willem V.[45] The Latin elegy to poet and classical scholar, Jeronimo de Bosch, prefixed to his *Italica* (1793, pp. xvii–xx) betrays ultimate disillusionment with the Patriot cause, as do a series of late French letters to book-collector, Johan Meerman, dated Groningen, 26 January 1793, 30 July 1794 and 8 February 1796.[46]

The aforesaid 'notable things' are those which Heerkens had observed during his travels in Italy, which we shall review in Chapter 4. Following the deaths of his mother in 1756 and father in 1758 his wanderlust had quickened. In 1759, armed with letters of introduction from assorted Dutch, French and German noblemen, priests and scholars,[47] the 34-year-old Heerkens – he was then entering a period of confirmed good health according to classical medical theory – set off, against the background of the Seven Years' War,[48] on what

[42] *Belgae*, a term used for Lowlanders from Roman times, was in the sixteenth century applied to the inhabitants of all 17 provinces of the Low Countries (*Ordines Belgici* = their States General). After the Revolt, *Batavi* was used specifically for inhabitants of the seven Northern provinces, or Dutch Republic, but *Belgae* continued to be used in contexts where Netherlanders in general were referred to. When a Northern institution such as the States General wished to present itself as the true representative or successor of the pre-Revolt Low Countries, it used *Belgicus, Belgae*, etc. I thank Jan Waszink for this clarification.

[43] See, however, n. 28 above where the reviewer of some of Heerkens's juvenile poems for the *Journal de Trévoux* regards his trumpet-blowing for the Stadtholder as a form of damage control.

[44] On the thought and influence of Luzac, see Wyger R. E. Velema, *Enlightenment and Conservatism in the Dutch Republic: The Political Thought of Elie Luzac (1721–1796)* (Assen: Van Gorcum, 1993).

[45] Indeed, the liminary verses to William in the *Notabilia* look forward to an opportunity to celebrate the history of the *Batavi* and that of the prince and his ancestors. Cf. Chapter 5, n. 18. (The poem is dated 1755, a typographical error.)

[46] In the 1794 letter, for example, he congratulates Meerman on the reception of his travel writings about Italy and Sicily, which have 'been read, this time, by the so-called Patriots themselves' ('soi-disant patriotes memes'). While Meerman's previous work, treating of the 'gathering of minds' ('reunion d'esprits'), was suppressed, Heerkens reports that this new one has found favour in Groningen, even within the ranks of that 'society of around one hundred and twenty (of whom at least a hundred are Jacobins)'. Indeed, parts of it have been quoted to Heerkens in a gloating fashion by one who 'knows that I am no democrat'. In the letter of 1796, the writer thanks God that out of 'the five priests who serve our [Catholic] church there is only one Patriot, and he is a man born here, and a nobody', but 'among your ministers it's much worse, and even among those of the University'. Cf. below, nn. 95–6, and Chapter 3, p. 109 and n. 14.

[47] The vital importance of such letters to Heerkens's scholarly and social movement and credibility is evident from the frequency with which he alludes to their success or failure, especially in his *Italica*. Cf. Ann Goldgar, *Impolite Learning: Conduct and Community in the Republic of Letters, 1680–1750* (New Haven: Yale University Press, 1995), pp. 24–5.

[48] He saw French and German troops ranged on either bank of the Lahn and spent a rough night in a tent ('sub velo') near Hessen; his chilly sleep was interrupted by a frightening call to arms in the middle of

he knew would be his journey of a lifetime. This was also, in some respects, a journey *backwards* in time, but, as we shall see in Chapter 4, Heerkens's Latin prose account of Italy and its people, published over two instalments in 1765 and 1770, reveals a genuinely practical and progressive spirit, as he is continually calibrating the literary and material remains of classical antiquity with contemporary Italian and Dutch building, engineering, agricultural and environmental and cultural conservation practices. And even as he was jotting down 'noteworthy things' in laconic and by no means unstylish, Latin prose,[49] our irrepressible Dutch Ovid was keeping a verse diary of his Italian 'exile' in the form of a series of elegiac letters to his friends, later published as the *Italica*. We shall sample some of these, as it were, reverse *Tristia* in Chapter 3. The first, on his journey through Germany and Austria to Venice (*Iter Venetum*), was dedicated to Nijmegen nobleman, Count Otto Frederick van Lynden.

Heerkens travelled by coach via Nijmegen and Neusz to Cologne, where he made a beeline for the Jesuit library and chanced upon several unpublished Latin poems by the Polish Horace, Kasimir Sarbiewski, S. J. (1595–1640), including some describing *his* Italian journey (*Italica* (1793), p. 7, and n. 6). In Cologne, thanks to the intercession of a well-connected uncle, he secured letters of introduction from the Elector, Clement Augustus, which would open doors for him to all the Jesuit houses in Germany and Rome (pp. 6–7, n. 5). At Koblenz the Jesuit alumnus was reunited with a beloved teacher from his Meppen days, Ignatius Beucker, and derived much intellectual nourishment from dinner with the local priests and a wise, elderly physician (pp. 10–14).[50] Thence he sailed to Bingen and observed the wine harvest. If we are to

---

the night, he was nearly mangled by the rushing carts and horses, and rather than entrust himself to the care of an Alsatian centurion, stole away to 'lonely haunts that would not be troubled by death-dealing wheels' ('Me ... in sola recepi, / Et loca funestis non nocitura rotis'). His salvation came in the shape of a coachman bound for Busbach, but he had to endure the latter's judgements of the respective merits of the generals; Heerkens 'mourned' for the French Marshal Louis de Contades, routed in the battle of Minden, 'for loose words, also around the camps, had insulted the vanquished leader' ('Contadio indolui, namque, et praetoria circum, / Victo insultarant libera verba duci', *Italica* (1793), pp. 22–3).

[49] Talented Latin poet Jacob Hendrik Hoeufft (1756–1843), addressee of the long dedicatory poem to *De valetudine literatorum* (1790), paid Heerkens the following backhanded compliment for his *Notabilia*: 'The shores of France and Italy saw you, and this one and that one applauded your verse; but you paint each so well in unfettered speech [prose], that it surpasses what you have written with feet bound [verse]' ('Gallica te vidit, te vidit et Italis ora, / Plausit et haec numeris, plausit et illa tuis. / Tam bene sed pingis sermone utramque soluto, / Ut superet vincto quae tibi scripta pede' (*Parnasus Latino-Belgicus: sive plerique e poëtis Belgii Latinis epigrammate atque adnotatione illustrati* (Amsterdam: Hengst; Breda: Bergen, 1819), p. 227).

[50] Cf. Chapter 5, p. 185, n. 78 on the senior doctor's dietary advice to his young colleague in advance of his Italian journey.

believe the elaborated version of the *Iter Venetum* printed in the 1793 *Italica*, Heerkens's departure from Frankfurt was delayed by a wily Alsatian Circe, the middle-aged mistress of an Italian merchant, who attempted to waylay our handsome humanist with the gift of a volume from the book fair, and to hitch a ride with him south of the border (pp. 24–31).

Happily disencumbered of his unwelcome baggage, Heerkens proceeded to Heidelberg, where he undertook an unsuccessful pilgrimage to the tombs of his Renaissance heroes Rudolph Agricola (fellow Groningener) and Petrus Lotichius (fellow physician and Ovidian elegist).[51] He journeyed to Ulm in the agreeable company of two learned Jesuits, Joseph Grangier and Francis Xavier Schwartz, and barely suppressed a titter at the quaint costume worn by the local ladies to church (p. 33). In Augsburg he would discuss faith and philosophy with a somewhat anguished Jacobus Brucker, Lutheran author of the influential 'Critical History of Philosophy'.[52] He arrived in Munich sick, but Providence sent him a kindly nurse in the shape of Willem Liedel, a Rotterdamer, and he recovered in time to accept a dinner invitation from the Elector and his wife – whose hand, he does not neglect to tell us, he was permitted to kiss (p. 39). Heerkens admired the Titians in the royal palace and thinks he just might have seen the manuscript of an unpublished Greek military text in the Elector's library; he suspects it may contain many unearthed treasures besides, since the Jesuits, the only educated men in this part of the world, are so little versed in Greek.[53] Of course, Heerkens also visited the magnificent Jesuit church and library (pp. 42–8).[54] Monkish and bookish delights competed with heart-stopping adventures en route to Innsbruck.[55] In Zirl he encountered a strange, grizzled, old man – 'you, Abraham, strolling in front your house in Canaan, could not have compelled my gaze any more' (pp. 54–5) – who had been present at the assassination of the Witt brothers and had loathed the Dutch race ever since. Of the rigours of the Alpine landscape, Heerkens groans: 'Whatever

---

[51] On Heerkens's Lotichius, cf. Chapter 3, p. 112, and n. 25.
[52] Brucker, *Historia critica Philosophiae*, 5 vols (Leipzig, 1733–63). See Leo Catana, 'The Concept "System of Philosophy": The Case of Jacob Brucker's Historiography of Philosophy', *History and Theory* 44 (2005), pp. 72–90.
[53] *Italica* (1793), p. 48; cf. *Notabilia*, Book 1, p. 3.
[54] Here he supplies an interesting prosopography of the Munich literary Jesuits.
[55] Taking a pedestrian shortcut to Zirl, Heerkens is confronted by a menacing local character on the path, to whom he is obliged to show his sword

winter weeps of snows, rains and hail, it stirs up here in spring, and in the middle of the harvest season. A more terrible region, to be sure, even though it approaches the stars, does not pass away to the ghastly realms of the Stygian God! Here it seems to a man that Nature is breathing out her last' ('Quicquid hiems nivium, nimborum, ac grandinis efflet, / Veris, et huc mediae tempore messis agit. / Horridior certe regio, licet astra propinquet, / Non abit ad Stygii lurida regna Dei. / Natura hic homini tanquam exspirare videtur', p. 50).

But Heerkens's philological-spiritual homeland was beckoning from beyond the Alps. He travelled by coach over the Brenner Pass to Trent and Rovereto, thence to Verona by boat. He opted for that means of transport having duly noted Sarbiewski's (verse) warning of bandits infesting the countryside; the unsteady craft was in the event all but overwhelmed by his fellow passengers, a mob of 'Genaunes', the feared ancient tribe of the Val d'Agno, wearing axes around their necks (pp. 63–6). In Vicenza, Heerkens was received most warmly by librarian and art patron, Parmenio Trissino, a descendant of the author of the *Sofonisba*; his obliging host even furnished him with an annotated copy of the library's catalogue (pp. 70–2, and n. 72). In Padua he sought in vain, at first, for professor of medicine, Giambattista Morgagni (1682–1771), the so-called father of anatomical pathology; for distinguished Latin lexicographer, Giacomo Facciolati (1684–1769); and for antiquarian and professor of experimental philosophy, Giovanni Poleni (1683–1761) (p. 77).[56] As will be clear even from this telegraphic survey, Heerkens was as much intent on viewing Italy's human treasures as its landscapes, libraries, art and antiquities. Of Padua, for example, he would observe that – in contrast to magnificent Vicenza – it 'seems to consist of ruins; but you should stay here a few days for the town's antiquities, churches and learned inhabitants. It's worth it, even for those who are not so keenly interested in learning and literature, to be able to visit men distinguished in letters, the arts, and sciences from the street ('ex via')'.[57] Thus Heerkens was making a *voyage littéraire* in many ways comparable to those undertaken by

---

[56] On Poleni's public electrical performances at the University of Padua see G. A. Salandin and A. Pancino, *Il 'teatro' di filosofia sperimentale di Giovanni Poleni* (Lint: Trieste, 1987). He is chiefly remembered, though, for his engineering advice to the Holy See on the stability and preservation of St Peter's dome. See also Dante Nardo, 'Scienza e filologia nel primo settecento padovano: gli studi classici di G. B. Morgagni, G. Poleni, G. Pontedera, L. Targa', *Quaderni per la storia dell'Università di Padova* 14 (1981), pp. 1–40.

[57] *Notabilia*, Book 1, p. 6.

Vossius, Mersenne and Gronovius in the previous century.[58] But we should not be deceived: he is no latter-day Charles-Etienne Jordan (1700–45) who, like his precursor Gronovius, scorned in his travels through France, England and Holland to visit monuments, and wasted little ink on gripping incidents such as attacks by pirates.[59] The pleasure which may still be had from reading Heerkens's *Notabilia* is the product of a nonchalant, roving eye for the amusing and seemingly insignificant detail, an artful blending of anecdotes of literary, archaeological and human interest with droll, conspiratorial asides and insider traveller's tips.

Venice was our eager tourist's principal destination in the north, but the Serenissima proved a little too quiet for the sociable Dutchman. He did not get off to a good start: a cryptic note in his verse letter to Groningen friend and farmer, Roelof Bernard van Sijzen, records that he has received a cool reception from the Danzig-born Dutch consul, Ros (was he perhaps suspected of espionage?).[60] Even more disappointingly, Cardinal Querini, Heerkens's chief contact in Venice, had recently died, and his conscientious protégé was treated with peremptory rudeness by the household of the surviving ancient brother. In both the *Notabilia* and *Italica*, Heerkens complains copiously of the lack of sunshine, public eateries and theatrical entertainment,[61] of the narrow streets (well-named *calles*, 'footpaths', by the locals), of the ubiquitous refuse, of the parlous state of the paintings in the churches, of the parsimony and stand-offishness of the nobles. He feels his national constitution for liberty being undermined by a servile fear lest he inadvertently give offence and wind up in one of the city's fabled underground dungeons! The local people are

[58] Goldgar, *Impolite Learning*, pp. 1–11; Paul Dibon and Françoise Waquet, *Johannes Fredericus Gronovius: pélerin de la République des Lettres: recherches sur le voyage savant au XVIIè siècle* (Geneva: Droz, 1984). It was only secondarily a *medical* pilgrimage such as Heerkens cautiously prescribes for the physician in *De officio medici* (Groningen, 1752), pp. 45–6, citing Thomas Bartholin's *de Perigrinationibus* [sic] *Medicorum* = *De peregrinatione medica* (Copenhagen, 1674). Plato and Cicero returned from their travels 'not sporting new cloaks or tunics, and with new clothes, but both with new interests and customs. You will excuse new clothes, however, as that is a matter of fashion; just let them not have returned with new vices' ('Non chlamide aut tunicâ ornate rediêre, novisque / Vestibus; at studiis moribus ambo novis. / Vestibus ignoscas tamen, ut sartoria cura est; / Si modo cum vitiis non rediere novis', p. 46). On medical travel, see Grell, Cunningham and Arrizabalaga (eds), *Centres of Medical Excellence?*
[59] Goldgar, *Impolite Learning*, p. 4.
[60] *Italica* (1793), pp. 112–17, at p. 113, and n. 1.
[61] In a note to his verse letter to van Sijzen, he complains that there is nothing worth seeing in the Venetian theatres apart from a few pieces of Goldoni; moreover, the performances start too late and only end near midnight! (*Italica* (1793), p. 116, n. 5). In the *Notabilia*, however, Heerkens concedes that he consoled himself with the opera, and especially enjoyed the lithe and expressive Italian dancers, who surpassed in grace even those of Paris (Book 1, pp. 12–13).

suspicious, closed-minded, pathologically proud of their city and ignorant of the world beyond. A well-born youth of the Grimani family whom Heerkens had got to know from the cafés and gaming tables (at least by his mask) would inquire, for example, whether his Dutch friend missed the mountains of his homeland, assuming that flat land could exist only in the Veneto (*Notabilia*, Book 1, pp. 7–8).

Heerkens was obliged to make side-trips to Vicenza and Padua to breathe more easily, both literally and socially. His luck and spirits lifted when he made contact, at last, with the learned men upon whom he had earlier called; and additionally, with scientist and inventor, Bartolommeo Ferracino (1692–1777), and with professor, publisher of classical texts and Latin poet, Gianantonio Volpi (1686–1766).[62] Morgagni encouraged Heerkens in his composition of medical epigrams, and Volpi in the versification of his journey to Venice. Back in Venice, our poet struck up friendships with the French ambassador, Le Blon, and with the Sardinian, Giulio Vittorio Incisa di Camerana. After three long months, however, he planted grateful feet and lips on *terra firma*. Making his way by sea to Ferrara, then Bologna, he followed the coast via Ravenna, Rimini and Pesaro, to Ancona. The polymathic Giovanni Bianchi (1693–1775), physician, naturalist and archaeologist, showed him around Rimini.[63] In Pesaro he called on Annibale degli Abbati Olivieri-Giordani (1708–89), a prominent scholar of the town's antiquities, and in the second book of the *Notabilia* proudly transcribed the contents of a flattering letter sent him by that distinguished personage (pp. 129–30).[64] Heerkens reached Rome via Loreto and Spoleto, having traversed the Apennines. Unfortunately, the poem which he addressed to van Lynden on this eventful leg of his journey was not recovered during his lifetime, and never published.

Rome and the Romans were certainly much more to Heerkens's liking than Venice and the Venetians, and he fully realized his good fortune in finding lodgings on the Pincio, near the beautiful Villa Medici.[65] He was soon befriended by two

---

[62] The human and architectural attractions of Padua are described in verse letters to Nicolaas Tenhove and Gerard Meerman (*Italica* (1793), pp. 84–96 and 98–106).

[63] Bianchi was Professor of Anatomy at the University of Siena, and author of works on medicine, geography, epigraphy and zoology (most significantly, *De conchis minus notis liber* (1739; 2nd edn 1760), on 'foraminifera'). See entry by Angelo Fabi, in *Dizionario Biografico degli Italiani* 10 (1968), pp. 104–12, available at <www.treccani.it/biografie/>.

[64] In 1787 Olivieri created the Biblioteca Oliveriana di Pesaro. For further bibliography see Ulrico Agnati, *Per la storia romana di Urbino e Pesaro* (Rome: L'Erma di Brettschneider, 1999), p. 249.

[65] He recommends the area to the addressee for its healthful and pleasant situation, its proximity to the sights and to the residences of the Pope and the 'Princes of the City' (nobles, or perhaps

eminent princes of the Church: antiquarian and art patron, Alessandro Albani (1692–1779), and firebrand Vatican librarian, Domenico Passionei (1682–1761), sworn enemy of the Society of Jesus. Passionei supplied the Dutchman with books and manuscripts, entertained him at his country villa, chatted happily to him in French and cherished the undisguised hope of making a priest out of him. Our worldly and erudite networker had other ideas, though. While he counselled the addressee of his *Notabilia* to avoid romantic entanglements with the lascivious and unlettered ladies of Rome, Heerkens was not ashamed to confess to a spot of promiscuity himself, albeit of the intellectual variety. Recalling Fontenelle's advice to him in Paris that he should not let on to Louis Racine that he was visiting the Jesuits of that city, Heerkens decided it was better to keep the irascible Passionei in the dark about his contact with the learned priests of the Collegio Romano. The Jesuit alumnus forged warm friendships with professor of Greek and editor of Cicero, Girolamo Lagomarsini (1698–1773);[66] with Archangelo Contuccio Contucci (1688–1768), curator of the museum of curiosities over which the polymathic Athanasius Kircher had once presided;[67] with Latin satirist and official historian of the Society, Giulio Cesare Cordara (1705–85), and with Bartolommeo Boscovich (1700–?) brother of the famous physicist, who regaled his fellow 'exile' with Latin poems pining for his homeland of Ragusa (*Notabilia*, Book 1, pp. 60–1).[68] It is worth noting that all the Jesuits mentioned here were accomplished Latin poets. In addition, Heerkens met in Rome the Theatine educationalist, Paolo Maria Paciaudi (1710–85) and the French Franciscan physicist and mathematician, François Jacquier (1711–88).

Passionei, of whom Heerkens was clearly fond, and who permitted him to consult books borrowed from the Vatican in his private library near Heerkens's

cardinals?), as well as to the Villa Medici, which is open to the public. In the evenings one can enjoy the *passeggiata* and cavalcade of carriages along the Via Flaminia. Best of all, the panoramic view of the city from the Pincio is not only beautiful but instructive (*Notabilia*, Book 1, p. 35).

[66] Passionei seems to have exempted Lagomarsini from his general odium for the order (*Notabilia*, Book 1, pp. 57–8).

[67] Maurizio Campanelli informs me, *per litteras*, that Contuccio's Horatian satire on Monte Testaccio (published in Giuseppe Brogi (ed.), *Arcadum Carmina, pars tertia* (Rome, 1768), pp. 107ff.), which treats of the number of contemporary poets and their pecking order, was written some 20 years before the much more famous *Lettere virgiliane* of Saverio Bettinelli, which was addressed to the Arcadians. As we shall see in Chapter 1, the 'mountain of the poets' was hotly contested territory in the Groningen pamphlet war that Heerkens himself sparked off in 1746.

[68] A special issue of *Povijeseni Prilozi/Historical Contributions* (24 (2003)) has been dedicated to Bara Boscovich: 'Znanstveni skup Tristota obljetnica rođenja Bara Boškovića'. See also *Croatiae auctores Latini (CroALa)*, Collectio electronica <www.ffzg.unizg.hr/klafil/croala/> for his Latin poetry. Dirk Sacré informs me *per litteras* that he is preparing an article, 'De Bartholomaei Boscovicii carmine c.t. "Patriae desiderium"', for the journal, *Vox Latina* (Saarbrücken).

lodgings, did not share his young friend's interest in antiquities. The only topics of learned conversation at Passionei's country estate, which he dubbed his 'Ruminatorium', were classical literature and theology. But forearmed with Livy's first decade and with the Jesuit Eschinardi's *Descrizione di Roma e dell'agro romano* (Rome, 1750), Heerkens padded religiously around the Roman countryside, sizing up ruined villas, comparing the visual evidence with ancient literary clues; and he commended the fun and fruitfulness of this exercise to the anonymous addressee of his *Notabilia* (Book 2, pp. 26–7). When he returned to Rome later in the year, our amateur archaeologist took the opportunity to strike out on a more ambitious expedition – to locate the site of Horace's Sabine farm, no less! While he affects indifference to the coolness with which his hypothesis was received at a meeting of the Academy of the Arcadians in Rome, he does not neglect to report that it was adopted by a Frenchman in attendance, an individual who was also party to subsequent discussions of the topic at the house of Laurent Pécheux (1729–1821), a learned French painter and friend of Heerkens.

Naples was the next port of call, and it too did not disappoint. Heerkens took the overland route through Velletri, Terracina and Capua, travelling by public coach (which he recommends here over the boat trip, *pace* Addison). The archaeology, geology and the history of habitation of the Pontine Marshes seem to have exercised a special fascination over our sometime peat-colonist, but the journey through this eerie landscape was by no means a familiar or comfortable one. In the *Notabilia*, and in his third, long verse letter to Count van Lynden, Heerkens expresses dismay at the desolation of the countryside – what we Dutch would do with such fields! – and with the lack of culture and lawlessness of the present-day inhabitants. A stray dog he had adopted in Verona proved its worth by sniffing out a robber lurking under the bed in one of the grim inns at which they were obliged to lodge (see Figure 5.2, for Heerkens's epitaph for this animal).[69] Renaissance antiquarian Biondo Flavio had written of a community of a hundred

---

[69] Following the lead of Castruccio Buonamici, who had composed an epitaph for the dog of one of his military comrades (*Notabilia*, Book 3, p. 60), Heerkens commemorated his own faithful friend in a verse inscription now preserved in the Groningen Museum. Its text, and that of another, in the dog's voice, appear in *Journal des sçavans* (October 1768), p. 286. Worp reports an unconfirmed story that Heerkens brought an unsuccessful court case against the local authorities who would not give him permission to bury the dog in the churchyard at Hoogezand or Sappemeer (p. 27)! In a footnote to one of his verse letters to van Lynden, Heerkens records that he had left two basset hounds in the care of his steward before departing for Italy, neither of which survived to greet their master on his return (*Italica* (1793), p. 142, n. 37).

monks that had lived in these marshes but had abandoned them shortly before his time.[70] Heerkens muses on the difference between those soft Italians and their Low Countries counterparts; the latter regard the conversion of swamp and forest into arable land as a point of pride and piety!

Between Capua and Naples, Campania was a revelation. After the unmitigated squalor of the Papal States, the sober citizen of Sappemeer marvelled at fields piled high with grain yet apparently bereft of labourers and at women in brightly coloured clothes singing and gesturing provocatively to passers-by. Naples itself was a city of almost obscene abundance, bursting at the seams with monks, lawyers and *lazzaroni*.[71] Heerkens was seduced by the emotional exuberance of the people, by their musicality, by the philosophical sophistication with which even the uneducated discoursed on the uses of pleasure, and by the native charm of the local intelligentsia. He tracked down Vonck's brightest Latin star, the hot-tempered historian, Castruccio Buonamici, a native of Lucca, who had fallen foul of the king of Sardinia and was now living in fear for his life.[72] During his southern sojourn Heerkens also met the superintendent of excavations at Herculaneum, Antonio Mazzocchi, an elderly man whose worthiness was unfortunately not matched by his spunk and curiosity. In a long section in the third book of the *Notabilia*, he barely represses his exhilaration at these recent discoveries, carefully describing the mosaics, villas and the painstaking techniques then being applied to unrolling and reading the papyrus.[73]

---

[70] *Notabilia*, Book 3, p. 19. Cf. his verse vignette on the Benedictines abandoning the basilica of San Paolo fuori le Mura at Rome, due to the poor quality of the territory: 'It may be sacred, it may be inhabited by the Gods, it may be a famous site for miracles, it retains none of its monks. Paul, they flee your hundred columns, and during the night, nor will there be anyone to guard your treasure! So malignant is the country surrounding sacred Rome, which was for a long time blessed – all the while she was pagan' ('Sit sacra, sit Superis habitata, sit inclyta sedes / Prodigiis, monachos non tenet ulla suos. / Paule tui fugiunt, et centum nocte columnas, / Nec gazam templi qui tibi servet, erit! / Usque maligna adeo est, sanctae circumsita Romae, / Illa diu felix, impia donec, humus!'; *Italica* (1793), p. 123).

[71] These were the poor inhabitants, immigrants from the surrounding countryside, whose simple clothing gave them the appearance of resurrected Lazaruses. See Chapter 4, pp. 142–3.

[72] Heerkens states that Buonamici, who was in the pay of the Genoese, had offended their enemy with a phrase suggesting that Charles Emanuel had 'played for time' ('insidiari temporibus'). The probable reference is to a passage from the second book of Buonamici's *De bello Italico*: the Sardinian sovereign is imputed to have cared less for the preservation of the peace and liberty of Italy after an outbreak of fresh hostilities between Austria and the Bourbons than to have desired 'to protract time, till he could see which side would make him the best offers; for both solicited his alliance with great promises' (review of the English translation by A. Wishart, in *The Monthly Review* (April 1753), p. 310).

[73] The *Enyclopédie* contributor on Herculaneum ('C' = Jean Pestré) writes that 'Personne n'a mieux décrit que M. Gerard-Heerkens, Hollan. 1770, la maison, où se sont trouvés les seuls livres qu'on

The return trip to Rome was marred by misadventure and is related in the fourth book of the *Notabilia* with our author's typical candour and nose for the comic, often at his own expense.[74] One of the travellers, a lovesick young Dutchman, had been foisted on him by the Dutch consul in Naples, Dirk Davel. The young man was sullen and silent for the first leg of the journey because, that morning, Heerkens had been obliged to tear him away from the arms of his Neapolitan sweetheart. When the horses took off at breakneck speed after Atella, the terrified youth sprung to his feet and made as if to jump out of the carriage, subsequently proving even more ill-humoured when his coachmate was compelled to restrain him. While the speed of travel precluded even the consolation of admiring the beautiful villas which Heerkens had enjoyed on the inbound journey, the tourists did visit the Bourbon palace at Caserta (at that time, of course, still under construction). In Capua, Heerkens had to come to the rescue of his hapless compatriot once again, when the latter was set upon by the avaricious coachmen in a dispute over payment. Heerkens ordered the young man's servant to charge into the fray, on horseback; then our hero and his own servant broke up the mob by brandishing their weapons at one or two of the drivers. This was only the beginning of their troubles, however. As a result of theft, or possibly sabotage, their coach, missing a bolt from one of its wheels, overturned. When righted, its collapsed roof rendered the cabin impossibly cramped. Heerkens's fellow traveller was by now so preoccupied with the adversities of the journey that 'his lovesickness only gave him sporadic pangs' (!). The passengers agreed to take turns riding one of the servants' horses, but the petulant Dutch Romeo, galloping ahead in an apparently face-saving show of bravado, was violently thrown. While the young man suffered only a graze to the knee, the travelling party was blamed for damage to the horse, and the exasperated Heerkens found himself having to make representations to the local police chief at Terracina. The story, in short, is like nothing so much as the plot of a comic opera, but its tempo and lightness, it seems, were not achieved as readily by Heerkens in verse. A similar tale of high drama on the

---

ait encore découverts depuis qu'on travaille à faire sortir de ses ruines cette ville ensevelie sous les cendres du Vésuve' (vol. 17, p. 319).

[74] No doubt the essential elements of this story are true, but Heerkens knew well how to embellish them. In fact he had already written an amusing verse satire on a disastrous journey, by coach and sea, complete with irritating fellow travellers, bad food, noisy inns and punch-ups. This, the fifth printed in his *Marii Curilli Satyrae* (pp. 33–9), was written in 1746 when he was bound for the University of Leiden.

highway, narrated towards the end of the *Iter Venetum*, provoked only dour disapproval from the Dutch reviewer of that poem.[75]

Heerkens lingered in Rome, where he fancied he walked among the true ancestors of the ancient Romans, until 18 September. He then began his homeward journey and set off for Florence via Sutri, Viterbo, Certaldo and Siena. He was so ill on arrival in Viterbo that the intrepid inscription-hunter had to forego an inspection of the forgeries of Annius; he suffered himself to be brought to 'some church or other' by a Florentine fellow traveller, a priest, where he admired the uncorrupted body of a certain St Rose whose youthful bloom had converted many heretics.[76] Heerkens's pious companion was, however, all for abandoning him at the lonely inn at Aqua Pendente where they spent the night, 'for I seemed to him to be afflicted by a lethal and contagious disease'. An unseemly battle for our author's body and soul is fought between the invalid and his faithful servant on the one hand, both anxious to make the onward journey, and the grasping innkeeper and fastidious priest on the other, 'of whom the first wanted to retain the patient and the other to abandon him, [and who] was agitating for the journey to begin before dawn, before the usual hour' (*Notabilia*, Book 4, p. 147). Heerkens ultimately prevailed and, tightly wrapped up in a woollen cloak, took his seat on the coach in spite of vociferous protestations from the priest 'that he would not make the journey with a corpse. What? He even tried to prevent my boarding with his hands' (p. 147). In the course of that journey Heerkens seems to have recovered his spirits sufficiently to notice that the country people were less oppressed by poverty in Etruria than in other parts of the papal states; and that the women wore the very garments 'in which painters dress pastoral nymphs, and which I had believed were the products of painters' fantasy, and were not the usual attire for women anywhere

---

[75] On the journey from Vicenza to Padua, Heerkens had refused to admit an unsavoury would-be traveller and his dirty servant to the coach, even threatening the driver with a gun to prevent them from boarding. The coach later crashed on the approach to a narrow bridge – sabotage is again mooted in the 1793 version of *Italica* – and the horses and passengers are strewn, semi-conscious on the road. When a mature lady traveller is revived she is restrained with difficulty from attacking the driver with her dagger, confirming – quips Heerkens – 'Menander's dictum that the desire for revenge increases in women with increase in age' (!). The author defends his relation of this cautionary tale for the benefit of tourists to Italy, but 'in The Hague Journal it ... was met with repeated strikes of the eraser, as incongruous and out of place, as if [the author] wished to share the annoyance he had experienced from the incident' (*Italica* (1793), pp. 74–5, n. 74).

[76] 'What heretics there may have been in Etruria in the thirteenth century the monks who looked after the Church could not explain to us, nor is it to be found in the annals of Christianity; unless those who took the side of Frederick II, who had well-known disputes with the Pope at that time or a little beforehand, were taken for and billed as heretics' (*Notabilia*, Book 4, p. 145).

in the world' (p. 150). But if he admired the exceptionally beautiful women in Siena, and mused on their fabled talents for singing, strumming and composing Latin verse (!), it was the libraries that tempted Heerkens in Florence. The Laurentian librarian, Angelo Maria Bandini, teasingly chided him for spending all his time at the books, for not taking time to see the city properly. (Bandini was unaware that his conscientious visitor in fact rose very early every morning for sightseeing.) In Florence Heerkens made the acquaintance of journalist and Church historian, Giovanni Lami (1697–1770), who had written a short notice of the *Iter Venetum* in his *Novelle Letterarie*.[77] And it was in Florence that he pored over the scholia of Ovid, transcribing annotations from a copy belonging to Poliziano that would be incorporated, with grateful acknowledgement, into the 1762 Paris edition of the *Opera omnia* by the abbé Joseph de Valart.

Homeward bound, Heerkens passed through Pisa and Lucca, making observations in his *Notabilia* on their respective political histories and architecture, if not, curiously, on the Piazza dei Miracoli. On the recommendation of the 'superintendent of Batavian affairs' ('Batavarum rerum procurator') he set off from Livorno to Genoa by boat. A terrifying night at sea is wonderfully described, Heerkens casting himself as a hapless anti-hero very much in the spirit of Ovid's *Tristia* 1. 2 (pp. 175–8). He had chivalrously invited a lady from Geneva to share his dinner on board. (She was returning home after working as a housekeeper in Livorno.) As the storm rises and the boat threatens to founder, the lady and Heerkens's servant pass out from sheer terror; the author himself frankly admits that, at that point, he had no thought for them, let alone his sodden luggage! The struggling sailors have noticed his watch, and he sustains them with feeble reassurances that it is almost dawn – in fact, he is unable to read its face in the dark, and when he holds it to his ear he thinks he hears the tolling of a funeral bell. At length the sun appears, and an uninspiring debate arises among the sailors as to which are the mountains in sight. When they put in at La Spezia, Heerkens dries off in the sun and resolves to continue his journey by land, to throw in his lot with a hinny on the steep, narrow, mountain paths rather than entrust himself again to the clueless boat crew. His poor, protesting manservant, however, is sent on by sea with the luggage, in spite of the fact that, since their arrival into port, one of the sailors has been revealed to be a murderer (p. 182).[78]

---

[77] Lami, *Novelle Letterarie*, 1st series, 21 (1760), pp. 376–7.
[78] His page was mischievously rumoured, according to Worp, to be a girl in disguise. I have not been able to find Worp's source.

The Swiss lady adamantly refuses to re-board, and despite Heerkens's lurid projections of the perils of the overland journey – they prove in the event to be understated ... – she persuades him to allow her to accompany him. She boasts of having scaled the mountains of the *Allobroges* by mule, and of having no fear of heights:

> I was pleased that she thought she could walk for a hundred days, as the time was at hand when I might admire her nimbleness. She was not much older than twenty-four, and of that sort of body which would have given a different impression of fleetness of foot on a road other than that which leads up and down without end through scratchy brambles. (p. 186)

Over the course of the day the poor woman gradually divests herself of her cumbersome clothes and enters the hamlet where they are to eat lunch wearing nothing but her slip, flatly 'declaring that one who is finished off by exhaustion and perspiration is not able to think about nudity' (p. 186). On the onward journey Heerkens persuades her to ride the mule, for fear that she might lose her balance and fall to her death over the cliffs. This was a mistake, as the goat path they were following was scarcely three feet wide, and the mule could not be kept to the middle of it, preferring to graze on the margins and to gaze down into the abyss (p. 187)!

After three days, during which Heerkens's lady friend proved herself a true Amazon, much to her reluctant escort's growing admiration, the dishevelled travellers arrived in Genoa.[79] Heerkens chanced to encounter some Dutch friends there and so lingered longer than anticipated. Genoa itself he found grim, dirty and unhealthy, and the lower-class women, due to their sedentary work in the textile industry, as pasty-faced as the ladies of Amsterdam (pp. 190–1). Moreover, Genoa had, according to Heerkens, evinced the least interest of all the Italian city–states in the Renaissance of letters, and its bookshops were a dismal disappointment (pp. 192, 194).[80] But he found a congenial companion in François Fagel, son of the famous Secretary of the States-General during the War of the Spanish Succession, who was about to embark on an Italian journey of his own. The poet-doctor dutifully composed his young friend an elegiac regimen.[81] He then proceeded via Ticino to Turin, was received with great

---

[79] She was good company, Heerkens concedes, and was very knowledgeable about cooking, so that she was able to whip up tasty meals 'with art and minimal work' at their wretched lodging places, where next to nothing could be found that was fit to eat (*Notabilia*, Book 4, p. 189).
[80] At least the Genoese outdid the Venetians in hospitality (p. 194)!
[81] *Italica* (1793), pp. 186–98.

kindness by the learned monk, Giacinto Sigismondo Gerdil (1718–1802),[82] tutor to the Crown Prince of Sardinia, to whom he was also duly presented (pp. 202–3). On 7 November, with the lady from Livorno still in tow, Heerkens undertook the crossing of the massif of Mount Cenis with some merchants from Geneva, arriving in Chambéry five days later.

\* \* \*

Had his rich and edifying Italian experiences trumped the giddier pleasures of his Parisian student days at the dawning of the *Lumières*? Had the journey to and from Rome been a pilgrimage as much spiritual as cultural, causing him now to regard with suspicion and distaste his former philosophical heroes? In November of 1760 Heerkens visited Voltaire in his chateau at Ferney. The old friends fell out. As he reports in the preface to the 1790 edition of his *De valetudine literatorum*, Heerkens subsequently destroyed 13 Latin poems he had written in his idol's honour; a family legend, relayed by Worp, has Voltaire shrugging off the physician's criticisms of his piety and personal life: 'Je crains plus vos medecines que vos reproches.'[83] In Paris, later in the month, Heerkens had a minor run-in with another well-known opponent of modern Latinity, Jean le Rond d'Alembert. But it is amusing to read that the cocky *philosophe* who scoffed at contemporary practitioners of Latin verse was so discomfited by Heerkens's rumoured aspersions on his classical learning, in an as-yet-unpublished Latin poem, that he made a personal appeal to the Dutchman to excise the offending lines, invoking their common membership of the Academy of Inscriptions and Belles Lettres.[84]

Having over-wintered in Paris, where he was reunited with old friends such as the Duke of Belle-Isle, and set about making new ones, Heerkens returned to Groningen at the end of 1761. Patriotic feelings began to stir afresh after what seems to have been an initially friendly reception in The Hague. But with the appearance of an unflattering review of his *Iter Venetum* in a Dutch journal, Heerkens buried himself in his little country house at Borgercompagnie with

---

[82] Gerdil was author of the pamphlet, 'Réflexions sur la théorie et la pratique de l'éducation contre les principes de J.-J. Rousseau' (1765).

[83] Heerkens's 'Satire to Corn. Valerius Vonck' (Groningen, 1751) gives a good indication of his former hero worship, as indeed does an ode 'To Envy, that it spare Voltaire', printed with *De officio medici* (Groningen, 1752) (p. 71).

[84] Cf. Chapter 4, p. 149. Heerkens may have been a corresponding member of this Académie but I can find no reference to him in the online records of the Institut de France: <www.aibl.fr/fr/membres/home.html>.

the paraphernalia of his Italian journey: marbles, inscriptions, portraits of famous men and, no doubt, cartloads of new books.[85] He set to work editing his Italian works. The verse letters of the *Italica* appeared in two editions in 1762 and 1793.

## Migrations ... and swan songs

It was not long before the restless Dutchman was on the road again, lodging first with poet and politician, Onno Zwier van Haren (1713–79), in Wolvega, in June 1762, at the height of the latter's legal troubles over accusations of incest; returning to The Hague later in the summer; searching in vain for his old student friend, Josua van Iperen, in Zeeland; spending the winter in Paris with Count van Lynden. Around this time a love affair, or at least a marriage prospect, briefly flared.[86] On the return trip to Groningen, Heerkens stopped at Brussels, where, he boasts, he was invited to dinner by the highly cultivated Governor of the Austrian Netherlands, Charles de Lorraine.[87] He was home again in June 1763, but January of the following year saw him in Middelburg, and February, Paris. Letters to his Dutch friends Vonck and van Haren, and from his French friend, le Franc, reveal that Heerkens was at this time considering a permanent move to France.[88] He seems to have thought better of it only because he was beginning to enjoy the patronage of the Stadtholder, Willem V, to whom, as we saw above, the first two books of the *Notabilia* were dedicated. The second pair were published by subscription, and dedicated to Heerkens's fellows in the Zeeuwsch Genootschapte Vlissingen, a scientific society established in 1769. Whether he took to Zeeland primarily for the warmth of its intellectual or physical climate we shall never know, but Heerkens would in any case spend a few months there each year for several years to come.

[85] The auction catalogue of Heerkens's estate (Groningen, 1805) lists some 5,000 printed works, 68 paintings, hundreds of drawings, prints, maps and coins and a respectable collection of antiquities, including a bas-relief in white marble of the story of Archimedes, a Roman inscription in white stone, two Roman bronze statues, a Roman urn, basin, &c.
[86] It seems to have fizzled by 1767 (Worp, pp. 36–7). The love interest to which Worp refers here may or may not be the mysterious Parisian girlfriend, 'Emily', celebrated in a poem appended to a letter to Vonck of 4 April 1761. In fact, Heerkens's parents had already sent him to woo a young lady in The Hague in 1756. See Chapter 3 for his letter to Vonck about that embarrassing and abortive mission.
[87] Indeed, he seems to have dined with Charles on some five occasions in 1761 and 1763 (*De valetudine literatorum* (1790), p. 81).
[88] I have not seen the letter from le Franc, formerly in the collection of Mr E. J. M. I. Canter Cremers of Rotterdam, but Worp suggests that it was to this effect.

He also shuttled back and forth from Paris, but after 1777 his wanderlust seems to have waned. In 1787 Heerkens published a set of ten Latin poems on 'the birds of Friesland' (i.e. of the Groningen countryside), at least two of which had been perused by the Comte de Buffon some ten years earlier. Heerkens had then nurtured hopes of being elected to the Académie des Sciences in Paris, and corresponded with both Buffon and Malesherbes on his prospects.[89] His tried-and-tested networking skills had failed him on that occasion; a second and third flock of Friesian birds never left the nest. Three hot summers beginning in the year 1779 saw our ageing physician succumbing to the ill health and low spirits his poetry had so often sought to forestall.[90] Family members and friends were passing away. In this melancholy period Heerkens took solace in his medical learning and turned to editing the epigrams on health, and not least old men's health, he had begun to compose with the encouragement of Giambattista Morgagni in 1759. Two editions of these poems, rather grandly entitled *Empedocles*, were released: five books in 1783, and seven in 1798.[91] We shall explore them, together with his earlier didactic poem on the duties of a doctor, in Chapter 6.

In the same year as his natural-historical *Aves Frisicae*, Heerkens assembled for publication his historical-biographical *Icones*, at least some of which, as we have noted, he had already begun to compose in Italy. We shall consider both of these collections in Chapter 5. The icon on 'Our Century' treats, *inter alia*, of the suppression of the Jesuit order. It also ranges under the great discoveries of the modern era, next to the hot-air balloon and the excavations at Herculaneum and Pompeii, Heerkens's own unveiling to the Republic of

---

[89] See J. A. Worp, 'Lettres de Voltaire, de Buffon et de Malesherbes à G.-N. Heerkens, médecin et homme de lettres hollandais', *Revue d'histoire littéraire de la France* 21 (1914), pp. 188-91.

[90] *Empedocles* (1798), p. vii.

[91] Heerkens was no slouch in his semi-retirement. In the preface to the first edition of the *Empedocles* (1783) he tells us that he is intending to publish, and has nearly ready, two books about 'Flemish painters', twelve 'Months of the agricultural year', three books of 'Friesian Birds', one on the 'Consuls of Groningen, at least of those who were at the same time almost dictators', twelve of 'Fasti of the Belgae', books six to eight of his 'Medical Epigrams', two books of 'Moral Epigrams'; and, in prose, one book on 'the Learning of the Famous Canters', two of 'Matters Pertaining to Myself', and sundry books of 'Noteworthy Matters'. As far as I can discover only one volume of *Aves Frisicae* (plus assorted birds printed separately, cf. Chapter 5, p. 184, n. 74), another two books of medical epigrams, four Dutch painters and perhaps a third of the *Annus Rusticus* (I have found 'January' (*Journal des sçavans* (January 1768), pp. 304-8) but not the first edition of Groningen, 1767, 'February' (*Journal des sçavans* (May 1768), pp. 561-6), 'March' (*Journal des sçavans* (October 1768), pp. 281-6), and 'April' (*Journal des sçavans* (March 1771), pp. 256-64) eventually found their way into print. It has proved impossible to trace the whereabouts of the manuscripts, if they still exist. They are not listed in the catalogue of sale of Heerkens's books and artworks (Groningen, 1805). For sundry other pieces not noted by Worp, see Appendix.

Letters of a Latin tragedy unknown to antiquity, a work he solemnly christened 'Tereus' and attributed to the Augustan poet, Lucius Varius. The long preface to the *Icones* records how Heerkens came to be in possession of this 'lost' manuscript and to identify its author – but his triumph was short-lived. Varius's 'Tereus' was duly exposed, in 1792, by Jacopo Morelli, librarian of the Marciana in Venice, as the *Progne*, a juvenile work by Italian Renaissance humanist, Gregorio Correr – not before Heerkens had gushed about Virgil's indebtedness to it in the *Georgics*.[92] While the learned world tittered gleefully at his gaffe – the story was retold in a handful of early-nineteenth-century biographical dictionaries and miscellanies – our irrepressible Dutch Ovid was undaunted.[93] In a last-ditch bid for scholarly celebrity he rounded off the 1790 edition of his poem on the health of scholars with the results of his research in Italy into the causes of Ovid's exile. The thin trickle of verse that winds through a dense forest of footnotes here might reveal, if the author had not already done so in the preface, that his 'poetic' digression was, in fact, a recycled scholarly dissertation he had once submitted to the Academy of Inscriptions and Belles Lettres. Alas, his erudite epilogue seems not to have registered a ripple.[94]

\* \* \*

It is difficult not to agree with J. A. Worp that the final years of our author's life will have been sad and lonely: ignored by the Republic of Letters, unloved by his countrymen, impoverished as the modest income from his French annuities has dried up,[95] and – perhaps the ultimate indignity – the lifelong Francophile obliged in his old age to billet boorish French soldiers who hindered him in

---

[92] See J. R. Berrigan and G. Tournoy, 'Gregorii Correri Venetae Tragoedia cui titulus Progne: A Critical Edition and Translation', *Humanistica Lovaniensia* 29 (1980), pp. 13–99, at pp. 18–19, who suggest that Heerkens set out to perpetrate a literary hoax, which in my opinion is doubtful. In the preface to the *Icones* Heerkens describes the circumstances under which he came to conclude that the play was sent to him by Divine Providence – he was at the time recovering from an illness – and betrays an unguarded, even childlike, credulity that is difficult to find insincere. See Chapter 5, pp. 165–6. The Latin text and English translation of Correr's play is now available in *Humanist Latin Tragedies*, ed. and trans. Gary Grund (Cambridge, MA and London: Harvard University Press, 2011), pp. 110–87.
[93] Indeed, he was still quietly crowing about his 'Tereus' in a footnote to the revised *Italica* of 1793 (p. 230, n. 2).
[94] Heerkens is not even mentioned in John C. Thibault's exhaustive survey of the topic, *The Mystery of Ovid's Exile* (Berkeley and Los Angeles: University of California Press, 1964).
[95] Due to his Jacobin enemies in France, he suspects, in a letter to Johan Meerman of 30 July 1794; letters sent to Paris lamenting the fate of French émigré friends have apparently been intercepted. Heerkens complains in the same letter to Meerman of having to sell off his medals and books 'at a very low price, which Latin books can but promise me'. He must now also put his house on the market, and without that, how can he accommodate a library which had once taken up four rooms? He exclaims,

his work.⁹⁶ Already before the Batavian revolution it seems that Heerkens's luck and cultural currency was running out: in a prefatory poem to his *De valetudine literatorum* (1790), to Dordrecht magistrate and Latin poet, Jacob Henrik Hoeufft, the perennially Ovidian Heerkens proves himself almost *tristior Tristiis*. He is rueful about his decision to return to his homeland: 'Once I was displeasing for not being a demagogue [sc. in his journalism] and, now, it is the same old story, others say I love the French too much' ('Displicui quondam, non demagogus; et idem / Nunc aliis Gallos dicor amare nimis', p. xviii). The old man is criticized for not 'shouting with the people' ('Vim populo clamare senem renuisse'); 'a certain cruel man of the mob' ('vir unus atrox plebis') flings the 'dire calumny' ('dira ... calumnia') of unpatriotism at him, and it smarts all the more because, 'if another country were dearer to me than my homeland, why do I live in my homeland, not France, known to me long ago? And I have beheld so many other lands under a smiling sky! And my homeland, more cloudy than the others, beholds me!' ('Carior ac patria si terra sit altera, cur me / Patria, non pridem Gallia nota, tenet? / Totque alias vidi ridente sub aethere terras! / Patria, plus aliis nubila, meque videt', p. xix). The blameless senior citizen even fears for his personal safety, as his house comes under hostile fire!⁹⁷ When it comes to high culture, 'the land of Tomi is better suited to the poet than Frisia, to whom you Rhodope, and you wide Haemus, deny your zephyrs' ('Aptior est vati, quam Frisia, terra Tomitis, / Cui Rhodope zephiros, latus et Haeme negas', p. xvii). In the preface to the second edition of his *Empedocles* (1798), Heerkens would describe himself as an exiled Ovid for the last time – but this time, it is the newly barbarian *French* who have transformed Groningen into Tomi.⁹⁸

poignantly, 'is there no employment in this town [sc. Groningen] or anywhere else for an old man, a man of letters, a catholic?' Cf. *Empedocles* (1798), pp. ii–iii.

⁹⁶ See, for example, the letter to Johan Meerman dated 8 February 1796, where he complains of being treated 'inhumanly' for the past five to six months, having boarded 'well beyond his quota share'. Groningen is 'swarming with troops, as many French as of our own nation'. As a consequence the cost of living has become exorbitant, with officers renting rooms in town. Heerkens disapproves especially of these French officers marrying well-born local girls, including one from his own family! He reports in a postscript that even a young Dutch councillor of the former regent class has found himself in prison for protesting the maltreatment of a soldier, leading to his death, by one of these officers. See Museum Meermanno-Westreenianum, The Hague, 95:16 / 242/265–/573 – six letters from G. N. Heerkens to Johan Meerman (1773–96).

⁹⁷ 'My villa was riddled with so many enemy bullets when we Dutch received our new guests from the [river] Havel' (sc. French soldiers returned from Prussia); 'Villa tot hostiles scloporum inpuncta per ictus, / De Spraea Batavis cum novus hospes erat' (p. xx). Billeted soldiers fooling around?

⁹⁸ For punishing recent violations of the peace he congratulates the dedicatee, Patriot magistrate and medic, Jacob van der Steege, who has recently 'returned from India more famous than Bontekoe' (*Empedocles* (1798), p. viii).

As for his character, Heerkens was certainly vain, ambitious and a self-publicist. But he must also have been, in his prime, lively, witty, amiable and eminently clubbable. If he sometimes evinced an aristocratic disdain for his fellow 'Frisians', preferring the company of those fancy foreign friends to the practical and profit-driven Dutch (in his own characterization), our study will reveal that he deeply craved the acceptance and admiration of his compatriots. He may even have entertained secret hopes of joining the ranks of the great Groningen humanists Rudolph Agricola, Ubbo Emmius and Menso Alting, commemorative statues of whom he proposed should be commissioned to adorn the city's *Grootmarkt*.[99]

This book is not intended as the intellectual biography of a figure who, even by the standards of his day, was no first-order scientific thinker, natural historian or even classical scholar. Nor do we pretend to offer a comprehensive analysis of each and every Latin work by Heerkens.[100] We present, rather, a study of the interaction of his Latin works and networks – the latter projected on multiple axes, to include, in addition to his contemporary correspondents, the various virtual networks of ancients and *recentiores* with whom he had daily commerce. We consider how these works and networks effectively created one another, combining to yield what we might call the 'literary life-work', the uniquely derivative, captivatingly composite, late humanist Latin subjectivity that was Gerard Nicolaas Heerkens. We shall see that Heerkens's compulsive cosmopolitanism and relentless self-promotion paper over the fault lines of a radically fractured identity, a northern Dutch identity compromised by his Catholicism; by his refusal to marry and fulfil the traditional obligations of the eldest son of a noble family; and, perhaps especially, by a confusion of vocations at a date when more exclusive choices were beginning to be demanded of the poet, philologist, philosopher and physician than a century earlier. It will be argued in this book, however, that the apparent incommensurability of Heerkens's poetic, scientific and social, aspirations is to some extent healed, made coherent, by his vociferous self-inscription into a modern *Respublica litterarum latinarum*; and by his adoption, perhaps not always fully conscious, of an Ovidian literary and life persona. Heerkens prescribes Ovid for himself as much as for his readers.

---

[99] *Notabilia*, Book 2, p. 126.
[100] Because Heerkens is relatively unknown today even within the Netherlands, and because his works are not all easily accessible online, I have erred on the side of generosity in supplying translated extracts. I have aimed to supply the original Latin for verse but, due to constraints of space, have omitted it from most of the prose quotations. Translations from other languages are mine unless otherwise indicated.

1

# Finding His Feet: Six or Five?

## The limits of chivalry: The poetic circle of Clara Feyoena van Sytzama

Clara Feyoena van Sytzama was a gifted Dutch poetess whose early life was marred by personal tragedy (Figure 1.1).[1] Born in Leeuwarden, Frisia, in 1729, to Pier Willem van Sytzama, an officer in the States' army and provincial member of the States-General, and Ebella Juliana Aebinga van Humalda, who died when Clara was just a year old, the girl moved with her father and brother to Winsum, in the province of Groningen, when Pier Willem married the young widow, Geertruida Foek van Burmania, and became lord of Bellingeweer. By 1738 Clara's new stepmother and three half-siblings had followed her own mother into the grave. A more enduring influence was the gutsy governess appointed by her father, Frederika Alida Tegneus, who nurtured her young charge's poetic talents. Clara's older brother, Pico Galenus, brought his talented sister to the attention of his student chums at the University of Groningen. Years later Clara would reflect fondly, perhaps strategically, on the literary circle that had crystallized around her in her youth and met in her father's house.[2] An *album amicorum* compiled by

---

[1] The still standard biography is Seerp Anema, *Een vergeten dichteres uit de achttiende eeuw* (Clara Feyoena van Sytzama) (Amsterdam, 1921). See also Annelies de Jeu, '*'t Spoor der dichteressen': Netwerken en publicatiemogelijkheden van schrijvende vrouwen in de Republiek (1600–1750)* (Hilversum: Verloren, 2000). Henrik S. van Lennep has written a brief biographical note for the *Digitaal Vrouwenlexicon van Nederland*: <www.historici.nl/Onderzoek/Projecten/DVN>.

[2] As Jacques Tersteeg explains, this cannot have been a formal literary society with set offices, rules and prizes, such as mushroomed in the Netherlands through the eighteenth century: Tersteeg, 'Clara Feyeona's dichterkring te Bellingeweer', *Info Bulletin Winsum* (Historische Verenigung Winsum-Obergum) 12.3 (2007), pp. 11–20, at p. 11. On literary clubs as an expression of Dutch sociability (*gezelligheid*) see Joost Kloek and Wijnand Mijnhardt, *1800: Blueprints for a National Community, Dutch Culture in a European Perspective* 2 (Assen: Van Gorcum and Palgrave Macmillan, 2004), chap. 7, pp. 93–114.

**Figure 1.1** The Dutch poetess, Clara Feyoena van Sytzama.
Source: Clara Feyoena van Sytzama, *Bellingeweerder Uitspanningen* (Groningen: Jurjen Spandaw, 1746), frontispiece. Courtesy of the University of Groningen Library.

one of the group, theology student, Arnoldus Kulenkamp, usefully supplies the 'Arcadian' names of many of its members. Among them was a certain 'Pylignus', the mercurial Gerard Nicolaas Heerkens.[3]

[3] C. W. Bruinvis, 'Album van Arnoldus Kulenkamp. De dichteres Clara Feyoena van Sytzama', *De navorscher* 54 (1904), pp. 389–94. Many thanks to Mr Harry de Raad of the Regioanaal Archief Alkmaar for supplying me with a copy of this article and of the album itself.

During this period in Groningen tensions were rife between the pro-prince Orangists (supporters of the 'stadtholderate', or hereditary stewardship, of the house of Nassau–Orange) and the pro-Republicans (or 'regents', a patrician class of rulers drawn from the richer merchant families).[4] Clara's loyalties, through her father, were with the Orangists, as proclaimed already in the title of her first poetic collection: 'Bellingeweer recreations ... together with a preface and appendix on the illustrious house of Orange and Nassau',[5] dedicated to the Friesian-born Stadtholder, Willem Carel Hendrik Friso (1711–51), his wife, Anna, and daughter, Carolina.[6] The political preliminaries by Clara's brother run to nearly a hundred pages; then follow some sixty pages of liminary verse by Clara's admirers, men and women. Most of these poems are in Dutch, two in German and just three in Latin, including one in elegiacs by Heerkens to which we will return at the end of this chapter. Four years later, in 1750, Heerkens would dedicate a *French* poem to Clara on the occasion of her marriage to Isaak Reinder, Baron of Raesfelt, Lord of Heemse in Overijssel. That party piece gives a good flavour of the young Heerkens's high spirits, subverting as it does the prevailing epithalamic conventions by commencing with a list of the suitors Clara has disappointed by marrying, and omitting the traditional reference to future children.[7] In his choice of language we perhaps get a foretaste of Heerkens's cosmopolitanism (although the use of French by educated Dutch in this period did not necessarily imply political *Francophilia*).[8]

Isaak was not Clara's first love. She had recently emerged from an unhappy affair with Justus (Joost) Conring (1725–48), Heerkens's best friend, the son of Groningen magistrate, Andries Conring. Heerkens, in his wedding impromptu for Clara and Isaak, rather tastelessly suggests that the then deceased Justus is being comforted in the afterlife by Sappho! Justus's precocious literary accomplishments had run to translating Thomson's *Seasons* into Latin and

---

[4] For the wider context, see J. E. Heeres, 'Stad en lande tijdens het erfstadhouderschap van Willem IV', *Bijdragen voor Vaderladnsche Geschiedenis en Oudheidkunde* 3.4 (1888), pp. 252–344.
[5] Clara Feyoena van Sytzama, *Bellingeweerder Uitspanningen ... Benevens een voorrede en aanhangsel, betreffende het doorlugtigste huis van Orange en Nassau* (Groningen: Jurjen Spandaw, 1746).
[6] A selection of Clara's Dutch poetry may be found in Lia Van Gemert, José van Aelst, Hermina Joldersma and Olga Van Marion (eds), *Womens Writing from the Low Countries 1200–1875: A Bilingual Anthology* (Amsterdam: Amsterdam University Press, 2011), pp. 385–95.
[7] See Tersteeg, 'Clara Feyoena's dichterkring', pp. 18–19. As he says, who could have expected a wedding poem from Heerkens after the fiasco of 1746? For the text of the impromptu, see Klaus Oosterkamp, 'Sneldicht ter gelegenheid van het huwelijk van Clara Feyoena van Sytzama barones van Bellingeweer etc. etc. met de heer Van Raesfelt, heer van Heemse, Den Alerdinck etc. etc.', *Info Bulletin Winsum* 12.3 (2007), pp. 21–4.
[8] Kloek and Mijnhardt, *1800: Blueprints*, pp. 404–5.

Dutch; he died having embarked on a Dutch translation of Voltaire's *Henriade*.[9] The regent party politics of his family, however, did not meet with the approval of Clara's father, although it is possible that Justus once served, Abelard-and-Heloise style, as her tutor.[10] Conring died at the age of 23, perhaps of a broken heart, and at any rate not long after Pier Willem had put an end to his liaison with Clara – but Heerkens, in the second edition of his didactic poem *De valetudine literatorum* ('On the health of learned men', Groningen, 1790), effectively attributes Justus's untimely demise to the young man's *own* father, for pushing him too hard. The early life of the scholar is a particular concern of Heerkens's in that poem, and Conring's premature passing serves as an example to all serious young men not to study too hard, not to rush to know everything too soon.[11] It is possible, of course, that Heerkens refrained from alluding to the love affair with Clara as a contributing cause of his friend's death because he wished to spare her feelings, since she was still alive at the time – or is that an overly charitable interpretation, given his apparent readiness to embarrass her on her wedding day?

Clara would dedicate poems to her lost love as late as 1794.[12] From that vantage point she would describe her poems in the *Bellingeweerder Uitspanningen* as 'kreupele verzen', crippled verses, overhastily despatched to the printer by her too-eager father.[13] Heerkens had no such complaints about *his* old man: Eppo's interdict on Gerard's scribbling became well known around Groningen from at least 1746.[14] This was the year in which a protracted poetic quarrel broke out between Heerkens and his friends and the local literary establishment. Lennep has dubbed it a battle between 'ancients' and 'moderns', but these labels need some qualification, as we shall see that the classicizing, cosmopolitan

---

[9] See Heerkens, *De valetudine literatorum* (Groningen, 1790), pp. 9–10, and nn. 8–11; and below, in the *Toesangh*. According to Anema the only writings preserved by Conring are in the Kulenkamp album (fols 55–8), but the short poem by 'J. C.' in the *Bellingeweerder Uitspanningen* is almost certainly by him.

[10] Thus Anema, *Een vergeten dichteres*, p. 66. In Kulenkamp's album, however, young Joost signs off 'vivat Oranje!'

[11] 'Nec dubito, quin sis documentum ultroque juventae, / Assideat studiis ne nimis illa suis. / Et qui scire cupit, scierit nisi tempore multum. / Passus agit modicus, non bene cursus iter' (p. 10). There is a certain irony in this admonition, since the poem was originally drafted in 1748/9, when Heerkens was himself still an adolescent according to classical medical theory!

[12] Although from this time she lived a quiet life on her husband's estate in Overijssel, Clara kept in contact with several poets and writers and became a member of the leading literary societies 'Kunstliefde Spaart Geen Vlijt' and 'Kunst Wordt Door Arbeid Verkregen'. She would endure and write about the death, in 1780, of her newly married daughter, Ermgard Ebella Juliana, whose small children she subsequently raised.

[13] Anema, *Een vergeten dichteres*, p. 52.

[14] Heerkens was close to his father and credited him with instilling a love of literature in him at a young age.

Heerkens may be viewed as both 'modern' *and* 'ancient'. What was really at stake here? The origins of the quarrel and the personal, political, perhaps even religio-political, motivations of the various parties remain partially obscure. In the following section I give a broad outline of hostilities in the context of the themes of our book. Not all the contributions were of high literary merit, and the Dutch poems, in particular, are often repetitive and rather ham-fisted. Some of the criticisms levelled by and against Heerkens, however, and indeed the very *interplay* of Dutch and Latin pamphlets, are revealing of our well-born Catholic author's ambiguous socio-cultural position in eighteenth-century Groningen, and of his literary aspirations and frustrations.

In order to understand Heerkens's future career, then, we must first come to terms with his rash and raucous entry into the world of letters. And we must try to resolve some *prima facie* paradoxes: the young satirist attacks established city poets, as well as the hack verses of the mainly student–poets who celebrated the regent-party wedding of Hermann Wolthers and Louise Christina Conring on 23 January 1746 – but on that occasion he had not refrained from tossing off a few lines himself, and was not embarrassed to say so later.[15] In the *poetenstrijd* Heerkens apparently lurks in the shadows and is branded a 'bat' and an 'owl' by his opponents – but if he really wished to escape detection, why did he assume the relatively transparent pseudonym of 'Curillus' (Heerkens = 'little lord')? Moreover, the old guard which Heerkens and his comrade-in-arms, 'Andreades' (= Justus Conring, in an equally obvious patronymic *nom de plume*), take on, turn out *not* to be that old, at least not in terms of collective grey hairs. Thus Heerkens sneers at the circle of student–poets around Clara Feyoena van Sytzama and brands her, with apparent sarcasm, a 'spirited virago'. What could have led him to, as it were, foul his own nest? Had he lost all sense of perspective, propriety, not to say chivalry, in a miscalculated bid for literary celebrity? That was certainly the complexion opposing poet Lucas Trip (1713–83) put on his peremptory characterization of Clara's followers as a 'dense and nameless mob' ('densum et sine nomine vulgus'). And yet Heerkens himself had joined the chorus of praise when the 17-year-old *virago* launched her *Bellingeweerder*

---

[15] The poems are collected in *Bruilofts-Gezangen opgezongen, ter Bruilofte van . . . Hermann Wolthers, en . . . Louisa Christina Conring* (Groningen, 1746), Pamphlet #1010 of the Van Alphen collection, held at the Groningen University Library. Pamphlets will be referred to throughout by their Van Alphen reference number. The collection is available digitally via subscription at 'The Early Modern Pamphlets Online', <http://tempo.idcpublishers.info/>. Heerkens's own elegiac epithalamium runs from pp. 16–20. See below, pp. 67–8.

*Uitspanningen*, which seems to have appeared shortly before the pamphlet war.[16] There is no reason not to believe Heerkens when he undertook to set the record straight more than a decade later.[17] His disparaging verses on the young men 'whipped into line' ('compellit') by the mannish Clara were not meant in earnest but are the residue of a sort of rambunctious, eighteenth-century 'battle rapping' between overgrown schoolboys.[18]

Be that as it may, Seerp Anema, in his 1921 biography of Clara, introduces Heerkens as a guest at the Wolthers–Conring wedding feast in the following sinister terms: 'a man with a strange, un-Groningish, un-Netherlandish character, a Libertine Catholic, a Mephistopheles by nature'.[19] And yet in 1750, as Tersteeg reminds us, this insidious interloper would appear as a guest at *Clara*'s wedding, and would even recite a few verses for his supper! What sort of a reception might Heerkens have anticipated, then, for his pseudonymous satires of 1746, and what could he possibly have hoped to gain by taunting some of the most powerful men about town? I wish to highlight the fact that Heerkens had the temerity not just to launch himself into, but to persevere in, a long and acrimonious feud, one that saw some thirty Latin and Dutch pamphlets fly into print in the space of two months.[20] The cocky teenager did not relent even after lawyer and future burgemeester Trip, the most celebrated Dutch poet of eighteenth-century Groningen, attempted to bring the affair to a close with his crushing *De Bescheiden Hekeldichter* ('The Coy Satirist').[21] As we shall see, Trip himself had been one of the original targets of Heerkens's satirical scattergun.

---

[16] Tersteeg correctly questions Anema's translation of *carmina iam eduntur* as 'songs have already been published', but it seems likely to me that the *Bellingeweerder Uitspanningen* were 'in press', at least, when the first volleys of the literary quarrel were exchanged. See the following note in which Heerkens seems to confirm that chronology.

[17] In the up-dated version of this poem in his revised (in fact, substantially rewritten) *Marii Curilli Groningensis Satyrae* (Groningen, 1758) Heerkens clarifies, in a note: 'since the author, and he who was Andreades, were most faithful followers of the poetess; since they had been members of the group you might think is being attacked here, and indeed had praised the girl's poems in their own poems published at the time ('quippe qui poematiis puellae tunc publicatis publicato carmine applauserant'); and finally, since she herself took the joke in good part and never asked for her name to be removed from this satire, now in its third edition, anyone will appreciate that these satires were not written out of any malice. They arose solely out of high spirits and boyish excess, for the author had then scarcely passed his nineteenth birthday' (p. 14).

[18] Tersteeg also views the quarrel as a student game that got out of hand. See 'Clara Feyoena's dichterkring', pp. 15–16.

[19] Anema, *Een vergeten dichteres*, p. 25.

[20] May–June 1746, #1013–#1037A.

[21] A concise biographical note on Trip by Groningen local historian, Beno Hofman, is available online from the Groningen Regional Archives, 'De dichtende burgemeester Lucas Trip' <www.groningerarchieven.nl/historie/stadsverhalen/taal-en-literatuur/de-dichtende-burgemeester-lucas-

## Ancients versus moderns ... or young Turks versus old fogeys?

Heerkens threw down the gauntlet in 'Curillus's song, bidding farewell to the Muses and summoning his energies for more serious studies', which begins in Juvenalian fashion: 'Semper ego insanus videar?'[22] From its opening line the *Carmen Curilli* revisits familiar anti-poetic themes from the Roman satirists: 'Curillus' reflects on the absurdity of writing verse in the vain hope of competing with the Horaces, Popes, Boileaus or Vondels[23] of this world, and in the company of so many modern poetasters. But already from the opening lines there is an Ovidian wink: 'will I have to keep listening to my Dad complaining?' ('totiesque querelas / Debuero sentire Patris?', p. 3). Heerkens initiates a game of autobiographical hide-and-seek that will be played out through his entire career. Who is the 'Hippus' to whom Curillus appears foolish, 'along with many others who don't know about poetry' ('audior *Hippo* / Et multis stolidus, quibus est ignota poesis')? Who is the 'immoral comrade' ('pravum ... sodalem') he must avoid, because he worships another God, as the pagans did of old – surely not the blameless, studious and Calvinist Conring?[24] What good is it, laments Curillus, to heed the advice of the great ENGELHARD,[25] when 'Dipsas' (an Ovidian bawd) loves to revile poets (p. 3). No, 'Andreades' (sc. Joost Conring), he must pander to old ladies (a future mother-in-law?) and bid the Muses adieu. His father's friend, 'Crispinus' (a

---

trip>. Hofman reports that after Heerkens fled Groningen, following the quarrel, the city council forbade him from publishing there again without their approval. It seems that Trip, to his credit, reacted with 14 sonnets attacking the proposed censorship. Trip's best days as a poet were ahead of him, as author of *Tydwinst in ledige uuren; of proeven van stigtelyken aandagt* (1764; 1774).

[22] *Carmen Curilli cum Musis valediceret et ad graviora studia animum appelleret* (#1013). The preceding pamphlet #1012, *Elegia ad Magistratum Groninganum ut restituantur Academiae Professores* ('Elegy to the municipal authority of Groningen, that the vacant university Chairs should be refilled'), is by an anonymous Heerkens, signing himself (in Greek) 'Palladophilos'. The prose 'monitum' makes clear that the author is a friend of 'Curillus', and that he was already embroiled in controversy; thus the pamphlet probably post-dates the *Carmen Curilli*. As for the latter, I cite the second edition, 'priori longe rectior' (#1014), which among other changes contains 'clarificatory' footnotes. One, for example, denies that 'Curillus' is derived from the Greek 'kurios' (and thus = 'Heerkens'); another disingenuously purports to soften the criticism of Meinard Hemsterhuis (see below, p. 40).

[23] The great seventeenth-century Dutch playwright and poet, Joost van den Vondel (1587–1679), was something of a lodestone in Heerkens's career. Vondel converted to Catholicism in 1641 (scandalizing Calvinist Utrecht), became a forthright advocate for religious tolerance, and lived to the ripe old age of 91. He was the author of anti-Calvinist satires.

[24] Curiously, in #1037A, by Erasmus Secundus (= Heerkens), the pseudonymous author exhorts Heerkens to suspend worshipping in his own Chapel for a while, and to visit Justus in his Church. This will upset his father, but he cannot refuse his friend.

[25] Nicolaus Engelhard (1696–1765), charismatic Swiss professor of philosophy at the University of Groningen; a much-loved mentor to Heerkens.

proverbial moralizer in Horace), chides him for frittering away the best years of his life. Does Curillus plan to withdraw to the country, 'where the wayward poet often wanders, the small-town residents marvelling at his zeal' ('ibi Vates devius errat / Saepe, suburbano studium mirante colono', p. 5). Go on, says Crispinus, you can appear learned and industrious out there; what country Corydon[26] will even be able to tell you are writing rubbish?

By casting his criticisms of the Groningen poets in the mouth of Crispinus, Heerkens/Curillus affects to avoid responsibility for his comparison of the venerable Meinard Hemsterhuis (1687–1774), assistant headmaster of the Latin school in Groningen, an established Latin and Dutch poet, to a certain hectoring 'Dominicus'; for describing the great Lucas Trip's verse as 'incomprehensible by everyone', and the Wolthers–Conring wedding poets as 'venal Baviuses'. Gerhard Alting – the father of one of Heerkens's university friends – is whining about the dearth of modern Maecenases, but forgets that poets should aspire to nothing beyond a good reputation. But perhaps Heerkens's most provocative gambit, aside from this brazen naming and shaming of his adversaries, is his reporting, *per* Crispinus, the Italian opinion that poets cannot be born beyond the Alps; that Frisia is a sterile land, a country of wethers that will never yield another farmer/*Agricola*.[27] As the Groningen *poetenoorlog* wore on and became uglier these lines would come back to haunt him, as Heerkens's religion and patriotism were increasingly called into question.[28] For now, his fictional preceptor commends him to the more 'profitable' ('lucrosa') study of the law, citing the example of (Joannes) Wolbers 'at whom Apollo perhaps glanced sideways when he was very young, and indeed Wolbers himself thought he was a poet then, but he has now ceased to rave in the deceitful art, having quickly come to his senses'

---

[26] A note to the second edition provides a surely superfluous (for a Latin-reading audience) gloss on the name of *Corydon*, namely that he is a *rusticus*. I suspect this is intended by Heerkens as a patronizing poke at his enemies, and is in any case a red herring: as the Kulenkamp *album amicorum* confirms, 'Corydon' was Conring's pseudonym in the literary circle around Clara. The passage continues: 'But someone, as he sees you going about the fields intent on your book, is amazed and pulls up his ponies, and leaning on his plough, says to his comrades: "this guy is studious and seems learned. He will know what our priest's son is always telling us here in the country, that the earth goes round in a day, and that the sun, on the other hand, is stationary – the same sun which we, however, see moving!"' ('Atque aliquis, per agros dum te videt ire libello / Intentum, mirans inhibet mannos, et aratro / Nixus ait sociis, studet hic doctusque videtur; / Ille sciet, nostri quod Mystae filius usque / Rure solet narrare, die quod terra rotetur, / Sol contra staret, sol quem tamen ire videmus!', p. 5).

[27] The great Northern humanist Rudolph Agricola (Roelof Huusman) was born near Groningen.

[28] The calibration of the classical theory of temperaments and climatic zones to intellectual aptitudes was a commonplace in the early modern Republic of letters. See Hans Bots and Françoise Waquet, *La République des Lettres* (Paris: Belin, 1997), pp. 76–8.

('quem primis forte sub annis / Viderat oblique Phaebus, seque ipse Poetam / Tunc equidem credebat, at insanire dolosa / Cessat in arte, cito resipiscens', p. 8). But see, adds Crispinus, Wolbers is now rich and famous! Forget about Tibullus and Ovid and turn your mind to higher things, Curillus, like natural philosophy and mathematics. Crispinus's homily moves the poet to hate the Muses, and he exclaims in the closing lines of the satire that 'a greater Apollo awaits me' ('melior mihi restat Apollo') – namely, the patron of medicine.

Pamphlet #1015 is a Dutch version of the foregoing poem, with explanatory footnotes – but it is immediately clear that the translator hails from the opposing camp. The epigraph from Hubert Poot's *Praise of Poetry* sets the tone: 'One who opens his mouth wide, in arrogance, and denies her honour, has an ignoble heart, full of ass-naturedness' ('Een die verwaant zyn' mond opspart / En haer haer eer ontzeit, / Heeft een onedelaerdig hart / Vol ezelaerdigheit'). The anonymous translator parodies Heerkens's Latin, rendering his infelicities of style into excessively rhymed Dutch (here reprising Crispinus's homily): 'Gy *styt* uw' *tyt* en *byt* met *vlyt*, om't geen niet *dyt*, / Uw' nag'len; maar ... gy *zyt* den Zang *stryt* toege*wyt*, en *ryt* en *splyt*, de *Nyt* ten *spyt*, uw hooft met rymen' ('You waste your time, assiduously biting your fingernails over that which is fruitless; but ... you dedicate yourself to the quarrel over poetry, tearing and splitting your head with verse, in spite of Envy', pp. 4–5). A note *ad loc.* clarifies that the translator is here attempting to capture Curillus's accumulation of Latin endings in -*is*. Other footnotes explain that he has sought, in bad Dutch, to give an indication of Heerkens's false quantities, and that he has replaced the word '*wiser* with *viser*, imitating the elegance of the Latin *recipiscere*, which the author consistently uses for *resipiscere*; perhaps because he prefers *capere* ('grasping') to *sapere* ('knowing')' (p. 6, n. (e)).[29] More darkly, the author chastises Curillus for his churlishness and lack of respect for the Wolthers–Conring wedding couple in describing their well-wishers as 'Slemppoeten', implying they had done everything for the sake of a dinner and not for their hosts. Moreover, he has it on the good authority of those poets that 'Curillus' is *really* a certain 'HEERTIE' ('little lord', p. 7, n. (k)).[30] In producing this Dutch version,

---

[29] 'Wat lachtge o Nar by uw' (e) *cinnen* bet te weezen': with a note, '*Cinnen* voor *zinnen* naargevolgt naar de sierlykheit van het Latynsche *recipiscere*, by den Autheur telkens gebruikt voor *resipiscere*, misschien om dat Hy meer houd van *capere* an *sapere*'.

[30] A sneering final note to the reader advises that, 'in order to avoid annoying [you] we have not taken into account in our notes the other errors in spelling and language which mar the Latin everywhere. We leave it to the reader to judge whether the author's ignorance or carelessness is to blame.'

of course, the anonymous translator is airing Heerkens's dirty linen in view of a wider reading public than that of the learned, closed, homosocial coterie for which it was originally intended. He is, as it were, transferring the jaunty Latin licence of the student rag to the front pages of the local, conservative broadsheet, thereby casting a dangerous shadow of slander over Heerkens's adolescent anti-authoritarianism.[31]

Well might Heerkens's enemies have hoped he would take his own advice in the *Carmen Curilli* and abandon the Muses, but a second Latin pamphlet was promptly unleashed: *Epistola Andreadis ad Curillum, Ut in Pindum Se recipiat, Musasque Defendat a malenatis Frisiae Poetis* ('Andreades's letter to Curillus exhorting him to get back to Pindus, to defend the sisters against the mongrel poets of Friesland').[32] Andreades/Conring, not impossibly Heerkens himself,[33] pleads with Curillus not to forsake his true vocation. The doctor will not easily leave his patients' bedside and the babbling lawyer exchange sweet forum and profits for Galen; the rustic born to the plough will not happily take up the weapons of war nor plough the swollen seas.[34] Poetry is in Curillus's blood. Is he seeking the peace of the philosophers, scrutinizing with a telescope the planets God has providently removed from our sight so as to banish them from our cares? Does he really want to know whether bold Copernicus was right to confiscate the Sun's horses and that 'ubiquitous chariot' ('decantatam quadrigam', p. 4)? 'These' – warns Andreades – 'are the new-fangled lies of the freethinkers who despoil Phoebus, as if God could challenge them by holding

---

[31] In the verse prologue to the *Marii Curilli Satyrae* he pleads: 'Curillus was a boy, younger than twenty, wanton and cheeky with the licence of that age' ('Puer Curillus, & viginti annis minor, / Petulans, & aevi garrulus lascivia'); cf. *Sat.* VI, 'To Vonck', in *Marii Curilli Satyrae*, pp. 46–7, where he begs for forgiveness, in accordance with ancient laws, for his youthful indiscretions; claims he wasn't *that* bad; and laments the fact that: 'what you were as a boy you will also be considered to be as a man, and ever thus. It's a harsh law, and not sufficiently lenient for a good poet, whose mind is like wax, pliant, and easily led wherever you like, especially before maturity has tempered the fires of his spirit' ('Qualis eras puer, & vir talis habebere, talis / Semper eris. Lex dura, bono neque lata poetae, / Cerea cui mens est, facilis, ducendaque quovis, / Praecipue ante ignes animi quam temperat aetas', p. 47). The adolescent poet thus suffers an irrevocable immortality similar to that of his modern counterpart on Facebook!

[32] Pamphlet #1016: I quote from the corrected edition, #1017.

[33] Thus Worp, 'Gerard Nicolaas Heerkens', p. 7, who points out that the poems attributed to Conring are later incorporated into Heerkens's own corpus, that is in the *Marii Curilli Satyrae* (1758). But could that not be interpreted as a gesture of piety towards his deceased friend, whom he had embroiled in the bungled publicity stunt that had demonstrably blighted his own career? Heerkens's note implies that 'he who was Andreades's shared in the fun and games. On the other hand, Joannes Lucaszoon Fockens, a fellow Clara-devotee, confidently identifies Andreades with Curillus (#1031, p. 8, nn. (f), (h)), as does Alting in #1025, and Trip in *De bescheiden hekeldichter* (#1037, p. 36).

[34] Cf. Horace *Sat.* 1. 1. 16–19.

the reins; Aethon and Pyrois [the horses of the Sun] are indefatigable, nor was the sacred chariot of Phaethon destroyed' ('Sacrilega haec sane nova sunt commenta sophorum, / Qui Phaebum spoliant, acsi lacesscere [sic] possit / Fraena tenendo Deus; non est fatigabilis Aeton / Non Pyrois, sacra nec Phaetonti fracta quadriga est', pp. 4–5).[35] Curillus protests that he has to earn a living somehow, and it is not possible to do that from poetry unless one prostitutes one's Muse like a *Hemsterhuis*, that hired hack who scribbles dirges for consuls, the rich and the unworthy. Or perhaps he should wield his verses like weapons, to keep the French at bay, as has *Alting*?[36] There is no little irony in Curillus's Ovidian claim: 'My Muse is milder, timid, defenceless, not up to attacking an armed enemy' ('Mitior & pavida est, nec in hostem tendat inermis / Armatum mea Musa', p. 6). Does Andreades seriously suggest he take on the patricians and senators of the city, as *Bakker* has done?[37] No, says Curillus, 'we have greater respect, and Apollo counsels the well-born poet against this' ('reverentia nostra est / Major, & ingenuo hoc dissuadet Apollo Poetae', p. 6). Besides, he has no girlfriend, no patron, no agent to bring his work to the ears of LAMAN,[38] since he would be too shy to do so himself ... But Andreades won't relent, reminding Curillus that van Swinderen favours the arts and would love to hear his lyre: 'as he himself is chaste/ beardless he protects, and will protect a chaste/beardless Muse' ('... ut tegit ipse / Impubes, musamque imbubem [sic] proteget ille', p. 7).[39] Just think, if the young man doesn't return to poetry people will think little of the art because of the prevailing low standards! What if there had never been an Apelles, only vapid landscape painters? What if

---

[35] Heerkens perhaps stages here, in light-hearted miniature, a genuine internal struggle between the new philosophy, even 'Enlightenment' on the one hand, and an older, more familiar world of (Christian) humanist poetry and scholarship on the other. Contemporary Jesuit scientific poets indicated a path to reconciliation, as we shall see in the next chapter.

[36] Not (as Tersteeg surmises) Heerkens's friend Willem Arnold Alting, later Governor-General of the Dutch East Indes, but his father Gerhard (1694–c. 1761), a lawyer and Groningen tax-officer who published many Latin poems in pamphlet form. The reference here is to Alting's pamphlet against Louis XV. His son W. A. Alting was a contributor of a Latin elegy to the Wolthers–Conring *Bruilofts-Gezangen* (#1010, pp. 45–6).

[37] The Groningen-born Pieter Huizinga Bakker (1713–1801) was an Amsterdam merchant and Dutch poet. The reference here is to a verse pamphlet *De Digtkundige Spectator*, attacking abuses in the election of public officers.

[38] Wink, wink! A footnote spells out that [Paul] Laman is 'a most distinguished consul of this city', but any hopes Heerkens may have entertained of securing him as patron were soon to be dashed. He would dedicate a funerary poem to Laman in 1747 (#1093), in which it is implied – but of course we will never know – that the elder statesman secretly favoured him in the Groningen pamphlet war. Heerkens's coy eulogy also casts a sly glance back at one of the original pretexts for the quarrel, as he scorns the writing of laudatory verse for personal gain.

[39] Wicher van Swinderen (1688–1764) was a magistrate, deputy to the States-General, and member of the Council of the State. He married Anna Maria Trip. See entry in the online New Dutch

everyone was to judge the art of sacred poetry with reference to the trashy verses of *Trip*? What if Homer had never existed, and *Alting* always – how rarely Pegasus would have flown! Now poetry is flourishing on the Tiber, Danube, Wisla and Rhine, in England and in France. It's true that Apollo has shunned our chilly Friesland for a long time ... at least, until recently, when so many wannabe bards have sallied forth and tried to scale Pindus, like Titans assailing Olympus. So far Apollo and the Muses have successfully fended them off, but Andreades urges Curillus to hasten to their aid:

> I nunc, I fer opem, te Pegasus efferet, ecce
> 
> *Hemsterhusus* adest, ferus, horridus, ore minaci
> 
> Ut furit! Heu Musae pallent, jamque acrius instat,
> 
> Hic venit *Altingus* dux agminis alter, ibidem
> 
> *Bolhusi*,[40] *Pabi*,[41] et quod secum animosa virago
> 
> Syztema compellit, densum et sine nomine vulgus.
> 
> Heu mihi, quam numerus crescit! Quis fervor ubique
> 
> Certantum, quam *Pabus*[42] ibi violentior urget!
> 
> Tam furiose ulli non pugnavere gygantum.
> 
> Verum age nunc, Musaeque vocant, ades o bone vates
> 
> Care Curille venis! Sic Pindo tuta Thalia est,
> 
> Pegasus exiliat, rursusque triumphet Apollo.

Go now, go bring help! Pegasus will bear you away, lo! *Hemsterhuis* is here, wild, bristly, how he rages with glowering mien! Alas, the Muses become pale, and now he is bearing down more fiercely. Here comes *Alting*, their army's other general, and in the same place the *Bolhuises* and *Pabuses*, and whatever the spirited virago Van Sytzama rallies, a dense throng of nobodies.

---

Dictionary of Biography, *Nieuw Nederlandsch Biografisch Woordenboek* (hereafter *NNBW*), P. J. Blok and P. C. Molhuysen, 'Wicher van Swinderen', Deel 9 (1933), available at <www.dbnl.org/tekst/molh003nieu00_01/>. Heerkens's pamphlet designates him a 'Clariss. Groningae Senator'. He was clearly not 'beardless' in 1746! In the expanded version of this poem published in 1758, Andreades exhorts Curillus to celebrate the deeds not of van Swinderen but of the Nassau prince.

[40] On Bolhuis see J. W. van Veen, *Michiel van Bolhuis: een achttiende-eeuws herenbestaan in Groningen*. He is the author of several occasional poems in the Van Alphen collection: #898 (1736); #952 (1741); #970 (1742).

[41] In the first edition (#1016) the name of 'Hulten' appears here: T. B. Van Hulten, 'doctor of both laws', was yet another occasional poet; he contributed the opening Dutch poem to the Wolthers–Conring *Bruilofts-Gezangen*. See below, n. 49.

[42] In the first edition Trip's name appears here.

Woe is me, how their number increases! On those surrounded by a sea of combatants how *Pabus* presses there more vehemently! None of the giants fought so furiously! But come now – and the Muses are calling you – o you are present, good poet, you arrive, dear Curillus! Thus Thalia is safe on Pindus, Pegasus may leap, and Apollo triumph once more. (p. 8)

Thus ends 'Andreades's' letter: a reverse gigantomachy in which Heerkens and his *alter ego* have the chutzpah to claim they are on the side of the angels. It is noteworthy that 'Andreades' refers to a contemporary international culture of Latin writing – in Rome, Poland, the German-speaking lands, England and France – and denigrates the efforts of at least the eighteenth-century 'Frisian' Latin poets. Both Conring and Heerkens were no doubt yearning for richer pastures.[43] Did Heerkens, chafing at the parochialism of Clara's Bellingeweer 'academy', already dream of the day his Latin satires would bring him to the attention of the Accademia degli Arcadi in Rome?

A rejoinder by none other than 'Poetry' herself was in the offing, the Dutch 'Dichtkunst aan Curil' (#1018). Poetry is incensed at Curillus's ingratitude. He was once well known for his literary gifts but is now a wolf-puppy grown to maturity and into savagery, a snail leaving a slimy trail. Let him listen to the old women who mock his poetry! Let him see if he can please them with better work! He should do as he promised and abandon the Muses – that will please his father, who had considered him lost to Catholicism for a pagan altar. But he should not expect any favours from Apollo in the science of medicine after scorning his patronage in poetry. Curillus's attacks on the esteemed Hemsterhuis, Trip, Bolhuis and Alting are motivated by envy. He has the gall to compare our 'hero of letters' to a madman! Will he (sc. Hemsterhuis) allow this owl to fly in his face, or, like a bat, shying the light, to attack him anonymously and escape punishment? The apostrophe is perhaps a clue as to the true identity of 'Poetry' – Hemsterhuis himself? – or at least an invitation to the cantankerous old schoolmaster to join the fray.[44]

Poetry's baleful threat did not intimidate our defiant student–poet. And if we ever had any doubts that the 'countryside Corydon' of his first satire

---

[43] Conring, however, apparently concentrated his efforts on the translation of foreign bestsellers.
[44] In #1019 Heerkens implies that Hemsterhuis is the author of this satire. According to the entry in A. J. van der Aa, *Biographisch woordenboek der Nederlanden*, Deel 8, Eerste stuk (Haarlem, 1867), available online at <www.dbnl.org/tekst/aa__001biog00_01>, Hemsterhuis had a high reputation as a scholar, but, according to those who knew him, was stiff and gruff by nature, and was particularly brusque and insensitive in his old age ('een uitmuntend literator, maar stug en norsch van aard, ruw en ongevoelig vooral in zijnen ouderdom', p. 543).

was, in fact, Joost Conring, Heerkens gives the game away in the title of his *Elegia G. H. qua queritur sibi imputari Satyram Curilli, quae nuper in Frisiae Poetas hic edita est, ad J. C. . . . Rusticantem* ('Elegy of G. H., in which he complains that the *Satire of Curillus*, recently published here against the Frisian poets, has been attributed to him, to J. C. in the Countryside', #1019). It begins: 'While you, friend, far from the noise of the city, pursue your leisure in the countryside, in complete and undisturbed tranquillity, the city detains me, and those city-chores of mine – and of course as I attend to them, I am obliged to suffer more of the same' ('Cum tu rure tuo procul urbis Amice tumultu, / Otia securae plena quietis agas, / Me tenet urbs, & in urbe mei, quos curo, labores; / Scilicet haec ut ago, debeo plura pati', p. 3). With the change of metre Heerkens aligns himself with the elegiac Ovid, Tibullus and Propertius (explicitly at pp. 3–4), and asks, if he really was 'this new Juvenal' everyone is talking about, why would he have dubbed the wedding poets 'venal Baviuses', since *he himself* participated in those festivities: 'As far as I know Horace didn't fulminate against himself; he spared himself when he wrangled the likes of Bavius . . .' ('Quatenus hunc novi, non saevit Horatius in se, / Parsit, cum Bavios strinxerit, ipse sui . . .', p. 4). Adding insult to injury, Heerkens bids T*** (sc. Trip) come and drink the waters he so craves: G. H. will not call him 'another Tantalus' or expel him from Pindus. I never said that 'you, A*** [sc. Alting] are held back by boozy gout – it is only fair that it should fetter your feet, lest you ascend too high' ('Non ego: te A—i retinet vinosa podagra. / Ne nimis altus eas, vinciit aequa pedes', pp. 4–5). And 'why', asks the poet, 'is H*** [sc. Hemsterhuis] raging and threatening me with punishments?' ('Quid furis H—e mihi, poenasque minaris?', p. 5). Let him mount Parnassus with my blessing – together with all his schoolboys! It wasn't me who carped at your art, 'learned W*** [sc. Wolbers]'. Keep on singing about your Dina, 'if that silly Curillus will just keep quiet' ('Nec nos docte tuam W – i carpsimus artem; . . . *Dina* tibi, sileat modo frivolus ille *Curillus*', p. 5). And Apollo doesn't need *my* help to eject B*** [sc. Bolhuis] from Pindus.[45] On the other hand, he *could* do with a hand defending Thalia: van Swinderen's 'abandoned Muse' might be enlisted to this end.[46]

---

[45] Cf. the finale to #1017, quoted above.
[46] I cannot find any trace of van Swinderen's literary efforts, presumably juvenile. Heerkens seems to be attempting to recruit him to his cause, but Trip will later name van Swinderen as one of the poetic elders whom Curillus has offended in the quarrel.

Returning to the pastoral theme, the author wishes that he could only enjoy C[onring']s peaceful life. It's *Curillus*, not G. H., who should be drinking this poison, Curillus 'who is pious to the Muses, impious to me' ('Ille pius Musis, impius ille mihi', p. 6). G. H. is reaping Bolhuis's criticisms and the wrath of Bakker. Is my boyish Muse, or even yours, Curillus, really worth all this fuss? (One can just imagine how that cute little provocation will have gone down with the grumpy old men of Groningen!) H[emsterhuis] is descending on me with his whole school! It's not safe to go to the forum either – a toady or student of yours, W[olbers], will point me out. Heerkens imagines himself being accosted by a stranger who inquires whether he is *the* Curillus who wrote those satires. The poet cannot convince him otherwise because, as the good fellow points out, his style gives him away![47] This stranger, the counterpart of Crispinus in the *Carmen Curilli*, has some frank advice for our poet: Is G. H. not afraid of how many enemies he is making, and how harsh Bolhuis's revenge will be? What his family and father will think? He should give up writing satire and allow that there is plenty of room for others in the Parnassan city of Cyrrha. Granted, W[olbers]'s poems are no good, but he *is* a good lawyer. What's the point of insulting him? The cockroaches will consume his songs and it is enough that *they* trample them underfoot. Don't worry about Trip's poems either; the only people who will buy them are the bookseller's hucksters . . . and so on. In fine, the exasperated G. H. imagines his friend, J. C., coming to his defence: 'How can they think you wrote those satires when you have never hurt anyone? Are you telling me they think *you* can write jibes? Believe me, you lot, he didn't write them, he is too much of an imitator of Ovid to sing [about others] what he hasn't first sung about himself!' ('Tene putent Satyras, cum nullum laeseris usquam, / Tene putent, inquis, scribere posse sales? / Credite non scripsit, nimium est imitator Ovidi / Quam canat ut, quod non praecinit ille sibi', p. 8).

Pamphlet #1020 contains two short Dutch poems. The first, 'Elegy to Curillus', mocks the latter for his French and Italian refinement and wonders whether he still understands our coarse Dutch language. The author can't believe he will give up Poetry: you who measure everyone else so mathematically, can you not get the measure of yourself? But no, get going, *pace* Andreades, you are no born poet! The elegy closes with a nice simile comparing Heerkens's

---

[47] A significant admission that suggests he never really meant to conceal his identity.

brilliance to that of the Northern Lights, which fades at dawn. Its companion piece, 'Lesson to Curillus', takes as its premise the Horatian cliché of knowing one's limits; warns Curillus that he has done nothing to tarnish the reputation of respectable men but has only brought disgrace upon himself; suggests that he 'burns incense for his own tinsel image' (hinting at his Catholicism?), and in the same breath compares him to an 'atheist' whose 'fine understanding' cannot make a common sense inference about the cause from its effects: that is, Curillus is a slanderer pure and simple!

At last a spirited Dutch reply issued from the Heerkens camp (#1021): 'Pindus stormed by a confused crowd of Poetic Rebels and Cowardly Cabbage-Poets, described by Eripanus, or Torch of Conflict'. The writer of this satire was almost certainly young Josua van Iperen (1726–80), a member of Clara's circle and contributor both to the *Bellingeweerder Uitspanningen* and to the Kulenkamp album.[48] In his defence of the *Zang-berg* ('Song-Mountain') Curillus has already fended off one 'Labeo'. With Andreades, who had dared to stand up to 'Hippus' (sc. in the *Carmen Curilli*), he engages with 'Sulcius', whose laurels end up in the mud; with the drunken 'Tigellus'; with 'Maevius'; and with 'twenty-seven pantomime Corydons' from the wedding feast.[49] Finally 'Cratinus' arrives with his well-arrayed troops, who turn out to be Curillus's men in disguise, and our heroes win the day. No doubt the target audience will have more quickly deciphered the Horatian code names than we can: but 'Labeo', a teacher of law in Augustus's day, is presumably Wolbers; 'Tigellus' is possibly Alting, as Heerkens had branded the latter 'boozy' in #1019 (assuming the allusion here is to Horace's uninhibited Sardinian singer, 'Tigellius', who sings 'Io Bacchae' from entrée through dessert).[50]

---

[48] Eripanus is an anagram of Iperanus. His pseudonym in the poetic consortium was 'Lycidas'. Van Iperen was studying theology in Groningen and graduated in Leiden in 1747. In 1752 he took a doctorate in mathematics and physics at Groningen. Author of assorted essays on literary, linguistic and scientific subjects, he translated, for example, Young's *Night Thoughts* into Dutch (Middelburg, 1767). Driven to the Indes as a result of opposition to his mild preaching, van Iperen ended his days in Batavia. (See the entry by Herderscheê in *Nieuw Nederlandsch Biografisch Woordenboek*, P. J. Blok and P. C. Molhuysen (eds), 'Josua van Iperen', Part 4 (Leiden, 1918), pp. 799–800, available online at <www.dbnl.org/tekst/molh003nieu04_01/molh003nieu04_01_1257.php>.) Van Iperen was a member of the 'Batavian Academy of Arts and Sciences', apparently 'the first association for intellectual pursuits established in a tropical European settlement', for which he wrote essays on 'natural curiosities and on Javanese history and historiography': Jean Gelman Taylor, *The Social World of Batavia: European and Eurasian in Dutch Asia* (Madison: University of Wisconsin Press, 1983), p. 86. Cf. Heerkens, *Italica* (1793), pp. 218–21, elegiac letter to van Iperen.

[49] This number puzzled me initially as only 13 poets contributed to the Wolters–Conring *Bruilofts-Gezangen* (Groningen, 1746). The opening eclogue by T. B. Hulten, however, contains precisely 27 capitalized 'Koridons'.

[50] Cf. Horace *Sat.* 1. 2 and 3 for Tigellius; 1. 3 for Labeo; 1. 4 for Sulcius.

The author of the Dutch Pamphlet #1022, 'Phoebus appearing in the Sign of the Twins of Curillus and Andreades', returns to the scene of Song-Mountain, and gains marginally higher poetic ground. Thalia introduces Andreades and Curillus to Apollo as he is emerging from the sign of Gemini.[51] While he doesn't recognize them, Thalia reassures him that they haven't climbed up Pindus step by step, but rather in a single bound – and they have produced excellent and exalted poetry to boot. Apollo is amazed that he doesn't know these boys: 'O brave Andreades, darling of the Muses, had I known you both earlier I would have turned to Groningen before now, happy Groningen, which will never be called Ass-country again, because of you, who have outgrown it.' Not only have they drunk from the waters of Hippocrene, they have licked up all the dirt and mud as well, like thirsty dogs after a long run. Now it falls to *them* to decide who keeps his place in the Parnassan choir. Let them be the twin stars that serve as infallible guides of poets! Though embarrassed by the praise, Curillus and Andreades are emboldened to approach Apollo: 'Will Castor and Pollux yield their places up to us?' 'No!', comes the furious reply, 'they will stay, as ever, and be the guides of sailors. You two will be the guides of shameless slanderers and those who poison poetry with envy' (p. 7). A brief 'Poem to Poetry' concludes this pamphlet, exhorting her not to spare Curillus, Andreades, nor yet Eripanus, however much he may call himself her 'priest, lover, comrade and courtier' (p. 9) – lest she be branded a lustful whore.

The stakes were clearly getting higher, and Heerkens seems to show the first signs of losing his nerve. In pamphlet #1023, a supposed Groningen friend of the satirists publishes two Latin letters allegedly sent him by Curillus and Andreades. In the first of these, Curillus vainly protests that he is not that unfortunate 'G. H.' – one would have thought a futile exercise given his playful and provocative self-outing in #1019! – and declares that he is on the point of confessing his true identity in order to save that young man from further unjust abuse. He concedes that he may have gone in a little too hard on Hemsterhuis: 'I am sorry and take it back, I certainly wouldn't want him to be considered stupid by one of his pupils' ('doleo & deprecor, nolo sane illum a discipulo stolidum haberi', p. 5). But the persona of the Andreades letter is more pugnacious, as it thrashes in the dark at the faceless authors of the anti-Curillan pamphlets. 'Andreades' concludes, for example, that 'Poetry to Curillus' (#1018) couldn't possibly be by Trip, as the latter's 'style is more

---

[51] Late May/early June, when the quarrel erupted, as explained in a footnote.

masculine and sharp', and Trip would surely not have sunk so low as to attack Curillus's *Religion*. Nor can the 'Lesson and Elegy to Curillus' (#1020) be Trip's work: 'I fear that you will find the antagonist of Curillus in some Doncker or other, or among those madmen of the *petits-maisons*' ('timeo ne *Curilli* antagonistam vel in *Donckero* quodam, vel ipsos inter fanaticos *dans les petites-maisons* invenias', p. 7). A footnote and the following pamphlet hint that 'Doncker' may have been a local *baker*, hence a moniker for Bakker: *petites-maisons* = 'mad-house' = 'dolhuis', thus Bolhuis.[52] The pamphlet concludes with Andreades squaring up against Bolhuis, letting him know that he has his Juvenal to hand and is busy composing a new satire.[53] Bolhuis and company should cease their *raving* (prolonging the pun on 'dolhuis') and leave poetry alone! Not only has Andreades nothing to fear from these mongrel Frisian versifiers, but – in a surprising, if not treacherous, twist – he suggests that Curillus has little use for van Iperen's services either![54]

The anonymous author of #1024, 'Apotheosis or Deification of Andreades and Eripanus, each on their own Parnassan summit, Eripanus taking the place of Curillus, who bade the Muses farewell', mocks the belligerent posturing of 'Andreades' in the foregoing letter. Even though Curillus has left, the lamenting Muses need not fear: they will have their Tweedle-Dum and Tweedle-Dee champions in Andreades and Eripanus. Andreades is ready to seek out the *Basters*[55] behind Jan Donckers's oven and smash their heads! There may be a sly dig at Heerkens's Catholic education when Horace and *Sarbievius* (i.e. the Jesuit Horace) shuffle along to make room for our anti-heroes on Pindus.[56]

Now comes the first open Latin counterblast from one of the much-maligned grizzled heads of Groningen, Gerhard Alting, in his *Exprobratio sive calumniarum depulsio ad Curillum* (#1025). Alting declares that he sees straight through Curillus's disguise: 'a youth who have recently withdrawn your hand from the [schoolmaster's] cane, you spit out your vile poison against the whole choir of the Pierians' ('Qui juvenis, ferulaeque recens subductus,

---

[52] The play on words is obliquely referenced in #1037, 'The Modest Satirist', pp. 21, 30 and n. 39. Pieter Huizinga Bakker dedicated a warm poem to his friend, Bolhuis (*Poëzy*, Part 1 (Amsterdam, 1788), pp. 134–9).

[53] Entitled *Vae, vae malenatis Frisiae Poetis*, apparently never published.

[54] This suggests that van Iperen probably *was* the author of #1021 and for some reason Heerkens wished to dissociate himself from it.

[55] Probably 'bastards', but not with the same semantic range as in English. The word seems to be a gloss on Curillus's *malenatus* for Trip's verses in #1013, and of course the subtitle of #1017, *malenatis Frisiae Poetis*. The Dutch word *bastaard* carries a sense of hybridization, hence I have rendered *malenatus* throughout as 'mongrel' rather than 'ill-begotten'.

[56] On the other hand both the *Carmen Curilli* and the *Epistola Andreadis ad Curillum* sport Sarbievian epigraphs, so Heerkens had made no attempt to conceal his Jesuit literary pedigree.

in omnem / Exspuis Aonium dira venena chorum', p. 3). He expresses both bewilderment and righteous indignation at the bile and ingratitude of one of his former acolytes: 'You used to be gentle, and you freely applauded in speech and writing – at that time our Muse could please you' ('Mitis eras, facilisque manu linguaque favebas, / Nostraque tunc poterat Musa placere tibi', p. 4). Heerkens's former mentor had initially consoled himself with the thought that the youth was afflicted by a *atra phrenesis* ('black fever') sent by Apollo. Perhaps he was just having a joke, and wanted to look clever – no harm in that – and if there is, he will repent and come to seek forgiveness. But no!

> Sed quia majori reparas jam bella tumultu,
>    Et cumulas probris probra priora novis:
> Immo, subornato jam nomine, carmina vulgas,
>    Reddis et haec stolidis lucidiora notis:
> Et nostrum nemo, nisi dente petitus, abivit,
>    Qui sumus Aonii pars aliquota [sic] chori.
> Tempus erit tumidum, malegrate, retundere fastum,
>    Ne tibi tam facilis, vane, triumphus eat!

> But because you now renew battle with a greater commotion, and heap fresh libels on the earlier ones – nay, under your false name you publish songs, and render these even more transparent with stupid notes: and none of us has retreated unless you have come snapping after him, we who form some part of the Muses' chorus – the time will come, ingrate, when we will beat down your swollen pride, lest you celebrate too easy a triumph, vainglorious one! (p. 5)

The second half of Alting's tetchy apology is devoted to refuting Heerkens's calumnies, line by line, in particular that the old man had complained about lack of patronage and sought to enrich himself by writing verse; and that he had forbidden his *own* son, Heerkens's friend, Willem, to write verse.[57] Alting proclaims that Andreades and G. H. are one and the same person, and that he will never be convinced otherwise (p. 7). He pulls him up on his quantities, and presses him on his self-confessed soft spot for Ovid (in #1019): 'Come on, then, you constant imitator of Ovid! If your guy wrote "knotty", why do you dream

---

[57] Answering the words put into his mouth in the *Carmen Curilli*: 'inutilis ars est / Noscere Pierides, non disces nate Poesin' (p. 8).

up, "boozy", ingrate, "gout"? But these are the vile hissings of your tongue' ('Tu verum, heus! *Ovidi* constans *imitator*, adesdum! / Cum tibi NODOSAM dixerit ille suus: / Quid mihi VINOSAM fingis, malegrate, podagram? / Sed sunt haec linguae sibila dira tuae', p. 8).[58]

It is difficult not to share Alting's judgement (if not approve his tired metaphors) that Heerkens has shown himself a sheep in wolf's clothing, licking and fawning; a tender rose concealing poison. The venerable senior citizen will have none of it: 'If this is your idea of fun and sport, I, already a man of a certain age, do not tolerate such jokes' ('Haec tibi si ingenii modo sunt lususque iocique, / Non ego, jam senior, ludicra tanta fero', p. 8). It is Heerkens's immaturity that prevents him from understanding Wolbers's love poems: 'no wonder, since Venus has not yet granted this Joseph to know his own desires and girlfriends' ('Quid mirum! Cypris cui nondum blanda Josepho / Scire dedit veneres deliciasque suas', p. 9). And if he is such an admirer of the 'language of power' ('dominae . . . linguae', p. 9), scorning his own, together with his homeland, he should remember that it isn't just the French and Italians who have distinguished themselves in Latin poetry. Has he forgotten about the Dutch Heinsiuses, Grotiuses, Secunduses? And if, Alting wonders, Heerkens is deserting the Muses in obedience to his father – which would be a feeble excuse – why does he feel the need to drag everyone else down with him? 'It is regrettable and distasteful that a youth favoured by Apollo should no longer wish to follow the Muses and their sacred standards; but ah, it is shameful to make his disgraceful exit thus, like a demon, with a big stink!' ('Est dolor, et taedet, juvenem cui favit Apollo, / Nolle magis Musas et sacra signa sequi. / Huncque ita, cum foetore gravi, Cacadaemonis instar, / Turpe, ah! discessum dedecorare suum', p. 11). In the end, Alting grudgingly offers the tiresome tearaway a way out – but he also delivers him a timely warning. If Curillus wants to return to poetry, well and good, he should ask for mercy and come back 'with a purer lyre' ('candidiore lyra', p. 11). If he intends to leave the Muses behind: 'believe you me, Curillus, you won't be so sorely missed that we will shed any tears. But I fear that grim Nemesis will then erect a sign for you with the following inscription: "Adversary of All Poets"' ('Crede mihi, tanti nec erit caruisse *Curillo*, / Propterea ut madidis ora rigemus aquis. / Sed vereor ne tunc tibi trux Rhamnusia lignum / Erigat, hoc titulo: PANTOPOETIMACHUS', p. 11).[59]

---

[58] Cf. Ovid *Epist. ex Ponto* 1. 3. 23.
[59] Notwithstanding the vehemence of these sentiments, Alting would be the recipient of a friendly elegiac Latin letter from an older and wiser Heerkens, dated Groningen, 28 November 1761

The author of the anonymous Dutch 'Lust for Slander attacked in the example of Curillus and Andreades' (#1026), possibly Lucas Trip,[60] isolates Curillus as the chief object of his censure, chiding him for leading a nice chap like Andreades astray. Andreades's bluster in the letter of Pamphlet #1023 is ridiculed, and he is warned to steer clear of poetry with which he has no business. As for Curillus, for all his affectations to be a new Pope or Boileau, for all his dressing up his deficiencies with Italian flair, he is like a 'negro who has painted himself white' ('Gelyk een Moor, die zich vergeesch poogt te blanketten', p. 4). While this latter is shocking to modern sensibilities, Heerkens may well have found more insulting the suggestion that his work would be judged by any educated person 'as monkish Latin, written by some boy or other who has just left the cloisters, who has cobbled together crazy fantasies from his befuddled brain and defiled good paper' ('en Munnike Latyn, / Van d'een of d'and'ren knaap, uit 't klooster pas gekomen; / Die uit 't beneveld brein zyn dwaaze herssendroomen / Te zamen heeft geflanst, en 'tschoon papier bevuilt', pp. 4–5). He is branded 'Lord-Inspector of Parnassus, Chief Inquisitor' ('keurheer op Parnas, en hoofd-*Inquisiteur*'), and he is accused of bringing back the age of the Spanish tyranny and Inquisition to the Netherlands after she had won her freedom of conscience and religion. The message is clear: Heerkens is untrustworthy and unpatriotic, he is not really one of us, but what else could we expect from a Catholic?

Heerkens engages principally with Alting's Latin 'Exprobratio' in his *Satyra Curilli: Licere juveni Poetae etiam, carpere malum versificatorem, licet sit senex* ('Satire of Curillus: That it is permissible for a young poet to attack a bad versifier, even if he is old', #1027). The poem itself is preceded by a prose 'monitum' in which the incensed Curillus adamantly refuses Alting's suggestion that he is a certain 'G. H.', his former pupil. Granted, he *is* young, and in his poem he

---

(published in *Italica* (1793), pp. 209–18), from which it would appear that the two men had by then buried their respective hatchets. Indeed, the pretext for that letter is Alting's attempted recruitment of Heerkens to his cause in a fresh Groningen literary quarrel about the value of Roman law, from which our repentant satirist recoils. On the latter quarrel, which revolved around controversial law professor, Frederik Adolf van der Marck (1719–1800), see Joris van Eijnatten, *Liberty and Concord in the United Provinces: Religious Toleration and the Public in the Eighteenth-Century Netherlands* (Leiden: Brill, 2003), pp. 269–70. Heerkens must also have made his peace with Trip, since he composed a Latin eulogy for the deceased burgemeester-poet. See the manuscript in the Rijksarchief in Groningen: Familie Trip, 465/112.

[60] References in #1031 (by Fockens) to Trip flaying Marsyas ('Zo moet de groote Trip, de geessel der gebreken, / Afbeelden op't panneel uw' Marsiasse treken', p. 9) seem to reprise a warning to Andreades in the present pamphlet to beware the fate of Marsyas ('En gy, om uw verwaande en reukelooze zangen, / Het loon van Marsias, zoo bloedig, moogt ontfangen', p. 6).

upholds his right to call a spade a spade, a pate a pate: 'Bald old man, what madness has possessed you? As if the gods gave you those white hairs so that the laurels of Phoebus might wilt upon them – how sad you are!' ('Calve senex! Quis mente furor? quasi numina canos / Dent tibi, turpe ut in his marceret laurea Phaebi, / Ut miser!', p. 4). *Pabus* couldn't get into Pindus when he was a youth so now he comes limping in on three feet.[61] Curillus tells him to get back; youthful Apollo and the Muses are laughing at him! But no-one should mock a poet for being beardless. Hercules was but a babe when he strangled the serpents, Bacchus unshaven when he conquered India: 'Stop counting the birthdays of a poet whose strength and manliness has come early. It's not his age, beard or experience that commends him to Apollo. Nature makes and polishes the poet, and she is bountiful with her gifts at every age' ('Parcite natales etiam numerare Poetae, / Cui vigor ante diem & sua virtus contigit, illum / Non aetas, non barba, nec experientia Phaebo / Commendat: natura facit politque Poetam, / Muneribusque suis cunctanti provenit aevo', p. 5). Yes, Curillus is young,[62] but he has dared to scale Mt Pindus, where Frisia has never sent any of its mongrel poets before. Responding no doubt to Alting's jibe that he was too immature to understand Wolbers's love poetry, Heerkens launches into a programmatic defence of his chaste Muse. If you want to know who Curillus is, know that he is, if nothing else, *pure*:

> Longe aliter vates, ac illum pinxit Athenis,
>
> Intus erat, nec ego morum traductor iniquus,
>
> Nulli (quod multi tamen audent) mordeo famam;
>
> Nemo mea ex satyra meretrices esse *Catulle*[63]
>
> Scivit, et hi quod sunt, illique fuere nepotes.
>
> Nostra lycambeo non sanguine musa rubescet,
>
> Archilochi detestor opus, Flaccumque licenter
>
> Mordacem, torvumque aegri Juvenalis acorem.
>
> Hunc nec ad obscoenum sequitur mea Musa lupanar,
>
> Protractura tuam generose Brittannice matrem.
>
> Haec mecum castae loca vitent usque Camenae.

---

[61] The old man's third foot is not just his cane: I suspect an allusion here to #1024, 'Apotheosis or Deification...', which is in tercets.
[62] 'I have scarcely passed my twentieth birthday.'
[63] Pamphlet #1027: *Catulles*.

The poet [Hipponax] was very different on the inside from how Athenis [Archaic sculptor] portrayed him, nor am I an unjust traducer of morals. I do not savage anyone's reputation – though many do. No-one has learned how to be a whore from my satire, Catullus; and that there are these and there were also *those* grandsons.[64] Our muse does not grow red with the blood of Lycambes: I hate the work of Archilochus, and of Horace biting too boldly, and the scowling sourness of Juvenal. Nor does my Muse follow him into the obscene brothel, to drag out your mother, noble Britannicus![65] Let the chaste Camenae, with me, ever avoid these places! (p. 5)

For attacking bad poetry Curillus's patriotism and religion have been impugned; he is menaced with black curses by Bolhuis, or by that 'impudent versifier' (sc. Alting) whose character may be known from his attacks on the crowned heads of France and Prussia (p. 7).[66] Curillus promises to go easy on his enemies if they will just leave the Muses alone. He could even wish that some of their songs will survive the moths and bargain-basement vendors to be read by their descendants – so long as the latter approve his judgement that they are rubbish!

After despatching this plucky little poem to the printer's our punch-drunk pugilist may have had a slight change of heart, if not the complete metanoia urged by Alting. Perhaps sensing the net tightening around him, Heerkens clutches at Alting's recent dismissal of his Ovidian aspirations in his *Elegia G. H. . . . ad Manes Ovidii se non esse Curillum, sicut creditum fuerat, & ferebant suspiciones vulgatae* ('Elegy of G. H. to the Spirit of Ovid that he *isn't* Curillus, as had been believed and as widely circulating rumours were suggesting', #1028). Of course Heerkens could never seriously hope to convince his enemies now that he was *not* Curillus, but in this charming poem he adopts a moderately more conciliatory tone. G. H. is up late at night, trying to compose something to prove his innocence to Trip, when he is visited by the ghost of Ovid.[67] The latter's arrival is heralded by a spooky blaze of light and a shaking of the floorboards. Half divine vision ('quasi praesentem testificata Deum'), half restless ghost, Ovid manifests here in his frightful post-exilic guise: 'Thus he appeared after the deeds of harsh Nero, complaining he had died from Scythian blows. He came to me, just as he was then, from Getic shores, wearing faded laurels on his sallow brow' ('Sic fuit immiti visus post facta Neroni, / Questus se Scythicis interiisse plagis. / Huc

---

[64] A rather obscure allusion, presumably, to *Cat.* 58, where Catullus's Lesbia 'peels'/'fleeces' (*glubit*) the 'grandsons'/'playboys' (*nepotes*) of Remus.
[65] Juvenal *Sat.* 6. 123, alluding to Messalina.
[66] See n. 36 above.
[67] The conceit of the sleepless satirist seems to be Horatian (*Sat.* 2. 1).

mihi, qualis erat! Geticis veniebat ab oris, / Lurida pallentis laurea frontis erat', p. 4).[68] His voice is kindly, though, and he laments the fact that G. H. has forsaken the elegiac genre for satire. Were you frightened of the troubles elegy might bring you, as they once did me? He chides his protégé's stupidity in attacking his countrymen – and the young poet can't conceal his true identity from the dead one, as the evil report has already arrived in the land of the spirits. These events, Ovid avers, have caused him more pain than all the sufferings he endured in life *and* death! His hopes for the young G. H. had been high: 'I had even heard at that time that a Frisian poet would one day provide a soothing balm for my wretched ghost ... but I am cruelly forsaken. I hear no song, no laments being sweetly sung over our grave. Naso was abandoned while he lived, a pitiable exile! And after his death Naso will be abandoned by all' ('Tunc etiam audieram, quod vates Frisius olim / Manibus afflictis blanda medela foret / At ... male destituor, cantus nullasque querelas / Audio dulce super nostra sepulchra cani. / Naso relictus erat, dum vixit, flebilis exul! / Postque obitum cunctis Naso relictus erit', p. 5).

The elegy to Ovid's ghost may not contain the flagrant *ad hominem* attacks of the previous satires but Heerkens was still far from offering a full and frank recantation. Ovid accepts that his disciple is scandalized by the very existence of poetasters, but he urges him to turn a blind eye to them. We had plenty of Baviuses in *my* day but I didn't banish my Muses on that account. Jupiter providently mixes a lot of bad in with the good so that the good may be better distinguished and appreciated. At the conclusion of his speech Ovid vanishes without giving the desperate G. H. a chance to reply; the latter wonders whither to direct his prayers. Is Ovid crossing the Styx or, God forbid, recalled to the chill Danube, or is he in the Elysian Fields? The poem closes with the author affirming, once again, that he has been unjustly charged: 'In whatever form you exist our complaint will follow you, if a case may be tried even in a Stygian court. The most just Minos hears the plea of an innocent man, my Muse seek this one out (let Ovid be present!). Let him thus learn, and all the shades and Persephone too, that I am unjustly called the *Trip* and *Alting* poet' ('Quo modo cunque estis, vos nostra querela sequetur, / Si quoque sit stygio causa probanda foro. / Innocui causam Minos justissimus

---

[68] The idea had already been tried out by Heerkens in his first published Latin poem, *Elegia ad Magistratum Groninganum ut restituantur Academiae Professores* (#1012). Here a more humble 'Curillus' appeals to the magistrates of Groningen to fill the Chairs of recently deceased professors, having been visited by Pallas while he was mourning at the tomb of the jurist, Jean Barbeyrac. She appears to him not as she once did to Paris on Ida, 'for she was gloomy, and she went about with tearful face, as she seemed at the death of Achilles' ('Tristis enim, riguoque ibat deformior ore, / Qualis Achillaeo funere visa fuit', p. 4).

audit, / Hunc mea (coram adsit Naso) Thaleia petet. / Immeritum sic me *Trippi, Altingique* Poetae, / Sic omnes umbrae, Persephoneque sciat', p. 8).

If Heerkens hoped that that would be the end of the matter, that the good citizen–poets of Groningen must now forgive and forget his boyish bravado, he was sorely mistaken. He was only just beginning to reap the whirlwind. First it was lawyer Joannes Wolbers's turn, in *G. H. Pseudonymi Curilli Furores repressi* (#1029). This elegiac poem opens with a statement of undying devotion to the art of poetry, answering Crispinus's allegation in the *Carmen Curilli* that Wolbers had renounced her charms in his youth ('Quae teneris fueras annis mihi grata, Poesis, / Nunc quoque grata mihi es, grata futura seni', p. 3). For the first three pages of his pamphlet Wolbers defends his art in purple, if predictable, terms: Poetry sings the praises of the gods and heroes, is a defence against tyranny, teaches arts and sciences, instils morals.[69] And then he gets personal. Base men who have no reputation use wicked verse to attack others: 'What moved you to brandish dire weapons against me? Why do you bark, Curillus, like a rabid dog?' ('Quid te commovit dira in nos tela vibrare? / Quid latras rabidi more, Curille, canis?', p. 6) But the more you carp at my songs, the better they please others, 'nor will your foul calumny give you the fame you desire; the Remnian law stands, and you should rather fear it!' ('Nec dabit optatam tibi foeda calumnia famam, / Remmia te magis at lex metuenda manet').[70] In fact there is no precedent for a man using a pseudonym to attack other poets, denigrating their writings, openly naming or indicating their names in footnotes! Wolbers claims he doesn't care that his verse hasn't met with the approval of a beardless youth: he is writing for men of distinction. The lawyer can't conceal his injured pride, though, when he protests: 'I would inspire envy if I cited the names of the great men who have sought out and applauded my verses' ('Invidiam facerem, si nomina magna referrem, / Plauserunt numeris quae apta meis', p. 7). Like Alting, Wolbers concludes by putting Heerkens in his place for his crimes against Latinity: 'Submit your hand to the cane again, and learn the Latin language, boy, and which case "beat" governs! But what gender is "fountain"? "Come to your senses", blockhead, and try to "win over" the injured poets!' ('Subde manum rursus ferulae, linguamque Latinam / Disce, puer, casum *pellere* quemque regat? / At cujus generis sit *fons*? *Resipisce* Vacerra, / Et laesos vates *conciliare* velis', p. 8). He should go back to school and let Master Hemsterhuis teach him the liberal arts and good grammar!

---

[69] One suspects – given the relatively late appearance of this poem after Heerkens's initial onslaught – that poor Wolbers had laboured over it long and *invita Minerva*.
[70] The Roman law against calumny – appropriately cited by the lawyer Wolbers.

The bitter Dutch *Roskam voor Curillus* ('Drubbing for Curillus', #1030; second edition #1031) is claimed by theology and philosophy student Johannes Lucaszoon Fockens, a younger man and yet another member of Clara's poetic circle[71] – from which, he snorts, Curillus and his ignominious accomplices also hail. 'Eripanus' used to have some genuine ability in Latin poetry but has stupidly entered the fray with an execrable Dutch poem to defend the slanderers who, for their part, insult him.[72] Fockens reminds Curillus that he has already taken a beating from Trip, Bolhuis, Alting, Wolbers and from Groningen's own Foquenbroch.[73] Bolhuis is set to 'draw a true likeness of him, a portrait of his ugly mug' ('Van u een ken'bre schets, en troonieteek'ning geven', #1031, p. 10): *he* knows, like Sannazzaro, how to deal with slanderers.[74] As for Hemsterhuis, he is preparing to teach Curillus a lesson in Horatian style. Indeed, Curillus should take Wolbers's advice and go back to school – but to *elementary* school! Fockens's invective seems to betray a genuine sense of grievance, or at least a desire to align himself with the powerful end of town. But if he can't resist a jab at Heerkens's 'crawling around in Roman verses' ('kruipt in Roomsche vaarssen', p. 9) – an ambiguous phrase which implies not only that his *Latin* is bad, but that he is in thrall to *Catholic* Rome – we shall see that it is Gerhard Alting who really takes a boot to that well-exposed Achilles' heel.

In 'Axiosis, or Prayers of Alting to Curillus that he be admitted to the company of Poets, if not on merit then at least by Your Grace' (#1032), Alting makes clear that he, for one, was not going to countenance Heerkens wriggling away under Ovid's skirts. With heavy sarcasm the pamphletist addresses a prefatory prose letter to 'Most Holy Curillus, Apostolic Legate of Phoebus', and makes a full confession of his sins against poetry. The flowery and obsequious prose is probably intended as a parody of the Ciceronian style cultivated in the Renaissance papal curia and savaged by Erasmus in the *Anticiceronianus*, but

---

[71] His pseudonym was 'Lysanthus'. Fockens was a contributor both to the Wolthers–Conring *Bruilofts-Gezangen* and the *Bellingeweerder Uitspanningen*. His is the first poem in Clara's collection, following directly after and describing her portrait. Did he perhaps command a privileged position within the literary group?
[72] Catching 'Andreades's' backhander in #1023 (see above, p. 50). Van Iperen's contribution to the Wolters–Conring collection was indeed a Latin ode (#1010, pp. 13–15).
[73] Possibly Quintijn Pabus, since Focquenbroch wrote a poem to Amsterdam as Pabus did one in praise of Groningen.
[74] The reference to Sannazaro may be a clue to the international aspirations of the Clara club, and of course carries with it an association of Arcadia. See now the 'I Tatti Renaissance Library' edition of Sannazaro's Latin poetry by Michael C. J. Putnam (Cambridge, MA: Harvard, 2009), *Elegia* XI ('In maledicos detractores'), pp. 188–91 – a poem in which, tellingly, Sannazaro defends his own circle of humanist poet-friends in the Pontanian academy.

perhaps also of the Jesuits. The poem itself opens with a nod to Juvenal (and of course to Curillus's first satire): 'Am I always just a "neighbour" and "dweller nearby to Pindus", I who have clung so many years to the "foothills" of the mountain?' (Semper ego tantum *vicinus* et *accola Pindi*, / Qui tot lustra tenax imis *radicibus* haesi / Montis, p. 5). Is this the shabby treatment Alting deserves for his assiduous service to Apollo and the Muses? Alas, 'why was he born under a Northern star, 'why not in Italy or the lily-bearing soil of France, most rich in geniuses?' ('cur me non *Itala tellus* / *Liligerumque solum, geniorum uberrima mater*, / *Progenuit*?, p. 6). Talent and experience are no use to him – Alting here closely echoes Curillus's satire #1027 – it is enough to be *Frisian* to be banished from poetry ('Te non *ingenium*, ipsa *nec experientia Phoebo* / *Commendat*, satis est *te Frisium*, ut arte *Poeta* / *Non fias*', p. 9). And yet, until recently he had thought he was in favour. What could explain Apollo's sudden change of heart? But there is no mistake, because 'a powerful satire and that celebrated poet, Curillus, said it himself, and lest it seem incredible, there is Andreades as witness, than whom no-one more distinguished has ever wandered the peaks of Parnassus. Thus, with one voice, Andreades and Curillus intone the sad decree of angry Minerva' ('Ille *potens Satyra* est *celebrisque Poeta, Curillus*: / Ipse ait, et ne quid longum vero simile absit, / *Andreades* quoque testis adest, quo clarior alter / Culmina Parnasi nunquam peragravit, uterque / Edocet iratae *decretum triste minervae* . . . Sic uno *Andreades* ita concinit ore *Curillus*', p. 7). Apollo is cast here as something of an Augustus figure, arbitrarily banishing the uncomprehending Ovid/Alting from Parnassus; Curillus and Andreades constitute a double-headed Pontiff: 'for as Peter, if the Gods will permit me, once entrusted the keys of the Heavens to *one* Pope, and gave him the absolute right to open or close them at will, without recourse to any law, so too Pythian Apollo gave the keys to the sacred thresholds of the Pierian temple to these *two*' ('Nam veluti Petrus Papae, si Dis placet, olim / Coelorum claves *uni* concredidit, et jus / Omne dedit coelos claudendi vel reserandi / Pro lubitu, sine lege ulla, sine limite certo; / Sic quoque Pierii sacrata ad limina templi / Pythius *his* claves concessit Apollo *duobus*', p. 7). We are not to enquire into the source of their authority – that would be sinful ('scelus esse puta, prope morte piandum', p. 8). The poetic envoys have been sent from Helicon bearing testimonials from Apollo; they have descended on the earth 'as frogs once did on Salerno, or as a foul turd drops from the bum of a cow, like an "alrunia", which – if we can believe the rumour – sprouts up from the bosom of the earth in one night, produced by the urine of a hanged man, and grows under the gallows' ('Depluit in terras (ut ranae aliquando Salernis, / Aut veluti vaccae teter editus excidit ano, / *Alruniaeque instar*, famae si credere fas est, / Ex suspensuri urina, quae nocte sub una / Provenit ex terrae gremio, et cita sub cruce crescit)', p. 8).[75] It is in the power of these two alone to say: 'I approve of you, Celsus, and pronounce you a poet worthy of ivy, for I like you'; or, 'I disapprove of you, Aulus, and whatever you do you won't please me, and your hat is cocked and your clothing shabby. I declare you unworthy of the laurel and I punish you with banishment from the waters of Pegasus, and you will never, Aulus, be a poet' ('*Celse probo, dignumque hedera pronuncio Vatem*: / *Tu mihi namque places*, et, nescio quid, tuus in se / Vultus habet, quod me trahit, ut cupiam tibi; contra / Te reprobo, fac, quicquid agis, *non Aule placebis*, / Pileus ut tibi stat transversus, ut horrida vestis, / *Te lauru indignam declaro*, et *Pegasi ab undis* / *Exsilio multo, nunquam eris, Aule, Poeta*', p. 10). In sum, it is implied that Curillus and Andreades have the power of poetic *excommunication*. In the final pages of his satire Alting notes that there is no point resisting – rather, he should try to win favour with his censors. This he does in language clearly spoofing 'Catholic' supplication and superstition: 'I venerate thee, I beseech thee humbly, my holy Curillus, be gentle and propitious; and thou who wert not long ago making free against Alting, and sharpening thy sword, more inclined to mercy, do thou rather bend thy gaze from the heights of Pindus here to me, I who live at the lowest foot of the mountain, and pour out thy favours, mild one' ('Te veneror, supplex precor, mi sancte Curille, / Sis facilis faveasque mihi, quique haud ita pridem / Liber in Altingos ibas, ferrumque acuebas, / Pronior ad veniam, potius de culmine Pindi, / . . . Flecte tuos in me, degentem montis in ima / Huc radice oculos, mitisque effunde favores', p. 11). Alting entreats Curillus and Andreades to 'intercede' for him with Apollo so that he will relent and show mercy to the abject poet. In return, he will honour them with twin altars and sacrifice and incense![76]

---

[75] A sinister reference to the humanoid mandrake root, 'Alraune', which, according to medieval German legend, was spawned by the ejaculate of hanged men. The mandrake was used in witchcraft, and Catholicism was associated in this period with superstition by 'enlightened' Dutch Protestants: Kloek and Mijnhardt, *1800: Blueprints*, p. 171.

[76] In the up-dated version in the *Marii Curilli Satyrae* (1758) Heerkens explains that Alting had sarcastically implored him in this pamphlet in the manner of a 'snub-nosed Indian', thus deliberately missing the Catholic point of the parody ('Sima ut nare Indus si supplicat, ante Cyrillum / Prociduus, geminas vultum demittit in ulnas, / Perque solecismos & Barbara verba precatur, / Sursum ire ut liceat', p. 16, and n. 3).

An anonymous Dutch 'Ghost of Sal. van Rusting to Curillus, Andreades and Eripanus, made sober by a drink of hemlock' (#1033) is almost certainly by Alting and, if anything, more bilious than either of his Latin poems.[77] Then young Petrus Lollema, yet another member of Clara's student-poet society, weighed in with his *Hekel voor Curillus, Andreades and Eripanus* ('Satire for Curillus, Andreades and Eripanus', #1034 and #1035).[78] No-one should give up poetry on Curillus's account. Poetry exists only in virtuous minds; Curillus has forfeited his right to her by his disgraceful behaviour, grabbing respectable poets by their grey hair! He has been blinded by the Italian proverb that no poets grow up north of the Alps – we are here to prove him wrong! Apparently unaware, or unconvinced of, Curillus's identity with Andreades, Lollema takes on the latter too, swaggering along, 'Juvenal in hand'. We Batavians who have wrested liberty from the hands of tyranny, we can only be conquered by mildness, never by slander and calumny! Finally, in clatters Eripanus, recognizable by his lame verse – but it would be cowardly for Lollema to mutilate him any further.[79]

The 'Poetic Spectator' (#1036), who 'takes a closer look at the characters and poetry of Curillus and Andreades', compares Curillus to the fox who declared 'sour grapes' and to the bullfrog who exploded in an attempt to imitate the ox.[80] The identity – or non-identity – of the 'Spectator' can perhaps be inferred from his reply to the snide remark made by Andreades in Pamphlet #1023, that the 'Lesson and Elegy to Curillus' were too awful to be by Trip (see above, pp. 149–50). The author claims not to be offended by Andreades's suggestion that those poems were the product of a *baker's* brain – Bakker would be proud to own them, but no, they are *not* his.[81] Anyway, Curillus can't prove it one way or the other, and the present poet – is it Bolhuis? – can't be bothered defending his work against an incompetent, beardless youth who lacks the skill and moral competence to make the proper distinctions. This satire contains all the by-now standard charges against our young

---

[77] The Dutch 'Geest van SAL. van RUSTING' yields the anagram 'Altingus Sr'. The conceit of the 'Ghost' must allude to Heerkens's poem on Ovid's visitation.

[78] His pseudonym was 'Ronduit', that is 'Frank'. Like Fockens he was a contributor both to the *Bellingeweerder Uitspanningen* and to the Wolthers–Conring *Bruilofts-Gezangen*.

[79] The stanza is rather catchy in Dutch: 'Daar komt nog een ('t is *Eripaan*) rinkinken; / Ik ken hem aan 't op lamme rymen hinken / Wat wil die bloed? Zal men hem meer verminken? / Dat war te wreed, en laf', #1034, p. 8).

[80] Cf. the end of Horace's *Sat*. 2. 3 for the fable of the puffed-up (mother) frog, retold by Damasippus to put Horace in his place.

[81] By a process of calibration and elimination (cf. Fockens, #1031), we can now offer the following tentative line-up of the anonymous anti-Curillan authors: #1015: Trip; #1018: Bolhuis; #1024: Pabus; #1033: Alting; #1036: Bolhuis (the title of this pamphlet seems to fulfil Fockens's promise that Bolhuis would soon reveal a true portrait of the malefactors).

pot-stirrers: of jealousy, arrogance, ambition, effrontery and narcissism – and of the inappropriate association between Curillus and Andreades: Curillus's father is afraid that his eloquent friend will prevail over his son, diverting him further from his 'art [sc. medicine] and altar' ('kunst en Altaar', p. 5 ). In his parting shot the satirist attacks their limping Latin verse, full of linguistic and stylistic errors.[82]

And so we come at last to Trip's 'Coy Satirist' (#1037). This is a much more ambitious poem than any we have reviewed so far, and runs to 36 pages. In his preface to the reader, Trip points out that G. H. has already confessed, and that he will suppress his real name on this occasion.[83] It's useless to engage with the anonymous slander of the 'cabbage poet'.[84] Trip is content that *his* poetry pleases sensible readers. But why is he criticized for writing in Dutch? Why is there an outcry ('wat schreeuwt men dan') that he is not fighting with equal weapons? Is he not free to parry a Roman/Catholic dagger with a Dutch sword? He admits that he doesn't care much for Latin poetry, but he knows enough to tell a Bavius from a Horace. Finally, Trip names the great men whose honour he will vindicate: 'revered [Wicher] van Swinderen, word-weighing [Albert] Alberthoma, pure [Michiel van] Bolhuis, ingenious [Gerhard] Alting, learned [Joannes] Wolbers, Ovidian [Jan Pieter] Driessen,[85] manly [Meinard] Hemsterhuis and upright [Pieter Huizinga] Bakker'.

Trip's poem is superficially didactic in the generalizing spirit of Horace's Letter to the Pisos, relaying as it does a lesson in the proprieties of satire from the goddess of virtue, Philarete. Preceptive didactic poems on the arts were all the rage in the eighteenth century in the wake of Horace, Boileau and Dufresnoy. On one level, then, Trip gives us Groningen's answer to Boileau's *Art poétique*. For all his advocating restraint and propriety, though, 'The Coy Satirist' is still very much an *ad hominem* excoriation. As Trip lays down the law, accompanying footnotes document the serial infringements of the muckrakers, citing pamphlet, page and verse numbers. The true satirist, says Trip, is like the good doctor, healing by cutting and burning the tumour but not causing unnecessary pain; his goal is to lead the reader to reason and he is motivated

---

[82] 'Aan een Latynsche maat en kreup'len tred gebonden, / Vol taal en kunstgebrek.'
[83] Confirming that he was the 'translator' of the *Carmen Curilli*?
[84] The term *Kooldichter* was first used by Eripanus in the title of #1021, in the sense of 'rubbish poet'.
[85] J. P. Driessen contributed a poem to the *Bellingeweerder Uitspanningen*: 'In poemata sacra nobilissimae virginis C. F. de Sytzama' (signed J. P. D.). There is nothing particularly Ovidian about it (it is in hexameters and references Virgil's fourth eclogue). I have not seen Driessen's *In nuptias pietate & doctrina insignis viri Johannis Huysinga, et lectissimæ atque ornatissimæ virginis Wyvæ Agnetæ* (1737), #902.

to eradicate the errors of mankind. Trip prescribes for the true satirist a combination of right aptitude ('geest'), rank ('rang') and judgement ('ordeel'). He will learn from the painter what should be in shadow; what should be in the back- or foreground; and what is too elevated to be sketched.[86] Some subjects are simply off limits, such as Religion and the Fatherland. Satirists should *glorify* their country as much as epic poets – unlike Curillus and Andreades, who have attacked the Frisian literary scene, spoken ill of the dead and flattered the French. Satirists should refrain from making fun of people's occupations, whether high or low, and they should not cruelly attack the poor. Here again, Curillus and Andreades have overstepped the mark. As for criticizing poets, that's for the likes of a Boileau, not a Curillus; a Gascon cannot comment on the niceties of courtly French, nor can a German farmhand/Roman Catholic ('Poep', p. 18[87]) be a judge of the pure Dutch language.[88] Women, the old and nobility also deserve respect. Here Trip takes it upon himself chivalrously to defend the 'soft-hearted Maid, another Tesselschade' (p. 22),[89] Clara Feyoena, from Curillus's bat-like sorties. Perhaps the most devastating pages of Trip's pamphlet, however, are those in which he separates out, and substantiates in his exhaustive footnotes, Curillus's and Andreades's faults of language and metre; their puerilities and inconsistencies; and, most seriously, their calumnies. The main text continues with a corrective to their flowery and ornamented style. Satire demands pointed, simple language – although a poet, *Dichter*, is not a *Dictator*, *pace* Curillus and Andreades. Trip has no patience with Curillus's puerile word games and silly pseudonyms. Assuming a benign, paternal tone ('myn zoon'), Trip gives the aspiring poet–addressee some advice on appropriate models. He should follow the good ship Huidekoper (a nautical metaphor is here elaborated).[90] A fulsome hymn to Modesty disarms the reader before the brutal finale: Curillus and Andreades are now openly upbraided for feigning

---

[86] 'Zoo wy de zaaken niet in hunnen eigen schyn, / Naturelyken dach, en ingeaarte trekken / Bespieg'len, on hun' stand en mistand klaar te ontdekken / Maar dat gezien, dan geest de leiding van 't penseel / Myn' schimppoëet een les, wat weinig of wat veel / Geschaduwt, 'tagterwerk of voorgrond moet beslaagen, / En wat, de kinst te hoog, geen schetze kan verdraagen' (p. 10).

[87] Corinna Vermeulen informs me that the word can carry both meanings, especially in Groningen.

[88] At this point (p. 18) Trip retells the fable of the conceited frog.

[89] She is compared to Maria 'Tesselschade' Roemers Vischer (1594–1649), poetess and engraver, one of two female members of the 'Muiden circle' of Dutch Golden Age writers and intellectuals. That Clara's circle was a far less formal affair than the Muiderkring is argued by Tersteeg.

[90] Balthasar Huydecoper (1695–1778) was a distinguished Latin and Dutch poet, linguist, critic, antiquarian, playwright and translator of Horace's satires, letters and Art of Poetry into Dutch verse and prose: Huydecoper, *Hekeldichten Brieven en Dichtkunst van Q. Horatius Flaccus* (Amsterdam, 1737).

homage to Apollo when their real intention was to crush honour and art. They are poets without name, writers without honour. They rape nature and art with their unnatural imagery. They should be silent or their disguises will be torn off, and 'Groningen's citizens will know precisely, by name, who the *gruff* so-and-so was who called their country a land of *billy-goats*; what French-minded cock benumbs the Batavian lion-hearts; which wild boar is rooting up their Helicon!' (p. 35). Trip's poem ends with a warning that the slanderers will suffer, if they do not relent, the fate of the Clazomenian youths,[91] that is, public humiliation by means of a sign affixed to Cirrha's temple doors proclaiming that 'Andreades, Curillus and Eripanus are free to go too far in shameless calumny'! (p. 36)

If Trip scolds the terrible trio of Curillus, Andreades and Eripanus without distinction, a 'necessary afterword' clarifies that he knows who is *really* to blame. Credible sources convince him that *Curillus* has disgracefully co-opted Andreades's name for his own work. While this seems to be the scholarly consensus even today, it is not impossible that Conring did draft at least the 'Letter to Curillus', albeit with Heerkens's collaboration. That is the impression we have from #1037A, perhaps Heerkens's only literary outing in the Dutch language. As 'Erasmus Secundus' he responds to Trip's 'Modest Satirist' with a provocatively *im*modest 'Serenade to Curillus and Andreades, both excellent poets and bosom buddies, to congratulate them on their newly acquired fame as poets' ('Toesangh aan Andreades en Curillus; beyde uytmuntende dichters en naeuwverknogte boezemvrinden. Ter verbreydinge van hunnen onlangs verkregen dichtroem'), a poem ostensibly published in Leiden in 1746.[92] The interest of this piece lies less in the outrageous and silly self-flattery – even Augustus's Rome counted only a handful of poets, so cold and barbaric Friesland should be proud that just two of its own have made it to Pindus – and exhibitionism – the Arcadians are longing to learn the true names of Curillus and Andreades, who are now triumphantly revealed to be . . . Heerkens and Conring! – as in Heerkens's teasing but affectionate vignette of his hyperactive, high-achieving young friend. Thus 'Erasmus Secundus' points out that, in the letter to Curillus, we can observe the workings of Justus's muddled brain, which is wont to skip from one topic (poetry) to another (mathematics), and from one language to another (Latin, French, English). Conring is in fact least interested

[91] Aelian *Various Histories*, 2. 15.
[92] Had he already fled Groningen or was the Leiden titlepage a fudge?

in writing Dutch, although he is coming around to it. While it might be tempting to read these remarks as an attempt by Heerkens to shift or share some of the blame for his own ill-fated satires – if so, would not the long-suffering Justus finally have objected? – they chime well enough with the poignant lines he published just three years later on the death of his friend, in the Latin didactic poem on the health of scholars we shall explore in the following chapter.

## A portrait of the satirist as a young man

I have provided a fuller synopsis of the Groningen pamphlet war than any to date, not in the hope of liberating any latent sparks of true poetry or wit from its often dry pages, but to illustrate, through the very repetitiveness of the insults exchanged, and from the vindictiveness with which the 'gang of three' was punished for its Clazomenian crimes, just how close-knit and claustrophobic the local literary scene must have been in Groningen mid-century. It seems unlikely that Heerkens aspired to be part of it – at least not long term. He was already an outsider by dint of his Catholic heritage and Jesuit education, to which fact, as we have seen, several of the pamphlets slyly advert. His preference for a classicizing Latin over a pious, Protestant Dutch is evident already in the Wolthers–Conring epithalamium – as is his exuberant sense of humour. In the following passage, foreshadowing one of the central themes of the pamphlet war, Heerkens suggests that on that happy wedding day:

> Quisque canit, cuivis Phaebus dedit esse poetam,
>   Largiflua sacras fonte propinat aquas.
> Gratia sponsa tibi est, quod Phocida Maevius intret,
>   Quodque canat Bavius, gratia Sponsa tibi est,
> Plausus, Hymen, & io, lyra & undique plectra resultant,
>   Non Hos concentus invida turbet Eris.
> Alma Venus, Venus alma, tuos sic quivis honores
>   Et Bavii pietas est modo grata, canit.
> Ille canit sponsum, sponsa stupet ille venusta,
>   Quisque sibi in sponsa credit adesse Deam.
> Hi genus amborum, proavosque patresque Loquuntur,

> Nobile sponsa genus, nobile sponsus habet.
> Atque aliquis jam sponsa refert genealogus, esse
>     Esse tuum patruum, quem stupet orbis adhuc,
> Certe etiam stirps est praeclara, vetustaque sponsi,
>     Fallor an in proavis Gruno sit ipse suis.

Phoebus allows everyone who sings to be a poet, offering sacred waters from his free-flowing font. Thanks are pledged to you that Maevius may enter Phocis; that Bavius may sing, thanks are pledged to you. Applause, Hymen, and Io! Everywhere the lyre and plectrum resound. Let envious Eris not disturb these concerts! 'Mild Venus, Venus mild', thus do all and sundry sing your praises, and the piety of Bavius is pleasing for now. This one croons about the groom, that one is astonished at the charming bride, everyone believes that the bride is a Goddess. These prate of the lineage of both spouses, of their progenitors and fathers. The family of the bride is noble; the groom has a noble family. And some genealogist now asserts that he at whom the world still marvels, he is your uncle! Ah, the line of the groom is illustrious indeed, and ancient – am I mistaken, or is Gruno himself counted among his ancestors? (#1010, pp. 17–18)

Heerkens clearly takes a risk in this passage, which provides an important and overlooked clue, I suggest, to the origins of the ensuing literary quarrel. No doubt the young man thought he was being very droll in parodying provincial Dutch social conventions. The picture he paints of the jolly wedding guests, competing to outdo one another in banal flattery, is certainly amusing and memorable, the responsorial anaphora creating an almost dance-like rhythm. It is not inconceivable, however, that once these verses had appeared in print, Heerkens received a visit and 'talking to' from some of the established gentleman–poets of the city (Trip, Alting et al.); and that his answer to their criticisms, and perhaps to the mounting concern and strictures of his own father, was, first, a cutting little number in the *Bellingeweerder Uitspanningen* (discussed below), followed shortly thereafter by the *Carmen Curilli*. Taken as a whole, the epithalamium for Louisa and Hermann is *not* disrespectful, and Heerkens may be forgiven for assuming that a joke at the expense of bad poets – effectively also at his *own* expense, and of his young friends, who constituted the bulk of the wedding singers – would not be taken amiss in the festive context. His attitude hardened, as did his sense of alienation, as that fateful year wore on.

The fact that the Wolthers–Conring wedding took place in January, in the depths of the Dutch winter, removes any suspicion, I think, that an unpatriotic slight was intended in Heerkens's teasing allusion to the bleakness of the venue and season.[93] The cold weather in Groningen and its effect on the poetic veins of the 'Frisians' is, however, a conceit exploited to more biting purpose in Heerkens's contribution to the *Bellingeweerder Uitspanningen*. In the company of the overwhelmingly pious Calvinist *Klinkdigten* of Clara's sacred collection, Heerkens's stands out for its worldly classicism. In his title he even praises the religious poetess for her physical charms: 'Elegy on the occasion of the publication of the songs of the most beautiful poetess, Clara Feyoena van Sytzama' (Cum Clarae Feyoenae â Sytzama pulcherrimae poetriae carmina ederentur. Elegia). Heerkens was already beginning to find his Ovidian feet. His elegy for Clara begins:

Dicebam, desiste bonas sperare Camenas,
    Quem procul a Latio tam rudis ora tuit.
Frisia cui patria est, Arctois crassa pruinis,
    Dissita Cimmeriis nec procul ipsa plagis.
Naso querebatur Getici de frigore coeli,
    Bruma quasi venam strinxerit atra suam:
Exulis & solito levius quasi corda subiret,
    Spiritus ille Deum, sacrificusque vigor.
Frisia at exilio tibi si Peligne fuisset;
    Justior illa tibi forte querela foret.

I was about to say, stop hoping for good Muses when an uncultivated shore bore you, far from Latium; you whose country is Frisia, stiff with northern frosts, the very place that was sown not far from the Cimmerian lands.[94] Naso [Ovid] complained about the freezing sky of the Getae, as if the black

---

[93] He bids his Muse bring lilies and roses for the happy couple, 'at which frosty Winter is stunned ... Come on Muse, come, bring me flowery garlands, garlands which Chloris and the frosty Garden cannot provide' ('Canaque quas stupeat Bruma rubere, rosas ... Eia age Musa veni, mihi fer tam florida Serta, / Serta, Chloris quae non, canus & Hortus habent', p. 16).

[94] Heerkens's footnote *ad loc.* is condescending to the patriotic reader, to say the least! 'Those who are rather fond of their Fatherland will wonder that it is said to be not far from those shadowy Cimmerian lands, until they are apprised of the fact that the Cimmerians, a nomadic race, when they left their Scythia, came into our neighbourhood, and that they were then called Cimbri, whence also the "Cimbric" (Jutland) peninsula, where they had a colony, continues to this day' ('Qui beatam suam Patriam plusculum ament, mirabuntur, dici illam tenebrosis istis Cimmeriis

winter had caused his veins to contract, as if that divine inspiration and sacrificial power was entering the exile's heart less predictably than it used to. But if, bard of the Paeligni, you had been exiled to Frisia, your complaint would have been more just!

Heerkens goes on to compare Ovid's good fortune with the Frisian poet's frigid lot. As for Ovid's place of exile, there is no more pleasing stream to Aurora than the Ister, and she smiles mildly on the neighbouring Getae. They receive the sacred waters of the Danube and Pegasus's font is nearby: 'What were you complaining about, Pelignian, there where Orpheus had drawn the wild beasts and the attentive grove (which even Rome marvels at)?' ('Quid quereris Peligne? feras ibi traxerat Orpheus; / Auritumque (stupet Roma quod ipsa) nemus'). Heerkens's homeland, by contrast, boasts of no Pindus, never sees the sun, cannot refresh itself with Aganippidan springs[95] – the river Aa is salty, and if it weren't for the perpetual rain there would be nothing to drink! Heerkens prolongs the melancholy theme for half a page, then suddenly breaks off: 'I was saying this, or something similarly frivolous about the harshness of our heaven – alas, how many times have I been so bold – when, I am either mistaken or the GODS, summoned by my lamentations, grant my Fatherland better stars!' ('Sic Ego, vel pariter dicebam frivolus, audens / Heu quoties! Coeli de feritate queri. / Verum aut fallebar, nostrisve vocata querelis / Sidera DI Patriae dant meliora meae'). Here begin the praises of Clara proper, who is described as a 'prodigy/monster, a female poet: Phoebus has hardly her equal in the better sex' ('. . . monstrum, femina vates, / Phoebus habet sexu vix meliore parem'). Ovid's daughter, Perilla, isn't her match, even though she was born in Latium and taught by her father; nor can the Greek Sappho compete. It does not require too cynical a reader to detect a note of irony, even snideness, in Heerkens's overpowering garlands. He imagines the young poetess climbing the sacred mountain (ambiguously of poetry and the Christian religion):

Vix tribus haec lustris, binos superaddidit annos,
    Jamque stupenda sacro monte cacumen adit,
Aggreditur juga celsa, sibi juga plena periclis;
    Ah ne te salebrae virgo tenella notent.

non adeo remotam esse, nisi sciant Cimmerios, vagam gentem, cum Schythiam suam linquerent, in nostram divenisse vicinam, & Cimbros tum apellatos fuisse, unde et Cimbrica Chersonesus, ubi illorum fuit colonia, adhuc Extat').

[95] Ovidian gloss for the Hippocrene font.

Ah tibi ne molles rupes secet aspera plantas;
> Quamque sacra est, utinam tam tibi tuta foret!

Quid loquor! Evicit felix audacia clivum,
> Evicit sacrae tanta pericla viae.

Quo nequit eniti labor & doctrina virorum,
> Pro, teneris annis nostra Virago petit.

She is barely seventeen and now the astonishing girl is approaching the peak of the sacred mountain. She makes an attempt on the lofty ridges, ridges full of danger to herself. Ah, let not the rough ground mark you, dainty little virgin! Ah, let not the sharp rocks cut your soft feet! If only that which is sacred were also safe for you! But what am I saying? Her happy boldness has conquered the hill, has conquered the many dangers of the sacred way! There where the labour and learning of men cannot strive to reach, just look, our Virago has gone in her tender years.

We might even see an implicit critique of Clara's theological pretensions in Heerkens's patronizing concern for the precocious girl's tender feet. She perhaps risks ridicule, even slurs on her maidenly virtue, by rashly attempting to join the public world of male sacred learning (*notent* carries a dual sense of 'mark' and 'stigmatize'). Moreover, the final lines of the passage here quoted yield an almost *Catholic* miracle, and a young, female saint whose victory over hard-won masculine doctrine may well have caused some stern Calvinist brows to crease! Indeed, was Heerkens's capitalization of the word *Virago* calculated to conjure the spectre of the Virgin Mary? However that may be, the lines that immediately follow, and the conclusion of the poem, carefully steer us away from thoughts of religion and to *belles lettres*.[96]

\*\*\*

In the Wolthers–Conring collection Gerard Heerkens signed himself *Phoebi utriusque studiosus* ('devotee of both Apollos'); in the *Bellingeweerder Uitspanningen*, simply as *Groninganus*. The Groningener who panted for the Roman Arcadia was about to enter a maelstrom of satirical abuse that was anything but pastoral. By the end of 1746 Heerkens would leave Groningen

---

[96] Thus Clara's epiphany heralds a *translatio imperii* of literary culture from Greece and Italy to the Northern Netherlands. Phoebus can't find a safe refuge in any other corner of the Old or New World: 'Et Latium bellat, nec ibi bene Phoebe lateres, / Ah Vaticano vix tegerere jugo'.

and his hexametrical battles behind him, at least for the time being.[97] As promised in the *Carmen Curilli*, he now pursued his medical studies in earnest, although he did not oblige his father by giving up poetry entirely. An exile poet before his time, the young Heerkens retreated into Ovidian elegiacs, and attempted to reinvent himself first as a medical epigrammatist in Leiden, then as a moralizing elegiac didactic poet in Voltaire's Paris. And it is to the elegant salons of that cultural metropolis that we travel in the next chapter.

---

[97] The collected *Marii Curilli Satyrae* (1758) seem to have been prepared for publication on the eve of Heerkens's journey to Italy in 1759. Koninklijke Bibliotheek, The Hague, 393 D 16 is a bound volume of *Curilli Juvenilia*, a miscellany containing some of Heerkens's previously printed poems, together with sometimes extensive manuscript additions in his own hand. It begins with a poem by his friend G. J. Draper, on the occasion of Heerkens's graduation in 'both laws', and is followed by one by Heerkens 'to the same'.

# 2

# Stepping Out: Healing the Republic of Letters

## A Dutchman in Paris

If the *Xenia* of Leiden were the first fruits of Heerkens's newfound scholarly poetic maturity, the massive didactic poem on the health of men of letters he produced during his student days in Paris was in many ways the most ambitious of his career – even if it withered prematurely on the eve of its publication. We shall see in this chapter that at least the first edition of the *De valetudine literatorum* (1749) proved to be a misjudged attempt to teach Heerkens's academic grandfathers to suck eggs. Not that his Dutch professors will have been averse to scientific poetry *per se*. The Linnaean Adriaan van Royen (1704–99) had already attained a modicum of international recognition as a Latin didactic poet for his *Carmen elegiacum de Amoribus et Connubiis Plantarum* ('Elegiac Song on the Loves and Weddings of the Plants' (Leiden, 1732) – which pre-dated Erasmus Darwin's *Loves of the Plants* by over half a century.[1] But Heerkens's *De valetudine literatorum*, significantly, was published in 1749, the very year in which a largely Jesuit anthology of *Poemata didascalica* ('Didactic Poems') appeared in Paris, under the aegis of distinguished French linguist, translator of the Classics, *académicien* and former Jesuit, Pierre-Joseph Thoulier d'Olivet.[2] Perhaps not coincidentally, 1749 was also the year in which

---

[1] Van Royen was himself trumped, though, by an Irish physician, Demetrius McEnroe, whose didactic poem, *Connubia Florum*, was first published in Paris, 1728. Van Royen's self-published collected poems (Leiden, 1778) are available on Google books. In addition to the two poems marking his accession to and retirement from the professorship in botany (both previously published) this collection includes medical elegiac didactics on 'the regimen for mind and body', and 'on the diseases of the ages' [sc. life stages].

[2] The behind-the-scenes editor of the *Poemata didascalica* was, in fact, the Jesuit François Oudin, in whose name the expanded edition appeared in 1813.

an Italian lexicographer, Jesuit alumnus Giampietro Bergantini, published in Italy the first in an ambitious projected series of editions of Jesuit Latin poems on the arts and sciences: *Botanicorum libri iv* ('Four books on Botany'), by the Neapolitan, Francesco Eulalio Savastano, S. J.[3] In his introduction to that volume, Bergantini records the titles of scores of Jesuit poems he had either sighted personally, in print or manuscript, or seen reviewed in foreign journals, treating subjects from meteorology to medicine, natural history to vampirology. It is likely that Heerkens, even before he arrived in Paris and befriended the elderly d'Olivet, was alive to this Enlightenment didactic 'buzz' through the Jesuit college network.[4] Indeed, sparks were flying even beyond the Society of Jesus. Jean-Antoine Nollet (1700–70), physics professor in Paris, invited the young medical student to commit his fashionable electrical experiments to Latin verse.[5] While Heerkens's muse did not fulfil that particular commission, it is nevertheless significant, I think, that he should have chosen to dedicate himself to a *continuous* didactic poem in Paris, rather than, say, a further series of epigrams on health, to gratify the guests of Fontenelle.[6] (Nearly 20 years later it was, tellingly, an Italian *Jesuit* who took up the challenge of committing the modern science of electricity to Latin verse: Giuseppe Maria Mazzolari.[7]) Heerkens sent extracts of the major work he was gestating to the abbé d'Olivet, and to Guillaume-Françoise Berthier, S. J. (1704–82), editor of the *Journal de Trévoux*, the Jesuits' international scholarly review.[8] It is not inconceivable

---

[3] See Y. A. Haskell, *Loyola's Bees: Ideology and Industry in Jesuit Latin Didactic Poetry* (Oxford: Oxford University Press, 2003), p. 312. Bergantini himself was a Theatine.

[4] In a verse letter to Jean-Jacques le Franc published with his didactic poem, *De officio medici* ('On the Duties of a Doctor', 1752, p. 58, n. (s)), Heerkens records that while he was in Paris he visited the Jesuits Boudori (sc. Joseph du Baudory, professor of rhetoric at the Collège Louis-le-Grand), Geoffroy (sc. Jean-Baptiste Geoffroy, professor of rhetoric at La Flèche for 22 years) and de la Sante (sc. Gilles Anne Xavier de la Sante, author of a didactic poem on iron, *Ferrum*, published in Nyon, 1707, and editor of a well-known collection of student pieces from the *Musae rhetorices* (Paris, 1732): cf. Haskell, *Loyola's Bees*, appendix 2, pp. 321–7).

[5] Nollet invited Herkens to attend his fashionable electrical demonstrations free of charge. On Nollet's activities at this time, see John Heilbron, *Electricity in the Seventeenth and Eighteenth Centuries: A Study of Early Modern Physics* (Berkeley: University of California Press, 1979; rev. edn; Mineola, NY: Dover, 1999), pp. 352–62.

[6] See Haskell, *Loyola's Bees*, chap. 4, passim.

[7] A passage in the third book of *De valetudine literatorum* (2nd edn, 1790) is effectively a retrospective advertisement for the shorter, didactic epigrams on health Heerkens had published in Leiden the year before his trip to Paris. Here Heerkens commends the usefulness of the epigrammatic form for, as it were, sampling and compressing the medical wisdom of the centuries and eliding the disputes which mar the works of learned physicians: 'I noted that there was scarcely a profession [lit. 'kind of life'] less peaceful than that which prescribes that souls be peaceful and wise' ('Vix genus, admonui, vitae minus esse quietum, / Quam quod pacem animos et sapuisse docet', p. 176).

[8] J. Corbett in *The Catholic Encyclopedia* notes that 'because of his powerful opposition to the infidel "encyclopédistes" [he] was bitterly attacked, especially by Voltaire' ('Guillaume-François Berthier',

that the Jesuit-educated foreigner was touting for a spot in d'Olivet's pending Paris anthology.[9] Its theme, after all, must have seemed a promising one for currying favour with hard-working Jesuit Latin humanists. If so, Heerkens's frank discussion of the sexual health of scholars (in the 1749 edition of *De valetudine literatorum*) may have damaged his poem's chances of inclusion – if not its great length.[10] Heerkens visited Rome ten years later, at the beginning of a boom in publication of Jesuit scientific didactic poems there. He was hoping to meet at least Carlo Noceti, professor of physics at the Collegio Romano and author of two celebrated meteorological poems, *Iris* (Venice, 1729) and *Aurora borealis* (Rome, 1747), reprinted in the Paris *Poemata didascalica*; unfortunately Noceti died shortly before his arrival.[11]

\*\*\*

*De valetudine literatorum* is one of just three Latin poems noticed by the author of Heerkens's short entry in the *Dictionnaire des sciences médicales* (Paris, 1820–5), the so-called Panckoucke. Only the telegraphic first edition of 1749 is mentioned. The history of the poem's publication is intriguing, and our curiosity is piqued all the more by the author's carefully finessed account

---

vol. 2 (New York: Robert Appleton Company, 1907), available online at <www.newadvent.org/cathen/02519b.htm>.

[9] In the 1790 edition of the poem, Heerkens writes of his affection for d'Olivet, whom he visited regularly during his first Paris period (p. 2); he writes also that 'by him, more than by anyone else, I was helped, and not a little, in emending this work' (p. 5).

[10] In the second edition, alas, the subject is passed over in a most perfunctory fashion: 'Much sex, and late nights tire the eyes, and a hunched posture' ('Multa venus, vigilesque fatigant lumina noctes, / Et si quis curvo vertice semper agat'). A footnote on this page explains: 'The author had included some 40 or 50 verses on the avoidance of too much sex by married scholars, following here, as in all these matters, Sanctorius. But since Berthier had warned him to get rid of those verses, if for no other reason than that the author's age had so often been mentioned – although everyone to whom he had read them had liked them – they were dropped, and the reason is also given here in the pentameter' [sc. in the couplet: 'I could indeed include further precepts and problems to be cured, but they are not the sort of thing a young man writes about' ('Plura quidem praecepta, et quae curentur, haberem, / Sed sunt, quae juvenis non bene dictat opus')] (Book 2, p. 126, n. 96).

[11] On this 'Roman school' of scientific didactic, see my *Loyola's Bees*, chap. 4. Heerkens met, among others, Contuccio Contucci, curator of the Kircherian Museum at the Roman College, author of an unpublished Latin botanical poem; and Girolamo Lagomarsini, professor of Greek and editor of Cicero, who seems to have taken a crucial behind-the-scenes role in the production and circulation of scientific poetry in eighteenth-century Rome. (He was himself the author of a modestly proportioned didactic poem 'on the origin of springs'.) It was to Lagomarsini that Bergantini dedicated his programmatic poem on the didactic-poetic empire of the Jesuits in 1749; at the same time he published and supplemented the first edition of Lagomarsini's poem, 23 years after its original recitation at the Roman College (*Loyola's Bees*, p. 195). It is the poem on springs which is quoted, under Lagomarsini's anagrammatic pseudonym, by Guatemalan Jesuit Rafael Landívar, as an inscription to the second edition of his didactic *Rusticatio Mexicana* (Bologna, 1782). Lagomarsini also surfaces in annotations to the Latin didactic poem on electricity by Giuseppe Maria Mazzolari, S. J. (Rome, 1767).

of its conception and fortunes in the preface to the expanded 1790 edition. It would appear that Heerkens was prompted to prepare a revised edition of his juvenile work after having been serendipitously reminded of its existence by a review in the *Journal Encyclopédique* of his *Aves Frisicae* ('Frisian Birds', 1787).[12] He claims to have been struck by the coincidence that his decision to revise and republish the poem on learned men's health was made in the same month, and perhaps on the same day, on which he had begun to compose it some 40 years earlier:

> But if the circumstances of the undertaking of the revision were remarkable, the writing and the fortune of the work, once known to the reader, will perhaps seem no less remarkable. I had come to Paris in the year 1748, a few months after my twenty-second birthday. Nothing could have been further from my mind, when I arrived, and even for some time afterwards, that within the year of my sojourn in that city I would have written around three thousand verses. (Latin preface to the 1790 edition, p. ix)

Hereupon Heerkens loses himself in a reverie about his student days in Paris. He writes with engaging frankness about his experiences as a star-struck denizen of the Procope café, the diffident manner he adopted in order to ingratiate himself with its powerful patrons, and the lengths to which he went to meet and impress Voltaire especially; he writes, too, of his deep disillusionment with the *philosophe*'s irreligious character and querulousness in later years, a disillusionment matched only by Heerkens's resignation to the irreversible decline of Latin letters in the second half of the century.[13] And why, he reflects poignantly, did he not follow his father's good advice and restrict himself to writing *prose*?[14] Of course, he had been blinded by recent praise for his poetic talents in the *Journal de Trévoux* (November 1748). His tentative first steps as a medical didactic poet had been applauded by some of the greatest literary men

---

[12] November 1788. Heerkens asserts that, 'in order to introduce me as a budding ornithologist to the learned world via my previous works, almost everything I had published up to that point was recorded in the article: and among those, the poem I had composed as a youth, "On the Health of Men of Letters"'. In fact, the *only* poems mentioned by the Bouillon journalist are the *De valetudine literatorum* and the *Iter Venetum*!

[13] A dedicatory poem to Dordrecht magistrate and Latin poet Jacob Hoeufft is, if anything, even more despondent, as Heerkens laments not only the decline of Latin letters but the accusations of lack of patriotism which have plagued his retirement in provincial Groningen.

[14] 'That I didn't follow his wise counsel grieves me now as I recall it, and it grieved me deeply when I contemplated my wasted efforts on the [work about the] kings of France, of which he had actually approved' (p. viii). Eppo's advice had been to eschew verse as it required a disproportionate amount of effort and was destined to be read by a very few cognoscenti. To whom would Heerkens send his drafts after his father's death?

in Paris, not least Voltaire and Crébillon, from whom he continued to receive regular advice and encouragement.

Returning to his homeland via Reims, where he graduated in medicine, Heerkens stopped at Leiden to have his precocious *magnum opus* printed. But where it had been received well enough in Paris, the poem now came up against some harsh criticisms from the Dutch publisher's all-too-learned academic readers.[15] According to Heerkens, still smarting from the insult four decades on, their 'judgements merited a quarrel, but since I had suffered them from teachers who had contributed not a little to my knowledge of medicine, and since I could hope for a perpetual spring in the grave at their hands, I shall say nothing of them' (pp. xiv–xv).[16] Whoever these disobliging former professors may have been, their reservations were evidently strong enough to give the printer, Johan Luzac, pause. A drastically abridged version of the original – more than 2,600 verses were cut – stumbled into print in 1749.[17] Undaunted, Heerkens commissioned 30 copies of the complete poem, in three books, to be sent to his friends abroad.[18]

The *second* edition, also in three books, was published in Groningen in 1790, with a dedication to wealthy Amsterdam merchant banker, Henry Hope (1735–1811).[19] How closely this text matches that of the original three-book version is hard to say, since the 30 complimentary copies of 1749 all but

---

[15] The identity of these critics remains a mystery. The professors of medicine and anatomy at Leiden in this period were Hieronymus David Gaubius, Frederik Winter and brothers Bernhard Siegfried and Frederick Bernhard Albinus. B. S. Albinus, Heerkens tells us in the poem, was 'known to me from the neighbourhood and as a teacher, and to all as the greatest of the Dutch anatomists and the most diligent of all that ever were. And that this testimonial was deserved by Albinus I have from the mouth of the Paduan Morgagni, an equally just and great man' (p. 136). Adriaan van Royen was professor of botany (1732–55) and only later professor of medicine (1755–75). In his poem *De officio medici*, Heerkens gently chides van Royen for fawning on Linnaeus (1752, p. 32), for aspiring to be remembered in the name of a plant rather than for his poetic efforts.

[16] Well, *almost* nothing. One of his readers had apparently sneered: 'Who dictated ['dictasset'] this work in France?' The hot-blooded young poet unwisely rose to the bait: 'Since that question seemed designed to bring down not only the work which was about to be published, but also those distichs I had published in Leiden nearly two years earlier, on preserving health [sc. *Xenia*], and were provocative, I responded more sharply than fairly, that is, by asking: "of the two academic orations he had published, who dictated the last one for *him*?" I said that if he would own up to *that*, I would confess to being the promoter ['adjutor'] of my work' (p. xi). The full import of the joke is obscure, but Heerkens seems to be implying that his Dutch critic needed help with his Latin. Suffice it to say that this offence to professorial dignity was not taken lightly, and Heerkens's hopes of seeing his poem published in its original form were quickly dashed.

[17] This edition 'appeared' simultaneously in Leiden and Reims. The scarce Reims 'edition' turns out to be the Leiden one with a new titlepage tipped in, perhaps in partial fulfilment of Heerkens's medical degree. I thank Ian Maclean for alerting me to this possibility, and Jan Waszink for comparing the editions in Paris.

[18] These were no doubt transcribed rather than printed. The Latin word is *describere*.

[19] He describes the Italian paintings at Hope's sumptuous summer villa near Haarlem, 'Welgelegen', as rivalling the Vatican collections. Did Heerkens meet Hope when he joined the Haarlem Maatschappij

disappeared in the poet's lifetime. What is certain is that the revised edition contains plenty of material that simply cannot have appeared in the original complete version. Heerkens refers to publications and events from the second half of the century,[20] larding his revision with generous footnotes, and, most significantly, bulking up the third book with a lengthy excursus on the causes of Ovid's exile, drawing on the results of original research he had conducted into the manuscripts and *scholia* during his Italian journey of 1759/60.[21] The mature Heerkens was no doubt seizing the opportunity, now, of saying everything he had ever hoped to say on the subject in 1749 – as well as everything he had subsequently learned. It is as if he is marshalling all the forces of erudition and seniority to silence, once and for all, those irritating critics of his youth.

If the younger Heerkens felt aggrieved at the butchery perpetrated on his text by the Leiden professors – we are not told, by the way, whether their criticisms were motivated primarily by literary or scientific considerations[22] – he was, of course, happy enough to allow the truncated version to go to print. Did Groningen's prodigal son feel a lingering obligation to redeem himself as a useful scholarly citizen, to publish his worthy new medical poem, by hook or by crook, before returning from his studies abroad? It is equally likely that he just didn't want to let good verses go to waste. Thus, while the poem that went to print was a very different beast from the 3,000-line monster hatched in France, most of Heerkens's verse works, in fact, would go through more than one edition

---

de Wetenschappen in 1772? In the dedication to the poem he says that Henry's four paternal uncles 'have been of much use to me in my life'; we also know that on his journey to Italy in 1759, Heerkens travelled between Bonn and Coblentz with Olivier Hope, presumably Henry's cousin (*Italicorum libri iii* (Groningen, 1793), p. 9, and n. 9).

[20] For example, the following lines appear in the first book of the second edition, in the context of a discussion of salubrious places for the scholar to live: 'but my Muse, who is only concerned about scholars, will not find them across the seas of the Indes' ('Sed mea, quae tantum studiosis consulit, illos / Musa per Indorum non reperiret aquas', p. 46). But a note explains: 'What seemed true in 1749 is no longer. For now learned men are found in India: in the Dutch Society established in the capital of the Indes [Batavia] some years ago, and growing in repute to the general delight of our nation, and to that of the author especially, because the founders of this institution, and its principal promoters, were Willem Arnold Alting, from Groningen, our governor in India, and also William Hogendorp and Paul Gevers, noblemen from Rotterdam, also both very old friends of the author'. Alting was, of course, the son of Heerkens's Groningen nemesis from the pamphlet war!

[21] He reports that 'the work was enlarged by some 300 verses, interwoven here and there, and with a few little notes ('notulisque'): mostly, though, [notes] to the verses which demonstrate the reasons for Ovid's exile' (p. xi). The second edition boasts 3,588 verses against the 366 published in 1749.

[22] There is a tantalizing aside at n. 93, pp. 124–5, where Heerkens reveals that a pentameter advocating extraction of peat fuel from the Dutch wetlands was 'one of the reasons why the original edition of this work was rejected forty years ago. As though he who provided many and for that matter impartial reasons for the preservation of his native soil (without which his country would not remain) was abusing the rights of a good citizen!'

and receive substantial touching up in the process. Literary perfection seems always to have been less of a priority for him than getting his thoughts down onto paper and out into print; consistency of content between versions less imperative than seizing the moment to make and remake his public image.

We might compare and contrast the literary habits of Nicolas-Claude Fabri de Peiresc (1580–1637), the renowned seventeenth-century French astronomer and antiquarian who regularly complained of, but never actually abandoned, his rural solitude in provincial Aix. Peiresc, as Peter Miller has shown, secured his high status within the early modern *Respublica litterarum* not by publishing books, but by a relentless exchange, in person and via post, of letters, manuscripts and objects. But the intellectual community with which our even more geographically isolated eighteenth-century Dutchman aspired to engage, and in an equally personal way, had to be reached primarily through print.[23] Heerkens's modern reader is frequently struck by the epistolary, gossipy, one is tempted to say, 'blog-like', quality of his printed paratexts, even of the texts themselves. Print for this young and rising literary-intellectual networker was a legitimate forum for airing and repairing work-in-progress. Only for the older and disenchanted citizen of the Republic of Latin Letters, disrespected at home perhaps especially after the Dutch Patriot Revolt of 1787, does print come to represent the final resting place for a learned legacy, for what even Heerkens must by then have realized could only ever be a provisional posterity.[24]

Both the older and newer editions of the *De valetudine literatorum* were then, as Heerkens himself was well aware, far from 'timeless' Latin verse; each was an imperfect compromise with the times. As such, however, the second edition may serve as a fortuitous instrument for surveying the changing intellectual landscape of the eighteenth century. In bringing his poem up-to-date, Heerkens is forced to reflect, almost continuously, on political and cultural developments since its first composition. The date of the first edition had closely anticipated

---

[23] On Peiresc's Republic of Letters, see Peter Miller, *Peiresc's Europe: Learning and Virtue in the Seventeenth Century* (New Haven: Yale University Press, 2000).

[24] Thus begins the mournful poem to Jacob Henrik Hoeufft which prefaces the second edition of the *De valetudine literatorum*: 'Friend – the only one who, unbidden, still cultivates and loves the Latin Muses [sc. without a commission], who is happy in tough times, and who by governing well the matters of state, well the matters of Helicon, tends to the wretched affairs of Phoebus and of our country – receive from one who is fleeing Pindus, in his later years, a work which may perhaps be the poet's last' ('Unus adhuc Latias, injussus, Amice Camenas / Qui colis, et, duro tempore laetus, amas, / Et bene res patriae, bene res Heliconis agendo / Res miseras Phoebi, qui patriaeque foves, / Accipe de seros Pindum fugiente per annos, / Vatis et extremum forte quod exstet, opus', p. xvii). Heerkens entrusts his posthumous reputation to Hoeufft.

what Hans Bots and Françoise Waquet, quoting d'Alembert's 'Tableau de l'esprit humain au milieu du XVIIIè siecle', have identified as an Enlightenment watershed moment, the dawning consciousness in France of a definitive break with past.[25] The date of the second, of course, follows hard on the definitive and shattering demise of the French *ancien régime* in 1789. In the United Provinces, the French-dictated Batavian Republic was just around the corner. The stereoscopic synthesis of viewpoints provided by Heerkens's 1790 *De valetudine literatorum* does not, to be sure, yield a crisp photographic image, that is a snapshot, of the Republic of Letters at *either* moment, but it might fruitfully be compared to a painted portrait, one that captures the evolving, living image of that community over the passage of 40 eventful years.[26]

## Whose letters, whose language?

An obvious first question arising from the title of this work is '*whose* letters?'[27] Is it written for the benefit of some sort of eighteenth-century continuation or offshoot of the early modern *Respublica litterarum*? The latter is a term we have been using somewhat loosely up to this point but which may now be refined. In its ideal configuration, the 'Republic of Letters' was an international, irenic, cross-confessional, community of primarily Latin-using scholars and scientists that had its heyday in the period between the Wars of Religion and the Thirty Years War.[28] Its existence and values, however, were invoked most frequently in the eighteenth century, and with a mixture of nostalgia and optimism.[29] It was in the eighteenth century, too, that its citizenry was first subjected to penetrating social scrutiny and census, for example in Charles Pinot Duclos's *Considérations sur les moeurs de ce siècle* (1751), which divided that once theoretically universal and socially permeable republic into three

---

[25] Bots and Waquet, *La République des Lettres* (Paris: Belin, 1997), p. 56.
[26] On the personification of the Republic of Letters see Ann Goldgar, *Impolite Learning: Conduct and Community in the Republic of Letters, 1680-1750* (New Haven: Yale University Press, 1995), p. 10.
[27] The 'letters' of the *Respublica litterarum* included experimental and natural science as well as historical and literary erudition. See Bots and Waquet, *La République*, pp. 14-18.
[28] In spite of its universalizing ideology, the 'space' of the early modern Republic of Letters was an hierarchical one, in which, for example, large swathes of southern and eastern Europe were considered beyond the pale. See Bots and Waquet, *La République*, pp. 63-90.
[29] In many ways the pre-Enlightenment Republic of Letters set the stage for the new collaborative enterprise of the *Encyclopédie*. See Bots and Waquet, *La République*, esp. 'Le temps de la République des Lettres', pp. 29-61; and Lorraine Daston, 'The Ideal and the Reality of the Republic of Letter in the Enlightenment', *Science in Context* 4 (1991), pp. 367-86.

distinct and hierarchized classes: 'les savants qu'on appelle aussi érudits', who are now going out of fashion; 'savants qui s'occupent des sciences exactes', who are well regarded and, generally speaking, better compensated than the former; and finally, those who are in the greatest demand: 'ceux qu'on appelle communément beaux esprits'.[30] But the constitution of this third class, especially, was contested, and Voltaire, for one, did not much care to be considered a *bel esprit*.[31]

What were the demographic and geographic borders of the Republic of Letters drawn up by Heerkens, or at least implied, for readers of his *De valetudine literatorum*? Does the fact that his work is in Latin, for example, suggest an affiliation with and particular concern for intellectuals of Duclos's first class, that of the increasingly outmoded (in France, at least) *érudits*? Heerkens's poem, it is true, is crammed with philological and antiquarian erudition, but, it should be noted, such material is often adduced to shed light on contemporary economic and social circumstances, and indeed on matters of public health. If Heerkens's choice of Latin is not dictated by mere backward-looking bookishness, then, does it speak to his professional (and progressive) aspirations as a modern humanist physician on the international stage? Latin was still, after all, a natural medium for scientific publication by university-trained medics, even the most 'enlightened', in this period.

Heerkens does not write a *De valetudine 'eruditorum'* in word or deed: the learned community on which he offers his comprehensive health report may not be entirely new-fashioned, but it is certainly wider and more worldly than that of Duclos's *érudits*.[32] The men of letters described by Heerkens in this poem either lived *by* their learning or applied their learning – as does Heerkens himself – to pressing contemporary concerns. They are philosophers and poets, historians, theologians and physicians, stretching from Protagoras, Juvenal and Ovid in antiquity through the Italian humanists and popular vernacular Dutch Golden Age authors, to modern writers in Dutch and French, professors of medicine, and, significantly, *philosophes*. There are, admittedly, distinct filters

---

[30] The quotations are from Chapter 10. Duclos's work is available via Google books. Heerkens knew and cited Duclos's history of Louis XI in the preface to the *De valetudine literatorum* (1790).
[31] Bots and Waquet, *La République*, pp. 58–9. Voltaire drew a line between original thinkers and writers on the one side (*philosophes*) and *parvenu* scribblers on the other (*beaux esprits*).
[32] The latter, observed the Frenchman wistfully, have been reduced in recent times to a sad, reclusive, if not eccentric, bunch: 'ils se produisent peu dans le monde qui ne leur convient guére, & à qui ils ne conviennent pas davantage'.

on Heerkens's intellectual demography. He does not discuss the careers and life expectancy of, much less the distinctive occupational hazards faced by, the 'hard-core' men of science of his and the previous century: the astronomers, mathematicians, experimental natural philosophers, natural historians, and, most curiously perhaps, not even the botanists.[33]

We must be wary, too, of an easy assumption that because this poem was written in *Latin* it was, *ipso facto*, destined for a wide and undifferentiated international audience. The first edition, shorn of the extensive notes that bristle in the second, was dedicated to Heerkens's one-time mentor, professor of medicine, anatomy and botany, and chief physician of Groningen, Hendrik Croeser.[34] This gesture of piety towards a beloved local teacher may already have predisposed Heerkens's Dutch readers to regard his poem as composed principally for *their* benefit. But many more passages in the second edition seem to indicate that the author had always had his countrymen (perhaps even the Groningeners specifically) in mind.[35] Thus, for example, sections on the evils of Dutch (over-)eating, smoking[36] and drinking (Book 1, pp. 27–37)[37]; on the relative longevity of painters, scholars and magistrates from different Dutch cities (pp. 38–40); on good and bad locations for scholars' houses primarily in the Low Countries (pp. 44–50); on the pre-eminence of Dutch, and especially Groningen, humanists (Book 2, pp. 73–80); on the reasons for the decline of the premium Groningen beer industry (pp. 99–101);[38] on the

---

[33] In this he differs from Samuel Tissot, discussed below, who addresses the separate risks to which different sections of the Republic of Letters are prone (orators, actors, lawyers, preachers, musicians, physicians, anatomists, botanists, chemists, etc.).

[34] The preface describes Heerkens's studies in medicine since Leiden, the great professors he frequented in Paris (such as Ferrein and Astruc) and his graduation in Reims. Much of the preface is given over to a description of the city of Reims and its antiquities.

[35] Expressly in a note on p. 156, where he explains that, on the recommendation of a learned reader, he has substituted for the name of an impious French poet, now forgotten (sc. François Linière), that of one 'Calaber Calabro' who had been incarcerated for blasphemy in the United Provinces and was thus well known 'to the Dutch for whom this work was written especially' ('Batavis, quibus hoc opus maximè scriptum', n. 27).

[36] Heerkens is expansive on the dangers of smoking, a particular vice of the Dutch and now of scholars – although in past times, as we may infer from the paintings and poems of Brouwer, Van Oestade and Cats, one predominantly of the lower classes (pp. 29–30). Heerkens interestingly associates the rise of rickets in Britain with the spread of tobacco smoking since Elizabethan times; the poison is transmitted from parents to offspring (p. 32, and n. 47).

[37] Not even the doctors give sufficient health warnings about the situation. Foreign professors of philosophy at the University of Groningen, Hendrik Croeser and Jean Bernouilli, preferred to decline the society of their Dutch colleagues than be obliged to partake of unmixed wine four hours after lunch (pp. 35–6, and n. 51)!

[38] Heerkens reports that Groningen professor of philosophy, Martin Schook, author of a 1661 treatise on beer, never published anything of note after he had left the land of the Cluny-drinkers (*Clunia*

ethnic origins of the Dutch and on historical waves of German immigration into the Netherlands (pp. 107–8); on Dutch versus Venetian water supplies (pp. 112–13); on travel destinations for Dutch scholars (pp. 114–15); on the particular dangers of idleness, causing phlegm, for Dutch scholars (pp. 117–18); on the unfortunate importation by the Dutch of German hypocaust ovens (pp. 123–4);[39] on recent reforms in the Dutch universities (Book 3, pp. 148–9); on the different effects of wind in the Low Countries and in Rome (pp. 161–2); on the Roman presence in Groningen (pp. 38–9; pp. 171–2); on the relative health of Parisian ladies vis-à-vis their Dutch sisters and how the latter can learn from the good example of the former by dressing more warmly in cold weather and taking regular exercise (pp. 175–6).

The preface explaining the poem's gestation in Paris, however, and the celebration of French manners, society and diet within it, hint that Heerkens the *student*–poet may have aspired, initially or additionally, to warm the hearts (if not the feet!) of his grand Parisian patrons.[40] Not a conspicuous seeker-out of female conversation, Heerkens goes out of his way to furnish the reader of his poem with eulogies of two learned Dutch women – a possible accommodation to French taste? Certainly his verses on Mme Scudery were included to honour Fontenelle, who was devoted to her memory (p. 133, n. 7).

Short of recovering one of the lost complimentary copies of the original long version of the poem we will never know how much editing it underwent between the first and second editions.[41] Chances are that some of the changes were not insignificant.[42] Heerkens's testy observations on Voltaire's character in the preface to the 1790 edition are something of a prophylactic against his

---

being the name of the Groningen beer) for Frankfurt-am-Oder, where he died three years later (pp. 115–16, n. 83).

[39] Heerkens specifies that they are made of iron, and that the resulting ferrous vapour damages the temples (causes headache?), lungs and eyes. Presumably some sort of *Kachelofen* is meant.

[40] Many footnotes supplying biographical information on Dutch writers and culture may have been designed for a French, if not wider, audience. For example, would Heerkens have felt the need to explain to his own countrymen that 'the *Treasury of Health* by Jan van Berverwijk was a book published in Dutch around 1630, and how much it was read may be gathered from the almost innumerable editions through which it went in the last century' (p. 30, n. 44)?

[41] Rarely does Heerkens provide such explicit advice on the introduction of new material as when in Book 2 he informs us that a passage on an unusually long-lived (172 and 179 years) corn-eating Dacian couple was added recently, and after he had a viewed pictures of them hanging over Charles de Lorraine's fireplace. But one suspects that the footnote was as much an opportunity to name drop – that he had dined with the Regent in Brussels on five occasions, in 1761 and 1763 – as to alert the reader to changes in the poem (pp. 80–1, n. 40).

[42] Judging, for example, from the cleaned-up 1758 edition of Heerkens's collected satires vis-à-vis their pamphlet originals from a decade earlier; or from successive editions of his *Italica*, poems from Italy (see next chapter).

more charitable treatment of the sprightly old man in the poem itself.[43] It is possible that he quietly removed any number of lines in praise of Voltaire from the reworked version, just as (he tells us) he burned the thirteen Latin elegies composed in his hero's honour in the eleven years since their first meeting.[44] On the other hand, Heerkens cannot resist dropping the name of so impressive an acquaintance in the occasional footnote to the published second edition.[45]

Take, for example, this revealing piece of self-congratulation from the opening pages of the second book: 'The author showed his poem, to his and its great benefit, to quite a few eminent critics in Paris, and because of their judgements on the work, or because of the praises bestowed in it on Voltaire, it followed that the latter wanted to see it for himself' (p. 56, n. 1). Heerkens relates how Voltaire had urged him to extend and carry over into the second book his discussion of the topic of suitable housing for the learned (and he obliges). Moreover, where Father Berthier, editor of the *Journal de Trévoux*, had suggested Heerkens drop from his first book a long digression on the ancient site of the city of Leiden, Voltaire had wanted to see that section preserved. Heerkens reports that he *would* have removed the verses in deference to the learned Jesuit, notwithstanding Voltaire's vote of confidence, but decided in the end that the information he had revealed there was 'more memorable for the most singular way in which it was received ('singularissimo modo acceptam'), and, for that matter, no less true'.

Singular indeed! Heerkens's antiquarian digression (pp. 47–52), which follows on a discussion of the health dangers of Dutch canalside-living, is relayed to him by the ghost of Joseph Scaliger . . . This was not of course our poet's first deployment of the conceit of the didactic ghost. Intriguingly, though, he maintains the fiction of the Scaligerian apparition even in the accompanying

---

[43] On Voltaire's temperate lifestyle, see *De valetudine literatorum* (1790), pp. 86–7.
[44] What would people have thought of him, Heerkens asks, if he had allowed those elegies to survive: 'I would be believed to esteem the worst philosopher, the worst citizen of his country even now, just as I esteemed him, foolishly, long ago' ('Pessimum philosophum, pessimum patriae suae civem, stulte diu aestimatum, aestimatum etiam nunc crederer', p. iii).
[45] Voltaire gets the date of Jean Barbeyrac's death wrong in his *Siecle de Louis XIV* (p. 22, n. 29); Voltaire and d'Alembert contend that the French and Italians cannot pronounce Latin correctly – as if it hadn't been in constant use in their churches since time immemorial (p. 25, n. 34);. Heerkens uses the periphrasis 'wise man of the Fibrenus' for Cicero and Voltaire seeks clarification, Heerkens explains that the Fibreno is the river near Cicero's birthplace, and Voltaire subsequently uses the phrase in his *Catiline*: 'Quoi, l'habitant obscur des rives du Fibrene, / Siege audessus de moi sur la pourpre Romaine?' (p. 84, n. 44); Voltaire always feared he was not long for this world (pp. 86–7, n. 46).

footnotes.[46] With the exception of a bird's-eye-view *aetion* explaining the Latin name of the 'goldcrest', *regulus*,[47] this is the only *fabula* to grace any of Heerkens's didactic verse – and Scaliger's crusty archaeological lecture, buttressed by long and learned footnotes, is hardly the sort of reader-refreshing metamorphosis or wondrous scientific vision he might have encountered in so many Renaissance or Jesuit Latin didactic poems.[48]

But to return to the opening footnote of the second book: it would seem to confirm that Dutch content was not necessarily earmarked, at least not exclusively, for a Dutch audience. Voltaire's acquaintance (very limited, in fact) with the Dutch language, if not the details of his early romantic adventure in the Netherlands, must have been rumoured to the young Groningener before their first meeting.[49] On that occasion, Heerkens teased and flattered the cosmopolitan *philosophe* by reciting some verses from a recent Dutch translation of his *Merope*, which he held to be as beautiful as the French.[50] Did he also aspire to tap into or foster a broader streak of Batavophilia among French readers of his medical poem? While his vignettes of Jacob Cats,[51] Joost van den Vondel,[52] Petrus Scriverius,[53] Hubertus Poot[54] and Sidron de Hossche,[55] seem to be pandering directly to Dutch cultural pride (and of Rudolph Agricola,

---

[46] That is, Heerkens writes as if this spectral Scaliger really did talk to him (p. 50, n. 77). For a discussion of truth versus fiction in eighteenth-century Jesuit didactic verse, see my *Loyola's Bees*, chap. 4, passim. Berthier's interference recalls that of Renaissance Cardinal Pietro Bembo, who exhorted physician-poet Girolamo Fracastoro to drop the 'Syphilus' myth in the third book of his *Syphilis, sive de morbo Gallico* (Verona, 1530) – perhaps the most celebrated neo-Latin poem of the Renaissance!

[47] In *Aves Frisicae* (Rotterdam, 1787), pp. 115–16. Cf. Chapter 5, pp. 180–1. Heerkens merely retells here a traditional story from Aristotle and Pliny (*Natural History* 10. 74) about the hostility between the eagle and the wren (Gk *basiliskos*).

[48] For example in the fourth book of Savastano's *Botanica*, where King Solomon is taken on a guided tour of the 'Laboratory of Nature' by Divine Wisdom. Heerkens owned a copy of this work.

[49] On this meeting, cf. Jeroom Vercruysse, *Voltaire et la Hollande* (Geneva: Institut et Musée Voltaire, 1966), pp. 91–5. Heerkens was bearing a letter of introduction from Dutch poet, Willem van Haren, over whom Voltaire had enthused for his populist (anti-French) poem, *Leonidas* (ibid., pp. 56–8).

[50] 'Et quoniam intellexeram, Belgicè eum scire, non dubitare me, dicebam, quin id idem de duobus saltem versibus [from a Dutch translation of the 'Merope', admired by Heerkens] judicaturus esset, eosque versus Gallicos et Belgicos hos esse.'

[51] For Cats, see pp. 29–30 (n. 41: 'a poet widely read by the Dutch, and most worthy to be read on account of the facility of his verse and the matters treated in them'; n. 43: Cats's verses describing the use of tobacco by his poor countrymen to assuage hunger); p. 116 (his wonderful facility with the Dutch language, exhorting the Dutch not to travel abroad in his autobiographical poem, 'A life of 82 years'); pp. 145–7 (his devotion to his deceased wife, in whose grave he temporarily interred himself to head off insistent admonitions by friends that he remarry); p. 160 (his physical attractiveness).

[52] Untranslated quotation in Dutch from the verse letter from St Agatha (in his *Brieven der Heilige Maeghden, Martelaressen* (Amsterdam, 1642), confirming his sensitivity (p. 145). Cf. untranslated verses of Cats, on smoking, p. 29, n. 43.

[53] See p. 38, and n. 55.

[54] See p. 37, and n. 53.

[55] See pp. 119–20, and n. 88.

Menso Alting[56] and Wessel Harmensz Gansfort[57] even to a certain Groningen provincialism), might they not equally be read as an audacious public relations exercise by the suave young Dutchman for his increasingly marginalized country and humanistic heritage?[58] Heerkens suggests as much in a note to his comments on Hubertus Poot (1689–1733), farmer's son and panegyrist of tea, who, once he became famous, forfeited his physical and intellectual robust good health to luxurious living: 'The author has used examples of some of the more celebrated poets who have written in the Dutch language because they are unknown to the French, and he saw that, in spite of this, the learned men to whom he read his little work did not find it displeasing' ('Exemplis poetarum celebriorum, qui Belgicè scripserunt, usus est propterea author, quod eos Gallis ignotos, virisque eruditis, quibus, hoc cum fieret, praelegit opusculum, ostendi haud ingratum esse videbat', p. 37).

These advisors, whose names and interventions pepper the footnotes, may be characterized as literary men but not necessarily scholars, Latin readers but not necessarily writers.[59] Indeed, Heerkens distances himself in the *De valetudine literatorum* from a certain kind of excessive classical erudition, which he considers an indecorous abuse of the 'good' of study: 'I would therefore not want you to look down on learning, haughtily, because some, through excessive love of learning, are scarcely wise' ('Nolim igitur, fastu studium ut contempseris alto, / Vix hujus nimio si quis amore sapit'). We are told that 'the critic must thus be deemed to have smacked too much of Horace; and he forces Ovid to speak with his own mouth' ('Sic criticus Flaccum, nimium sapuisse videndus, / Nasonemque suo cogit ab ore loqui', p. 23). A note clarifies that the 'Englishman Bentley ordered Horace, the German Curtius, Lucan, and the Dutchmen Nicolas Heinsius and Peter Burman, Ovid, to speak in accordance with their own taste'.[60] Such hubristic

---

[56] On 'our Belgian Strabo', see pp. 39–40, and n. 57.
[57] See pp. 77–8. See Fokke Akkerman, Gerda C. Huisman and A. J. Vanderjagt (eds), *Wessel Gansfort (1419–1489) and Northern Humanism* (Leiden: Brill, 1993).
[58] Heerkens claims that no other culture ran with the baton of the Italian Renaissance more enthusiastically than his own: 'Conatus Italum gens nulla adverterat aeque / Nulla priusque sequi, quam mea visa fuit' (p. 73). The associated note (n. 30) makes clear that 'my' country refers in the first instance to Groningen, but may be extended to other 'Belgians of that time, of whom there was a greater number of famous teachers and practitioners of the liberal arts than from any other race beyond the Alps'.
[59] It seems, however, that Heerkens did not seek the opinion of his Parisian medical professors!
[60] Towards the end of the poem, in his digression on the causes of Ovid's exile, Heerkens scoffs at the blindness of such textual critics to historical evidence: 'Those who have written commentaries on the *Pontica* and *Tristia*, what in those prolix and often useless notes of theirs can they claim to be slightly memorable? Nothing in the variants of Micyllius, Pontanus or Burman [sc. the Elder], that most boring collator, or what each sees as unsafe readings, has made any difference' (p. 179, n. 53). Contrast his championing of a *useful* philology in *Notabilia*, Book 3, pp. 106–7, there as a handmaid to archaeology.

scholarly ventriloquism is matched – in a somewhat tendentiously logical leap – by the perversity of the physician who prescribes only exotic medicines, and by the nerve of 'that famous philosopher over here [sc. in Paris], who bids the lovers of a better life live in the wilderness on four feet; thus, likewise, if fortune dictates that one must live in community, our wise man prohibits all cultivation of the mind, everything!' ('Sic sophus hic celeber, vitae melioris amantes, / Vivere deserto quadrupedesque jubet. / Sic pariter, si fata jubent convictibus uti, / Cultum omnem prohibet mentibus, omne sophos', p. 24).

This curious little outburst against Jean-Jacques Rousseau[61] builds to a three-page rant on the decline of the Latin language in antiquity, of the French language in modern times, and finally, on the increasing contempt for *Latin* literature among the French, even for Latin literature by their own countrymen. It is worth reproducing and reflecting on the climax of the tirade, where Heerkens singles out Jean le Rond d'Alembert as something of an evil genius presiding over the downfall of French Latinity:

Linguam operis nostri, scriptamue per omnia saecla,
    Scriptamque a Gallis tam bene, tamque diu,
Linguam illam ut scribas, negat, et pronuntiet ut quis,
    Idque caterva hominum tam bene docta negat.
Idque sibi credi, propriae tot lumina gentis
    Ut non respectes, imperiosa jubet.
Scilicet absurdis, quae plurima fundit in auras,
    Causa deest: ingens causa sed hujus erat.
Contemni sua scripta videt. Prius omnia, Galli
    Quae dederant, populos sparsa per orbis erant.
Praeterito quidquid vix Gallia scripserat aevo,
    Mox pavit Batavos terque quaterque typos.
Quid modo Germano, Batavoque recuditur orbe,
    Quam Latium si quod Gallia prodit opus?
Scripta Poligniacus, sua vix Vanierius edit,

---

[61] 'That philosopher was Rousseau from Geneva, who at that time used to hold forth daily in the café Procope, not far from the author's lodgings, with the most insane fanaticism, on subjects on which he published not long thereafter' (n. 32).

Anglus, et haec Ubius, moxque Batavus amat.
Idne Dalambertus ferat, et sua quisquis amari
    Sola, vel a lingua censet amanda sua?
Gallica jure placet, nec et altera notior orbi.
    Sed minus unde legi nunc sua scripta facit?
Quid, calamistratis pascam mea pectora nugis?
    Frivola, res nullas, jamque pudenda sequar?
Quid video scribi, via Jacobaeaque vendit,
    Illa novit fluvii plenaque ripa libris?
Si pauca excipias, data nuper et optima, quaeque
    Et nimio et vano pars aliena dabat:
Estne, quod ad Batavos bene sana mente reportem?
    Meque relecturum vel semel ipse putem?
Quotque locis illis scripta aurea, caraque terris,
    Verae mirata est Gallia laudis amans!
Tanta fuit clades, Veterum contemnere linguas!
    Tanta fuit, nugas et nova monstra sequi!

The language of my work, which has been written through all the centuries, and written by the French so well and for so long, he [sc. d'Alembert] denies that you can write it, and that anyone can pronounce it – and a throng of such well-educated men denies it![62] And they imperiously command you to believe this so you will have no respect for the numerous talents of their own people! To be sure, so many of the absurdities they pour out to the breezes lack a reason: but there was a great big reason for *this* one. They see their own [sc. vernacular] writings being despised. Before, everything that the French published was spread to the four corners of the globe. In the past, whatever France had written would soon see three or four Dutch editions. What else was printed in the German and Dutch worlds until recently if not French Latin

---

[62] That is, in d'Alembert's dissertation 'on the harmony of languages, and in particular on that which one is believed to hear in the dead languages, and, on this occasion, on modern Latinity', where he argues that neo-Latin writers cannot possibly be sensitive to the sounds and subtleties of the ancient language, just as we see that foreigners, with all the learning resources available to them, including access to contemporary speakers, hardly ever write good French.

[63] Cardinal Melchior de Polignac was the author of a modern *De rerum natura*, the *Anti-Lucretius sive de Deo et Natura* (Paris, 1747); Jacques Vanière, S. J., of a 16-book poem on the management of a country estate. Both went through multiple editions and were acclaimed as modern Latin classics. An excellent recent article on Polignac is T. Tsakiropoulou-Summers, '*Tantum potuit suadere libido*:

books? Polignac and Vanière had scarcely published their works[63] before an Englishman, a German and soon enough a Dutchman, was in love with them. Could d'Alembert bear this? Or anyone who thinks that only *his* writings should be loved, or are fit to be loved only if in *his* language? The French language is nice, there's no denying, nor is there another more celebrated throughout the globe. But why does [France] now render its own literature less read? What, should I feed my soul on flowery nonsense? Should I chase after the frivolous, the trifling, and now the shameless? The stuff I see being written and hawked in the rue Saint Jacques, or what that bank of the Seine [sc. Quai des Grands Augustins] which is bursting with books has come to know? With a few recent and excellent exceptions, and the books which some have published against this excess and vanity, is there anything I could take back to the Dutch in my right mind? Anything I would consider reading again, even once? And how many golden writings, dear to the world, has France, the lover of true praise, admired in those places [sc. the *bouquinistes*]? It has been such a disaster, this contempt for the ancient languages, such a disaster to chase after nonsense and monsters of novelty! (pp. 25–6)

A footnote reveals that anti-Latin sentiments were expressed publicly by d'Alembert at the time of the poem's composition, but Voltaire was to commit them to writing shortly thereafter. Heerkens finds the latter's hypocrisy breath-taking: 'since I heard him, in front of d'Alembert, confess that nothing reasonable could be gainsaid of this note of mine, and Reinallius,[64] who is still among the living, is urging this, and asserting things in praise of my argument which modesty would prevent from being repeated, even if a greater need dictated' (p. 25, n. 34). Heerkens had given us a bit of back-story to Voltaire's volte-face already in the preface. The courteous *philosophe*, we were told, had sought his learned guest's opinion on the vexed question of the pronunciation of Latin, since 'quite a few men in Paris were claiming that it could not be spoken any more'. Heerkens would set him straight: Latin had been used in France since the earliest Christian centuries until the end of the eleventh, in some provinces even later. If it had changed in France more than elsewhere the correct pronunciation was still recoverable, for example, from modern speakers in the hills of Tuscany. It was not a dead language! Heerkens says that Voltaire approved his judgement at the time and asked him to repeat it on

---

Religion and pleasure in Polignac's *Anti-Lucretius*', *Eighteenth-Century Thought* 2 (2004), pp. 165–205. On Vanière, see Haskell, *Loyola's Bees*, chap. 1.

[64] The *philosophe* Guillaume-Thomas Raynal (1711–96)?

numerous occasions, in front of many people. It was all the more remarkable, then, that he should be so 'forgetful' ('immemor') to assert, 'a hundred times later in his writings, with astounding fickleness, that the Latin language could not be pronounced/spoken' ('centies post mirabili levitate in scriptis suis asseruit, linguam Latinam pronuntiari non posse', p. xiii).

The significance of these asides lies, I suggest, in Heerkens's identification of *personal*, in fact rather petty, motives and moral failings as the drivers of apparently ineluctable intellectual climate change. Voltaire he had long trusted and admired. He claims in the preface to the poem that, in the early days of their friendship, his solicitous mentor had warned him against that 'dangerous philosopher', Nicolas Boindin (1676–1751);[65] and when commenting on a draft, Voltaire had 'approved of nothing more than those passages in which I demonstrated respect for religion, and that nothing made him more unhappy than the fact that his poetic writings, through the interpolation of verses, and his prose, through the interpolation of sentences and often long periods, might become harmful to religion or morals' (p. vi). Hence Heerkens's bemused disenchantment when, a decade later in Ferney, he found Voltaire's character apparently so changed.[66]

Heerkens's feelings for d'Alembert, however, must have been cooler from the start – and vice versa. As a party game, the health-anxious Voltaire had once invited his tipsy dinner guests to jot down the reasons why he should expect to live a long life. Heerkens had tossed off a lightly edited epigram from his Leiden *Xenia* to the effect that keen senses, a sharp mind and aesthetically pleasing bodily proportions were all sure signs of longevity. D'Alembert challenged him, but Heerkens was quick to reveal that his couplets were simply a verse rendition of the irrefutable opinion of the great Francis Bacon: 'and that they were particularly apt to their host, no-one, not even d'Alembert, could deny' (p. 87, n. 46). One suspects that d'Alembert was irked less by Heerkens's medical opinion *per se* than with the medium – Latin verse – in which it was delivered.

---

[65] Boindin was a writer of comedies, a *moderne* in the Querelle, and professed atheism. His name appears also in a note to Heerkens's sixth satire in the *Marii Curilli Groningensis Satyrae* (Groningen, 1758), as a defender of the outspoken and maligned (by Voltaire) French poet, Jean-Baptiste Rousseau (1671–1741) (p. 47).

[66] Is Heerkens a little disingenuous in expressing surprise at Voltaire's change of heart on the Latin question? Earlier in the preface he had confessed to being anxious about their first meeting because 'he had heard that [Voltaire] despised beyond measure modern poets who had written in Latin'. On the other hand, Voltaire may have given Heerkens cause to believe that reports of his antagonism to Latin literature were exaggerated. For example, he seems to have requested from Heerkens a translation into Latin of the first 20 verses of Jacob Cats's Dutch poem in praise of Anna Maria van Schurmann, which he subsequently circulated among his friends (p. 146).

Something about the affable, obliging, linguistically talented Dutchman seems to have rubbed him up the wrong way. Was this, at root, Heerkens's Jesuit humanist education, recently advertised in his poem in praise of the Westphalian Jesuits?[67] D'Alembert's assumption that the young man's attachment to Latin verse put him on the wrong side of a steadily rising intellectual-political fence?

## Enlightened education: *mens latina in corpore sano*

Did, then, our mercurial Dutch Catholic betray anything in his Latin didactic poem like an anti-philosophical spirit, or, for that matter, a reactionary religiosity? On the second point, Heerkens by and large takes a pragmatic, non-confessional and 'rational' view of Christian faith more or less consonant with that of the early Voltaire.[68] He has little patience for fire and brimstone religion. He tells us in the *De valetudine literatorum* that a little spark ('scintillula') of madness planted in the developing mind can derange it, leading inexorably to the mental hospital, and confesses to have narrowly escaped that fate as a Jesuit schoolboy under the surveillance of an over-exacting director of conscience.[69] If Heerkens's opponents in the Groningen literary quarrel had sought to denigrate his Catholicism with the smear of superstition, that very faith is vindicated in the *De valetudine litteratorum* as a brake against deranging self-doubt, and shown to be perfectly compatible with the moderate, modern intellectual life.[70]

Heerkens objects not so much to the ideas of the *philosophes* as to their conceit and posturing. A discussion of the abuse of indoor fires in the third book is the pretext for a footnote diatribe on the intellectual pretensions of Rousseau, the *parvenu* from Geneva (pp. 164–7, n. 36). Heerkens was aware that the most ancient Greek physicians had attributed a general decline in human health and

---

[67] Cf. the preface to *Empedocles sive Physicorum epigrammatum libri septem* (Groningen, 1798): 'Among the less frequent guests [of Fontenelle] was D'Alembert, who had widely spread a rumour that my Elegy was dictated to me by the Jesuits' (p. vi).

[68] His views fit comfortably within the framework of 'Religious Enlightenment' outlined by David Sorkin, *The Religious Enlightenment: Protestants, Jews, and Catholics from London to Vienna* (Princeton: Princeton University Press, 2008); cf. Ulrich Lehner, 'What is Catholic Enlightenment', *History Compass* 8 (2010), pp. 166–78. Significantly, as Sorkin notes, 'many of its fundamental ideas, Protestant and Catholic, first appeared in the Dutch Republic, which maintained a precarious toleration' (p. 6).

[69] See Chapter 6, pp. 202–3.

[70] For further discussion of Heerkens's views on the spiritual and emotional lives of scholars, see my 'Physician, heal thyself! Emotions and the Health of the Learned in Samuel Auguste André David Tissot (1728–1797) and Gerard Nicolaas Heerkens (1728–1801)', in Henry Martyn Lloyd (ed.), 'The Discourse of Sensibility: The Knowing Body in the Enlightenment', Special Issue of *Studies in History and Philosophy of Science* (forthcoming).

longevity to the discovery of fire, and he suggests in a footnote that this was the likely origin of the myth of Prometheus unleashing disease throughout the earth. In Paris, the conscientious medical student would discover, in the library of the Count of Belle-Isle, the works of Arnaud de Villeneuve, a thirteenth-century Catalan physician who had expressed much the same view but in probable ignorance of the Greeks. Since it was confirmed by Villanovanus's experience, not just by authority, the ancient doctrine thus seemed all the more sound to Heerkens, and he proceeded to promulgate it among the learned men of Paris. Only after the doctrine and its double provenance had become established did Rousseau, apparently, begin to 'proclaim' ('personare') it. The younger Heerkens consequently came under the unwelcome suspicion of being a disciple of the older Rousseau and was warned to keep away from the 'most paradoxical one' ('ὰ παραδοζωτατω'). Our prudent medical student avers that he was able to live with the fact that '[Rousseau] was putting it about that writers not even known to him by name, and indicated to him by *me*, had been rescued from the darkness, read by him, and were most worthy of everyone's attention – but as soon as he abused the information I had provided for the purposes of corroborating his own ill-omened opinions, I fled from his side' (p. 166).

In the continuation of this footnote, which runs over four pages, Heerkens provides a devastating portrait of Rousseau the *faux savant*, the anti-type of the diligent and deserving Latin *vir literatus* who is the poem's *de facto* addressee:

> Rousseau had come to Paris not long, or at least not very long, before I did; and he had come, like so many of his countrymen, in the hope of making his fortune – but this was a hope given him by a little knowledge of music, of skilfully painting the notes of songs. He had withal no knowledge of the ancient languages, but a smattering of the scientific terms of French learning common enough among peoples speaking French. That he should become recognized as a philosopher in such a short time he owed to the Procope café, an establishment, that is, near the Comédie française, where the more idle *érudits* used to gather, and among them, too, the most famous *philosophes*. That he who was for a long time their daily auditor should later dare set himself up as their detractor and adversary, he owed to his tongue, which was glib enough, and to the fact that he had equal tickets on his own judgement[71]. (pp. 165–6)

---

[71] 'linguae debuit satis disertae, et quod de judicio suo haud minus praesumebat'.

It wasn't so bad at the outset, Heerkens continues, when Rousseau was attacking the 'free-thinking philosophers' ('philosophis licentiosis'), although his ignorance of the principles of philosophy and his bullying demeanour meant that he did so with more anger than justice. Indeed, his ignorance and offensiveness alienated none so much 'at first as those who were dedicated to the field in which he would become famous' (presumably the *philosophes*). It was not ever thus. During his early days at the Procope, the learned Dutchman had felt sorry for the boorish Swiss, plying with maxims from the ancient authors and attempting to dissuade him from venturing into topics beyond his depth. Alas, Rousseau fell into supporting the most absurd opinions and soon enough into publishing them. His impertinent attacks in speech and print on culture and science 'procured him the hatred of the learned, all of whom deserted this monstrously rude and bad-tempered man. And a comedy soon gave an indication of this odium, the "Badly Educated Man", the *faux savant*, written by him' (p. 166).[72]

Thus, as with his observations elsewhere in the poem on Voltaire and d'Alembert, Heerkens's intellectual appraisal of Rousseau is predicated on his personal experience of the philosopher's bad manners and flawed character. He is impatient with Rousseau's impertinence, his lack of moderation, his obstinacy, and, above all, with his ungracious treatment of his intellectual fellows. The anti-humanism of Rousseau's thought is viewed as the logical counterpart to his egregious transgressions of an unwritten code of polite conduct within the Republic of Letters – and vice versa.[73] Heerkens hints, too, that it is the lack of an adequate *Latin* education that has created this monster of misanthropy.

\*\*\*

Physician Samuel Auguste André David Tissot (1728–97) was probably *not* known to Heerkens personally, but the tone and tenor of his writings earned him a tarring with the same brush as his Swiss compatriot. Heerkens, having warned ambitious parents against hot-housing their children, is careful to

---

[72] 'odium fecit eruditorum, qui hominem immaniter incivilem et iracundum destituerunt omnes. odiique huius signum mox dedit comoedia, Male Doctus, le faux savant, ab ipso inscripta'. Presumably not the work of this title by Jacques du Vaure, which was first performed in 1728. Heerkens may be referring, muddle-headedly, to Rousseau's *Narcisse ou l'amante de lui-même* (1752), the preface of which 'provides some evidence for the view that, whether real or imagined, Rousseau's sense of being persecuted by "adversaries" was anything but an acquisition of old age': B. R. Barber and J. Forman, 'Introduction to Jean-Jacques Rousseau's "Preface to Narcisse"', *Political Theory* 6 (1978), pp. 537–42, at p. 540.

[73] See Bots and Waquet, *La République*, pp. 113–14 on 'Le savant et la "civilisation des bonnes manières"'.

balance these apparently Rousseauvian strictures with a deep nod to the dignity of learning:

> Non certe a morbis decet irridere juvantem
>> Aut cupidum studio te recreare chorum.
> Turpiter id facis, si qua ulla, facetus inepte,
>> Praecepta huic dictas, auxiliumque feres.
> Id, quia ridiculus Latio blateraverat ore,
>> Nec criticos ideo, grammaticosque ferat,
> Ducat id esse sibi Tissotius unus honori
>> Risus ab auxiliis non semel ipse suis.
> Ille omnem pingit tibi Pindum, et Palladis aulam,
>> Ut plenam aegrotis, mente inopemque domum.

> You who help to ward off disease [sc. physicians] should not, to be sure, mock and entertain yourself at the expense of the chorus of scholars. You act disgracefully if you relay any precepts and prescriptions for them in a sarcastic manner. Let that – since he blathered laughably in Latin, and that's why he can't bear scrutiny by critics and philologists – let that be considered a badge of honour by Tissot alone, he who has been laughed at more than once for his remedies. He paints the whole of Pindus for you, and the court of Pallas, as brimming with the sick and the mad. (p. 60)

In the years between the first and second editions of Heerkens's poem, Tissot, celebrated public health advocate and Chair of Medicine at Lausanne, perhaps best known to posterity for his writings on migraine and masturbation, had published his Latin academic oration on 'the health of men of letters'.[74] Heerkens does not neglect to assert the priority of his own *De valetudine literatorum*.[75] It seems to have galled him to see Tissot's work go through not only a second *Latin* edition (Lausanne, Frankfurt and Leipzig, 1769) but no less than five in French, one unauthorized, by the date of the second edition of his poem! In his 1790 poem, Heerkens refers sporadically, and never charitably,

---

[74] *Sermo inauguralis de valetudine litteratorum habitus publice die 9 Aprilis 1766 cum novam medicinae cathedram auspicaretur* (Lausanne, 1766).
[75] 'Tissotius, qui xvii post meum annis, suum de Literatorum Valetudine opusculum vulgavit' (p. 105, n. 68).
[76] Reprinted Paris, 1768; thanks to Anne Vila for clarifying this.

to his copy of the expanded French edition of Tissot's *De la santé des gens des lettres* (Lausanne, 1769).[76]

Superficially, these exact contemporaries cover a lot of common ground: they both warn against the dangers of abuse of tobacco and tea,[77] of changes in the weather, of late-night study vigils; identify the stomach as the crucible of scholarly complaints; advise a frugal diet[78] and daily exercise[79]; caution parents who ruin the health of their children with unrealistic educational expectations; commend society, cheerfulness and religious faith for the modern man of letters; and they both, for that matter, embellish their arguments with examples drawn from ancient literature.[80] But Tissot approves only such education as is necessary to a child's future career, and evinces a fundamental impatience with learning as an occupation in its own right.[81] Indeed, one detects an almost perverse delight in his recitation of the bizarre and unsavoury bodily symptoms associated with abuse of the life of the mind: from bad breath, mouth ulcers, flaccid skin and gum disease, through alopecia, gallstones, flatulence, shortness of breath, haemorrhoids from long sitting and constipation as a result of retaining faeces in order to continue studying.[82] The scholar of Tissot's

---

[77] Of hot ('fumivora') beverages Heerkens warns: 'It's not just the common people who indulge in this; even the scholar drinks those poisons among his piles of books' ('Nec facit hoc vulgus tantum: studiosus et inter / Librorum cumulos ista venena bibit', Book 2, p. 109).

[78] Eating less, and a near-vegetarian diet, is Heerkens's most frequently prescribed preventative and remedy. An interesting passage in the second book directly relates overconsumption to loss of memory and intellectual acuity (pp. 82–3, and n. 41).

[79] The younger Heerkens knew from personal experience the excruciations of the scholarly stomach. During his studies he had had recourse to various medicines and waters, without success; he was not attended at the time by his father, whose common good sense, he suspects, would have prevailed. Relief came, in the end, *not* from abandoning his studies, but from an unexpected source: his long rambles around suburban Paris (Book 1, pp. 18–19).

[80] On the topics treated by Heerkens in his 1749 edition, see: Yasmin Haskell, 'A Dutch doctor's observations on the health of scholars, young and old: Gerard Nicolaas Heerkens' *De valetudine literatorum* (Leiden and Rheims, 1749; Groningen, 1790)', in Maria Berggren and Christer Henriksen (eds), *Miraculum eruditionis: Neo-Latin Studies in Honour of Hans Helander* (Uppsala: Uppsala Universitet, 2007), pp. 151–66.

[81] Tissot's treatise concludes with an unconvincing rider, anticipating the objection that he has little personal experience or appreciation of the scholarly life, and that he is endorsing the radically negative view of learning advanced by Rousseau in his first *Discourse*. As Anne Vila observes, Tissot proceeds to take 'a moderate stance in the debate then raging over the relative merits and risks of striving to become learned: he argues that the pursuit of knowledge, while not entirely beneficial, can at least be benign to fledgling scholars, as long as they meet certain conditions'. These conditions make of the scholar a 'type of patient who must submit to constant control, not only physical control ... but also moral control, which Tissot exerts by exhorting his readers to cultivate the arts and sciences in a manner that is cool-headed, self-disciplined, and socially acceptable': Vila, *Enlightenment and Pathology: Sensibility in the Literature and Medicine of Eighteenth-Century France* (Baltimore: Johns Hopkins University Press, 1998), p. 103.

[82] But his long meditations, apparently, also have the effect of excessive evacuation (p. 38).

[83] On this subject Tissot recommends a dissertation by German physician I. Z. Platner, *De morbis ex immunditiis* ('on diseases from lack of cleanliness', Leipzig, 1731). Heerkens also took perspiration seriously, but perhaps especially after his Italian journey, where he imbibed Giambattista Morgagni's admiration for the theories of Santorio Santorio (see Chapter 6, p. 219).

treatise is a pathetic and rather revolting creature, who suffers from 'obstructed perspiration' because of his slovenliness (p. 97),[83] who cannot sire illustrious sons because his semen is impoverished (p. 84), and who is as unamenable to correction as the lover who is told that the beloved is flawed (p. 136). The physician Tissot implies that the 'passion' for learning is a variant of Renaissance love melancholy.[84] We might note, *en passant*, the relative and curious absence in Heerkens's *De valetudine literatorum* of discussion of 'melancholic', 'hypochondriac' or 'nervous' illness – the disease(s) of scholars par excellence from the early modern period through the eighteenth century.[85] Tissot, for all his modernity, is still invoking humoral models of melancholy in addition to the newer nervous variety.[86]

For Tissot there is almost always something pathological about learning, and hence it merits a half-treatise worth (some 130 pages) of remedies: from diet to drugs, purging, bloodletting, rubbing, spas – and strictly no visits to libraries! An intellectual life might be appropriate for the truly gifted and constitutionally robust, but unfortunately, since the Renaissance, the world has been overrun by 'érudits', a species of men unknown in antiquity that tortures itself like the *Fakirs* of India – but with cold as opposed to sunshine, with manuscripts, medals and inscriptions, and physical inactivity, rather than with whips and chains. Moreover, most modern learning is futile, frivolous often not even produced with the public in view.

Had he known or read Heerkens, Tissot might well have deemed him just such a distracted dilettante! What would he have made, for example, of his Dutch colleague's fastidious gloss on a verse describing the hearths that scholars construct in their studies as 'altars of learned Vulcan' ('Docti Mulcibris aris') – a pun, Heerkens makes sure we get it, on the Roman temple to 'Womanly Fortune'

---

[84] See for example Jacques Ferrand's *Treatise on Lovesickness*, ed Donald A. Beecher and Massimo Ciavolella (Syracuse, NY: Syracuse University Press, 1991).

[85] In the second edition, Heerkens observes that lack of sleep leads to stagnation of food in the stomach, enfeeblement of the body and embittering of the blood, and that 'there is no other cause of the melancholic's lamentable disease and, like the blackish bile, consumption itself proceeds from here [sc. the bitter blood]' ('Causa melancholico non flebilis altera morbi, / Bilis et ut nigricans, hinc phthisis ipsa venit', p. 121). Perhaps his most interesting observation on 'hypochondria' is relegated to a footnote: that 'valetudinarians, melancholics and hypochondriacs' who are confined to bed and a frugal diet are observed to live long lives (pp. 167–8, n. 39).

[86] On the variety of such 'illnesses' in the early modern period through eighteenth century, see the essays in Yasmin Haskell (ed.), *Diseases of the Imagination and Imaginary Disease in the Early Modern Period* (Turnhout: Brepols, 2012).

[87] 'This note was necessary', Heerkens claims, 'because, when I sent this work to a learned friend when it was first published, he was of the opinion that the adjective "learned" did not agree with "Vulcan"; but when he understood my reason [analogy with "womanly" Fortune, signifying that the temple had been built *by* women] he not only conceded the poetic expression but also praised it' (p. 124, n. 92).

('Fortunae Muliebris') (p. 124)?[87] Indeed, Tissot might have diagnosed pathological learning in Heerkens from a perfunctory appraisal of the poem's *mise en page*, where sometimes the thinnest vein of verse pulses feebly over an intestinal tangle of footnotes. Yet Heerkens's footnotes are, on closer inspection, as much about the lived society and observed emotional lives of scholars as any dusty book learning.

\*\*\*

While his *De valetudine literatorum* (Figure 2.1) opens on a sombre note – Heerkens's dismay at the untimely death of so many learned men, and an outpouring of personal grief for the loss of his young comrade-in-letters, the over-industrious Justus Conring – the poet regards learning, in proper measure, as a *good* thing. It is true that the *militia studiorum* can be unhealthy: 'I have seen those to whom a whole winter spent in their studies denied a journey of a hundred steps in the spring; I have seen those who so unlearned sleep through learning that it would not return except with the help of soporific drugs' ('Vidi, musaeo quibus omnis bruma peracta, / Ad centum passus vere negabat iter, / Vidi, qui somnum sic dedidicere studendo, / Non nisi somnifera post ut adesset ope', p. 41). But he will have no truck with Tissot's scare-mongering:

Nullus ibi, qui non studio te absterreat omni,
    Nullus ibi, cuperes quo praeunte sequi.
Crede mihi, mentem studiosam, avidamque sciendi,
    Non nisi propitius dat cuicunque Deus.
Vult sua, vult operum secreta patere suorum,
    Deque aevis veterum te sapuisse jubet.
Rideat a Graecis doctos, et ab orbe Latino:
    Cultus ab hoc exul redditus orbe fuit.
Et nullum studii genus est inamabile, quodque
    Tristem animum, vitae triste genusque facit.
Laetus apud tetricam caperata fronte Minervam,
    Laetus apud laetas sis Helicone Deas.

There is no-one there [in Tissot's book] who would not frighten you away from all study; no-one there, you would wish to follow. Believe me, none but a propitious God gives anyone a studious mind, eager for knowledge. He wants, he wants to reveal the secrets of his works, and from ancient times he

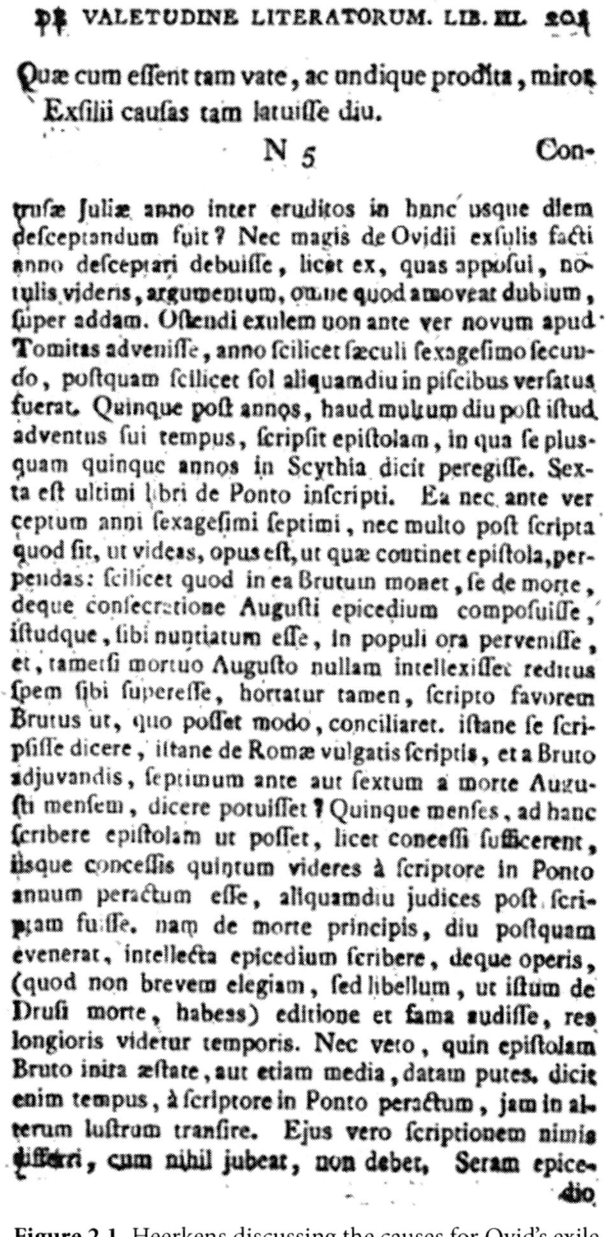

**DE VALETUDINE LITERATORUM. LIB. III. 201**

Quæ cum essent tam vate, ac undique prodita, miror
Exsilii causas tam latuisse diu.

N 5         Con-

fusæ Juliæ anno inter eruditos in hunc usque diem
desceptandum fuit? Nec magis de Ovidii exsulis facti
anno desceptari debuisse, licet ex, quas apposui, notulis videris, argumentum, omne quod amoveat dubium,
super addam. Ostendi exulem non ante ver novum apud
Tomitas advenisse, anno scilicet sæculi sexagesimo secundo, postquam scilicet sol aliquamdiu in piscibus versatus
fuerat. Quinque post annos, haud multum diu post istud
adventus sui tempus, scripsit epistolam, in qua se plusquam quinque annos in Scythia dicit peregisse. Sexta est ultimi libri de Ponto inscripti. Ea nec ante ver
ceptum anni sexagesimi septimi, nec multo post scripta
quod sit, ut videas, opus est, ut quæ continet epistola, perpendas: scilicet quod in ea Brutum monet, se de morte,
deque consecratione Augusti epicedium composuisse,
istudque, sibi nuntiatum esse, in populi ora pervenisse,
et, tametsi mortuo Augusto nullam intellexisset reditus
spem sibi superesse, hortatur tamen, scripto favorem
Brutus ut, quo posset modo, conciliaret. istane se scripsisse dicere, istane de Romæ vulgatis scriptis, et a Bruto
adjuvandis, septimum ante aut sextum a morte Augusti mensem, dicere potuisset? Quinque menses, ad hanc
scribere epistolam ut posset, licet concessi sufficerent,
iisque concessis quintum videres à scriptore in Ponto
annum peractum esse, aliquamdiu judices post scriptam fuisse. nam de morte principis, diu postquam
evenerat, intellecta epicedium scribere, deque operis,
(quod non brevem elegiam, sed libellum, ut istum de
Drusi morte, habess) editione et fama audisse, res
longioris videtur temporis. Nec vero, quin epistolam
Bruto inita æstate, aut etiam media, datam putes, dicit
enim tempus, à scriptore in Ponto peractum, jam in alterum lustrum transire. Ejus vero scriptionem nimis
differri, cum nihil jubeat, non debet. Seram epice-
dio

**Figure 2.1** Heerkens discussing the causes for Ovid's exile.
Source: Gerard Nicolaas Heerkens, *De valetudine literatorum* (Groningen, 1790), p. 201. Courtesy of Google Books.

bids you to be wise. Let him [Tissot] laugh at those taught by the Greeks and by the Roman world: our exile has returned from this world a cultured man! And there is no field of study that is hateful, none that depresses your spirits, and there is no sad way of life. You can be happy in the company of severe Minerva with a wrinkled brow; you can be happy on Helicon with the happy goddesses [of poetry]. (Book 2, p. 61)

In fact, there is one significant exception to Heerkens's claim that no branch of learning is inherently injurious to the health, and that is *medicine*. Medicine, moreover, is injurious to the health of doctor and patient alike:

Illa suis cerebrum cultoribus una lacessit,
    Illa suis vitam finit et ante dies.
De centum studio quocunque juvantibus aevum,
    Gaudere haud parcos, et senuisse, vides.
De centum medicis, liquet ut ratione fideli,
    Plurima pars infra septima lustra perit.
Nam, velut experiens medicamina perdit amicos,
    Seque pari, et nimia pars bona perit ope.
At sibi nec Cous nocuit, nec et ante Machaon,
    Nec tum aliqua celeber quisquis ab arte fuit.
Ars se perdendi saeclis fuit abdita priscis.
    Jungat et inventis hanc medicina suis.

She alone injures the brain of her practitioners, and she alone cuts life short before its time. From a hundred men pursuing any profession you like you will find not a few enjoying a good life and who have grown old. From a hundred physicians, as is clear for good reason, most perish before the age of thirty-five. For most, just as they destroy their friends by testing out their cures, destroy themselves equally by their excessive interventions. But the Coan [Hippocrates] didn't harm himself, nor Machaon before him, nor was anyone famous in those days for any art. The art of destroying oneself was hidden from ancient times. Medicine may add this to her discoveries! (Book 2, p. 62)[88]

---

[88] Cf. *De officio medici* (1752), p. 48, on the physicians who have died prematurely through intemperate, if selfless, study: Giorgio Baglivi and Heerkens's own Groningen mentor, Egbert Wyard (for whom he wrote a funeral elegy in 1747).

On the whole, though, learning can be 'protective'. Not only do those without culture not live well, they don't live as *long*. Heerkens asks us to consider:

> Vulgus agris manuum vel in urbe labore salubri
> > Quod se alit, haud crebros cur dat ubique senes?
> Cultus abest. potus, cibus, imber, frigus et aestus,
> > Jamque nocens labor est, jam diuturna quies? (*)
> Morbus et hinc quibus est, par ignorantia morbi,
> > Quae fuerat vitae, quid nisi fata ferat?
> Sic quoque Roma diu cum vixerit, ante superbo
> > Quam cultum populo Graecia capta dabat,
> Quid mirum est, primis si rara Quiritibus aetas,
> > Et Xenephontaeae par prope nulla fuit?

Why is it that, wherever you look, the mob which feeds itself in the fields, or in the city, by the healthy labour of its hands, does not yield a rich crop of old people? Culture is absent! Is it that drink, food, rain, heat and cold, and now work are harmful, now long periods of leisure? (*) And the ignorance of the disease, which is equivalent to an ignorance of the life that was, what, apart from death, can take it away? And so too, though Rome survived long, what wonder is it if, before captured Greece brought culture to that proud race, the earliest citizens rarely reached old age, and almost none to the age of Xenophon? (p. 63)

In his footnote *ad loc.* (*) the author sneers:

Tissot may consider this kind of life [sc. of manual labour] to be healthy, and healthy an ignorance of the evils that proceed from this kind of life. According to Tacitus, those who brought barbarism to Europe lived in this way, the Germans and Goths. [He paraphrases here from Tacitus *Germania* 15, on the Germans' laziness and delegation of manual work to women and the weak during periods of respite from war.] Behold, in Tacitus' words, that famous way of life, which is proof of a great longing for barbarism in those, whether like Tissot, for whom the 'most paradoxical' Rousseau is an object of admiration, or for whomsoever has no regard for the benefits culture confers!

While it is tempting to scrutinize such passages for evidence of sympathy with Tissot's Parisian rivals, Antoine Le Camus (1722–72) and Charles-Augustin

Vandermonde (1727–63), who advocated the cultivation of sensibility and self-improvement through learning,[89] Heerkens was less interested, I suspect, in any such project of Enlightenment eugenics. Rather, he sought to renew hope in latter-day humanists like himself who wished to persevere in an older style of intellectual life, one predicated first and foremost on Latinate literature and learning. On the other hand, this will be a tempered, new-fashioned and even *fashionable*, Latin learning, an *honnête* erudition that may have seemed a contradiction in terms to some of Heerkens's contemporaries.

\*\*\*

It was Heerkens's poetic prerogative, perhaps, to use terms of art creatively, if not ambiguously. In the *De valetudine literatorum* it is difficult to pin down just quite what our medical poet means by the Latin *cultus*, although there are moments when this word is distinctly redolent of eighteenth-century French *politesse* (if not *so* much as to offend the sensitive noses of his Dutch readers[90]):

> Cultum aliquem, et mores studiis nisi jungere possis,
>
> > Tam cessasse ferè, quam studuisse, juvat.
>
> Abnormis sapiens cultis coram auribus apta
>
> > Vix loquitur: quid si rus, vitiumque sonat?
>
> Amotus, veluti quod foetet naribus, inque
>
> > Rus, aut cauponam rejiciendus erit.
>
> Par erit huic, coram qui posteritate libellos,
>
> > Rus simul ac sordes qui sapuere, feret.
>
> Sit sophus, et doceat nova multa, vel omnia sancta,
>
> > Sit medicus, qualis Villanovanus erat.
>
> Sitque, amor Aonidum qui culta mente fuisset,
>
> > Et data scintillent scripta, mephitis erunt.

Unless you are able to combine a certain degree of culture and manners with your studies, it is almost better to have stopped than to have studied.

---

[89] See Vila, *Enlightenment and Pathology*, chap. 3, pp. 80–110.
[90] See Wyger R. E. Velema, *Republicans: Essays on Eighteenth-Century Dutch Political Thought* (Leiden: Brill, 2007), chap. 4, pp. 77–91, on the increasingly strident Dutch polemic against *politesse*, which identified in this French cultural ideal effeminacy, hypocrisy, addiction to appearances and the whims of fashion and slavery to social distinctions – in short, the very antithesis of Dutch social freedom.

> The irregular philosopher[91] says hardly anything fit for the hearing of the cultivated. What if he sounds boorish and ungrammatical? He will have to be banished to the country, like something that offends the nose, like an innkeeper! On a par with him is the one who will offer books to posterity as soon as they smack of the countryside, of filth. He may be wise and teach many new things, or even all things holy; he may be a physician, as was Villeneuve. And there may be a love of the Muses, such as ought to have dwelled in a cultivated mind, and his writings may flash with brilliance – they will be of the swamp. (p. 91)

Did Heerkens have Rousseau in mind in this rather curious characterization of the *abnormis sapiens*? However that may be, the example elaborated in the pages that follow is of a Renaissance Latin poet, Helius Eobanus Hessus (1488–1540), indeed, a fellow medic. But Hessus, famously uncouth and a drunkard, is far from the modern Latin-writing physician–poet Heerkens aspires to be (pp. 90–4). Hessus's boozy biography is followed by one celebrating the longevity of the French – precisely on account of their *cultus* (pp. 94–7).

The vernacular indications of Dr Heerkens's Latin *sensile, sensus* etc. in the *De valetudine literatorum* are similarly vague; he is perhaps deliberately evasive. The successful man of letters is no impassive Stoic but must be endowed with a certain 'sensitivity' ('sensus') and feel himself the emotions he wishes to express: 'Do you think that those who persuade the general mob, who have been its saving, who were able to consult the interests of their country, do you think their minds lacked sensitivity, and that they did not grieve themselves whilst others were grieving?' ('Et, qui hominum turbae suadere, salusque fuisse, / Consulere et patriae qui potuere suae, / Horum animos sensu caruisse, nec ex alienis, / Credis et hos propriis non doluisse malis?', p. 144).[92] This capacity for feeling is not a sign of mental weakness, however: 'The more sensitive the mind is, and the more affected for worthy reasons, the sharper it usually is' ('Quo sensibilior mens est, affectaque dignis / Quo magis ex causis, acrior esse solet', p. 144). Heerkens adduces the example of his revered compatriot, the poet Jacob Cats, who jumped into the grave of his deceased wife in order to put an end to his friends' incessant entreaties that he remarry (pp. 145–7). Sure, the mind of the sensitive man is 'driven' ('acta') by more 'fibres'/'nerves' ('nervisque') (p. 213),

---

[91] Cf. Horace *Sat.* 2. 2. 3.
[92] Heerkens seems to have been influenced by (L.-J. Levesque de Pouilly's) *Théorie des sentimens agréables* (Geneva, 1747).

but it is rare for a feeling heart to exist in a sickly body. Indeed, Cats's pleasing bodily proportions disprove the theory of Jesuit Jacob Balde that intelligence and longevity are incompatible with good looks (p. 160 and nn. 30, 31). Special care must be taken, however, when the subject is young, and his 'fibres' are weaker.

Heerkens seizes on the Catonic harshness implicit in the Tissotian/Rousseauvian censure of a soft and self-indulgent learned culture, giving it a characteristically Ovidian twist:

Non mea convictum Musa, aut contemnere cultum,

    Humanum quadrupes nec jubet esse genus:

Deque Sopho nihil ut videatur docta Lemani,

    Restare, et felix vita sit unde, docet:

Et quos corrupit tenerum mala cura per aevum,

    Et data delitiis prima juventa suis,

Consilio cunctos studet haud morosa tueri,

    Contentam quovis seque Catone, probat.

My Muse does not bid you shun society and culture, nor the human race to be four-footed.[93] So that you may know she has not been instructed in the least by the Philosopher of Lake Geneva [sc. Rousseau], she stays [sc. in the city], and teaches the origins of the happy life. And those whom bad education has corrupted in their tender years, and all those whose first youth has been given over to indulgence, she strives, and not in an ill-tempered way, to fortify with advice, and she is satisfied with any attempt at self-discipline. (pp. 166–7)

Nevertheless, says our young/old doctor Heerkens, it is better to attempt to change one's ways before the critical age of 35.[94]

---

[93] In a letter of 30 August 1755 Voltaire had written to Rousseau: 'On n'a jamais tant employé d'esprit à vouloir nous rendre bêtes. Il prend envie de marcher à quatre pattes quand on lit votre ouvrage'. Five years later, a quadrupedal Rousseau grazed on lettuce in Palissot's satirical play, *Les Philosophes*, a *succès de scandale* at the Comédie française to the great vexation of the philosophical party. My thanks to Stéphane Schmitt of the Centre national de la recherche scientifique, Paris, for this reference. Cf. Chapter 6, p. 210 for a quadrupedal Linnaeus.

[94] There is hope for the elderly, too, though, as is proved by the long life of the Duc de Belle-Isle, who modified his intemperate eating habits towards the end of his life, saying that 'he feared more verses [sc. from Heerkens], but that he had read those that were written with a grateful heart' ('versus dixit novos se timere, scriptos tamen grato animo legisse', *De valetudine literatorum* (1790), p. 88, n. 47).

## Medicine from below

Perhaps the most significant, and easily missed, difference between the published 1749 and 1790 editions of Heerkens's poem on the health of the learned is his concession in the first of the necessity of doctors versus his implicit undertaking, in the second, to help the reader keep the doctors *away*. Thus, in the longer version of his poem:

> Magnum operae pretium, medicis gaudere remotis:
> Et certum sani corporis esse juvat.
> Burhavi instituens medicum liber, estque Galeni,
> Corpus per partes notius unde facit.
> Haec quisquis legit perpensa, lubentius omne
> Si quod amet, medicae post leget artis opus.
> Et satis est, modo scripta legas tuitura salutem,
> Nostra quibus junges, si breve carmen ames.

It is really worth the effort to enjoy having your doctors far away! And to have decided to be healthy helps. And there is Boerhaave's textbook, and Galen's, in which he makes the body better known through its parts. Anyone who reads and considers these may read every book on the medical art more freely, if he pleases. And it is enough if you just read works about protecting your health, to which, if you like a brief [!] song, you may add ours. (p. 7)[95]

Again, in the 1790 version, Heerkens writes about a simple old nurse of his acquaintance who lived to a ripe old age, and about peat-farmers from his district who flouted the Roman Corbulo's law, and have done well by refusing physicians admittance to their community. Of course the abbreviated edition was published in partial fulfilment of the doctoral degree at Reims: this was perhaps not the ideal place for Heerkens to show disrespect to his chosen profession.

---

[95] Near the end of the 1749 edition he is more cautious: 'Blessed is he who has a strong body and can take care of himself, and does not seek to engage doctors for ills of the mind! But there is something useful in a Doctor for those whose mind is injured, just as certain medicines command the healthy to act foolishly' ('Felix qui valido sibi corpore consulat ipsi, / Nec medicos animi quaerat habere malis! / Est tamen in Medico, mens laesa juvetur ut aegris, / Desipere ut sanum pharmaca certa jubent', p. 19).

In both the long and short versions of his poem Heerkens is apologetic about his young years, about his presumption to teach his seniors. In the 1790 version this apology is programmatic – and double-edged:

Forsitan aspectis monitor contemnar ab annis,
    Aestimer auxiliis et minor esse meis.
Res ingens, oculisque abstrusa scientia, laesae
    Mille malis vitae ferre potenter opem.
Sed partes ars vasta aliquas, ultroque recludit,
    Perfaciles scitu jussit et esse Deus.
Nam non ad morbos sumus et suspiria nati;
    Obvia res homini vivere scire foret.
Cura tamen vitae, miseras distracta per artes,
    Cum dubia inciperet, res fierique latens,
Jussa docere homines Junonia dicitur Hebe,
    Jussa ididem, Phaebi neptis, Hygeia fuit.
Quod famulae Junonis erat, scitumque puellae,
    Non nisi de medico nunc sene fiat opus?

Perhaps I will be spurned as a teacher because of my years, and I may not seem up to my remedies. It is a great thing, and a science hidden from the eyes, that of powerfully administering cures for the thousand ills that ail our life. But the vast art reveals some parts of itself freely, and God ordained that they should be easy to know. For we are not born for diseases and sighs, and it should be an obvious thing for a man to know how to live. But when the care of life, torn apart by so many miserable arts, began to be doubtful, and to be a hidden thing, it is said that Juno's daughter, Hebe, was commanded to teach it to mankind, and Hygeia, Apollo's granddaughter, was commanded to do the same. Can only an elderly physician write a work about that which was known to Juno's maid, and to a girl? (pp. 3–4)

Heerkens's precociousness, his arrogation of the mantle of youthful Hebe is close in tone to his relatively recent satire against old-man Alting in the Groningen literary quarrel. If the younger Heerkens who wrote these lines had done his medical homework – he makes sure we know that – he was not, of course, speaking from experience. He was no grey-bearded

Alvise Cornaro (1484–1566), the amateur Paduan health guru who shared the secrets of his own long life in his celebrated *Discorsi*. Heerkens's *De valetudine literatorum* is medicine from below, from the perspective neither of the authoritative, professional physician (at least, at the time of original composition) nor of the venerable lay Nestor, but very much of an insider in the work's imagined scholarly community – especially literary community.

Heerkens confesses that he has learned much from sitting at the tables of cultivated Frenchmen: 'O lucky me, to whom it was given to learn these things, during the incautious years [sc. of my youth], even from their presence and from their mouths!' ('O me felicem, male cui prudentibus annis, / Horum etiam viso discere ab ore datur!', p. 94).[96] And if the poem's learned addressee can derive instruction from everyone God puts in his path, including the 'bad, stupid, proud and harsh', he should strive to 'get to know more, know more thoroughly your peers in your field, whether your homeland or a journey has given you the opportunity to visit them. And select from those who are fashioned after your temperament, and from the peaceful ones, those whom you might wish to follow in all their actions' ('Nosce magis, studiique tui pernosce coaevos, / Patria, visendos seu via facta dabit. / Deque tuos factis ad mores, deque quietis / Selige, quos cupias cuncta per acta sequi', p. 213). Heerkens favours Ovid, naturally, and, in this century, Fontenelle, whom he 'keeps before his eyes if ever quarrels come' ('Et lis, ante oculos, si mihi fiat, erunt', p. 213).

Despite its ambitious length and breadth, and even allowing for interpolations in the second edition, Heerkens's *De valetudine literatorum* betrays the limits of the writer's experience at the time of writing. The young Dutchman's Latin networks were beginning to ramify, to be sure, but the cultural axis of the poem remains a Dutch–French (if not a Paris–Groningen) one. In the following two chapters we shall find our redoubtable scholarly networker making friends and conceiving projects from further afield.

---

[96] He notes, however, that one of his most generous hosts, the Comte de Vence, died from eating oysters (Book 2, p. 85, n. 45).

3

# Tomi Calling: Letters to/from Italy

## Cornelis Walraven Vonck and the Road to Rome

No sooner was Heerkens back in Groningen after his Parisian adventures than he was beginning to form plans for an even more ambitious cultural pilgrimage. We are fortunate to have access to a series of 19 letters, mostly from the 1750s, which he sent to Latinist, magistrate and ultimately burgemeester, of Nijmegen, Cornelis Walraven Vonck (1724-68).[1] These letters shed invaluable light on Heerkens's scholarly inclinations in the context of contemporary Dutch humanism, and in particular, on his growing awareness of and orientation towards *Italian* horizons. A precocious philologist, Vonck, rather like Heerkens himself, seems to have been torn from an early age between his vocation for classical scholarship and the demands of a paying profession (in Vonck's case, law and public office). The promising young man who impressed leading Latinists such as Tiberius Hemsterhuis (1685-1766) and Pieter Burman, Jr (1713-78) quickly assembled and published two volumes of textual-critical observations, mainly on later Latin writers. In the preface to his *Lectiones Latinae* (Utrecht, 1745) Vonck announced his intention to prepare editions of Flavius Cresconius Corippus (6 CE), Martianus Capella and Boethius on Cicero's *Topica*; his choice learned labours never came to fruition, however, much to the disappointment of the diligent friends who had helped him procure manuscripts. In the meantime Vonck managed to put the backs up of the Utrecht theological faculty, weighing into a controversy over an unorthodox graduation thesis by a certain Valentijn Blondeel, a student of his former law professor,

---

[1] Biographical details are drawn from Y. H. Rogge, 'Cornelis Walraven Vonck', *Oud Holland* 17 (1899), pp. 95-119; and Christian Adolph Klotz's eulogy in *Acta Litteraria* 6 (1771), pp. 54-67. Vonck's correspondence is held in the Leiden University Library, collection reference BPL 746: C-F.

**Figure 3.1** *Cornelius Valerius Vonck.*
Source: Jacob Folkema after Willem den Hengst, engraving, 1752. Courtesy of the Rijksmuseum, Amsterdam.

Abraham Wieling (1693-1746).² Vonck's nineteenth-century biographer finds him a prickly character, caustic in criticism, with a talent for making enemies. If so, this did not prevent him from securing an impressive series of public offices, if not the academic posts to which he initially aspired. With Hendrik G. Bornman and Philip Lotichius, respectively 'Conrector' and 'Rector' of the Nijmegen Latin School, he conceived the ambitious plan of re-launching the old *Gymnasium Illustre* which had closed its doors in 1679.³ Though thwarted in those efforts, effectively to promote his friends to more lucrative professorships, Vonck was acknowledged by his fellow councillors, for better or worse, as a man of unusual learning.⁴ He participated in a busy international network of scholarly correspondence stretching from Switzerland to Southern Italy.⁵

Vonck's and Heerkens's circles of correspondence notably overlap in the persons of Cardinal Angelo Maria Querini (1680-1755) and Otto Frederik, Count van Lynden (1716-88). A patron of contemporary Latin writing, the avuncular Count Otto arranged for Vonck to publish and furnish prefaces to historical works by Latin-writing Italians, Girolamo Falete, Guido Ferrari and Castruccio Buonamici.⁶ But if it was van Lynden who encouraged Vonck

---

² Wieling published a satirical commentary, *Mercurii Stygii Iter Subterraneum sive Adriani Hardy Somnium, et alia cum commentariis perpetuis* (Oneiropoli, [s. a.]).
³ On this style of institution in the Dutch Republic, intermediate between the Latin School and the Academy, see Willem Frijhoff and Marijke Spies (eds), *Dutch Culture in a European Perspective: 1650, Hard-Won Unity* (Houndmills: Palgrave Macmillan, 2004), pp. 253-4. Rogge ('Cornelis Walraven Vonck', p. 113) points out that Vonck conducted significant unpublished research into the history of the Nijmegen gymnasium. His manuscript notes on the learned men of Nijmegen are held at the library of Arnhem (Centrum, Magazijn KLUIS MS 69).
⁴ To Vonck they entrusted an unpublished manuscript found at the Auditor General's office, 'Gulielmi de Berchem Chronicon Gelriae'. He was to prepare it for publication and supply a commentary – another unfulfilled project.
⁵ This Latin correspondence merits further investigation. It would be interesting, for example, to compare the preoccupations of Vonck's generation of Dutch Republicans of Letters with those of the correspondents of D'Orville (1697-1751). A substantial collection of Latin Letters to D'Orville, a classical scholar born in Amsterdam to French Protestant parents, may be consulted in Oxford, Bodleian Library, MS D'Orville 483. See <www.bodley.ox.ac.uk/dept/scwmss/wmss/online/1500-1900/dorvilleCLD/dorvilleCLD.html> for a brief description of the whole collection, MSS D'Orville 1-618. In fact there is some overlap between D'Orville's circle of correspondents and Vonck's (e.g. Burman, Hemsterhuis and Meerman).
⁶ Castrucci Bonamici, *De rebus ad Velitras gestis Commentarius ad Trojanum Aquavivum Aragonium S. R. E. Principem Cardinalem*, ed. Cornelius Valerius Vonck (Amsterdam, 1748); idem, *Commentariorum libri tres de Bello Italico* (Leiden, 1750 and 1751); Girolamo Falete, *De bello Sicambrico libri IV; praemissa est epistola Cornelii Valerii Vonck ad virum illustrem Janum de Back* (Nijmegen, 1749) [a poem]; Guido Ferrari, *De politica arte oratio*, ed. Cornelius Valerius Vonck (Nijmegen, 1750). Falete was a sixteenth-century author; Jesuit Guido Ferrari and Pietro Giuseppe Maria Bonamici (= Count Castruccio Buonamici) (1710-61) were still living. See the respective articles in the *Dizionario Biografico degli Italiani* on Bonamici by Claudio Mutini, 11 (1969), pp. 525-7, and Ferrari by Luisa Narducci, 46 (1996), pp. 620-2, available at <www.treccani.it/biografie/>,

to dedicate his edition of Buonamici's 'Commentary on the Italian War' to Cardinal Querini,[7] it seems to have been Vonck himself who arranged for Heerkens his coveted contact with that influential churchman; Vonck, once again, who introduced his friend to the Italophile van Lynden, with whom Heerkens lodged when he was bound for Italy in 1759.

Before we appraise the dynamics of his friendship with Vonck, let us first consider Heerkens's broader epistolary network. Though frustratingly fractured, what survives of his correspondence constitutes a precious witness not just to our author's character and career, but also to the use of language as a precision instrument for self-definition and – promotion within the eighteenth-century Republic of Letters. For the modern reader, Heerkens's language choices may seem at times counterintuitive. He will write in French, for example, to the perfectly Latinate Querini, to whom, elsewhere, as we have seen, he dedicates his Latin didactic poem on the duties of a doctor, prefaced by an autobiographical epistle in Latin verse. Querini, for his part, always replied to Heerkens in Italian – a gesture of paternal intimacy, perhaps?[8] The use of French in the letters to Heerkens by Dutch poet and politician, Onno Zwier van Haren (1713–79), and presumably *vice versa*, may surprise.[9] Is it a function of the 'French school' phenomenon identified by Kloek and Mijnhardt, namely that educated Dutch people of the period sometimes felt insecure writing in

---

accessed 20 May 2012. On Ferrari, for a more recent discussion, see Maurizio Campanelli, 'Settecento Latino II', *L'Ellisse. Studi storici di letteratura italiana* 3 (2008), pp. 85–110.

[7] At the suggestion, in turn, of Basel jurisconsult, Rudolph Iselius.

[8] Querini's correspondence was voluminous, and he counted many learned luminaries of the day, from Muratori to Voltaire, among his friends. Some 10,000 letters to Querini are scattered throughout the libraries of Europe, and an unknown number of autographs. (See the useful biographical note at the Biblioteca Queriniana: <http://portale.comune.brescia.it/NR/exeres/FD734508-12FB-4BD3-B529-14165401EFB2.htm>.) I have seen photocopies of six letters in Querini's hand to Heerkens, dating from March 1752–March 1754, in the private collection of Mrs Canter Cremers of Rotterdam. The first encourages Heerkens to persevere with his Latin poetry, which he was threatening to renounce; advises him that a gift of a silver medallion is on its way; and sends news to Vonck. The second answers Heerkens's letter of 11 July, thanks him for the first instalment of his poem, *De officio medici*, and looks forward to delivery of the remainder by 'the Jesuit fathers you mentioned'. A French letter by Heerkens dated 7 January 1753 (in the Biblioteca Queriniana in Brescia) proposes an edition of the translation of the Greek anthology by Hugo Grotius. Heerkens hints that Querini's assistance might be useful in extracting the autograph manuscript from the French Jesuits: 'le sanctuaire de leurs muses est impenetrable'. The third of the Canter Cremers' letters by Querini, dated 25 February 1753, responds to this last.

[9] The friendship dates from the beginning of 1762, during van Haren's trial for incest. See Pieter van der Vliet, *Onno Zwier van Haren (1713–1779): Staatsman en Dichter* (Hilversum: Verloren, 1996), especially pp. 281–8 for the correspondence with Heerkens. The letters to Heerkens from Onno and his brother Willem are collected in H. E. Moltzer (ed.), *Hareniana: Brieven van W. en O. Z. Van Haren* (Groningen, 1876).

their native language?[10] But apart from an early Latin panegyric, van Haren's literary oeuvre was exclusively in Dutch, and it seems unsafe to conclude – although it is theoretically possible – that he wrote Heerkens in French to spare his friend's linguistic blushes.[11] Given that Heerkens wrote in Dutch to at least two other scholars,[12] the use of French by/with van Haren may have betokened something more – if not a shared political Francophilia,[13] then at least the affirmation of a certain kind of élite, literary–cultural identity. But this was an identity, or persona, that was subtly different from the one Heerkens shared with Vonck, and different again from the one he contracted, as it were virtually, with the addressees and readers of his *published* Latin verse letters from Italy. That Heerkens writes consistently in French to book collector, Johan Meerman (1753–1815), son of the famous jurist, statesman and (Latin-writing) historian of typography, Gerard Meerman (1722–71), may be a sign of the changing times; it should not, at any rate, be taken as a sign of informality.[14] Meerman *senior* emerges from Heerkens's Latin letters to Vonck almost a figure of fun, a stuffy old pedant who turns out gargantuan and unreadable learned tomes; Heerkens even once satirized him in a Latin poem.[15] A more respectful Heerkens would address a Latin verse epistle from Italy to his erudite and well-travelled compatriot, soliciting a testimonial to smooth his path in Venice (*Italica* (1793), pp. 96–106).

---

[10] Joost Kloek and Wijnand Mijnhardt, *1800: Blueprints for a National Community* (Assen: Van Gorcum and Palgrave Macmillan, 2004), p. 404. They point out that 'for French there were separate language teachers and governesses. Furthermore, thanks to the *Académie française*, French had already been standardised, with fixed spelling and grammatical rules'.

[11] O. Z. van Haren's letters are liberally sprinkled with quotations from Latin literature.

[12] Christophe Saxe (1714–1806) and Hendrik van Wijn (1740–1831). Saxe was the author of a Latin biographical dictionary, *Onomasticon literarium* (Utrecht, 1775–1803), in which Heerkens himself features.

[13] Van Haren's later thoughts on the decline of the Dutch Republic under the bad influence of French *politesse* are rehearsed in his address on the occasion of the 1779 bicentennial of the Union of Utrecht: *Proeve van eene nationale Zedelyke Leerreeden van een oud man aan de jeugd van Nederland over de woorden van Ezra*, cap. III, v. 12: 'ter geleegenheid van't begin van de derden Eeuw van de Unie van Utrecht'. See Wyger R. E. Velema, *Republicans: Essays on Eighteenth-Century Dutch Political Thought* (Leiden: Brill, 2007), p. 77.

[14] The six extant French letters from Heerkens to J. Meerman held at the Museum Meermanno-Westreenianum in The Hague (running from 1773–96) are written by an older man in need of favours, plaintive but proper. In the letter of 12 January 1793 Heerkens attempts to persuade Meerman to order a dozen copies of his *Italica* to sell on in Leiden, appealing to the latter's parents' kindness to the author until their death, and to the inclusion in the work of a letter and tribute to Meerman's father. He believes that the book will sell well if 'Professor Luzac, whose father and uncle were my friends, announce it in his gazette'. But cf. n. 31 below for Heerkens's perhaps misplaced confidence in the partiality of the Luzacs!

[15] See, for example, letter to Vonck of 9 (?) March (?) 1751. On 11 September 1751 he confesses to Vonck that 'I don't particularly like that weird ('abnorme') work of Meerman's – and I'm annoyed by almost

Heerkens's letters to Vonck are at first ingratiating, increasingly affectionate, intimate – 'my most learned/excellent/beloved Vonck; my Valerius . . .' ('mi doctissime/optime/amantissime Voncki; mi Valeri . . .') – and appreciably less formal than what survives of the French correspondence with another regular confidante, the religious poet, Louis Racine.[16] They are almost certainly *not* drafted with an eye to future publication. While it may seem an obvious point, the choice of Latin, even by the same writer, could be motivated by different, indeed multiple, considerations in different contexts. In his letters to Vonck, Heerkens establishes, in the first instance, a relationship of workaday scholarly solidarity, but he is also using Latin to draw his esteemed correspondent into an almost conspiratorial confidence. And so he ranges over subjects from the doings of mutual friends and mentors (such as 'our' professor, Nicolaus Engelhard[17]) to Vonck's health problems (alternating advice not to ignore his studies and not to overdo it) to the publication and reception of their respective works (seeking Vonck's advice on his poetry, including some unpublished hendecasyllables pining for a Parisian girlfriend, 'Emily'[18]), the vagaries of the post, university politics (Vonck's failed attempt to win the Chair of Law at Groningen; the odium professor J. J. Schwartz has incurred for breach of promise to marry the daughter of professor Eck[19]), through to Heerkens's

everyone who writes books in folio. I'd prefer to be the author of the letter to Langius [sc. Justus Lipsius] than the producer of such a heap of books'. In another, undated, letter, Heerkens claims that 'as much as [A. A.] Iddekinge disapproves my inconsiderateness and irreverence towards the learned fathers [sc. Calvinist professors at Groningen?], he seems to approve my joke about the learned Meerman. I see today in the public newspapers that the fourth volume of Meerman's *Thesaurus* was announced, and that, from the same publisher, Hondius, the satires of "L. Sectanus, Q. filius" have appeared [pseudonym for the Italian Jesuit, Giulio Cesare Cordara, of which Heerkens was as yet unaware]. But if that work was written by the same author [sc. Meerman], I am fearful, for I know that the most learned gentleman took my poetic licence badly'. On Meerman see the biographical entries in the *Digitale Bibliotheek voor de Nederlandse Letteren* (*DBNL*), available at <www.dbnl.org/auteurs/auteur.php?id=meer049>. His massive *Novus Thesaurus Juris civilis et canonici* was published posthumously, with a supplement by his son, Johan (8 vols; The Hague, 1780). Meerman's most famous work was the *Origines Typographicae* (The Hague, 1765). A selection of his letters was published as *Gerardi Meerman et doctorum virorum ad eum epistolae atque observationes de Chartae vulgaris seu lineae origine* (The Hague, 1767). Cf. Chapter 4, p. 152.

[16] Granted, only Racine's side of this correspondence survives. Worp sighted 46 of his letters to Heerkens, dating from 3 February 1749 to 1 May 1758, in the collection of Mr E. J. M. I. Canter Cremers in Heerenveen. Forty-seven were apparently sold at auction by Sotheby's in the late 1960s (cf. *Cahiers Raciniens* xxi (1969), pp. 78–9). Only four are still available for public consultation, three in the Groningen University Library, and one in the Houghton Library at Harvard College, MS *69M-91. I thank Paris autographs dealer, Thierry Bodin, for sending me a copy of another now in private hands.

[17] The warmth of Heerkens's feelings for Engelhard may be gauged from the elegiac eulogy he published in the *Journal des sçavans* (August 1765), pp. 263–4.

[18] 4 April 1756, Heerkens (in Venloo) to Vonck (in Nijmegen).

[19] Letter of 2 October 1758. Cf. Heerkens's Latin 'Phaleuques' in the *Journal des sçavans* (June 1758), *Supplément*, pp. 174–6: 'Sur le Mariage de Mrs. Schwardz & Van Douveren, (Professeurs de

indignation at being treated like a naughty schoolboy by his parents after returning from The Hague empty-handed when sent to woo a marriageable young lady![20] In this letter, dated 21 February 1756, the not-so-young Gerard Nicolaas petulantly declares that he is on the point of leaving home, of defying his father's threats to cut off his allowance; that he can make enough to live on by practising medicine; that 'serious friends' have exhorted him to extricate himself from his humiliating domestic situation, to emigrate and live more comfortably abroad:

> but I am not so soft that I cannot inure myself to hardship ... As I am better known to my countrymen I am also closer to them, and among them you are the one, Vonck, who knows what I am, and what I am not. You, I think, have perceived better than others who are more distant from the Muses and literature whatever exiguous merit there is in me.

Heerkens pumps his comrade-in-letters for a fresh vote of confidence in his poetic prospects, and alludes to a potential obstacle to patronage which Vonck had raised on an earlier occasion:

> You said when we were together in The Hague that it was my religion that stood in the way of the generosity of friends. But, my excellent Vonck, can the Muses not be separated from the altar? If our Church ('Gubernatrix'), to whom I have sung so often to prove myself a poet and a devotee of letters, not one who stirs up religious controversies and seeks converts for the Pope – I would certainly not be one of those, even if the Roman cardinals were paying their taxes to my Muses – if that most generous leader could be persuaded that my Muses merited his beneficence, or that I could become like a Suetonius in the imperial household, I am sure that, provided you commended me in some way, he would not deem an annual stipend unreasonable, and send away his champion and poet empty-handed.[21]

One can only guess at the context of that earlier conversation about religion, but we do know that in 1763 Vonck left Nijmegen for Cologne, where, possibly

---

l'Université de Groningue) avec les deux Filles de feu Mr. Eck, Professeur de la meme Université: Et sur le Mariage de Mr. Holbeeck, Professeur en Théologie, avec le Fille du Célébre Professeur Gerdes.'

[20] 'Dura dicunt dura agunt suspicantur quae ferre non possum. Vir prope trigesimum annum, philosophus qui de moribus scribo, quique cum gravissimis viris foris versor, domi ut puer adolescens observor.'

[21] How much better are things in France, Heerkens muses, where noblemen and members of the public alike will make provision for a good poet from some portion of their property!

under the influence of the Jesuits Reiffenberg and Harzheim, if not Heerkens himself, he converted to Catholicism. With letters of recommendation from his Jesuit friends – according to Rogge sporting a black robe himself, but this seems unlikely – Vonck entered the service of Karl Theodor, Count Palatine and Elector of Bavaria, and was rewarded with a professorship in Mannheim. The valetudinarian politician who had struggled all his life with debilitating migraines would retire after just two years in academic post due to ill health.[22]

While always deferring to Vonck's taste, judgement and superior connections, Heerkens seeks to forge an almost Atticus-and-Cicero-like bond with his dilatory, or perhaps chronically indisposed, correspondent. He is forever pressing him to send news or books or to forward letters, cajoling him into cosy familiarity with gossip, learned jokes and the odd wry anecdote from the Frisian frontier. There is, for example, a deliciously tart account of the tedious and inappropriately political eulogy by Leonard Offerhaus on the death of Stadtholder Willem IV, which, Heerkens reports, was subsequently printed in both Latin *and* Dutch, as if to compound the audience's agony.[23] As for historians, Oudendorp[24] has been bitchy about Querini's autobiography – it seems that he and Heerkens nearly came to blows over this – and has augured that the 'Chronicle of Gelria' which Vonck is preparing for publication will be 'awful and old-fashioned' ('horridum et antiquatum'). 'Perhaps one day it will be possible to curb the follies of that grammarian', Heerkens snorts, but what can we expect from one who prefers the elegies of Philippe D'Orville to 'my' Lotichius?[25] In another letter, signed 'Groningen, the day before Easter', probably 1752, Heerkens asks Vonck to send him, post-haste, one of his medals bearing the image of Cardinal Querini (Figure 3.2); this he intends to have engraved to adorn his forthcoming poem on the duties of the doctor,

---

[22] See the poem complaining about his headaches reproduced in Klotz's eulogy in *Acta Litteraria*, p. 66.
[23] Offerhaus (1699–1779) was a German professor of history at the University of Groningen. Heerkens seems to have taken a shot at his gloomy historical writing in a satire (unpublished?) on 'the praises of ignorance', reviewed in *Journal des sçavans* (August 1753), p. 201. In another letter to Vonck we read about 'that Berthelingius [sc. a local theologian], who almost calls our Engelhard an atheist', who was granted a second day to continue his preaching on the humility of theologians.
[24] Frans van Oudendorp (1696–1761) had been Rector of the Latin school in Nijmegen (1724) and from 1748 was professor of history and rhetoric at Leiden.
[25] Petrus Lotichius Secundus (1528–60), poet and later physician. Heerkens's copy of his *Poemata* (Leipzig, 1580) is held at the public library of Leeuwaarden. At the end of this volume are several pages of manuscript notes in Heerkens's hand, including a prose *Vita*. I thank Gerda Huisman for sending me a digital copy of these. Heerkens also devotes some lines to Lotichius's career in his elegiac letter to Peter Burmann Jr, 'about to publish his Lotichius in Amsterdam' (*Italica* (1793), pp. 225–9, esp. pp. 226–7).

Figure 3.2 Elegy to Cardinal Angelo Maria Querini.
Source: Gerard Nicolaas Heerkens, *De officio medici* (Groningen, 1752), p. 3. Courtesy of the University of Groningen Library.

*De officio medici*. The request is urgent because Heerkens wants to call in a favour from a local artist, Theodor Beckering, whom he has recently furnished with an *epinicium* for the front matter of a geographical atlas.[26] Why? 'Here is the little story . . . ' Preparations for a rival atlas from Amsterdam were underway, 'with this difference – that one was for profit, this one for glory'. The Batavian publisher had written something uncomplimentary about his Frisian counterpart, and the latter had approached Heerkens for assistance, declaring: 'I don't believe that Batavian champion will dare anything further against me if I have the satires of Curillus on my side!' Heerkens smiles: 'Look how formidable I am! What the King of Prussia is to the rulers of Europe, that's what Theodore thinks I am among our writers! But I should finish this tale, lest in continuing it you perceive there to be more vanity in me than *he* judged there to be muscle in your puny little Curillus ('Curilliolo tuo')!'

The little charade of self-deprecation is poignant. Over the course of their correspondence one has the impression from Heerkens's rising refrain that he has been forgotten by his friend that the conversation must have been relatively one-sided: he hasn't received a letter for so many months, even years;[27] he is very anxious about Vonck's poor health, would he please write?; he is passing through Nijmegen and could Vonck possibly spare him half an hour in the evening? Heerkens identified in Vonck a kindred spirit, one who shared his interest in both classical and contemporary historiography.[28] Vonck was also a connoisseur of Latin letters who, for all his philological acumen, was no narrow-minded 'grammarian' like the aforementioned Oudendorp. In his 'Satire to Corn. Valerius Vonck' (Groningen, 1751), an apology for *not* writing satire, Heerkens nevertheless resumes his role as literary bouncer at Mount Pindus, this time taking it upon himself to eject from those hallowed haunts all

---

[26] Presumably the epigram which appears at p. 68 of the volume containing *De officio medici* (1752), 'In Tabulam Geographicam Frisiae a Theododo [sic] Beckeringh JCto descriptam', said to be 'forthcoming'. Beckeringh was a cartographer but seems to be tagged here as a jurisconsult.

[27] Heerkens's final letter in the Leiden collection dated 10 June 1764, is curt and reproachful: 'Why will you expunge me from your mind through long oblivion? A third year has passed in which I have had no letter from you, and meanwhile I have been back to France twice, and spent the winter. I wonder whether I will emigrate there one day, having had enough of the travelling life' ('quid me longa oblivione animo tuo expunges? Tertius annus abiit ex quo nihil a te literarum. Galliam interim bis revidi, per hiemes. Dubito an non aliquando illic sedem figam, vitae viatoris satur').

[28] See Chapter 4 for discussion of Heerkens's historiographical speculations and of Vonck's inaugural professorial oration at Mannheim, *Meditatio Politico-Historica de Felici Integritatis ac Prudentiae in Historia Temperamento* (Utrecht, 1764). Rogge concludes that Vonck was most productive as an historian, and contributed almost nothing to legal science besides his dissertation ('Cornelis Walraven Vonck', p. 118).

pedantic Teutonic textual critics.²⁹ For his part, Vonck, in a letter to Rudolph Iselius prefacing his edition of Guido Ferrari's 'On Prince Eugene of Savoy's deeds in the Pannonian War' (The Hague, 1749), wrote warmly of contemporary Italian Latinity and lashed out at those 'gloomy wranglers' who 'spread their Scholastic manure over them [the Italians], who, while they willingly join in futile gladiatorial combat over 'barbarism', are themselves most exceptionally barbarians, just as they repeatedly betray themselves by their own evidence to be shrew-mice, much to the discredit of the times, indeed, but much more so to their own'.³⁰ Above all, Vonck was Heerkens's Nijmegen node, a clearing house for news and books from the east, his intermediary between the worlds of an increasingly beleaguered Dutch Latin humanism and the tantalizing new world of enlightened Catholic Italy.

\* \* \*

In a letter of 25 May 1751, Heerkens congratulated his friend on the favourable review of 'your Ferrari' in the *Journal des sçavans*, noting that Racine, 'the son of the famous tragic poet, has promised me a similar kindness for my satire'.³¹ He wonders, though, whether he really deserves to be known in Italy: 'You, my friend, can be the judge of whether the praises of your Ferrari, Bonamici and Querini will suffice to smooth out and erase my stylistic blemishes and poetic vices' ('mi Amice penses an laudes Ferrarii, Bonamici et Quirini tui aequare

---

[29] While true poets and philosophers have their place, there are 'no grammarians', says Heerkens, 'the race of Saumaise is not here unless it is sweating underground, like the Cyclopes in your caves, Mt Etna. They are a kindred species, but this one serves the Gods and fashions arms and terrifying thunderbolts for Jove, *that* one [sc. grammarians], files down, as it were, your words, and of those who are skilled at speaking. And so the servile Critics, a race of manual labourers, bereft of mind, does not enjoy the light, or at least not the upper light, on Pindus's curved peak; those who are prepared to quarrel, dispute, wage war over a mere letter are swollen with bile: only Bentley [Richard Bentley (1662–1742)] and Gronovius [Johann Friedrich Gronow (1611–71)] dwell at the foot of the mountain. Here grave Graevius [Johan Georg Greffe (1632–1703)] also clings – he has been admitted through the intercession of the Umbrian poet [sc. Propertius] and the prayers of Catullus' (p. 8).

[30] 'Eant jam, Scholasticorum iis sordes objiciant tenebricosissimi Vitilitigatores, qui dum in Barbariem necquicquam depugnant voluntarii Mirmillones, ipsi quam insignissime sint Barbari, veluti suo se sorices indicio, produnt identidem, magna quidem temporum, sed majore multo sui infamiâ' (p. ix). Ironically, Christian Klotz's eulogy for Vonck in *Acta litteraria* (pp. 56–7) characterizes him as somewhat overconfident in his own textual-critical powers.

[31] Probably the Satire to Vonck (1751). Two years later the Dutch publisher and bookseller, Elie Luzac, chastised Fomey, editor of the *Bibliothèque impartiale*, for praising Heerkens 'because Mr. Racine praised him & because his poetry was presented and recommended to you by Mr. de Lohman. But are these reasons for an Author of a Bibl. Imp.? Admit, Monsieur, that such determinants must do harm to a Journal' (trans. Ann Goldgar, *Impolite Learning: Conduct and Community in the Republic of Letters, 1680–1750* (New Haven: Yale University Press, 1995), pp. 110–11, from Deutsche Staatsbibliothek (now Staatsbibliothek Preussischer Kulturbesitz), East Berlin, Correspondence of Jean-Henri-Samuel Fomey, fol. 112 (film), letter of Luzac to Fomey, Leiden, 27 February 1753).

et delere possint naevos sermonis et vitia Poetae'). One senses a mixture of excitement and apprehension as the provincial Dutchman contemplates these potential peninsular readers, an imagined community of discriminating Latinists far superior, he assumes, to their French contemporaries.[32] Italy, for Heerkens, is the Parnassus of modern Latinity; his 1751 Satire to Vonck culminates in a rather sycophantic celebration of the latter's reception into the Academy of the Arcadians in Rome, and of Cortona in Tuscany:

> Sed dum Ferrario, Bonamicis, atque Nocetis
> Amplexus partiris, amicitiamque QUIRINO
> Dividis, haud subeant oblivia Vatis amati,
> Qui tantisque viris unà, magnoque QUIRINO
> Corde tuo junctus, merito sibi plaudet, & illis
> Ut Soli Dea noctis, erit, Lunaeque satelles.

> But while you enjoy the embraces of Ferrari, Bonamici and Noceti, and share the friendship of QUERINI, do not forget your beloved Poet, who is joined in your heart with such men, and with the great QUERINI; and he will be well pleased with himself, and he will be to them as the Goddess of the night is to the Sun, and as a satellite to the Moon. (p. 12)

References to 'your' Bonamici, Ferrari and Querini are dotted throughout Heerkens's letters to Vonck. He must have nurtured hopes of one day meeting his Italian idols in person, of converting that hankering 'your' into a nonchalantly mutual 'our'. As is clear from the above-quoted verses, though, Heerkens knew very well the Italian name out of which he could make the most capital. A considerable part of the correspondence in the Leiden collection revolves around his (attempts to establish) contact with the great Querini. In a letter of 1751 he is casting around for something to dedicate to him and seeks Vonck's opinion as to whether his poem on the duties of the doctor, which is 'almost ready, in my writing desk', would be suitable. He worries that 'the material is pedestrian and almost unworthy of such an illustrious authority'. On 1 July 1752 Heerkens is despondent because there has been no word from Italy about his verse dedication. He wavers over writing to Querini again, fearing the worst:

---

[32] And so in another letter he writes of 'a certain Burgundian Jesuit, a Latin poet, but the last in France, I fear', who is preparing an edition of the excellent didactic poems of the Italian, Carlo Noceti, on the rainbow and aurora borealis (15 August 1750?).

It embarrasses me, grieves me, pains me to have written. This recent action of mine has occasioned more loathing and bitterness than I have ever experienced pleasure in praise and commendation of my talents. What have I done, fool that I am? There is a section in the poem on the duties of the doctor which is a bit sharp and obscene, and yet I had the gall to dedicate that poem to a pious old man, and a prince of the church, and of that church to which I belong! I have always had a rash character, foolish and impetuous ... But, my friend, if you can, correct with your discretion the indiscretion of your silly little friend.

In lamenting the failure of his literary powers, Heerkens invites comparison with the exiled Ovid: 'They say I am losing my touch, and that whatever I have composed since a year ago is far inferior to my previous work – whether my health, which is beginning to fail, has affected my talent, or whether it's not possible to be a poet in Frisia after your twenty-fifth birthday.'[33] Just a few days later, however, it was an entirely different story: 'On the eighth of July, my birthday, I received a most friendly letter from your Querini, and together with it a little packet which he intimated he had also sent to you. By Hercules, what a kind man he is! "He will always be a God to me, and on his altar I shall sacrifice oft a tender lamb from my flocks."'[34] Another letter begins: 'Your Curillus is in Heaven!' Querini has been showering him with letters and literary gifts from Brescia, and the ecstatic acolyte rejoices in the friendship with Vonck which has procured and ensures the cardinal's continuing favour.

In 1759, as he was making preparations for his Grand Tour, Heerkens wrote to Vonck proposing a stopover in Nijmegen.[35] While he may indeed have 'greatly desired to embrace' his old friend and to consult him on the details of his itinerary, most of all, one suspects, he needed a personal introduction to Count Otto Frederik van Lynden, 'for, as I hear, he has left many friends behind in Italy'. That introduction secured, Heerkens sojourned with van Lynden en route to Italy. On 13 March 1760, Heerkens wrote Vonck from Rome that his

---

[33] 'ajunt enim me deficere, et inferius multo prioribus esse, quiquid ab anno composui, sive valetudo, quae labascere mihi incipit, transierit etiam in genium, seu non licet esse poetam in Frisiâ quum quintum et vigesimum annum excesseris.'
[34] Virgil, *Ecl.* 1. 7–8. The letter is incorrectly signed 11 June 1752.
[35] The revised, collected volume of his satires had just appeared (1758), and Heerkens jokingly refers to getting out of town: 'in three or four months I am going to Italy; while I am away they will be less angry with me – if there are any who are going to get angry with the republication of my poetic trifles.'

letters of introduction had been favourably received, and that he had been treated very kindly by the Jesuit Cordara; unfortunately he had not arrived in time to meet Carlo Noceti, professor of physics and scientific poet at the Collegio Romano, who had recently died. But Italy, 'my excellent Vonck, if you consider the poverty of her inhabitants, is everywhere wretched, especially the Papal States; and it is absolutely contemptible if you consider the characters of its utterly untrustworthy men. I believe that greater faith survives among the Turks and the Numidians'. To Count van Lynden, Heerkens dedicated the first and longest of his published elegiac verse letters on his journey to Italy: *Iter Venetum* (Venice, 1760).[36]

## Wish you were here ... letters from a lovely exile

The 'Journey to Venice' was followed in 1762 by an *Italicorum liber unus*, dedicated to Dutch politician and poet, Willem van Haren (1710-68), comprising six elegiac epistles to Heerkens's mainly Dutch friends.[37] In 1793 a three-book collection of the same title appeared in Groningen.[38] Like the second edition of his *De valetudine literatorum*, Heerkens's revisited *Italica* was significantly emended and expanded; not only did some of the original poems double in length, but eight completely new letters were added, five

---

[36] An unauthorized shorter version appeared in Utrecht in the same year. In his definitive *Italica* (Groningen, 1793) Heerkens tells us he despatched three verse letters to van Lynden during his Italian journey: this one (= *Iter Venetum*); a second, lost, which was sent from Naples on 20 April 1760 and described the leg from Venice to Rome; and a third, sent 'around the ides of September', a few days before he left Rome for Florence (p. 118, n. 1). The first edition of the *Iter Venetum* was rounded out by an elegiac epistle to (Roelof) Bernhard van Sijzen (pp. 26-9) which would reappear in both editions of the *Italica*, and an ode to the Dutch envoy to Hamburg, J. Jac. Maurits (pp. 30-2), which is also the final poem in the 1793 *Italica*.

[37] This volume comprises an elegiac letter to Nicolaus Tenhove, a Dutch noble, collector and traveller in Italy, author of 'Memoirs of the House of Medici', whom Heerkens knew from his Leiden days; to Giulio Vittorio d'Incisa, Count of Camerana (misspelt 'Ircisio de Camerana' in both editions), Sardinian Resident in Venice 1744-74; to Heerkens's Groningen friend, Bernhard van Sijzen; to Count Otto van Lynden; to Groningen philosophy professor, Nicolaus Engelhard; to François Fagel (1740-73), son of the eminent *Griffier* (principal secretary) to the States-General during the War of the Spanish Succession; and finally, an ode to Claude-Alexandre de Villeneuve, Comte de Vence (1703-60), whose hospitality Heerkens had enjoyed ever since his first visit to Paris.

[38] At the top of the preface, to Johan Andreas Canter (who was related to both Heerkens and Willem van Haren), the author states: 'you have been demanding for many years, and in the last few more strenuously, that I should gather together my *Italica* which were separately published, and that I should try to unite the large number of unpublished poems with those that have been published' (1793, p. i).

of which either pre- or post-date his Grand Tour.³⁹ Again, very much like the *De valetudine literatorum* of 1790, the 1793 *Italica* opens with a long autobiographical preface detailing the circumstances of its production, the wonderful treatment the Latin poet had enjoyed outside his native land, and the hostility he would experience on his return – albeit after an initially warm reception in The Hague. Even his friends would then counsel him to give up poetry, and Heerkens is resigned to the fact that he will never live down the scandal of his student days.

By modern standards of peer review, the lukewarm appraisal of Heerkens's *Iter Venetum* in the 'Hague journal written in French' (sc. *Bibliothèque des Sciences et des Beaux Arts*, 1760) seems hardly to merit the attention drawn to it by the aggrieved author.⁴⁰ It is true that the reviewer begins on a mildly sarcastic note, observing that Heerkens had alarmed his friends with the 'doleful songs of his lyre' by threatening to retreat from the literary scene – but lo, he has returned,

---

³⁹ The first book of this second edition is now given over entirely to the *Iter Venetum*, which has grown from 354 to 1,110 verses. The first and second letters of the second book are now addressed to Nicolaas Tenhove (the first a revised version of the letter printed in the 1762 edition, now twice as long; it is dated here Groningen, 25 April 1762); the third to historian of printing, Gerard Meerman; the fourth to the Count of Camerana (some 20 lines longer than in the first edition); the fifth to Bernhard van Sijzen (here only slightly longer than in the first edition); the sixth, to van Lynden (nearly 780 verses, up from 394 in the first edition). The third book opens with two letters to Nicolaus Engelhard (the first slightly enlarged from the 1762 version, but dated here Naples, 12 April 1760); a third to François Fagel (50 lines longer than in the first edition; now signed Paris, 12 January 1761); a fourth to Prime Minister of Naples, Bernardo Tanucci, omitted from the original edition, Heerkens reports, out of deference to the opinion of a 'friend of thirteen years, a reasonably good arbiter of my Muse' (Vonck?; since he was a long-standing supporter of Castruccio Buonamici?); a fifth to Heerkens's old sparring partner in the Groningen literary quarrel, Gerhard Alting (Groningen, 28 November 1761); a sixth to his student friend and satirical accomplice, later missionary in Batavia, Josua van Iperen (sent from Middelburg, 29 December 1762); a seventh to Johan Andreas Canter (sent from Onno Zwier van Haren's estate, 13 August 1764; cf. *Journal des sçavans* (December 1764), pp. 461–3); an eighth to Pieter Burman, Jr, 'about to publish his Lotichius among the Batavians' (signed Groningen, 25 March 1754), which had first appeared in the front matter to that edition (*Petri Lotichii Secundi Solitariensis Poemata Omnia* (Amsterdam, 1754)); and a ninth to Jesuit historian and prefect of the Innsbruck college, Ignatius Weitenauer (dated Rome, 25 August 1760). Two odes complete the volume, the one to Villeneuve, the Count of Vence, from the original edition of the *Iter Venetum*, and another to the Dutch envoy to Hamburg, J. Jac. Maurits, from the 1762 *Italicorum liber unus*.

⁴⁰ But it seems that the 'writer of the Hague Journal, and reviewer of this poem' had also criticized Heerkens (subsequently? in print?) for being 'an admirer of a weak prince [sc. William V of Bavaria], and a collector of titles less intelligent than Keysler' ('principis imbecillis admirator, et titulorum collector Keiselerio minus sensatus ab Hagani Diarii, et poëmatis hujus arbitro scriptore, dictus fui'). These charges occasion a defensive note by the poet on the life and virtues of the Catholic Duke William: *Italica* (1793), pp. 42–3, n. 47. Heerkens also alludes to criticism by the Hague Journalist of his account of the Council of Trent, but this, too, does not appear in the *Bibliothèque* review of 1760 (p. 61, n. 62). Cf. p. 121, below, on the probable identity of the critic.

accompanied by good health and the Muses!⁴¹ Its most damning allegation, no doubt, is that Heerkens's 'Venetian journey' is no great read: 'To tell the truth, Mr Heerkens could have made the description of his trip more entertaining or more instructive than he has. One encounters nothing really interesting in the 354 verses he has composed.' The reviewer stops short of imputing this defect to Heerkens's lack of talent: 'One can't be cheerful when one is suffering. Boredom, tiredness, bad food, the cold, acts of violence and danger, pursued our author all the way to Munich.'⁴² Although Heerkens's health and spirits had improved by the time he reached Verona, 'unfortunately for the Poet, and for the Reader, the company was awful between Vicenza and Padua. We were on our way – one of the coach wheels broke. The Author, on arrival [in Padua], did not manage to locate a single one of those *savants* who adorn the University. Morpheus was his only refuge, and, forced to depart for Venice the next day, all that he adds is that he arrived' (p. 477). What the reviewer misses in Heerkens's elegy, he says, is the 'affability ('aménité') of a Horace or a M. Le Franc, the cheerfulness of a Bachaumont or of a de la Chapelle'. He does not entertain the possibility that Heerkens's Venetian journey was, to some extent, a *deliberate* whinge.⁴³

Heerkens would have his revenge on the anonymous reviewer in the republished *Iter Venetum* (the first book of the 1793 *Italica*). He reveals in a final footnote that he knew the man – but not, at the time of the poem's first airing, as the writer of the review. It seems that the gentleman in question ran into our returning hero in Genoa; he was chaperoning a noble youth who was about to make his own Grand Tour. Heerkens gave the Dutch travellers advice, wrote fulsome letters of introduction for them, and even accompanied them on an aborted excursion to Ticino and the river Trebbia to visit the site of Hannibal's victory. The party set out in convoy. Heerkens had agreed to take the rear coach, with the youth, so that his learned friend could ride in front with the Dutch consul. But the lead coach driver charged ahead:

---

⁴¹ The reference is not to Heerkens's juvenile satires but to an elegiac poem about his near-scrape with death after drinking from a copper vessel (elegy to 'Sissinius', sc. Bernard van Sijzen, published in the same journal, Jan/Feb/Mar 1759, pp. 239–40).

⁴² 'On ne peut guere être de bonne humeur quand on souffre. L'ennui, la fatigue, la mauvaise chere, le froid, des brutalités, & les périls suivirent l'auteur jusqu'à Munich', p. 477.

⁴³ Already the dedicatory poem to van Lynden begins to point in this direction: 'Believe me, it would have been better for one who has been borne through bloody camps, over the Alps, and through so many life-threatening perils of the unreliable road, to have emerged from Getic grottoes and to have dragged myself forth from a Pontic hut' ('Crede mihi, vecto per castra cruenta, per Alpes, / Perque tot infidae dira pericla viae, / Utilius fuerat Geticis exisse cavernis, / Meque Borysthenia proripuisse casa', *Italica* (1793), pp. 1–4, p. 2).

like someone who was going to complete the whole journey in half an hour, and indeed like someone who has in fact completed it [in that time], as far as he was concerned ('ut qui iter omne intra sequi horam confecturus erat, et ut revera illud sibi confecit')! For then, jumping down from his horse, first with entreaties, then with threats, and presently by striking the face of his customer three or four times with his rod, he exacted, and exacted the entire, fee which had been agreed for a three-day journey. When [our man] had been ordered to get down with his old friend [sc. Dutch consul], he saw his coach driver disappear into the mountains with their luggage. (pp. 75–6, n. 74)

This unfortunate tourist, 'a man in his forties, and who, like Vitellius, had hung a dagger around his neck when entering the coach, did not dare to demand, did not dare to reclaim it [sc. the luggage]'. Heerkens paints an unflattering picture of his cowardly compatriot, sulkily nursing the *stigmata* of his shameful ordeal, and having far more animated words with his adolescent charge, who now wished to return to Genoa with Heerkens, than he had ventured with the surly coach driver. Our poet chivalrously offers his own coach, and proceeds with the youth by foot. In conclusion:

He, the same man who, before this, had so hissed me off stage in his review, was the very same man who, when he returned to Holland and became important, was not to be seen having any memory of this, or of any other service I had provided for his journey. But although I wondered greatly for some time at the bizarre character of the man, I would cease to wonder when I realised, late in the piece, that he had been the writer of that review in the Hague Journal.

While Heerkens does not name his antagonist here, he lets slip his age and place of birth, Geneva, so that we might infer that the reviewer was, in fact, co-editor of that journal and Calvinist clergyman, Charles Chais (1701–85).

\* \* \*

If Heerkens usually played the Ovid card to characterize his Dutch provincial homeland as a climatic and cultural backwater, in his elegies to Tenhove, Meerman, Van Sijzen and Camerana on his Venetian sojourn, the poet mischievously assumes the mantle of warm-hearted, down-at-heel, Dutch exile in the land of the lugubrious lagoon-dwellers. One can only assume that he hoped to win some points for patriotism with what the close reader cannot fail to suspect is a sort of reverse *Tristia, from* Italy. In the elegy to Camerana, for example, the poet, having barely survived the perils of the Alpine journey, declares that he is 'now dwelling in an unknown place, instead of my homeland; let me complain about the sky and the earth and the natives!' ('Nunc ignotam habitans, pro qua mihi patria sedes, / De caelo et terra terrigenisque querar', p. 107). That place is Venice, where:

> Quà fera suspicio regnat trepidoque pavori
>   Advena cum miseris civibus usque litet,
> Quà me angunt vici, qua lubrica marmore quaevis
>   Perfida poplitibus, diraque ponte via est,
> Quà mea simplicitas illuditur omnibus horis,
>   Voxque fere nullo comis ab ore sonat,
> Quàque oblitum hominem solatur epistola rara,
>   Quà videor patriae non superesse meae,
> Quàque malo immerito, laceranti viscera, morbo
>   Luxuriae atque gulae, me superesse, stupes.

harsh suspicion rules, and the stranger is always making amends, in trembling fear, to her wretched citizens; where streets press in on me, where every marble path is slippery and treacherous to the knees, and that of the bridges is fatal; where my candour is mocked at every hour, and a friendly voice scarce issues from any mouth; and where a forgotten man is consoled by the rarest letter, where to my fatherland I seem not to have survived; and where you are amazed that I have survived an undeserved illness, an illness of excess and gluttony, that wracks my guts. (pp. 107–8)

We are informed in a long note *ad loc.* that Heerkens was seized by an attack of dysentery, which his Venetian doctor wrongly put down to poisoning since he had personally observed the Dutchman's abstemious dietary habits.[44] Poor Heerkens feared for his life, and that he would be despatched to the mortuary island which the Venetians reserved for commoners and foreigners: 'and always before my eyes was that sad island, and the beach, full of unknown bones and naked cadavers, which terrifies the waves of the retreating sea' ('Semper

---

[44] In fact the poet-doctor's less dramatic self-diagnosis and cure proved correct: 'the reason for the illness was to be attributed to unfamiliar air, the trials of the journey, and that I had just passed through a more than usually hot summer in my country' (p. 108, n. 2).

et ante oculos insula tristis erat, / Ossibus ignotis, et plena cadavere nudo / Lida, maris refugi quae pavefactat aquas', p. 109). But he recovered promptly, he says, because of the friendship of Camerana, and promises to remember and extol his name in verse forever more. The Italian should not imagine that the Dutch have cold hearts: 'If Corbulo found us rough, and Alba ferocious, whatever recent rumour reports, and an old woman's rumour, the Dutchman has nothing of ice and wind in his breast: our hearts are soft, and we know how to love with tender faithfulness' ('Corbulo nos duros, et senserit Alba feroces, / Quidquid fama recens, famaque cantat anus, / Nil habet à glacie ac ventis in pectore Belga: / Molle cor est, tenera scimus amare fide', p. 110). In this poem, then, Heerkens alternately assumes the persona of Ovid in Tomi (Dutchman in Venice) and warm-hearted Belgic 'barbarian' who longs to return to Tomi (Groningen), but will never forget his friend, even though 'many mountains, and immeasurable distances between places' ('Et multi montes, spatia infinita locorum') separate them.

In fact, it was not just the Venetian leg of his tour which gave rise to invidious comparisons with Heerkens's homeland. In the sixth elegy of the second edition, to van Lynden, recounting his journey from Rome to Naples through the Papal States, the poet paints a grim genre scene of Campania sometime Felix. The journey is dangerous and the road is littered with the corpses of those who departed Rome in the wrong season.[45] Heerkens's explanation for the unwholesomeness of the countryside, and for its infestation with disease-bearing insects is worth noting – a lack of habitation, a lack of smoking hearths.[46] But the Pontine Marshes were cultivated in antiquity, and from Heerkens's perusal of the rich coin collection of the Duke of Noja[47] he confirms that they once sustained great cities:

---

[45] 'But to wish to make the journey when the sun is vomiting fire, when the straw on the bridges catches fire spontaneously, and the split earth yawns into the abyss, is madness! And the road is often not felt to be suitable and safe for setting out until autumn. We saw them go, whom Fate followed with a swift wheel, and whom the Appian Way paved with their very horses' ('Sole sed ignivomo, paleae cum pontibus ardent / Sponte, et in immensum scissa dehiscit humus, / Carpere velle viam, furor est. Nec saepe profectis / Apta sub autumnum, tutaque sensa via est. / Vidimus ire, rota quos praepete Parca secuta est, / Et quos ex ipsis Appia stravit equis', p. 121).

[46] A 'Corycian gardener' interlude in *De valetudine literatorum* (1790) had Heerkens receiving advice from an elderly Scots doctor living near St Germain, who had known the great Sydenham; he counselled scholars against living in the countryside or near the walls of cities: Book 1, pp. 44–5.

[47] Giovanni Carafa the 3rd Duke of Noja (1715–68), a partly self-taught polymath whose interests ranged from literature and antiquities to mathematics, optics, electricity and the natural sciences. By the time Heerkens met him he had already made extensive scientific journeys throughout Europe and Russia. In his second verse letter to Engelhard, Heerkens complains about the general laziness

> Sed nunc, dicta diu felix, plaga vera laborum est,
>   Et fortunatis incola squallet agris.
> Lipsius Amiseo vicina per oppida risit:
>   Visa sed hic risus oppida, gensque negant.
> Rara ibi munditie domus et placitissima mensa,
>   Obvia sed probitas et solet esse fides.
> Utque ibi non cimex, et scorpio bestia pejor,
>   Repit et in lectum nulla lacerta tuum:
> Utque hospes nullis ibi dicitur hostis, et aer
>   Obvius haud hostis, quique venenat, erit:

But now, long called 'happy', she is truly a land of labours,[48] whose inhabitants are wretched in their fortunate fields. Lipsius laughed at the towns around the Ems:[49] but the towns around *here*, and the people, are beyond laughter. There, a clean dwelling and a good meal are rare, but there frank decency and good faith usually prevail. Just as there, you don't find bugs, and a beast worse than a scorpion, and no lizard creeps into your bed! Just as there, nobody calls a host 'hostile', and you will not encounter a hostile air which poisons you! (p. 120)

After Anxur, which 'is not located on the cliffs, as Horace says, but *hangs* from them and looms over the briny waters' ('Non positum saxis, ut Horatius inquit: ab illis / Pendet, et aequoreis imminet Anxur aquis', p. 140), the Via Appia traverses the wide plain of Fondi. Heerkens exclaims in frustration: 'O what fields! But the weeds and brambles in them, and there are those which are even uncultivated! You will not look upon them without bile. If such a sky were granted me in my homeland, and such fields: what joy there would be from these acres!' ('O quales agros! Sed in his sentesque rubosque, / Hos etiam

---

of the Neapolitans and reports that Carafa was the only man he regularly visited there who was not to be found lying in bed when the sun was up! ('Unicus isque vir est, quem visere saepe, nec alto / Contigit extensum sole videre thoro', p. 181). His biographical note on Carafa in this letter records that he died in 1769; and that Heerkens had perused his descriptions of his extensive ancient gem collection, and his famous topographical map and commentary on Naples and environs, not yet published, and that he was 'equally devoted to mathematical study as to antiquarian' (p. 181, n. 7).

[48] Heerkens's footnote: 'she is called *Terra Leporina* by Pliny, that is, from *lepore*, "charming"; during the barbarian centuries she was called in Italian *terra di Lavore*, "land of labours", and such she seemed to me, except between Capua and Naples.'

[49] Heerkens's footnote informs us that Lipsius's humorous letters on his experiences in some Westphalian inns are periodically reprinted at Emden, 'with notes, when the printing presses are not running hot'.

incultos non sine bile vides. / Tale mihi in patria caelumque, et talia dentur / Jugera: jugeribus gratia quanta foret!', p. 141). The town of Fondi itself is delightfully situated:

> Monte latus tegitur, pars altera cingitur Urbis,
> > In queis naturae luxus abundant, agris.
> Hic inter virides fulgent poma aurea fructus,
> > Hic cerasa, et ficos, munera veris, habes.
> Latior hic oleis se silva perennibus offert,
> > Dixeris hic homini posse deesse nihil.
> Sed quia cultus abest, et adest ignavia genti,
> > Depravant hominum qualiacunque manus.
> Rancidius nusquam est oleum: nec in arbore fructus
> > Deligitur: ramos pertica coeca ferit.
> Hospitium rhedis licet ardua praebeat aedes,
> > Lectulus ex stipula, foedaque mensa fuit.
> Adde, quod occuluit latronem lectus, et uni
> > Debuimus socio non periisse cani.

One side of the city is shaded by mountain, the other ringed by fields in which the luxury of nature abounds. Here, among the vigorous fruits gleam golden apples, here you have cherries, and figs, the gifts of spring. Here a wider wood of olive trees offers itself: you would say that a man here lacked nothing. But because culture is absent, and the idleness of the people is present, the hands of men ruin whatever they touch. Nowhere is the olive more rancid. Nor is the fruit plucked from the tree; a blind pole batters the branches.[50] And while a lofty dwelling provides hospitality for coaches, the bed was made of straw, and the food was foul. And throw in, that the bed concealed a thief, and that I owe my life solely to my canine companion! (p. 142)

Luckily for Heerkens, his assailant at that insalubrious inn was a local, *not* a Roman: 'The great boldness of Rome is up for any crime; nowhere else in Italy are hearts more courageous!' ('Quodlibet ad facinus magna est audacia Romae / Nusquam plus Itali corde vigoris inest', p. 143). Where Romans boys will kill

---

[50] Cf. for example Ovid, *Tristia*, 3. 10, on the agricultural indifference of the Tomitans.

one another in the streets, 'the mob from Fondi is enfeebled by the Calabrian winds from the south: whether it wants to or fears to, it does not submit to any dangers' ('Fundanum Calabris resolutum vulgus ab austris, / Seu cupit aut metuit, nulla pericla subit', p. 144). Thus pronounces the enlightened doctor Heerkens, and probably in medical earnest.

\* \* \*

It should certainly not be imagined that Heerkens's *Italica* are an unmitigated dirge. They are punctuated by moments of high adventure, antiquarian, geographical and even prehistoric curiosity,[51] intertextual wit[52] and comic romance.[53] While relatively discreet about his romantic adventures, Heerkens plays the erotic Ovidian card more freely in his letters to van Lynden. Both the first and third (second published) of these include narrow escapes from more or less comely 'cougars' intent on leading the studious tourist astray. On the road to Velletri, the travellers are obliged to negotiate a steep path by foot: 'Here, while thoughts of not a few friends from my homeland steal into my heart, not a few sweet girlfriends, and while I am wracked by this useless yearning for those who are absent, behold, a letter is lying on the ground, and the letter has been recently lost!' ('Hic, mihi dum patria atque animum non unus amicus, / Et non una animum dulcis amica subit, / Cumque amor absentûm me torquet

---

[51] On a visit to 'the Island of Aeaea, now no longer an island as it was in the ancient times of Homer's Circe [= Monte Circeo], your tomb, Plancus, detained my gaze, which has bestowed so very pleasant a setting on no-one [else]' ('Insula et AEaeae, jam non magis insula, Cyrces / Moeonidis prisci tempore sicut erat. / Detinuitque tuum mea lumina Plance, sepulcrum, / Quod nulli sedes tam peramoena dedit', *Italica* (1793), p. 148). The corresponding footnote supplies further information about this out-of-the-way monument and its inscription. Heerkens was clearly intrigued by the discovery of human bones a hundred feet underground during excavations for the aqueduct bringing water to the palace at Caserta (a modern marvel in its own right). The reason for such deep burial of these remains provoked speculation from 'all of Naples, who flew to see them'. After weighing the different theories, Heerkens concludes that the ground has risen due to run-off from the mountains, but only after thousands of years: thus the bones must date to the time of Noah (pp. 156–8).
[52] Does he perhaps allude archly to the barbaric/bestial language of Ovid's Tomitans ('omnia barbariae loca sunt vocisque ferinae, / omniaque hostilis plena timore soni, / ipse mihi videor iam dedidicisse Latine: /nam didici Getice Sarmaticeque loqui', *Tristia*, 5. 12. 55-8) when he complains that he cannot commit the names of the Innsbruck Jesuits to verse? 'Do you want me to tell their names? River Inn, an oracle imitating your sounds would not yield harsher matter for my verse. But the crashing of your stream did not terrify any of their hearts, nor does the Seine, nor even the Tiber, feed hearts more cultivated' ('Nomina vis dicam? Numeris magis aspera nostris / Non daret, AEne tuos sors imitata sonos. / Pectora sed nulli fragor horrificaverat amnis: / Sequana culta magis nec quoque Tibris alit', *Italica* (1793), p. 57).
[53] In addition to those already mentioned, there is a case of mistaken identity on the road from Capua to Naples, when the travellers descend from their coach and Heerkens is affectionately embraced by a local girl who takes him for her brother (*Italica* (1793), p. 159).

inutilis, ecce, / Charta jacet terris, perdita charta recens', *Italica* (1793), p. 125). Heerkens snatches it up stealthily ('surripio') and 'the first things I read attest to the love of a mistress, for whom a boy is ablaze with a mad passion' ('Surripio, et, quae prima lego, testantur amorem / Pellicis, insano quam puer igne coquit', p. 125). The unsatisfied 'Penelope' is announcing her husband's absence for nine nights. When the party reaches town, Heerkens gallantly resolves to return the misplaced missive to its writer, a lady who was 'well-known in the city' and whose 'door was not unyielding to a stranger's knock' ('Moxque reperta fuit, bene cognita scilicet urbi: / Dura nec ignoto janua pulsa fuit'). She appeared with her three children, 'nicely dressed, and most alluring'; she was older than Heerkens, 'but there was no lack of sparkle in the eye or colour in the cheeks of the so-frequent parent' ('Vixque admissus eram, comta, et blandissima, cum se / Penelope natis obtulit aucta tribus. / Vicerit utque meos annos, tam saepe parentis / Non oculis aberat flamma, nec ore color', p. 127). Heerkens politely declines her invitation to dinner.

Though permeated, to be sure, by a wistfulness for familiar friends and places,[54] Heerkens's *Italica* evince an open-minded appreciation of the Italian countryside and culture(s). Even his gloomy *katabasis* to the remains of the theatre at Herculaneum leaves the poet feeling 'close to Elysium, not where sad Avernus holds the souls of the guilty. A land once happy, and for so many centuries, will have been even more dear to the Gods, below' ('Namque ibi me Elisio censerem adstare propinquo, / Non, quà animas sontes tristis avernus habet. / Tam quondam felix, et tot per saecula tellus, / Infra etiam fuerit Dîs quoque cara magis', p. 162). He has an almost religious experience at the Liris stream, where Cicero and his ancestors once drank, and where the god of the place seems to speak to him, exhorting him to follow a level path in life, to cultivate books, shade and friendship ... and not to expect too much from the Muses (*Italica* (1793), pp. 149–50). True, his eyes moisten when he compares Lazio with his own land – not because the latter is unpleasant or uncultivated,

---

[54] His first letter to Engelhard begins with a deft synopsis of the journey so far, and plans for his return to Groningen, via Paris: 'You know well how sweet the Seine is to me, with so many friends: Here the first kindness was showed to my Muse. Here love, here, if the kindness shown to the young man remains, beguiling kindness, beguiling love remains for the man. But love from our country is more beguiling and, for me, more reliable, a country ruled by liberty and fair Justice' ('Scis bene, quam multis mihi Sequana dulcis amicis: / Venerat hic musae gratia prima meae. / Hic amor, hic juveni si praestita gratia restat, / Blanda viro restat gratia, blandus amor. / Blandior à nostro tamen et mihi certior orbe, / Quem pia libertas, et Themis aequa regit', *Italica* (1793), p. 170).

but 'clouds and winds must be endured for eight months, and now, with the harvest scarce well collected, a fire. For whom does a fire blaze here, unless for him who sees a second December?' ('Sed nebulae, et venti, mensesque per octo ferendus / Et jam, omni lecta vix bene messe, focus. / Cui focus hic lucet, nisi mense Decembre reviso?' p. 150). The brief spring in Rome is more beautiful than anywhere else in the world, but Heerkens can easily bear the summers too, for all his days! 'I like the mildness of the zephyr, I like the heat, to arrange my limbs on a lazy couch and to write on my lap, and listen to the sonorous fountains, which, following the example of the ancients, Rome approves even now' ('Me mitis zephyri clementia, me juvat aestus / Tempore languidulo ponere membra thoro, / Scribereque in gremio, et fontes audire sonoros, / Quos veterum exemplo nunc quoque Roma probat', p. 151). With Rome as his destination, our professional exile couldn't complain *too* much. She looks good in ruins; she is kind to foreigners; one can lodge and eat well here; the water is healthy; the site was well chosen in antiquity and the streets of the new city are wide (*Italica* (1793), pp. 168, 172–4). She welcomes 'wretched exiles' to this day.[55] Best of all, Rome is *città aperta* for the arts.[56] Heerkens's was an educational journey, after all, and in our next chapter we shall follow the conscientious note-taker as he records his experiences and observations of Italy for the unnamed friend who might wish to follow in his footsteps.

---

[55] 'And her [nobility] does not shut away its paintings from the lover of the arts, and her coins and the marbles of the ancients, if anyone loves those. The ancient books are accessible, and their use, books which elsewhere you might not even hope to flick through' ('Et sua non claudit picturam, et amantibus artes, / Nummosque, et veterum marmora siquis amat. / Accessumque libri veteres patiuntur, et usum, / Volvere quos alibi nec quoque velle potes', *Italica* (1793), p. 173).

[56] 'Exsulibusque favet miseris, sedemque tuetur: / Montgo boni exemplum nobile cujus adest': that is, the nobleman and French diarist, Charles Alexandre de Montgon, who, according to Heerkens, was exiled for criticizing Cardinal de Fleury; he lived in freedom at Rome, and published his books in Switzerland (p. 173, and n. 7).

# 4

# Writing Home: Lessons from Italy

## Museless amusements

Not only did Heerkens write up his Italian journey as a series of poems, but also, and unusually for him, he committed his travel experiences to prose.[1] How do the four books of his *Notabilia*, in two volumes published in 1765 and 1770, articulate with the verse *Italica* published in 1760 and 1793? How and when were they written? In fact the prose text mirrors many of the events and impressions relayed in verse, especially in the long, narrative letters to van Lynden, and it is not a simple matter to determine which came first. In a note to his third verse letter to Count van Lynden,[2] Heerkens confesses that he had begun writing him a fourth letter in Florence, but that 'the things I endured in the subsequent journey and recorded in my Commentary [sc. *Notabilia*] wiped all care of the Muse from my mind' (*Italica* (1793), p. 118, n. 1). This might lead us to suspect that he jotted down his thoughts in prose first, or at least more readily. In *Notabilia*, Book 3, however, he writes that he had speculated in that same verse letter to van Lynden that the Appian Forum lay at the site of the modern Casanova; *now* he believes he can prove it is at least 12 miles closer to Rome (Book 3, p. 9). Of course, we are reading this in his *published* prose account (in the case of the third book, published nearly a decade after his return from Italy). It seems safe to conclude that, whatever form Heerkens's travel notes/journal may originally have taken, the *Notabilia* that went to print will have undergone, like so many of his other works, considerable fine-tuning and enhancement.

---

[1] The only other prose work which survives, and one which has no particular pretensions to stylistic elegance, is the *Quaestiones Medicae Parisinae* (Groningen: Jacob Bolt, 1754).
[2] The second and last published, as Heerkens's original second letter was never retrieved from its dedicatee for publication.

Having said that, the Latin of the *Notabilia* is fresh, apparently spontaneous, the prose style less periodic than that of the sometimes frustratingly convoluted prose prefaces to Heerkens's volumes of verse. Part of the work's undoubted appeal lies in the agreeable tempering of a wide-eyed enthusiasm and earthy Dutch frankness with a lightly-worn erudition and dry wit. But if he gives the impression of straight-talking and unguardedness, Heerkens was as aware as was his favourite poet that 'it is an art to conceal art' ('ars est celare artem'). The *Notabilia* is no travel diary scribbled *in situ* from the cabin of a rickety stagecoach; it is larded with choice, often substantial, excerpts from poets, historians, travellers and antiquarians, from antiquity to present times (notably Biondo Flavio, Paul van Merle, Julius Caesar Capacius, Bernard de Montfaucon and Joseph Addison).[3] Nor does it ever deteriorate into a stodgy didactic pilgrimage. All four books are enlivened with dramatic incidents and curious characters: stubborn, strange and lovelorn fellow travellers, violent coach drivers, crooked innkeepers, shifty money-changers, bitchy cardinals, impressively learned men and beautiful, if not always so learned, women. A long section in the first book, for example, is devoted to the question of why Roman women are relatively uncultured vis-à-vis their Parisian sisters: the urbane men of Rome are clerics and thus off limits to the female sex; the local women have to content themselves with young, uneducated lovers. Heerkens quips that the ladies of Rome are as 'addicted to love as ours are to tea and sweets'![4]

The basic organizing principle of the work is the author's chronological progress through the peninsula,[5] but there are no date entries or marginal notes, no breaks in the text. Footnotes are sparse and supply nothing beyond the short titles of books cited. This is an interesting departure from the *mise en page* of Heerkens's poems, where, as we have seen, footnotes can be long and digressive,

---

[3] Biondo Flavio is usually cited with respect; Merula was wrong in suggesting that Capua abounded in inscriptions (Book 3, p. 41). Recurring targets of Heerkens's scorn are the Jesuit Athanasius Kircher (always incorrectly cited 'Anastasius') and travel writers Misson and Keysler (on the latter, see below).

[4] They also eat too much fennel, an aphrodisiac according to Christina of Sweden, in a book published in Rome which Heerkens read at Cardinal Passionei's place! (Book 2, p. 40). Cf. *Italica* (1783), p. 191, to François Fagel. In his *De officio medici* (1752), Heerkens had primly conceded that he fancied the Linnaean conceit of plant marriages, whether monogamous or polyandrous: 'only that which is permitted to the girls born of Earth, let *our* girls consider unlawful and a disgrace. For if a Frisian wife were to learn your morals, she is no wife of mine, and would never be one!' ('Dummodo quod liceat genitis Tellure puellis, / Illicitum nostrae dedecorique putent. / Nam vestros mores si Frisica discreet uxor, / Uxor nulla mihi est, nulla futura foret', p. 33).

[5] With the exception of some of the later Roman material which is redirected to the first, primarily Roman, book.

sometimes verging on minor scholarly dissertations in their own right.[6] In the *Notabilia* the digressions are all contained within the body of the text, so that the text *itself* comes to resemble something of an extended footnote. There is no preface – again, unusual for our compulsively autobiographical author. At the outset Heerkens simply states that, 'since the observations in this book for the most part concern Italy, I did not think it would be out of place to prefix to my little work ('opusculo') a short treatise ('commentariolum') I had given a certain friend of mine, on the manner in which to undertake A BRIEF JOURNEY TO ITALY' (p. 1). There follows the presumptive text of this *commentariolum*, which begins: 'He who desires to make a journey to Italy from Holland, following my lead or advice, and who has little time to spare, should commence his journey through Germany and leave at the end of March.'

Heerkens proceeds to give us the heads-up on when to travel, modes of travel – it is better to use your own coach and horses than to put yourself in the hands of the public companies – numbers of days to be allocated to the various northern Italian cities, and sundry tips on eating houses, entertainment, the dangers of back-street money-changers, of over-eating and of embroilment in amorous affairs.[7] Exhortations and asides to the unnamed addressee are frequent and familiar in tone. The future traveller is encouraged, for example, to visit this or that learned gentleman whom Heerkens himself had visited. We begin to suspect that what we are reading is, essentially, the much-elaborated text of a *letter* composed by Heerkens for this friend, a letter offering practical advice on how to make the Grand Tour from the Low Countries and interspersed with the returned traveller's reminiscences of his own journey. Indeed, I would suggest that the recipient of the original letter was none other than young François Fagel, whom Heerkens had befriended in Genoa, and to whom he had addressed, from Paris, his versified travel advisory about Italy (*Italica* (1793), pp. 186–98). At least, many of the precepts on food, wine, sex and tourism from the first book of the *Notabilia* are directly paralleled in this poem.

At no point, however, does Heerkens's 'brief' *commentariolum* definitively end and the *opusculum* proper, to which it was supposed to be 'prefixed',

---

[6] As indeed they do in the verse *Italica*, some of which parallel or supplement the text of the *Notabilia*.
[7] You run the risk of a priest coming in the middle of the night and forcing you to marry an unsuitable girl – the dreadful fate that befell a young German nobleman of Heerkens's time, who had come to Rome with a Venetian a mime-actress in tow (p. 47).

discernibly begin. Indeed, the first book closes with a statement promising that his *commentarium* will continue into the next: 'But I conclude the first part of my journal/notebook ('commentarium') here, so that I can begin the next one, about the present-day inhabitants of Rome, from good omens, and not without praise' (p. 90).[8] Nearly 50 pages into the second book comes a sort of 'proem in the middle' which, at last, orients us to the origins and evolving aims of this idiosyncratic work:

> I had set out brief tips for a journey to Italy in a short letter. Into it, while I was transcribing my little work for the printer, and judging that certain things could be fitly added, I piled them in, one thing leading to another, many and various things which I had meant to broach in separate chapters. If I do not preserve the order of things too scrupulously in this cobbled-together narration – an order which would not exist in separate chapters – let me appear to have followed the order of the traveller, since I am writing for him. You will have seen temples, monuments, statues, pictures, old and new, as they appeared, in turn, and often together. The kind of person who is so punctilious about order would want to visit all the churches before looking at a monument or anything else. That's not the way you live when travelling; that's not the way to write a book of travels. Busbequius, whose notebooks ('commentariis')[9] on the embassy to the Turks I would hope my own work resembles, writes, in the space of one page, now something about Rustan, now about Hungarian matters. To know, and to know how to choose, what will delight the reader most is a very different gift from frigidly preserving order in writing! Far be it from me to arrogate to myself what I judge to belong to Busbequius, that sweetest of writers. I claim only to strive to write like the excellent Busbequius, and after that, to strive with all my might to keep as far as possible from the obscure and dull diligence of a Misson or a Keysler. Misson in the description of sacred or pagan buildings is affectedly scrupulous, counting steps; he measures

---

[8] Indeed, it is possible that the four published books of *Notabilia*, all on Italy, were conceived as the first instalment in a longer series of autobiographical reflections. Heerkens alludes to manuscript books of *Notabilia* in the preface to his medical epigrams of 1783, and in his *De valetudine literatorum* (1790), to 'books of *Notabilia* soon to be published' (Book 2, p. 120, n. 88).

[9] In fact, Busbecq's Turkish travel writings are autobiographical *letters*. See Z. R. W. M. von Martels, 'Augerius Gislenius Busbequius. Leven en werk van de keizerlijke gezant aan het hof van Süleyman de Grote: Een biografische, literaire, en historische studie met editie van onuitgegeven teksten' (unpublished dissertation, University of Groningen, 1989); and idem, 'The Colouring Effect of Attic Style and Stoicism in Busbequius's *Turkish Letters*', in Martels (ed.), *Travel Fact and Travel Fiction: Studies on Fiction, Literary Tradition, Scholarly Discovery and Observation in Travel Writing* (Leiden: Brill, 1994), pp. 140–57.

bedrooms, dining-rooms and sanctuaries in temples – as though he had promised to observe nothing besides that which anyone who shared his strange obsession could very easily observe and follow up [for themselves]. Keysler, who is completely devoid of judgement, who is one of those crazy writers who render the invention of the printing press a curse to the world of letters, not only raves on every page of that immense and awful book of his, but stands convicted of the densest ignorance. For example – you will know this man and 'observer' beautifully from one example – he had lived two years in Italy, and two years, I think, among men of the Catholic faith in other countries, and he writes that they are forbidden on Easter day to eat lamb's meat if the previous night they have slept with their wives ... But I know for a fact that the Pope has not forbidden lamb's meat to any men on Easter day. (pp. 137–9)

Here, then, is our best explanation as to how Heerkens's 'short' letter to a friend blew out to an autobiographical travelogue of four fat books in two volumes. His *commentarium* has, in effect, cannibalized his *opusculum*, however that was originally conceived to run. But the passage quoted is also illuminating of Heerkens's views on the purpose and proprieties of travel writing, period. We note that he favours something like a 'stream of consciousness' style of reportage, an organically evolving narrative as opposed to the fastidious and systematic distribution of facts. Moreover, he censures those writers who cram their travelogues with superfluous, dull or inaccurate detail. And yet, we might well ask, *who* is to be the judge of what is genuinely worth noting as opposed to what is trivial or irrelevant? Is Heerkens any less of a pedant than Maximilien Misson (1650?–1722) or Johann Georg Keysler (1683–1743)[10] when, for example, he estimates for the reader the dimensions of buildings excavated at Herculaneum (Book 3, pp. 80–2); or transcribes in full the text of a panegyric to Pope Benedict XIV (Book 2, pp. 181–9) or indeed Castruccio Buonamici's epitaph to a fellow soldier's dog (Book 3, p. 60); or comments on a rescript by the Emperor Antoninus repealing a law forbidding a wife's ashes to be disinterred and reburied with those of her husband, which he viewed in the Museum Kircherianum at the Jesuit College in Rome (Book 1, p. 64)?

---

[10] Misson was a French Huguenot and author of *Nouveau Voyage d'Italie* (The Hague, 1702). The German Keysler visited Italy in 1729–30.

What is it that compels our attention – and strangely it *is* compelled – to such minor details? I suspect the answer lies in the work's unerased origins as a letter, the sustained illusion that it is addressed to *us*. We find ourselves believing that the writer is concerned for our personal welfare, edification and amusement; in short, that *we* are the travelling friend. The epistolary fiction creates a sort of counterfactual trust, inviting us to indulge, if not to share, our affable friend's excursions and detours, idiosyncratic judgements and confessions. Thus the *Notabilia* is both memoir and letter, past and prospective, private and public – but public only up to a point, as Heerkens makes some rather sensitive admissions in the course of his travelogue, winks at us, invites us to share a joke that he trusts we, his ideal and complicit reader, will readily understand. While no explicit rationale is ever given for the multifarious facts and miscellaneous scholarly curios selected for inclusion, there is, of course, a pattern to Heerkens's note-taking which may be reconstructed from the text itself. In what follows, then, I offer a tentative typology of what Heerkens deemed 'noteworthy' in his Italian journey – and assumed that his readers would as well.

## Reading a Latin landscape

When arduously picking his way along the mountains of the Ligurian coast, Heerkens certainly admired the sublime view, but landscape for him was, above all, *Latin* landscape:

> However great was the exertion, it gave satisfaction not just in its completion, but now and then during the journey. For while I was labouring greatly on that long walk, I thought to myself that I was in that very region which, on so many occasions, had exhausted the armies of Rome; that I was seeing those Ligurians which, as Livy said, were easier to conquer than to find. And the region, in its distinctiveness, revived my spirits. The view from the high mountains down to the sea was wide open, and that down into the groves and little cottages, from village to village, was no less admirable. (Book 4, pp. 188–9)

The natural charms of the Italian countryside were enhanced for our learned pilgrim at every step by the satisfaction of calibrating them with choice passages from the Roman historians and poets. Of Umbria, for example, he raves that there isn't a stream or lake that 'history and all the nine Muses haven't described' (Book 1, p. 22).[11]

Of course, even vernacular-writing visitors to Italy embellished their travel diaries with excerpts from the classical authors, but Heerkens's sources and quotations are usually more recherché, and most frequently deployed, I would suggest, in the prospect of turning over some previously unturned stone. For example, he rejects the view of those who believe that the hill of Monte Testaccio in Rome grew up from the rubble of ancient buildings or from heaped-up broken pots. Extrapolating from some verses of Juvenal,[12] he concludes that it must have been formed from sacred vessels and pottery used in sacrifices (Book 2, pp. 150–4). Heerkens's consistent and independent attention to such minor details of text and turf casts him as a rather different kind of tourist – in any case not a very grand one – from the typical 'bear-led' British *milord*.

The Kleinemeerian's keen eye for the history and geography of the Pontine Marshes (Book 3), his probing comparison of Italian and Dutch drainage techniques and land use, are dictated by peculiarly patriotic sentiments and considerations.[13] He proves a good Dutch citizen, too, when he commends to the reader the excellent wall-strengthening techniques of the Romans, still practised in Italy (Vitruvius's *insertum parietum*), and especially the cement made from the sand of Pozzuoli: 'Our ships, since many of them go to Centocelle, and many to Naples, could carry this sand away in great quantity, or at least as ballast: which, as soon as our people got wind of it, would then seem worthy of our merchants' attention' (Book 1, pp. 83–4).

Not that our pragmatic Dutchman was dour and passionless. On his return trip to Rome from Naples we learn 'that the love and admiration which have always drawn me to that philosopher–poet [sc. Horace] caused me to long, when I was in Tivoli, to seek out the site of his villa'. Five pages of philological-

---

[11] Cf. the second verse letter to Engelhard: 'I saw Alburnus green with holm-oaks, as before, certainly the mountain before my eyes was the same in Virgil's time' ('Et vidi Alburnum ilicibus, velut ante, virere, / Mons nempe ante oculos quando Maronis erat', *Italica* (1793), p. 185). Or this note from the second book of the *De valetudine literatorum* (1790): 'and the farm of Accius [sc. the Roman tragic poet, Lucius Accius], as it was long famous among the ancients, exists to this day in the region of Pesaro: it was shown to me, to be sure, when I was passing through those parts, by Annibale d'Olivieri, a noble and famous antiquarian, son of the sister of the Cardinal' (pp. 63–4, n. 11).
[12] *Sat.* 6. 342–5.
[13] Cf. the sixth elegy, to van Lynden, in *Italica* (1793), especially pp. 130–1, for Heerkens's comparison of this land to the Omlandia of Groningen he knew so well.

cum-topographical detective work ensue. Heerkens infers, first of all, that the town of *Vico vari* was probably the 'Varia' of Horace's *Epistle* 1. 14. 1:

> When I had arrived there on a hired mule – that's the way Horace used to make the journey – and inquired about the names of the places and streams, I heard the word 'Licenza' pronounced. Realising this was 'Degentia' I asked them to take me there. *Gelidus Degentia rivus* [*Epist.* 1. 13]. But 'Licenza' is a village. When I saw it, towards the south, protected from the sun by a mountain, I saw that Horace's 'Mandela', a village shrivelled with cold, a habitation of five hearths, had lost its name with the passage of time and had taken on the name of the stream which flows through the town, and flows through with chilly water; since, as I said, it receives only the shortest rays of the highest sun. Therefore I could not doubt that at Mandela I was near the site of Horace's villa. (Book 1, p. 30)

The *fons Bandusiae* is located, and Heerkens and his attendants drink a libation, purify their hands and faces and pray to Horace and the *genii* of the place to be well. In triumph, he hastens to announce his exciting discovery to a meeting of the Arcadians in Rome – but his Italian colleagues are sceptical and in any case dismissive of its significance. The hint, however, seems to have been taken by a French abbé in attendance, an account of whose own discovery of the site of Horace's Sabine farm was later published in three fat volumes.[14] Heerkens professed not to care that this Capmartin de Chaupy had effectively poached his hypothesis – although the latter, ironically, proved most vociferous in defending his own vaunted intellectual property![15]

## Human monuments

Heerkens makes no apology for the fact that so many pages of his first book, largely concerning Rome, are devoted to imposing personalities and not to buildings:

> I am not worried about seeming excessively diligent in describing the men I have indicated to you. Although they differ very considerably from us

---

[14] Bertrand Capmartin de Chaupy, *Découverte de la maison de campagne d'Horace*, 3 vols (Rome, 1767–9).
[15] Giuseppe Lugli, *Horace's Sabine Farm*, trans. G. Bagnani (Rome, 1930), records de Chaupy's intolerance of alleged pretenders to his theory. See also Bernard D. Frischer and Iain Gordon Brown, *Allan Ramsay and the Search for Horace's Villa* (London: Ashgate, 2001).

in their customs, you will find that you will happily and usefully frequent them. And then, above all, I bid the traveller study *men*. Plato, and all of the ancients who made journeys, often reminisce in their writings about the people they met; not, to the same extent, about the temples or dwellings they viewed – and in Rome, those buildings have been described and painted *ad nauseam* by one and all. (Book 1, p. 80)

The portrait of Cardinal Domenico Silvio Passionei (1682–1761) stands out among several vivid vignettes of notable personages (Book 1, pp. 50–8). The fiery-tempered Passionei has severe morals: he won't endure music at mealtimes and turns away even the musicians of the exiled James Stuart when he comes to lunch. He cannot abide the female sex, although Heerkens repeats a rumour that he once relaxed his stern brow and enjoyed the company of the famous Portuguese lady poet, Bocage;[16] that the Lambertini pope, Benedict XIV, had drolly declared of this aberration in his misogynistic cardinal: *et homo factus est* ('and he has become a man', p. 53)! Now, however, Passionei flies into a rage at the mere 'shadow of a woman'. Heerkens had made the mistake of mentioning a chance encounter with the 'honoured and noble Mrs Boccupadula' in the gardens of the Villa Medici, only to be transfixed by the cardinal's glare as though he had 'praised the entire order of the Jesuits' (Book 1, p. 54). Passionei's hatred of the female sex was, it seems, matched only by his loathing of the Society of Jesus. After the Jesuit order had been expelled from France, Passionei took pleasure in riding in his coach, at dusk, down the Via Flaminia, taunting any Jesuits he met with, 'you will pay, fathers, you will pay!'[17] But the Jesuits outwitted their old foe in the end, sending him to an early grave through apoplexy. They contrived, says Heerkens, to have the Pope oblige him to sign a document condemning a book written by one of his Jansenist friends. Back in the United Provinces, Heerkens says that he had learned that the Society had placed this 'notable' inscription above a memorial to Passionei in one of the churches of Rome: 'To Dominic Passionei, Cardinal of the Holy Roman Church, [from] the Society of Jesus, which Survives' (DOMINICO. PASSIONEO. S.R.E. CARDINALI. SOCIETAS. JESV. SVPERSTES).

---

[16] Heerkens incorrectly records that she is French.
[17] A reference to the English capturing ships from the lucrative Martinique mission, causing the enterprising Superior, Antoine la Vallette, to go bankrupt. In 1760 the creditors appealed successfully to the courts in Paris to oblige the Society to pay their debts.

Memorable anecdotes are also told of the friendly rivalry of octogenarian physicians Giambattista Morgagni and Giulio Pontedera;[18] of Jesuit satirist and historian, Giulio Cesare Cordara, who bids Heerkens leave off reading to him from a work of Hugo Grotius, since the only Dutch Latin he could bear to hear was that of Erasmus; of Jesuit professor, Girolamo Lagomarsini, whose gargantuan editorial labours on the text of Cicero are destined to oblivion, and who, 'considering his unhappy books, not infrequently heaved a great sigh and addressed them, "*povretti mei*"'. In Book 3 we meet soldier–historian, Castruccio Buonamici, a native of Lucca and a cultural celebrity in Naples. Buonamici's martial demeanour was well-matched by his muscular Latinity: 'you could hear the strong and sinewy style of Sallust breathing through his speech and writings' ('Stylum Sallustii, fortem & nervosum, in ore et verbis ejus spirare sensisses', p. 56). He had a hot temper to match Passionei's: 'When I saw him in Naples – and I saw him almost every day – he in no way moderated his language whenever a discussion arose about the powerful men who did not support him.' Indeed, he leapt out of bed in a rage early one morning when Heerkens, who was paying him a visit, failed to condemn his nemesis, Bernardo Tanucci (1698–1793), whom Heerkens had visited the previous day. Buonamici blamed Tanucci for barring him an honourable retreat to France after he had offended the King of Sardinia. He had spoken so intemperately to Heerkens on this occasion that:

> I admonished him not once that his servant was in the room, and mine outside the door, and that he was a Neapolitan man. 'It doesn't matter', said he in Italian, '*he* knows that I dare to express my own mind, and that if I live, I will make it known to everyone – now and in the future, not just to you – that he [Tanucci] did not get away with treating me shabbily!' (Book 3, p. 59)

Prime minister in Naples from 1754 and anticlerical champion of enlightened absolutism, Tanucci features in Heerkens's verse letters to Count van Lynden and to the philosopher, Engelhard, though more in his capacity as philologist, philanthropist and antiquarian than as a politician or free-thinker.[19] Ever the social operator, Heerkens included a letter to Tanucci

---

[18] Pontedera laughs at Morgagni for weighing his food, but Morgagni has the last laugh. When Pontedera ails first, he confesses himself beaten and summons his friends and students to his bedside to confirm the validity of Morgagni's fastidious diet (*Notabilia*, Book 1, p. 5).

[19] It is perhaps significant that Tanucci, 'a not untrustworthy author', confirms for Heerkens the location at Formia of Silius Italicus' altar to Cicero, which he watered with his tears: 'and Rome, more a slave thereafter [sc. after the murder of Cicero], was taught, on a narrow shore, that righteous Freedom

in the second edition of his *Italica* – and not, curiously, one to Buonamici, darling of van Lynden and Vonck.[20] (Indeed, while he features prominently in the *Notabilia*, Buonamici is not even mentioned in the *Italica*.[21]) The 40-year-old Castruccio, 'free and ferocious' ('liber & ferox'), lived almost monastically, and without children: 'an aged wife was all his bondage' ('annosa mulier omne erat servitium').[22] Unlike Passionei, however, he seems to have enjoyed mixed company, and invited Heerkens along to the salon of the poetess, Morelli.[23] There Castruccio and that 'most talented woman' would endure in good humour the ribald verses of the mainly impromptu poets who convened there every evening ('ingeniosissimam faeminam, ipsumque Bonamicum ferre benigno animo insulsissimos versus...omnes propemodum a subitaneis illis poëtis, qui *improvisatori* dicuntur, facti sunt', p. 59).

Already in his first book Heerkens had generalized that 'when [learned] Italians are good, they are better and wiser than any men I have ever seen' (p. 48). He finds erudite Neapolitans, in particular – when they are not chasing or litigating court cases – the most wise, lovable and hospitable of men (Book 3, p. 55).[24] They do not, however, escape his affectionately exaggerated caricature in the *Italica*. With the exception of the industrious Duke of Noja, southern intellectuals 'languish' ('marcessere') in bed until 'late in the day' ('alta dies'): 'If someone were to raise themselves up onto an elbow, it was a big deal, something that made an impression and was remembered. But many of them

---

could win empires for her in secret, and she made vast empires for the righteous, and she tarried a while for the righteous in the Dutch and Scottish worlds' ('Serva magis post Roma, edoctaque, litore in arcto / Clam pia Libertas quod sibi regna daret, / Vasta piis fecit sua regna, piisque Batavo, / Inque Caledonio praestitit orbe moram', *Italica* (1793), p. 146).

[20] Vonck's role in promoting van Lynden's name in Italy through his publishing ventures is noted in Heerkens's third letter to the latter (*Italica* (1793), p. 164).

[21] And vice versa: Tanucci is a more shadowy figure in the *Notabilia*. Cf. above, Chapter 3, p. 119, n. 39.

[22] Unlike Passionei, however, Castruccio seems to have been a favourite with the Jesuits, if that is how we are to read: 'he was popular in the colleges, into many of which he introduced me; and when he spoke, he turned all eyes and ears toward himself' (p. 56). It was in any case a Jesuit, fellow historian, Giulio Cesare Cordara, who mollified the Sardinian envoy (sc. Tanucci) who had bad-mouthed Buonamici at the Papal court for insulting the king of Savoy. Cf. Introduction, p. 22, n. 72.

[23] This was Maria Maddalena Morelli, herself an improviser. See Elisabetta Graziosi, 'Revisiting Arcadia: Women and Academies in Eighteenth Century Italy', in Paula Findlen, Wendy Wassyng Roworth and Catherine M. Sama (eds), *Italy's Eighteenth Century: Gender and Culture in the Age of the Grand Tour* (Stanford: Stanford University Press, 2009), pp. 103–24, at pp. 121–2.

[24] Cf. *Italica* (1793), where Heerkens tells Engelhard that, 'as a learned man you love learned men, and I shall attempt to describe the ones I saw, those who, to be sure, merit first place in number and quality. And they are moderately renowned in both your and my fields – but how well their fame will endure, only time will tell' ('Doctos doctus amas, visosque ostendere coner, / Quos certe, ut numerus, primus et ordo decet. / Suntque satis celebres, studiisque tuisque, meisque: / Sed, sua quam perstet fama, futura sciet', p. 180).

have a reader sitting by, bought for a copper, and the master feasts, each day, for one copper. Food is so cheap, and the food is so healthy, that each thereby increases its own number of the lazy' ('Si quis et in cubitum corpus sustolleret, ingens, / Quaeque animum afficeret, res, memorantis erat. / Pluribus assedit lector tamen, asse coemptus, / Datque dies epulas unius assis hero', *Italica* (1793), p. 181). Heerkens seems to imply that Castruccio's straight-talking Sallustian style and tolerance of free banter bloomed on his liberal Lucchese roots. If asked for his medical opinion, he may well have attributed his lay-a-bed friend's alternate timorousness and touchiness to the influence of the Neapolitan climate.

## Airs, waters, places: Case notes on the common people

If Heerkens laments the general dishonesty of the Italian populace (especially in the Papal States) there are significant exceptions to his contempt.[25] His final comment on the Venetians is, it is true, a watery compliment at best: 'That I may conclude my discourse on a note of high praise, the Venetians have a reputation in Italy for probity and candour – which virtues in the other Italians, especially the southerners, who are men of quick wit, do not please, to be sure, so much as a certain admirable cleverness' (Book 1, p. 15). But Heerkens writes almost romantically about the modern-day Romans, that they are proud, fierce and public-spirited, just like their ancient ancestors. Indeed, they compare favourably with the Dutch in their reverence for their own heritage:

> The common people back home seem more fierce, intemperate and rough than the plebs of Rome. So many gardens, villas and temple porches crammed with numerous statues lie open at Rome – yet none of these monuments suffers any injury. Many of the statues are naked: there are many Venuses and many Priapuses among them, but they are not defaced, nor are they subject to the lechery of the mob. And what if similar objects were placed before the eyes of our people? They wouldn't last a year, not a month! That's for sure, since the one public statue of Erasmus to be found in our cities, in Rotterdam, is molested, and forever endures on its toga stones, mud and the

---

[25] Heerkens warns us especially against money-changers, toll-collectors, coachmen and innkeepers.

assaults of the people. The people of Rome are much more self-disciplined, and if it were not the case and had not always been so, how is it that so many of the ancient marble statues have hands, noses and fingers? (Book 1, pp. 88–9)[26]

The true flame of the Roman character burns most brightly, Heerkens confirms, in the Trastevere district, and he describes the engaging pomp with which even its poorest citizens dress and process in the streets on holidays, girt with swords, and preceded by their own sons as if by Roman lictors. They honour the memory of their ancestors and retell fabulous tales of the deeds of the ancient Romans which even the most superstitious Christian would not credit of the saints.

As a good humanist physician, Heerkens ascribes the persistence of these putatively Roman character traits to the influence of the air. Enlightened physician that he is, he makes the climatic explanation primarily with reference to Montesquieu,[27] but also finds good classical precedent in Livy, who had celebrated the invigorating properties of the Roman air in many passages. If, as Heerkens claims, the Calabrians, Neapolitans and the inhabitants of Fondi and Cuma, are 'as women' by comparison with the Romans, and if the Swiss and Scots residents in the southern cities are similarly enervated, shouldn't the virile vapours of Rome, by rights, have the reverse, masculinizing effect on her long-term residents? But the city's good influence was not, it seems, so quickly felt by the *peregrina plebs*; Heerkens evinces an unrelenting contempt for the vagrant riff-raff which, under the guise of religious pilgrimage, pours into the city from the furthest regions of Europe – including his own! – and camps in the Borgo.[28]

\* \* \*

---

[26] Indeed, he imputes to the Italians generally a fascination for their past, and applauds the practice, widespread even among the 'most unlearned', of decorating their houses with the 'trinkets of antiquity' ('vetustatis xenia') (Book 3, p. 89), a practice which the returning tourist will emulate in his own country house (*Italica* (1793), p. 83, and n. 6: 'Vestibuli muris insertaque prisca videbit'). The modern Romans are claimed to have a particularly solicitous concern for their ancient monuments – an attitude that perhaps would not have been shared by many of his Italian contemporaries (a contention I hope to explore separately with Maurizio Campanelli).
[27] 'Whoever knows the ancient Romans from history and from their writings will be amazed that the citizens of this city, having suffered so many wars and such vicissitudes of fortune, having been so many times changed and mixed with foreign dregs, have preserved in their customs, rites and in their very characters, something from which they can be recognised as the most ancient of Romans. That the climate and environment shapes men and their customs and laws, as Montesquieu has recently taught, you will surely understand from Rome, if from nowhere else' (Book 2, p. 94).
[28] Heerkens uses the phrase *conchis imbricatis obsitum* ('tiled with shells'), recalling Erasmus's colloquy on a pilgrim to Compostela, 'Peregrinatio religionis ergo'.

The peasants of Southern Italy are subjected to more thoroughgoing, almost natural-historical, scrutiny than even the Romans. Heerkens devotes several pages in his third book to the physiology, temperament and costume of the Campanian peasants who crowd the city of Naples:

> The common people of this city are innumerable and of a much greater quantity than necessary. Few are born in town, but they flow down rather from the Lucanian and Calabrian mountains completely destitute, almost completely naked. The Neapolitans call them 'Lazaroni' because they appear as Lazarus resurrected from the dead. An outer tunic of coarse linen, boots of a blue colour and a red felt cap are their first purchases; nor do they don any other clothing during the entire course of their life. The foot even into advanced old age is bare, without covering. All these men have a wild expression, the eyes very alert, the neck squat, the body muscular, and since they are different in appearance and in their whole bearing from other Italians, they appear to some to betray a Greek origin. But I believe it is the climate and the nature of the mountains where they were raised, their harsh way of life, and the labour of their parents that gave them that physical constitution.... It's without doubt sufficient to prove that the Neapolitan mob arose from Calabrian grandparents and great-grandparents that the Romans and Tuscans are as unlike them as the sons of the Dutch born in India seem to our people. Is it not the case that one Indian generation seems to have wiped out all appearance of Dutch blood? (Book 3, pp. 51–2)[29]

The citizens of Naples also exhibit a baffling – to our phlegmatic Dutchman – emotionality:

> You will see them arguing in the streets at every step, and arguing so furiously that at any moment you might expect bloodshed or a battle. But nothing that bad ever happens. With great gestures and blazing looks they set hands to hands, heads to heads – but they don't strike one another, and after the most terrifying rows, when their anger is all sweated out, they part in the best of spirits. Nor does one hear of frequent murders in Naples, for they do not come

---

[29] Naples' Campanian peasants may not owe their stocky physiques directly to Greece, but those ancient genes are carried, Heerkens opines, in her distinctive domestic architecture: 'There is no-one to whom Naples does not seem distinguished among the well-built cities of Europe. I doubt there are more buildings, raised to such a height, to be seen anywhere else. A fifth and sixth floor is common, and a seventh is found in not a few. Nor perhaps should it be called a storey ('contignatio') so much as a vaulting ('fornicatio'). An arch is built on top of another arch, and so on up to the roof, which is flat on all the buildings and shared by all the families living on the different floors of those buildings. At dusk nearly all the tenants meet on the roof, which is not surrounded by any

to blows except with those who are their kin, or known to them. They see with remarkably sharp insight that it is dangerous to fight with just anyone, and if one of them is bolder and, in the hope of a fat profit, gets into an argument with a foreigner or stranger so that a fight, or the threat of a fight, ensues, the most intense dispute will die down immediately, and the same man can seem in the same moment tiger and lamb. (Book 3, pp. 69–70)

Where the spirits of the thief from Fondi were simply 'enfeebled' by the ill winds blowing up from Calabria, the Neapolitan spirit of self-preservation identified here seems to command a grudging respect from our author. Rather than indicating a craven pusillanimity, is it perhaps the last gasp of an ancient *cultus* which, as in Rome, breathes through noble and commoner alike?

> These men are marvellously born for the appreciation of pleasure, since they understand its sweetness and consider it foolish to put in danger a life made for everyday delights. And that prudence seems to come to the aid of these men in their anger so that they are always able to temper it with reason. And we might add that their more vigorous enjoyment of pleasure weakens their nerve. . . . Two Neapolitan rowers from the Pompeian coast had conveyed me [to Capri] with the help of a light sail, and since the waning day had not yet shown me all that was to be seen on the island, I asked them to postpone our return journey until the following day so that I could see the sites more easily. But after I had shown them that, with the promised tip, they could live it up at an inn, they swore that they would spend the night very badly, as there was no girl there – and they were going to enjoy a very pretty one back in Naples. And I was thus unable to prevail on them not to bring me home the same day by rousing their hopes of reward. And something not heard almost anywhere else, the common people prattling ('ut argutetur') about the enjoyments of life and the use of pleasure, you may hear in Naples if you happen to have a conversation with a coach-driver or a rower. And the philosophising about these things is so frequent and earnest it is as though everyone had learned something from the precepts of Aristippus [sc. the Cyrenaic]. (Book 3, p. 71)

---

fence. But custom ensures that no-one's eyes are affected by the dark; and while they are chatting, or the mothers and fathers of the families are enjoying the magnificent panorama, you will see boys playing about in that perilous space as if it were on the ground. Nor is any sad experience recounted to them to forbid that carefree behaviour. In other cities of Italy there are no flat roofs on the buildings, nor were there in Rome in antiquity, but from Greece, its founders – where from the time of Homer to this very day it is practised and common – Naples has taken and retains this building custom' (Book 3, pp. 122–3).

## Pagan presences and Gothic superstitions

The foregoing reference to the precepts of Aristippus is, no doubt, somewhat arch, but Heerkens is earnest and diligent in his quest for survivals of ancient culture in contemporary Italy, both psychological and material. At Priverno, in Lazio, for example, he is delighted to be approached by boys selling milk in woven baskets, just as they had in Tibullus' day (Book 3, p. 20; cf. *Eleg.* 2. 3. 15). But local colour and authentic souvenirs aside, just how tolerant was our enlightened humanist when it came to the persistence of certain aspects of pagan religion?

A fascinating ethnographical description is given of the maritime rituals of the fisherman of Posillipo, as reported to the author by Castruccio Buonamici (Book 3, pp. 61–2). When one of their number dies at home he is taken to have his feet bathed in the sea before burial. The corpse is followed by a large group of women, their hair loose and oiled, which they tear and toss into the grave, each according to her degree of proximity to the deceased. Then, holding hands, they leap around the grave 'weeping, or as if weeping' ('flentes aut flentibus similes'). Such rites are held not just for the dead, however. When winter sets in, on a fixed day, the fishermen and their families rush down to the sea to splash themselves in the icy brine. Even the very elderly are not spared: 'Old men are dragged down to the water, if there are any who are unwilling to participate. And it is believed that the sea is placated by this custom, in this way: that by the right which the waves have over the fishermen, they will abate, and the winter fishing will be much safer.'[30] There is nothing supercilious or even disapproving in Heerkens's account of this picturesque but essentially pagan ceremony.

Some superstitions, however, are deemed to be 'very stupid', such as the 'insane' belief 'found today not only among the common people, but even among men of some education', that the Roman ruins are inhabited by demons, installed there by the invading Goths to guard the treasure they could not carry off until such time as they should return; and that these demons were hostile only to Italians, not to those whom they took to be of their own race (Book 2, pp. 164–5). Bernard de Montfaucon (1655–1741) had attempted in vain to

---

[30] 'Neque ultimae senectuti licet, huic solemnitati abesse. Protrahuntur ad aquam senes, si qui socii esse non velint. Crediturque mare placari ea consuetudine sic, ut de jure, quod in piscatores habent, remittant undae, & hiberna piscatio multo securior fiat' (p. 67).

dissuade the Italians from this inveterate opinion, which continued to cause northern travellers much inconvenience and indeed physical danger from hostile locals.[31] And yet, as we have seen, the light of human reason is not the exclusive privilege of the educated. On one of his early morning walks around Rome, Heerkens was exploring the 'Arch of Janus' (in the Forum Boarium) and poked his finger into a crack to gauge the thickness of the marble sheets with which it was clad. A 'common old lady' ('plebeia anus') appeared at his side and, 'with an ironic smile' ('ironico risu'), told him that 'behind this bull there used to be a treasure, but it is not there anymore' ('Dietro questo toro stava un tesoro, ma non è più'). Heerkens and the old crone have a good laugh, he learns that she is a Sabine, he gives her some money, and she goes off 'to the church to seek her treasure in heaven' (Book 2, pp. 165–6).

An almost homeopathic tincture of irony suffuses Heerkens's account of the miracle of San Gennaro (liquefying of the blood) which he witnessed in Naples on 3 May in the company of the son of the Duke of Noja. He is astonished not so much at the miracle itself, but at the fervent piety of the *lazzaroni* who throng the Cathedral and can hardly be restrained from stampeding the *taberna*[32] by the armed guard which surrounds it. At the moment at which the miracle is declared to have occurred by the ringing of a bell, they surge forwards: 'I saw many breasts slashed and bloody from the spears [of the guards], but I think I shall never in my whole life lose sight of them, in my mind's eye, their hands clasped in prayer, their ardent gaze transfixed on the ampoule' (Book 3, pp. 124–5). If Heerkens was moved spiritually by this experience, he does not let on. In the next sentence he remembers asking his escort whether they might hope for another miracle to escape the crush! The miracle is said to preserve the citizens of Naples against the flames of Vesuvius; it last extinguished them in 1470, 'at least, that's what the pious believe' ('ut saltem piè creditur'). Jesuit-trained he might be, but Heerkens barely suppresses a smile at a purple account of the flames of Diocletian's furnace bowing down before Saint Januarius: 'You would

---

[31] He returns to this theme in the third book (pp. 117–19), and reports on his visit to an old man at Ocriculi (in Umbria) who had broken open a column in front of his house because everybody believed there was treasure inside. Heerkens suggested that there might yet be treasure in the ruins with which his house was decorated: '*Dio mi guarda!* He said that I was a foreigner and probably unaware that the Goths had placed a curse on such ruins and installed demons who would suffocate those who were greedy and lusted after treasures, and that this had often happened, and through the sad experience of many was known to all' (p. 119). Even in Venice, the custodian of a monastery library had wished Heerkens sincere good luck in finding treasure on his journey south.

[32] Apparently some sort of temporary structure erected outside the cathedral.

think it was a holy preacher talking, but it is the Jesuit, Recupito, in an historical work about the eruptions of Vesuvius!' (Book 3, p. 126).[33] While anti-volcanic properties are imputed to the blood of San Gennaro alone, Heerkens points out that miraculous liquefactions of blood are also conceded in Naples to Saints Stephen, Pantaleon, Patricia, Vitus and John the Baptist, and of milk, to the Virgin Mary: 'For, after the miracle of Saint Januarius created such fame for its church and such a rush of pious men, this sort of miracle seemed necessary for the other churches, and through the prayers of the priests who were in charge of those churches it is said to have been accomplished' (pp. 126–7). The 'seemeds' and 'said-tos' of Heerkens's narrative may indeed betray an enlightened scepticism with regard to these beliefs, but we must always bear in mind his audience.[34]

Our Dutch Catholic indulges, for example, even applauds, the wisdom of the early Church in assimilating pagan cults in the churches of its Christian saints. He may well be pre-emptively admonishing the more iconoclastically inclined of his Calvinist countrymen to keep an open mind, to show due respect for local beliefs when travelling in the heartland of Roman Catholicism:

> It's wrong for Christians who practise different rites ('diversis sacris dediti') to blame this kind of tolerance. They are wrong to mock at the retention of some pagan ceremonies among the rites of the Church. Is anything corrupt or wrong, then, because, whatever it is, the pagans happened to like it? The pagans liked to make sacrifices in a white toga. Is it sacrilege for our priests to wear that colour in front of the altar? Those who want their brothers to change their outward appearance, or clothes, waste their days, years and life – to be frank, they actually have too little thought for the souls of those men. (Book 2, pp. 102–3)[35]

A compatriot who accompanied Heerkens on a visit to the catacombs must have been a Grand Tourist of sorts, but he was hardly a pilgrim. The foolish young man was emboldened to attempt to open a sarcophagus, thereby

---

[33] *De Vesuviano incendio nuntius* (Naples, 1632); Heerkens cites from the third Louvain edition of 1639.

[34] The sincerity of Heerkens's piety may be gauged from a passage in the *Iter Venetum*. Descending the Zirler Berg alone, by foot, by means of a perilously steep and narrow track, and cursing his coach driver who had suggested the shortcut, Heerkens suddenly catches sight of the cross to which he must orient himself and falls to his knees, regretting his intemperate anger, forgiving the driver and vowing to himself to reward him with an increase in pay. At this point the poet feels the guiding presence of his father, who had died a year before to the day, and resolves to complete the journey on his knees, keeping his eyes fixed only on the path (*Italica* (1793), pp. 52–3).

[35] See *Notabilia*, Book 2, pp. 99–107, for the whole fascinating discussion.

endangering his companions' lives when the outraged monks extinguished their candles (Book 1, pp. 85–6). The Dutch vandal had conceived his wicked plan, according to Heerkens, from a reading of the misleading (in all senses) Keysler, who had boasted about carrying off just such an exploit during his own Italian journey.[36]

## Setting the record straight

Perhaps the favourite pastime of our down-to-earth Dutchman, however, might be characterized as 'myth-busting'. We have already had a taster of his disdain for sensationalist writers such as Keysler and Misson.[37] In the first book of the *Notabilia*, the long section on Venice is in effect an exposé of the Doge's new clothes: 'I know that it is celebrated in writings, and put about by travellers everywhere throughout Europe, that Venice is the homeland of delights, and that at the time of the Saturnalia [sc. Carnevale], it is a paradise on earth' (p. 10). It will seem a great paradox that the cheery Heerkens, who professes himself 'not born to gloom and quarrels', found nothing delightful in Venice after a sojourn of three whole months! He believes, though, that he has discovered the reason for the city's exaggerated reputation. Most of these eulogies are centuries old, and most come out of Germany – from a time when the latter was especially uncultivated and the Venetians were flourishing over all other Italian cities. The extent of Venice's wealth became known through documents at the time of the war and treaty of Cambrai. In Regensburg in 1510, in order to stir up the Germans, the French ambassador, Louis Hélian, fulminated against Venetian luxury:

> Luxury, the parent of the arts, of pleasure, of games; all things which are most pleasing to young men. From that time and ever since it became the custom for Germans to send their noble youth to Venice – who, since they had seen nothing of the sort at home, were easily impressed. The great-grandchildren follow their forebears, and they have not ceased to praise what they have heard from them. And so a legend was born which is easier to confirm than to destroy or attack: especially since educated men, frequenting the Venetian

---

[36] Cf. the letter to Fagel, where he exhorts his young friend: 'A decent respectfulness is always useful in the churches, so that a voice reprimanding the foreigner does not issue forth.' ('Expedit usque decens templis reverentia, templis / Quo minus, externum vox monitura, venit', *Italica* (1793), p. 194).

[37] Misson is scolded for his casual underestimation, based on a thirty-minute perusal, of the extent of the Elector's library in Munich (*Italica* (1793), pp. 48–9).

holidays for a few days, as if a show, have not denied that it is an absolutely singular and must-see event. (Book 1, pp. 10–11)

Again, contrary to popular belief, Italian men are not especially jealous. And Heerkens vigorously contests the (disingenuous?) report of British surgeon and letter-writer from Italy, Samuel Sharp (†1778), that Italians in general, and Neapolitans in particular, are unmusical. While Sharp had not heard any noble Neapolitan lady singing at dinner, 'can anyone, indeed, conceive that those reasons are sufficient – that some thousand musicians, performing music of every kind in all the streets of Naples, were not only not heard by Sharp, but even made themselves invisible to him?' Heerkens sneers: 'It is a deceitful thing, one that boggles belief, to want to contrive something new; and for those admiring paradoxes the truth doesn't even appear obliquely' ('Insidiosa et vincens judicium res est, velle aliquid novum adstruere, et paradoxa admirantibus veritas ne a latere quidem apparet', Book 3, p. 49).

Most interesting, though, is Heerkens's vocal appreciation of the merits of the ancient Italians vis-à-vis the modern French, whom he seems to enjoy bringing down a peg or two. His friend Voltaire had vaunted the superiority of French roads:

> Voltaire, in his *Siècle de Louis XIV*, had the nerve to write that the roads of the French kingdom surpassed those of the Romans in elegance, but not in solidity – as if in works of that nature solidity were not more important than elegance! But the Roman roads far surpassed the French ones even in splendour! In the French roads the stones are the same and set together in the same way as those you see in our Dutch cities. So anyone will understand how often some of the hard stones laid in sand subside under the weight of coach wheels, not only spoiling the appearance but also the surface and utility of those roads. Not even then, when the French roads were new and well preserved did their surface, made level out of rough stones, have the smoothness of the Roman roads, which are like the most polished pavement. And how great and how eternal is their durability! (Book 3, pp. 20–1)

*À propos* French ignorance of Roman roads, in the verse letter to van Lynden about his journey to Naples, Heerkens spits bile at his old foe, d'Alembert, for having scoffed, in a dissertation which 'he had read some years ago in Paris, in front of me and others', that Horace 'had said almost nothing memorable in his account of the journey to Brindisi unless – he said – you consider memorable the fact that he, a young man, had been fatigued by a journey of five leagues'.[38] But Heerkens had now experienced first-hand the rigours of that passage, which had cost him seven long hours by coach. On his return journey from Italy he stopped in Paris, where he read his as yet unpublished poem to a select group of friends, including Charles Le Beau, perpetual secretary of the Academy of Inscriptions. D'Alembert got wind of the fact that he had been criticized both for his ignorance of geography and his tin ear to Horace's recherché joke about the 'city of the Mamurras', a joke which required, according to Heerkens, 'some knowledge of the ancient writers, and one that would have been fitting for a fellow of so many academies'. The disgruntled *philosophe* urged the upstart poet not to quarrel with a fellow member of the Academy, and promised for his part to strike out the disobliging things he had said in his dissertation about modern Latin poets and about Horace. But it appears that d'Alembert honoured only half of the bargain, and Heerkens decided against altering his own text.

More surprising, in the *Notabilia*, are Heerkens's snide remarks about the venerable Fontenelle – a figure revered by the poet of the *De valetudine literatorum* where he is set on an equal footing with Ovid as a model of scholarly equanimity. In listing the fine distinctions of duties recorded in the tomb of the slaves of Augustus and Livia, which had been discovered just beyond the Porta Capena, Heerkens reports that:

> Bernard de Fontenelle, a very famous man and an antiquary of the Paris Academy, behaved unadvisedly, not to say stupidly, in mocking Antiquity for having an office of 'wool-weigher'. If only Fontenelle, who was very clever, eloquent and knowledgeable about many things, were a more diligent and insightful student of the writings of the ancients! Then he would not have sullied his own writings with so many false judgements about Antiquity, which are certainly more fit to be ridiculed in a man like that than Greek and Latin Antiquity are by him. So what about the 'wool-weigher'? Different strokes for different folks. Does the learned gentleman demand that the customs of all countries and all times be like those of Paris? . . . Fontenelle sees no use in the inscriptions in the sepulchre apart from the fact that they appear to be in good Latin. But don't they additionally demonstrate something about the customs of ancient times, about the Roman household, about the luxury and magnificence of those

---

[38] *Italica* (1793), p. 144.

times? ... And finally, doesn't it appear from those inscriptions alone that the delights and comforts of life were born well before the last century in France, which is when Fontenelle and his colleague Perrault imagine they came to be? (Book 2, pp. 177–8)

It is not just the French, of course, whose cultural blind spots render them incapable of seeing others in anything but their own image. Heerkens is amused, for example, when an amiable, beslippered aristocratic gentleman of Capua is unashamed to reveal that he has no notion of the whereabouts of the United Provinces (Book 3, pp. 40–1). And on the road to Naples, Heerkens's Italian travelling companions, by no means unlearned men, are incredulous when:

I swore to them that we [in the United Provinces] had no *castrati*, that no man was emasculated, that we would fear an uprising of our women! He [an old lawyer] retorted that we would buy that merchandise from elsewhere and sell it on at an enormous profit. The lawyer won, and it seemed incredible to his companions that a people not entirely savage could live without *castrati*, that we could wish our music to lack that sweetness. (Book 3, pp. 46–7)

## Scarcely noted?

Heerkens was apparently drawn more to the study of Roman domestic architecture and to the harvesting of useful inscriptions than to rapturous reviews of the big-ticket ancient sites.[39] The owner, moreover, of an original Titian portrait of Ariosto,[40] writes almost nothing in his travelogue about Renaissance and baroque Italian art. He does, it is true, commend ancient and modern Italian mosaic work, but with an eye more to its technological than to its artistic merits.[41] He offers his opinion of contemporary painters at Rome (Book 2, pp. 112–22), from Piranesi to the learned Laurent Pécheux (1729–1821), a sort of eighteenth-century Poussin manqué, who had been passed over

---

[39] In the first book (pp. 82–3) he passes straight from, as it were, human monuments to contemporary building techniques, suggesting that Dutch builders and masons should travel to Italy to glean some know-how, just as painters' sons used to in the previous century.
[40] So he tells us in *Notabilia*, Book 1, p. 17.
[41] In fact he passes a negative judgement on the mosaics at Praeneste/Palestrina, essentially for their lack of verisimilitude in the depiction of food on the floor pavement (Book 2, pp. 113–15).

for a scholarship at the French School and had, says Heerkens, helped him to understand painting better.[42] Catholic though he was, Heerkens seems rarely to have set foot inside a church during his travels in Italy – or, at least, any such visits did not seem to merit recording. Most curious, perhaps, is the relative absence of discussion in the *Notabilia* of contemporary topics in medicine, botany and natural history, aside from some early passages on diet, wine and on the rarity of birdlife in the Roman countryside. When later in the preface to his *Aves Frisicae* Heerkens described his approach in those 'four books on the right way to undertake a journey to Italy' as 'wholly antiquarian' ('antiquarius totus') he stated a curious truth. After all, we might have expected something a little more 'scientific' from our travelling physician, if only because the second two books were dedicated to the new Flushing scientific academy (Zeeuwsch Genootschap der Wetenschappen te Vlissingen).

But while Heerkens's eye is certainly humanistic – it is trained on topics in history, archaeology, literature and language[43] – he seems also to be making a concerted effort in the *Notabilia* to notice *new* and different things, everywhere eschewing the obvious.[44] And despite his censure of Sharp's and others' exaggerated or false claims, he is not averse to spicing up his narrative with a few choice curiosities: an inscription in a chapel in Venice commemorating a Veronese prostitute, testifying to her beauty and wealth – and if that weren't 'notable' enough, her insignia hang over the altar in the form of three testicles (Book 2, p. 124); a digression on the exotic Maronite Christian community in Rome (Book 1, pp. 67–8); his observation in the Kircherian museum at the Roman College of 'ancient seals, with which inscriptions and titles and whole epigrams were printed in various ways'. These objects put Heerkens's Jesuit guide, Contuccio Contucci, at a loss to explain how the ancients, from such beginnings, could not have discovered printing. The Dutchman's response is telling:

> The reason for this has been explained by one of our countrymen. That most august man, G. Meerman, who is Mayor, sharing Grotius' glory, of

---

[42] Sylvain Laveissière (ed.), *Un peintre français dans l'Italie des Lumières* (Milan: Silvana Editoriale, 2012).

[43] He commends to his addressee the sonority of the Italian language as spoken by Romans: 'it is by far the most useful of modern languages, and knowledge of it will help your Latin; the origins of which, partly to be sought in the German language, the footprints made by our ancestors in Lazio will indicate, not without shedding great light on ancient things [?]' (Book 1, p. 25).

[44] Marie-Noëlle Bourguet has suggested to me that Heerkens may even have been setting out to write an *anti*-Grand Tour. I am not convinced he was trying to be so controversial, but it is true that he (explicitly) makes a virtue out of *not* repeating that which the traveller can glean elsewhere.

the city of Rotterdam, teaches in his work on the 'Origins of Typography' that the ancients did not know that kind of ink which doesn't flow, which is composed from oil. Before the age of Coster, the Van Eick brothers, Flemish painters, had mixed oil into their colours. That invention, Meerman showed, assisted Coster, and it was the only thing that prevented the ancients from inventing printing. (Book 1, p. 65)

In the roll of subscriptions to Heerkens's work we might note that Meerman's name is down for 15 copies.

## A Dutchman 'downunder'

Heerkens's narrative in the *Notabilia* assumes an ideal and, I would argue, ideally *Dutch* audience. He was disgusted, for example, to observe on a bridge in Genoa, erected by some nobleman or other, an inscription in capital letters gloating that he had been disinherited by his father but that his fortune had been restored by God. This breach of filial piety evidently went against the Dutch grain, and Heerkens and his companions sent their horses across the stream to avoid using that impious and stupid structure (Book 4, p. 195). This in spite of the fact that 'we are among those . . . who believe that free states are happier and more enduring to the extent that they allow privileges to the aristocracy'. Who is this 'we'?

'Gerard Heerkens the Kleinemeerian', as he pointedly styles himself on the title-page of the first instalment of his travelogue, can hardly have anticipated that his Italian reminiscences would be read and enjoyed 200 years on by an Australian female neo-Latinist. But neither, perhaps, did he anticipate that his *prima facie* open Latin letter would find readers in Italy, France and further afield. Indeed, the constitution of the work's original target audience may be gleaned from the subscription table printed at the head of the second volume, listing the 'names of patrons, of the friends and learned men for which/by which ('quibus') this work was published'. Six pages of almost exclusively Dutch names confirm, I suggest, that Heerkens was writing here primarily for the *Dutch* province of the eighteenth-century Republic of Latin letters.

Thus, while it is a *Latin* voice that speaks, it speaks from an identifiably Dutch standpoint; it speaks primarily to a Dutch audience, indeed, to an audience of fellows of the Flushing Academy.[45] That is not to say that it is a chauvinistic voice. As we have seen, Heerkens believes that his countrymen have much to learn from both ancient and modern Italy. He would hardly have objected to his Italian, if not French friends, 'overhearing' this frank conversation with his learned compatriots. But I suspect that the deep-seated hope of our roving Dutch Ovid, who had put himself beyond the pale with those naughty satirical poems, who had been seduced by Parisian *politesse*, and who had recently failed to impress as a journalist in his native language, was to get *home* with Latin; to be welcomed back in his own land as a productive and patriotic scholarly citizen.

Heerkens had marvelled in his first book at an Italian reverence for their literary celebrities:

> You will be amazed in Ferrara that the relics of the Este princes are less famous than those of its poet. The Ferrarese seem hardly to remember their princes, excellent as they were, and of whom there remains a great palace. But you will be invited by one and all to see the house of Ludovico Ariosto, his painted likeness, and his tomb, each in their several places; and boys in the street will impress this upon you. (Book 1, p. 16)

Thus the Romans' respect for their traditions and ancient monuments is paralleled in their enduring respect for literary culture – even for foreign writers. So much so that, when the ashes of the Scottish writer John Barclay, once held at the church of Sant' Onofrio on the Janiculum, were anathematized and tossed into the Tiber on papal orders, the resident priests rescued his statue and gave it a home in their domestic library. Even heretics, the priest-guide informed Heerkens, deserved sanctuary within a library of so learned a city (Book 2, pp. 135–6). Torquato Tasso spent his final days in a cell here, dying on the eve of his coronation in Rome as poet laureate. In return for a meagre and rather miscellaneous legacy – a few bad paintings, a piece of petrified wood – the priests of Sant' Onofrio erected a marble monument to him.[46] Heerkens was even invited to compose a new Latin inscription to adorn his cell.

---

[45] Klaas van Berkel, 'Science in the Service of the Enlightenment: 1700–1795', in Klaas van Berkel, Albert van Helden and Lodewijk Palm (eds), *A History of Science in the Netherlands: Survey, Themes and Reference* (Leiden: Brill, 1999), pp. 68–94. According to van Berkel, the Flushing Academy 'grew out of a reading circle in Vlissingen of which almost half the members were ministers and which had as its aim monthly discussions of French journals and learned works' (p. 86).

[46] Contrast the shameful vandalism of Philibert Prince of Orange who destroyed Sannazaro's villa at Mergillina (*Italica* (1793), p. 161, and n. 52).

'When I had learned in Italy how much a monument can adorn a city–state', he writes, 'I often wished, after I had returned home, that there might be in our people some share in that veneration with which the Italians honour the memory of their great men' (Book 2, p. 126). If Heerkens never persuaded the magistrates of Groningen to install statues of the town's humanists in the main square, he would indulge this newfound passion for civic commemoration in historical verse portraits of the governors, statesmen and birdlife of his homeland. It is to these minor monuments that we turn in the next chapter.

5

# Patriots in Portraits:
# From National to Natural History

## The purpose of history

In 1755 Heerkens published in Groningen an annotated edition of Einhard's 'Life of Charlemagne', dedicated, *prima facie*, to enlightened scholar-Pope Benedict XIV.[1] But celebratory verses to the history-loving Lambertini pontiff are followed by a long prose letter to Heerkens's aristocratic French friend, Jean-Jacques le Franc, Marquis de Pompignan, six years before the latter's debacle of a debut at the Académie française. Following Heerkens's original life of Einhard (again addressed to le Franc), with a list of earlier editions of that author, we come across a dedicatory elegy to the papal legate in Belgium, Giovanni Carlo Molinari. From this we glean that the volume was originally destined for Cardinal Angelo Maria Querini (1680–1755), recently deceased, whose friendly shade now commends it to his Muse-loving successor ('Umbra boni Tibi me commendet amica QUIRINI, / Ipsa in morte mei quem meminisse ferunt', p. 62). In lining up high-level contacts for his projected Italian Grand Tour – first stop Venice – Heerkens was presumably having a ducat each way!

The edition of the 'Life of Charlemagne' was the product of a long-standing passion for history dating back, according to Heerkens's letter to le Franc, to his early childhood:

> As a young boy my father used to tell and read me those famous Romance tales, and especially those which La Calprenède, your countryman, published last

[1] *Eginharti de Vita Caroli Magni Commentarius cum annotationibus* (Groningen, 1755).

century. I can remember nothing sweeter in my life than listening at that time to the speeches of the great-souled Juba or Artabanus. I was captivated by their words and courage when those bravest of heroes joined some battle or other. By Hercules I shivered, and rejoiced, and wept at times with as much emotion as a boy can muster. And from that moment on I loved history perhaps more passionately and earnestly than any other subject in the world of letters.[2]

Curiously, Heerkens suggests that this interest was foreign to his chosen field of medicine, although he has no regrets about the value he once placed on stories, and now on history: 'I believe that all our studies should be referred to the science of morals and life' ('Omnia nostra studia ad morum credo & ad vitae scientiam referenda esse', p. 8).[3]

Whatever his commitment to poetry, then, we must not underestimate our humanist physician's aspirations as an antiquarian[4] and, indeed, modern historian. As we saw in the last chapter, the letters Heerkens despatched to Cornelis Walraven Vonck in the lead-up to his Italian journey of 1759–60 are studded with references to the latter's editions of historical writers Guido Ferrari and Castruccio Buonamici. That journey was undertaken first and foremost as a pilgrimage to the land of Livy, but Italy was also, in the estimation of both Heerkens and Vonck, the land of *neo*-Latin historiographical best practice.[5]

---

[2] 'Puero infanti narrare mihi ac legere solebat Pater fabulas sub Romanensium titulo notissimas, illas praecipue, quas Calprenaeda popularis Tuus, priore saeculo edidit. Nihil mihi in vita memini tam dulce fuisse quam audire tum, magnanimum Jubam aut Artabanum loqui. Voce & animo captus eram, cum isti fortissimi heroes aliquod praelium committerent. Horrebam hercle, gaudebam & lachrumabar aliquando tanto affectu, quantus esse potest in puero. Exinde ardenter & impensius forte historiam quam quidquam aliud litterarum studium amavi', *Eginharti*, Letter to le Franc, pp. 7–8.

[3] See Nancy G. Siraisi, *History, Medicine, and the Traditions of Renaissance Learning* (Ann Arbor: University of Michigan Press, 2007); and Gianna Pomata and Nancy G. Siraisi (eds), *Historia: Empiricism and Erudition in Early Modern Europe* (Cambridge, MA: MIT Press, 2005) for the pursuit and uses of historical learning by an earlier generation of humanist physicians.

[4] Antiquarian material is strewn, unsurprisingly, throughout Heerkens's Italian works. In the preface to the *Aves Frisicae*, as noted in the previous chapter, he describes himself as having been a 'complete antiquarian' in the *Notabilia* (p. ix). But such material may also be collected from the *Aves Frisicae* itself (e.g. disquisition on the use of quill pens by the ancients, 'Anser', pp. 105–8, n. 2), from the medical epigrams (e.g. long first epigram and footnote on Roman antiquities in Groningen, *Empedocles* (1798), Book 4, pp. 114–15) and *De valetudine literatorum* (1790) (e.g. footnote on murrhine ware, p. 102, n. 64).

[5] In a prefatory letter to Basel juriconsult, Rudolph Iselius, at the front of his edition of Guido Ferrari's *De rebus gestis Eugenii Principis a Sabaudia in Bello Pannonico* ('On the deeds of Prince Eugene of Savoy in the Pannonian War') (The Hague, 1749), Vonck commends the Jesuit writer's pure Caesarean style. That commendation is further elaborated by Giulio Cesare Cordara, S. J., the young Ferrari's mentor, in a dedication to Cardinal Alessandro Albani. Vonck also praises Italian Latin writing in the preface to the first book of his edition of Castruccio Buonamici's *De bello Italico* ('Commentary on the Italian War') (Nijmegen, 1750). Significantly, this edition is dedicated to Angelo Maria Querini, paving the way for his Groningen friend's own overtures to the learned cardinal a couple of years later. Cf. Y. H. Rogge, 'Cornelis Walraven Vonck', *Oud Holland* 17 (1899), pp. 94–119, at pp. 104–5.

The letter to le Franc is a manifesto for an edifying and exemplary style of history writing which, in some respects, harks back to a pre-Machiavellian Renaissance. Heerkens begins by observing that not all times and nations are equally deserving of our scholarly notice. While the Greeks may have scorned, to their cost, to learn the lessons of Roman history – Alexander knew nothing of the impressive deeds of Horatius Coccles, Mucius Scaevola or Coriolanus – today we are afflicted with the opposite vice, excessive curiosity:

> Whatever you like in barbarian history is now too much revered and valued by civilised peoples. He who made a journey into the vast and trackless wilderness would not find anything worth writing about; but he who skims through the annals of an uncultivated and savage race encounters things which will also offend him: bloody, foul and unremitting crimes, unredeemed by any noble or brilliant deed.

In fact *all* history is to some extent horrible, but more through the fault of its writers than its actors. Heerkens commends the historian who, like Voltaire in the *Siècle de Louis XIV*, excuses men's faults and generally tries to show them in a good light. He takes aim at the modern 'apes of Tacitus' who exaggerate human failings for sensational effect.[6] Tacitus, an admirer of the Roman Republic, is unfairly censorious of the Julio-Claudians, whereas in fact Tiberius, Caligula and Nero have their redeeming qualities (!).[7] As for Otho, Heerkens can think of no more noble subject for a tragedy: where Corneille hadn't succeeded, the author of the 'Dido' (le Franc) may yet![8] The villains of a great culture such as Rome cannot help but evince some admirable traits: 'Thus, once a state is rightly established, especially if it has flourished for some time, it cannot be deflected suddenly from the habitual practice of the virtues' ('sic semel recte instituta

---

[6] The classic point of departure for early modern Tacitism is Richard Tuck, *Philosophy and Government 1572-1651* (Cambridge: Cambridge University Press, 1993); cf. Peter Burke, 'Tacitism, Scepticism, and Reason of State', in J. H. Burns (ed.), *The Cambridge History of Political Thought 1450-1700* (Cambridge: Cambridge University Press, 1991), chap. 16, pp. 479-98; Robert Bireley, *The Counter-Reformation Prince: Anti-Macchiavellianism or Catholic Statecraft in Early Modern Europe* (Chapel Hill: University of North Carolina Press, 1990); Jacob Soll, *Publishing the Prince: History, Reading, and the Birth of Political Criticism* (Ann Arbor: University of Michigan Press, 2005). See also the useful introductory matter to Jan Waszink's edition of Justus Lipsius's *Politica* (Assen: Van Gorcum, 2004).

[7] Is Heerkens trying to butter up the modern-day Romans whose hospitality he is hoping soon to enjoy? We have a better measure of his views on Tiberius, Ovid's nemesis, in the notes to his digression on the causes of Ovid's exile near the end of the *De valetudine literatorum* (1790). See below, p. 180.

[8] In fact Corneille had written a fine Tacitean drama, *Otho* (1664). Le Franc's *Dido* (1734) played 18 times at the Comédie française in its first year.

civitas, praesertim si aliquamdiu floruit, deflecti a virtutum consuetudine subito nequit'). Even Marius, 'born among our Cymbrian ancestors, a man of inhuman barbarity', was capable of demonstrating brotherly mercy to his enemy, Sulla, under the influence of Rome. In short, if you are born bad and live in a barbarian land you have no hope of becoming good; if you are raised in a civilized country you may at least improve.

In the same way, Heerkens contends, the historian cannot help but be improved by the intrinsic interest and grandeur of his subject matter. He accords Livy almost poet status for conveying sense through syntax, for example when he reveals agitated emotion in describing how the evil Tullia Minor, wife of Tarquinius Superbus, drove a chariot over the body of her murdered father, Servius: 'This consummate perfection of writing, which the rarest of poets achieve, is frequent in the narratives of Livy' ('Summa haec scriptionis perfectio, quam rarissimi poetae assequuntur, crebra in narrationibus Livii', p. 24). However, that ability is not merely a result of Livy's native genius or art, but is due to the outstanding material ('res praeclaras') with which the Roman historian was blessed to work. We are bound to write more movingly when we contemplate Coriolanus departing Rome and returning with an enemy army, to be repelled by his mother's tears, than 'he who has before his eyes the exiles and barbarous deeds of some cowardly king Chilperic or Childebrand or Childebert' (p. 25).

These sentiments are telling of Heerkens's relative lack of interest in the New World, Far East, or, for that matter, the margins of Western Europe – apart from his own, of course![9] What mattered for him, and not least for the rhetorical purposes of this volume, was *Roman* civilization, first in Italy, and then, as admired and imitated throughout the Empire:

> But he who considers that, when the seat of empire was exported to the conquered races, the Romans remained unchanged either by the oppression of the Caesars or the idleness of a gentler clime, that Citizens survived in Asia, he may rightly marvel at how much sway virtuous habits have among men, how much the memory of ancestral glory.[10]

---

[9] The catalogue of his library (*Catalogus bibliothecae: quam reliquit Gerardus Nicolaus Heerkens*; Groningen: Bolt, 1805) tells a slightly different story, with numerous books in Dutch, Latin and French, learned and popular, on the Middle East, Africa, East Asia, North America, etc. Suffice it to say that Heerkens never writes about non-European cultures.

[10] 'Sed translata apud victas gentes imperii sede, nec oppressione Caesarum, nec mollioris coeli ignavia mutatos esse Romanos, superfuisse in Asia Quirites, qui considerat, miretur sane quantum recta instituta & quantum gloriae avitae memoria apud homines valeant', *Eginharti*, Letter to le Franc, p. 18.

Heerkens's straining to extol everywhere 'what the Romans have done for us' sometimes results in an almost perverse blind-eye-turning. Appealing to the rule of France's 'incomparable jurisconsult, Montesquieu, who in his immortal work on the nature of laws, asserts that those peoples are the best who are able to be governed with the lightest of punishments', he claims that the Romans should be especially venerated for their lack of cruelty (!). So-called civilized nations today are in fact much more savage, since they love to gawk at the most atrocious punishments exacted in public ('adstare & inhiare, populusque concursu & frequentia', p. 23).

Our patriotic Dutchman suggests, moreover, that those who undertake the writing of national histories will be greatly aided by love of country ('multum & libenter scriptor suadet, ut proavos suos quam felicissime depingat', p. 26). Unfortunately, such a history has yet to be written in France because its early annals are so uninspiring. On the other hand, where Voltaire had dated the rise of French civilization from as late as the reign of François I, Heerkens is, in fact, more generous:

> I like the French under Charles VIII, after they returned to France; and I consider the times of Louis XII, such a good king, just as happy, memorable and worth knowing about; and French affairs also seem bright and admirable during the preceding two centuries, under the Crusader kings who fought to recover Judaea: whether that expedition gives pleasure *per se* because of its piety, or whether the events take on the character of a happier sky, and the barbarian heroes seem less barbarous as they clash with the Caesars of Greece. And then, the Caliphs form part of this history, those cultured Caliphs, outstandingly humane, who in every virtue (apart from piety and Religion), in mercy, learning and elegance of life, far surpassed the Princes on our side. (p. 27)

No doubt this backhanded compliment to the French should be read less as an Enlightenment gesture towards the Islamic 'Other' than as a shrewd attempt to flatter the main target audience of Heerkens's Einhard edition: the learned Italians he looked forward to meeting on his Grand Tour. And, as we saw in the previous chapter, the Latinate intellectuals of eighteenth-century Italy were, in the event, happy enough to embrace the obliging foreign doctor who tended, so gently, to that growing Gallic chip on their shoulder![11]

---

[11] Cf. Françoise Waquet, *Le modèle français et l'Italie savante: Conscience de soi et perception de l'autre dans la République des lettres (1660–1750)* (Rome: École Française de Rome, 1989).

The take-home message of Heerkens's letter to le Franc is that it is impossible to explore every corner of world history: priorities must be made. No doubt Scythia has produced some good citizens, but if they can point to their one Anacharsis,[12] who would not prefer to read the annals of the Athenians? Heerkens betrays an anxiety about the perceived demand – how well-founded by this date is moot – for a universal history accommodating all peoples and times.[13] Even if such a history were achievable, and even if the lives of its subjects were uniformly admirable and edifying, such diligence on the part of scholars would constitute a sort of intellectual gluttony. We *do* need examples to live by, but we should be content with a few choice ones, just as Epicurus drew more profit from observing the goings-on in his small garden community than the busy Athenians who spent long days in the agora, hungry for the latest news from Sparta and Thrace.

However, if our career Ovid exhorts us not to wander off in our historical and ethnographical studies to a metaphorical Thrace ('non evagemur in Thraciam', p. 30), he concedes that it may look as though he has done just that in writing the present work, which, after all, retails a series of less-than-inspirational events from an unlearned century in France's history. Somewhat inconsistently, Heerkens claims that he has undertaken the edition not for the sake of French history, not for the sake of Charlemagne, but for the sake of *Einhard*. An admirer of Plutarch and Suetonius for their lives of great men, he cites Pierre Bayle's invitation to modern authors to imitate Suetonius when composing histories of popes, emperors and kings. Surprisingly, no-one has ever risen to that challenge apart from Einhard, and as the first and relatively successful imitator of Suetonius he deserves our attention, as would the first competent imitator of Raphael in painting. And respect and attention Heerkens has certainly lavished upon his barbarian author, for whose sake, he tells us, he has been obliged to grapple with the writings of Rabanus Maurus, the monks from St Gall (Notker Balbulus) and Angoulême (Adémar de Chabannes)[14], and the Saxon poets – a burdensome task which he compares to making a journey

---

[12] A Scythian, perhaps proto-Cynic, philosopher who made his name in Athens as an outspoken 'barbarian' (Diogenes Laertius, *Lives of the Philosophers*, Book I, §§101–4). Heerkens is writing here before the publication of the imaginary journey through Greece of Anacharsis, Jr, by Jean-Jacques Barthélemy (*Voyage du jeune Anacharsis en Grèce dans le milieu du IVe siècle* (Paris, 1788)).

[13] Cf. Anthony Grafton, *Bring out Your Dead: The Past as Revelation* (Cambridge, MA: Harvard University Press, 2002), chap. 9, 'The World of the Polyhistors: Humanism and Encyclopedism', pp. 166–80.

[14] An eleventh-century monk and chronicler. My thanks to Professor Sarah Foot for this suggestion.

to Lapland from Italy, or from le Franc's precious Aquitaine! If this labour has not yielded great fruit, Heerkens trusts that he has at least done some service to the Republic of Letters in bringing together, in economical format, material that has hitherto lain neglected in fat volumes and dense commentaries. Pointedly, he remarks that while his own notes are 'not much abbreviated, nor cursory, they have the advantage of lacking that obscure diligence of critics who, in the cheap quest for variant readings, prefer to bury ('ponere') a work than to present it' (p. 33). Heerkens cocks a snook here at precisely the kind of close textual scholarship for which many of his own countrymen were justly famous. Good history, like good letter- and travel-writing, must not be pedantic. And as we will see in the next section, it must be *personal*.

## Speaking pictures

The first two *Icones* published by Heerkens in his eponymous collection of historical verse portraits[15] were, it happens, of men known to him personally. Charles-Louis-Auguste Fouquet, Duc de Belle-Isle (1684–1761), he had met on his first trip to Paris, dined with frequently and sumptuously during a winter sojourn in 1752–3, and ministered to medically in 1760.[16] Belle-Isle, Marshal of France, a veteran of the Wars of the Spanish, Polish and Austrian Successions, was the grandson of the notorious Nicolas Fouquet, disgraced Superintendent of France under Louis XIV. A passage in the third book of Heerkens's *De valetudine literatorum* (1790) commemorates Belle-Isle's careful parenting of his only son, the Duc de Guise, who was tragically killed in battle at the age of 26. And in the preface to that poem we learn that it was Belle-Isle who inspired Heerkens to embark, all those years ago, on a series of poetic portraits of the kings of France, from Charlemagne to present times.[17] None of those royal *icunculas* ever found their way into Heerkens's published *Icones*, a volume dedicated to Belle-Isle's friend and fellow war hero, Charles Eugène Gabriel de la Croix, marquis de Castries (1727–1801). Again, the *De valetudine*

---

[15] Utrecht, 1787; 'Paris', 1788. As Worp already observed, these are in fact the same edition.
[16] In a note in the second book of his *De valetudine literatorum*, Heerkens reports a conversation with Belle-Isle towards the end of 1760, and claims that he was then acting as the Duke's 'head physician' ('archiater') (1790, p. 88, n. 47).
[17] He claims there to have completed 30–40 verses on each king, but some 700 on Louis XI, presenting completely new material drawn from unpublished commentaries in the Duke's possession (1790, p. vii).

*literatorum* preface provides an indication as to why Heerkens decided not to publish, in 1787, the icons apparently so admired by his late father: the changing political climate seemed to render a work on the French monarchy unfashionable, to say the least. We should also note that 1787 was the year of the (anti-Stadtholder) 'Patriot' Revolution in the United Provinces.[18]

The five portraits Heerkens has assembled for his, as it were, late exhibition, were carefully chosen to complement Belle-Isle's.[19] He writes that he was prompted to publish the latter's long-intermitted icon after a disagreeable conversation in Amsterdam the previous year with two British scholars, who had perversely persisted in their negative judgement of Belle-Isle in the face of Heerkens's personal testimony to his honour (pp. viii–ix). Next to Belle-Isle's icon hangs that of Abraham van Hoey, Dutch ambassador to France from 1727 for two decades, who, not unlike Heerkens himself, had incurred the displeasure of his countrymen for getting too cosy with his foreign hosts.[20] Van Hoey, 'who had lived the best and most famous part of his life with Belle-Isle, and was among his friends and companions, seemed to demand to be joined to our hero, crying out from the grave' (p. x).[21]

The preface to the *Icones*, like so many of Heerkens's paratexts and indeed texts, is unabashedly autobiographical. The poet explains that he had first conceived the idea of composing 'icons of famous men' during his teenage years but that he was persuaded to write about famous *Dutch*men when

---

[18] Heerkens seems to have maintained friends on both sides of the political fence. Worp views his dealings with Patriots van der Cappellen, van der Steege and Hendrik Hooft as at least a faint trace of his true allegiances (p. 45). But another friend, Nicolaas Tenhove, was an ardent Orangist, having a hand in the publication of the pro-Stadtholder tract, *The Old-fashioned Dutch Patriot* (W. R. E. Velema, *Republicans: Essays on Eighteenth-Century Dutch Political Thought* (Leiden, Brill, 2007), p. 119). Heerkens preserves two letters to Tenhove in the second edition of his *Italica* (1793), pp. 78–96. In a letter to Johan Meerman of 30 July 1794, the down-at-heel Heerkens even entertains the possibility of writing the lives, 'little known', of the princes of Nassau who have governed Friesland and Groningen, 'if our good prince' (sc. the present Stadtholder) will only meet the shortfall from his suspended French annuities. Cf. Introduction, p. 30, and n. 95.

[19] The icon of Belle-Isle was apparently first composed some 25 years earlier (p. ix; p. 16).

[20] Van Hoey's reputation was subsequently rehabilitated when he supported a profitable neutrality for the United Provinces during the Seven Years War.

[21] In a final note to this portrait, Heerkens reports that he met van Hoey during the last five years of his life, at his country villa outside The Hague. The younger man was bearing a letter of salutation entrusted to him in 1761 by yet another general and French marshal, Gaspard Clermont de Tonnerre (1688–1781). He found the elderly but spry van Hoey promenading in his garden, oblivious to a chill wind; he received Heerkens cheerfully, and bustled him inside to compose a reply to Tonnerre's letter (p. 52, n. 21). On 8 June 1764 Heerkens addressed a highly laudatory elegiac letter to van Hoey (published in the *Journal des sçavans* (July 1764), pp. 524–6). He enjoyed conversations with the retired ambassador (and with Belle-Isle and Fontenelle) on the character of Cardinal de Fleury (*De valetudine literatorum* (1790), Book 3, p. 132).

he was in Italy, where he discovered that his learned friends were largely oblivious to the talents and memorable achievements of his countrymen (p. iii). He resolved there and then to send off a sample of poetic sketches of the most eminent candidates to Cardinal Domenico Silvio Passionei, subsequently Heerkens's chief patron in Rome. The cardinal was captivated by these poems, not least because he had himself spent some years in the United Provinces and had been present at the Peace of Utrecht, 'so to speak representing the Pope' ('tanquam res pontificis videns'). Passionei was apparently in the habit of reciting Heerkens's political *icunculas* to the assorted intellectuals who convened daily in his private library. He had urged the poet to compose more – especially of men known personally to *him*, Passionei! He had even indicated a potential subject in Antonius Heinsius, Grand Pensionary of Holland from 1689 until his death in 1720, whom Passionei had 'seen, known, engaged with' ('quem viderat, norat, accesserat', p. iv).

The pushy prelate's none-too-subtle encouragement precipitated a minor crisis in our poet, since Heerkens did not feel that Heinsius was intrinsically worthy of commemoration: 'as many words and phrases are inappropriate for correctly fashioned verses, only those things which are noble and which greatly move the cultivated soul should be expressed in them' ('ut multa vocabula & verba versibus recte factis inidonea sunt, per eos nullae nisi nobiles, & res animum cultum maxime moventes ostendendae sunt', p. v). However, as he was wandering in the region beyond the Ponte Milvio on one of his regular visits to the ruins, he chanced to find himself at the site of the gardens of Ovid, 'which had so often inspired that poet's writing' (p. v).[22] He recalls appealing 'to the *genius loci* for help with the work that had been commissioned'[23] and saw in a flash how he could fulfil the cardinal's mandate and salve his own historical conscience – he would record the deeds of Heinsius, 'but merely as an adjunct to the fate of his country, like an Automedon in Achilles' chariot'.

Whatever became of that half-hearted Heinsius – we are told that 200 verses were duly executed within a few days of this Ovidian epiphany – it was not one of the five icons selected by Heerkens for publication in the

---

[22] Cf. *Notabilia*, Book 2, pp. 168–73, for Heerkens's description of the site and scholarly speculations on the supposed sepulchre of Ovid's family discovered in 1674.
[23] Compare the vision of Scaliger during his archaeological ramble in Leiden, discussed in Chapter 2!

*Icones*.²⁴ Nor was a portrait of the good cardinal himself, which the latter had stipulated should be 'as long and free as possible' ('quam longissimam sui & liberrimam', p. vii) – but note, Passionei had taken it upon himself to prepare a dossier of suitable materials for inclusion.²⁵ For Heerkens's 1787 collection, 'four little works previously published, which had experienced no bad press and even some praise, were sought out and joined to the Belle-Isle' ('Fuerantque conquisita & jungenda Bellilio quatuor opuscula pridem edita, nullamque ut adversam famam, laudes etiam aliquas experta', p. x). Patriotism, he says, dictated that he incorporate an icon (the third) of William Louis, Count of Nassau-Dillenberg (1560–1620), Stadtholder of Friesland, Groningen and Drenthe, co-commander with his cousin Maurice of the Dutch States Army in its struggle against the Spanish. And to provide context for the more recent martial exploits of Belle-Isle and van Hoey, he decided to republish a synoptic 'Icon of our Century', ranging over the various international conflicts of the modern age as well as its most significant (to Heerkens) cultural developments.²⁶ This, then, was the fifth and final portrait in the 1787 collection – but what of the fourth?

So as not to dishonour the memory of Belle-Isle, Heerkens must, above all, avoid associating with him anything 'that could provoke envy or controversy' ('nihil videbatur sociandum, invidiam aut crisin quod excitaret', p. xi). The icon of the 'Governors and Kings by whatever title [sc. Stadtholders] of the United Provinces' might seem to have been liable to do just that, but it slips under the radar curiously unremarked in Heerkens's preface.²⁷ The opening verses of this fourth icon announce the Dutch muse's right to pass judgement on Dutch monarchs, if France and England are allowed to pass judgement on theirs. By

---

[24] For a succinct and not very flattering appraisal of Heinsius, cf. Heerkens's 'Icon on the Governors ... of the United Provinces' (*Icones*, p. 111, n. 51).

[25] It seems these were not, however, dispatched to Heerkens before Passionei's sudden death in 1761. As we saw in the previous chapter, though, a colourful prose portrait of Passionei graces the second book of Heerkens's *Notabilia* – one that was probably truer-to-life than the authorized verse version contemplated by the 'sitter' himself!

[26] This had appeared pseudonymously, without the extensive Latin notes which accompany the text in the *Icones*, as 'Eppii Lucumonis de casibus nostri saeculi elegia', in *Journal des sçavans, combiné avec les meilleurs Journaux Anglois*, 28 (November 1779), pp. 242–56. The updated version is some 160 verses longer; the new verses are simply appended to the text of the earlier version, which remains essentially unchanged. Heerkens's more usual practice, as we have noted, was to amend and interweave verses from edition to edition.

[27] Previously published as 'De Belgii Foederati Gubernatoribus Elegia', in *Journal des sçavans* ('Extraits des meilleurs journaux de l'Europe') (January 1781), pp. 183–91, again, under the pseudonym 'Eppius Lucumon', and with mimimal notes.

the third verse, Heerkens has bombarded us with a catalogue of *displicuits*, supported by copious footnotes, regarding the Stadtholdership of William the Silent. His harshest censure, however, is reserved for William III, of Orange; Mary's behaviour vis-à-vis her Catholic father is even compared to that of Livy's unnatural Tullia.[28]

If Heerkens anticipated an anti-Orange audience for his *Icones*, in line with his then political allegiances, the remainder and indeed bulk of the preface (pp. xi–xciv) is devoted to a less inflammatory subject: the author's triumphant restitution to the world of letters of (what he mistook for) a lost Latin tragedy by Augustan poet, Lucius Varius. In the early nineteenth century, Simon Chardon-la-Rochette would cattily suggest that Heerkens's publication of the *Icones* was, in fact, an elaborate pretext for publicizing this 'discovery', which is not only propounded in the preface at embarrassing length, but reprised in the revised finale of the closing icon, on the major events of the eighteenth century.[29] But it is more likely, I suggest, that Heerkens was simply trying to kill two birds with one stone. The times were changing for neo-Latin literature. Heerkens had published his 1783 collection of medical epigrams, *Empedocles*, at his own expense, and admits it had found 'hardly any buyers'; most of the copies went to friends, as gifts (p. xii). When Heerkens wrote to the Baron de Breteuil seeking permission to dedicate an edition of his 'Tereus' to the king of France, and to have it printed at the Louvre, the king's minister sought advice from the Secretary of the Academy of Inscriptions and Belles Lettres. The *académiciens* declined to make a judgement on the basis of the extracts Heerkens was offering, and asked to see the full manuscript. Heerkens made his excuses: the paper was too fragile; the writing so faint as to be almost illegible; it had been returned to the religious house whence it had come to Heerkens as a gift, after his *trop*

---

[28] 'Your holy wife flies into her father's palace and strips the sheets from the paternal bed. It is a marvel! The turncoat shudders at the [woman's] lack of feeling. And soon everyone sees that you [sc. William] are no less heartless!' ('Tua sancta uxor patris invola aulam, / Detegit & patriis strata toris. / Miratur! Sensuque carentem proditor horret. / Nec minus excordem te cito quisque videt', *Icones*, pp. 102–3). In the accompanying note, Heerkens observes that some of the couple's new followers 'had whispered that it was nearly Tullian' ('aliqui prope Tullianum esse mussitaverant').

[29] 'Anecdotes littéraires sur Heerkens', in the *Magasin Encyclopédique* 9.5 (1804), pp. 75–98: 'Heerkens n'a probablement publié ses *Icones* . . . que pour placer à leur tête la préface dont je viens de rendre compte, d'autant plus qui les soixante-dix-sept derniers vers du cinquième portrait, qui est celui du dix-huitième siécle, sont entièrement remplis et d'éloges de la tragédie et de lamentations, sur ce qu'il ne trouve aucune facilité pour la faire imprimer' (p. 84).

*vifs remercîmens* had alerted the monks, to their great embarrassment, to its true identity and value.[30] Cold-shouldered in due course by the *académiciens*, Heerkens took matters into his own hands.[31]

\* \* \*

We can trace the literary pedigree of Heerkens's galleries of the great to two related and long-lived Renaissance genres. The first is that of the illustrated portrait book.[32] The tradition of the *Bildnisvitenbücher* begins with the *Illustrium imagines* ('Images of the Illustrious', 1517) by antiquarian and numismatist, Andrea Fulvio (1470–1521). Paolo Giovio (1483–1552) was arguably its most shining and prolific exponent, in his 'Praises of Illustrious Men' (Venice, 1546), 'Praises of Men Distinguished in Martial Virtue' (Florence, 1551) and 'Praises of Distinguished Men of Letters' (Basel, 1577).[33] Physical portraits of Giovio's subjects hung in his villa–museum on Lake Como, and engravings after the portraits graced some, if not all, the printed editions of his *Elogia*.[34] In antiquity, *elogia* were inscriptions on Roman funeral busts which celebrated the achievements of the deceased. They were paraded at funerals and subsequently affixed to permanent busts or statues, to be displayed in the houses of important families to serve as an inspiration for future generations. As T. C. Price Zimmerman has pointed out, though, Giovio's *Elogia* differed from their essentially positive ancient prototypes in being 'rhetorical in

---

[30] It was sent in return for a copy of his 1783 *Empedocles*. We learn the identity of the sender from a note in the 1793 *Italica* (p. 230, n. 2): Ignatius Weitenauer. Weitenauer was professor of philosophy and oriental languages at the University of Innsbrück, who, after the suppression of the Jesuits in 1773, accepted an invitation from the abbot of the Cistercian Salem Abbey to continue his literary studies under their protection. Presumably this is the monastery to which Heerkens mysteriously alludes.

[31] The correspondence is assembled in 'Anecdotes littéraires sur Heerkens', pp. 85–98. Cf. the résume of the affair in Louis-Gabriel Michaud, *Biographie universelle ancienne et moderne*, new edn, 85 vols (Paris, 1857), XIX, pp. 34–5 (q.v. 'Heerkens'). No doubt Heerkens embellished the story of the mortified monks, to say the least, so as not to lose control of his manuscript – Chardon-la-Rochette draws delighted attention to inconsistencies between the version of events in Heerkens's second letter to the minister (1785) vis-à-vis that of the *Icones* preface – but it also seems likely that he was convinced of the text's antiquity and authenticity.

[32] See Milan Pelc, *Illustrium imagines: Das Porträtbuch der Renaissance* (Leiden: Brill, 2002).

[33] But Pietro Crinito's *De poetis Latinis*, 1st edn (Florence, 1505) was the first Renaissance history of Roman literature containing prose biographies of the Latin poets.

[34] See Paul O. Rave, 'Paolo Giovio und die Bildnisvitenbücher des Humanismus', *Jahrbuch der Berliner Museen* 1 (1959), pp. 119–54; and T. C. Price Zimmerman, 'Paolo Giovio and the Rhetoric of Individuality', in Thomas Mayer and Daniel R. Woolf (eds), *The Rhetorics of Life-Writing in Early Modern Europe: Forms of Biography from Cassandra Fedele to Louis XIV* (Ann Arbor: Michigan University Press, 1995), pp. 39–62.

accordance with the humanist historical conception of furnishing examples of good and bad conduct for moral reflection.[35]

Giovio was, significantly, a *physician* as well as a prelate and an historian. His *elogia* were paired in his Como museum with images that reflected his belief in a manifest correspondence between character traits and physiognomy.[36] It was only a matter of time before biographical portrait collections were devoted to the lives of medical practitioners themselves, starting with those of Hungarian humanist physician and emblematist, Joannes Sambucus (János Zsámboky) (1531–84), whose *Icones veterum aliquot ad recentium medicorum philosophorumque* were published in Antwerp in 1574.[37] However, Sambucus's title, as in other portrait collections entitled *Icones*, refers primarily to the engraved portraits which *accompany* the biographies: Heerkens's *Icones* are, interestingly, portraits in verse only.[38]

It is possible, of course, that Heerkens entertained hopes of adorning his verse biographies with engraved images, perhaps at the expense of the dedicatee. He was by no means oblivious to the historical as well as aesthetic value of the visual arts, collecting coins, medals, inscriptions and portraits. In Rome he had commissioned from local painters, for the price of one ducat apiece, copies of the portraits of famous men which he had admired in the Vatican (*Notabilia*, Book 2, p. 116). Perhaps the work which best illustrates Heerkens's recourse to art as an historical source, however, is the *De valetudine literatorum*, which contains any number of embedded third-person 'icons' of learned writers. Heerkens frequently compares the evidence of written and visual sources on

---

[35] Price Zimmerman, 'Paolo Giovio', p. 45.

[36] See T. C. Price Zimmermann, *Paolo Giovio: The Historian and the Crisis of Sixteenth-Century Italy* (Princeton: University of Princeton Press, 1995), p. 282; for Giovio's 'never-failing surprise when physical appearance belied the mental gifts within', see p. 19.

[37] See A. S. Q. Visser, 'From the Republic of Letters to the Olympus: The Rise and Fall of Medical Humanism in 67 Portraits', in Jan Frans van Dijkhuizen (ed.), *Living in Posterity: Essays in Honour of Bart Westerweel* (Hilvershum: Verloren, 2004); Siraisi, *History, Medicine*, pp. 109–13. Siraisi mentions Eobanus of Hesse's *Chorus illustrium medicorum*, which 'consisted only of brief verses to accompany imaginary portraits of ancient physicians in a private library' (p. 113). Heerkens knew Hessus's work but did not admire him (*De valetudine literatorum* (1790), Book 2, pp. 90–4).

[38] The title, *Icones*, had also been used by the Calvinist Theodore Bèze (1519–1605) for his biographies, accompanied by engraved portraits, of the Protestant Reformers: *Icones, id est verae imagines virorum doctrina simul et pietate illustrium ... quibus adiectae sunt nonnullae picturae quas Emblemata vocant* (Geneva: Jean de Laon, 1580). Other collections include Nicolaus Reusner's *Icones sive imagines viuae, literis claris virorum, Italiae, Graeciae, Germaniae, Galliae, Angliae, Ungariae* (Basel, 1589) and Theodor Zwinger's *Icones aliquot clarorum virorum Germaniae, Angliae, Galliae, Ungariae. Cum elogis* (Basel, 1589). Closer to home, Heerkens might have perused Johannes van Meurs's *Icones, elogia ac vitæ professorum Lugdunensium apud Batavos* (Leiden, 1613).

the physiognomy, life events and even lifestyle, of his subjects: 'that van den Vondel was thick-set and almost all muscle was not only asserted by all his contemporaries, but can be seen in his exceptionally lined face in the very numerous pictures of him. For he was painted by almost all the more celebrated painters of his time, and three times, as is reported in his *vita*, by that most esteemed disciple of Rembrandt, [Philip] Koninck' (1790, pp. 21–2, n. 28).[39] In the encounter with Scaliger's ghost described in the previous chapter, Heerkens identifies the old man from his 'gloomy face, already meditating death', recalling the *insignia* he had seen at Scaliger's two residences in Leiden, and from his distinctive philosopher's cloak (pp. 47–8 and n. 72).[40] He also suggests that the painters of his country are much better known than its scholars: 'While scholars neglect the memory of their peers, a painter was found, as early as the sixth year of the last century, who, by writing their lives and displaying their images, rendered the painters of the Low Countries up to that time most famous; and the same was done by his followers, and continues to our own day' (p. 38, n. 54).[41] Two hitherto unremarked sets of icons of Dutch painters appear in the *Journal des sçavans* (December 1764), pp. 464–7 and (January 1770), pp. 241–6.[42]

Giovan Battista Egnazio's *De Caesaribus* (Venice, 1516) launched a related tradition of humanist biography that diverged somewhat from that of the illustrated portrait book: comprehensive genealogies of rulers from Roman times to the present. This genre was cultivated particularly in Germany with

---

[39] In another footnote, Heerkens describes a 'large picture' in his possession, of the family of his ancestor, Jan Canter, from which he first deduced that Canter had visited Italy: 'from the monuments and tombs of the Tiber in the background, which you see through a window, as if of a home' (p. 74, n. 30).

[40] One of these *insignia* was captioned, 'image of Scaliger contemplating death' ('Scaligeri mortem meditantis imago'). In his note, Heerkens does not seem to recognize this as the first line of Hugo Grotius's brief verse portrait of his beloved teacher, which accompanied the physical portrait by Jan van der Leeuw/Jan de Leeuw (*c.* 1660–?) executed in 1707. For the portrait, Latin elegy and translation by Arthur Eyffinger, see the 2005 Annual Report of the Huygens Institute, available at <www.huygensinstituut.knaw.nl/wp-content/bestanden/Jaarverslag2005ned.pdf>, pp. 31–3.

[41] In fact Dominicus Lampsonius had already published his *Pictorum aliquot celebrium Germaniae inferioris effigies* ('Portraits of Some Celebrated Artists of the Low Countries') in 1572, and these were accompanied by his own Latin poems. A later collection of images of artists with accompanying Latin verse biographies, Hendrick Hondius the Elder's *Pictorum aliquot celebrium, præcipué Germaniæ Inferioris, effigies* (The Hague, 1610), may be perused at the Courtauld Institute's 'Picturing the Netherlandish Canon' website: <www.courtauld.org.uk/netherlandishcanon/>.

[42] See Appendix, and Introduction, p. 29, n. 91, on the unpublished works listed in the first edition of his *Empedocles*. In a note in Book 2 of his *De valetudine literatorum* (1790), Heerkens reports that he was questioned by the Comte de Vence (Claude-Alexandre de Villeneuve) about the decline of Dutch painting in the present century, and that he was able to provide an answer (in the referring verse) because the 'illustrious man had collected lives of the Dutch painters, written in Dutch, from Amsterdam, and the author had almost daily access to these so that he could translate them for him' (p. 89, n. 48).

the aim of demonstrating the continuity and legitimacy of the Holy Roman Empire.⁴³ Johannes Cuspinianus (= Spiessheimer, 1473–1529), poet and medical teacher in Vienna, produced *Consules* and *Caesares* (from Julius Caesar to Maximilian I, via medieval and Byzantine rulers and including recent Ottoman sultans).⁴⁴ Each of Cuspinianus's *Caesares* bore a verse inscription (and the author hoped for accompanying portraits by Dürer). As Marc Laureys has pointed out, such genealogies could also be written wholly in verse, as for example was the series of Latin lives of Ottoman sultans by sixteenth-century Flemish humanist, Philippus Meyerus.⁴⁵ If not Meyerus's catalogue, Heerkens must have known the poetic serializations of kings, popes and other great men by Caspar Ursinus Velius (1493–1539), and of the 'German Caesars' by George Sabinus (1508–60), stretching from Charlemagne to Charles V. The latter, especially, puts one in mind of our poet's unpublished series of icons of the kings of France.

Laureys has suggested that the quality most prized in such metrical historiography was brevity, and that the elegiac list of counts of Flanders which Philippus Meyerus's father, Antonius, appended to an edition of his better-known uncle's *Commentarii sive annales rerum Flandricarum* (1561) had a 'mnemotechnic and didactic purpose' insofar as each count was commemorated in a single line (p. 282, n. 30).⁴⁶ Now in Rotterdam, in 1776, Heerkens published, under the pseudonym 'Eppius Lucumon', the first book of a planned verse chronicle of the Dutch Republic: *Annalium foederati Belgii, liber primus, ab origine tumultuum ad usque inducias historiam foederati Belgii comprehendens* ('Annals of the United Provinces, Comprising its History from the Origin of the Troubles up to the Truce').⁴⁷ This work, while not organized

---

⁴³ See Peter Hutter, *Germanische Stammväter und römisch-deutsches Kaisertum* (Hildesheim; New York: Olms, 2000), pp. 25–36; for Habsburg panegyrics cf. Johannes Ammann-Bubenik, 'Kaierserien und Habsburgergenealogien – eine poetische Gattung', in Manuel Baumbach (ed.), *Tradita et inventa: Beiträge zur Rezeption der Antike* (Heidelberg: C. Winter, 2000), pp. 73–89.

⁴⁴ On Cuspinianus see Siraisi, *History, Medicine*, pp. 198–206. He adopted the monograph 'CMP', *Cuspinianus Medicus Poeta*, on many of his books.

⁴⁵ Laureys, 'History and Poetry in Philippus Meyerus's Humanist Latin Portraits of the Prophet Mohammed and the Ottoman Rulers (1594)', in Yasmin Haskell and Juanita Feros Ruys (eds), *Latinity and Alterity in the Early Modern Period* (Turnhout: Brepols; Tempe, AZ: ACMRS, 2010), pp. 273–300, at p. 282.

⁴⁶ Velius wrote monostichs and distichs, but the poems of Sabinus were somewhat longer (26 lines for example, devoted to Charlemagne).

⁴⁷ The title page says 'after the Venice exemplar', which I have been unable to trace. If it existed, did Heerkens intend his *Annales* to do dual duty as a potted Dutch history for foreigners? I have consulted the (uncatalogued) copy in the National Library of the Netherlands, The Hague (489 K 92). In the preface to the first edition of his *Empedocles* (Groningen, 1783), among 'works on which

along genealogical lines, certainly fits Laureys's minimalist didactic bill. Each year from 1564 through to 1609 (the Twelve Year Truce) is accorded a mere three distichs by the laconic poet. The prologue gives a flavour of a style which, even as it pays tribute to the proem of Ovid's *Ars amatoria*,[48] is much more telegraphic and paratactic than any we have encountered from Heerkens's pen thus far:

> Historiam Patriae Batavis referemus, & unde
>   Cognita libertas, parta, retenta fuit.
> Vera loquar. Verum gens libera spernere nolit.
>   Sin minus, haec Batavus non legat, alter amet.
> Tempora prisca tegunt tenebrae, tegit horror, & alta
>   Barbaries; longae tempora noctis erant.
> Nos Belgas, claros memorandaque facta canemus,
>   Famae cara, suam quae terit inde tubam.
> Sed, neque cuncta placent, nec scribere cuncta vacaret,
>   Rerum summa brevi carmine dicta leges . . .

We relate the history of our nation to the Batavians, and whence we knew liberty, obtained it, retained it. I shall tell the truth. A free race does not know how to spurn truth. If [our race] is not [free], let the Dutchman not read this, let another enjoy. Darkness shrouds the ancient times, terror and deep barbarity. They were times of a long night. Let us sing of brilliant Belgae and deeds worthy of memory, dear to Fame, who wore out her trumpet from that time on. But neither are all things pleasing, nor is there space to write all. You will read a compendium of events, told in brief verse. . . . (p. 3)

Heerkens's *Annales* are certainly not without bias or idiosyncrasy. The work was cited off and on during the nineteenth century for its defence of the seemingly indefensible 'Iron' Duke of Alba (Fernando Álvarez de Toledo).[49]

---

we have expended labour, for the most part complete', Heerkens lists 12 books of *Fastorum, sive Dierum Belgicorum ab eventis maxime notabilibus descriptorum* (p. xxiv).

[48] Surprisingly, perhaps, not the *Fasti*.

[49] A long footnote accompanies this distich for 1569: 'The executioner's axe too often brandished banished many thousands, but the madness that was said to be the Duke's was the King's' ('Millia multa fugat nimis ostentata secures, / Ira sed illa ducis credita, regis erat'). Heerkens notes that the great-great-grandson of Alba had informed him personally that he was in possession of 'letters and documents, in the Duke's hand, from which it was clear that he was led to those harsh edicts with an extremely unwilling heart, and would not have executed Count Egmont and Hoorn had Philip not repeated the order' (!) (p. 6). He would also balance Philip's and Alba's cruelty against that of William

Nevertheless, the crisp, almost prosy, style, enlivened by simple rhetorical effects such as anaphora, sustains the impression, if not the illusion, of plain speaking.[50] The pithy *Annales* are closer, perhaps, to Heerkens's medical epigrams (see next chapter) than to the dense and strenuous *Icones* published in 1787.[51] The length of the latter, ranging from 164 to 567 lines, also militates against the notion that Heerkens was striving after brevity or memorisability. The *Icones* recall not so much the succinct character sketches of Paolo Giovio's *Elogia* as his major biographical works, in which character emerges, almost by default, out of the narration of events. Price Zimmerman finds an important general distinction between the history-driven genre of humanist biography on the one hand, and 'lives' of the Plutarchan variety on the other, where events are always secondary to the personalities being illustrated by them. He suggests a reason, moreover, why the Suetonian model may not have been readily adopted by Renaissance biographers as an alternative to the Plutarchan: 'historical biography, or biographical history was eminently suited to the humanists, for whom, in most instances, a frank analysis of the moral dimensions of their princely subjects would not have been convenient. In general, humanist biography relied only vaguely on classical precedents'.[52] Heerkens's first four *Icones* allow morally problematic events to, as it were, speak for themselves – with a little bit of help from his footnotes – while at the same time retaining the fiction of a first-person protagonist narrating those events from *their* point of view.

---

of Orange in a note to his 'Icon of the Governors . . . of the United Provinces': 'Philip and Alba are said to have been cruel in persecuting the iconoclasts. But William, his brothers, and their followers devastated the Morini and the coastal Dutch with slaughter and pillaging; and as perpetrators of more than barbarian savagery they were extolled to the heavens because they commanded the writers and the reports arising from those events ('. . . quod scriptores & inde natam famam sibi deditam habuere')' (*Icones*, p. 80, n. 4).

[50] In the entry for 1564, the Catholic Heerkens does not pull his punches in describing the reaction of the Dutch to Philip II's harsh treatment of Protestant 'heresy': 'When the court of Philip was promulgating the laws which the Tridentine fathers decreed among the Dutch peoples, it had ordered an inquisition into those who followed the new rites, a harsh inquisition, and the punishment was grim. The nobles obstructed, Orange skilfully obstructed, and the Council of State banished you, Perenot' ('Belgarum populis cum mitteret aula Philippi / Jura, Tridentini quae statuere patres: / Jusserat inquiri contra nova sacra sequentes, / Inquiri durum, poenaque tristis erat. / Obstabant Proceres, obstabat Orangius arte, /Consiliumque aulae te Perenotte fugat' (p. 4).

[51] It is possible that Heerkens, even if he did not have an exclusively schoolboy audience in mind, composed his *Annales* with a sly sideways glance at pedantic history professor, Leonard Offerhaus (see above, p. 112), whose *Compendium historiae foederati Belgii per modum annalium in usum juventutis academicae concinnatum* ('Compendium of the history of the United Provinces, in the form of annals, for the use of the youth of the Academy', Groningen, 1763), was much more prolix!

[52] Price Zimmerman, 'Paolo Giovio', p. 40.

In the preface to the *Icones*, Heerkens remarks that Passionei had furnished him with so much material for his portrait of Antonius Heinsius that, 'for one lacking [access to] Dutch sources, there seemed to be an abundance rather than a shortage of them; I was therefore not at liberty to look back to my earlier icons, which I had enclosed in at most thirty or forty verses, following the epigrammatic poets'.[53] But there *is* something of an epigrammatic edge to Heerkens's longer *Icones*, too, one not confined to local pockets of sententiousness. Heerkens's individual personal biographies are *auto*biographies in which the speaking subjects are given a posthumous right of reply to their potential critics – or, at least, to those not in full possession of the facts. In this respect they recall the speaking tombstones of the Greek Anthology, where the deceased narrator regales the passer-by with a verse cameo of his or her life. Even though Heerkens's *Icones* are lengthier by comparison they are predicated on a similar conceit of the subject reaching out – from the frame, if not from the grave. They convey an impression of striving to arrest the attention and sway the emotions of posterity, the illusion of which is sometimes rather poignant. And in a sense not fully articulated by Heerkens himself, the first three *Icones* might also be read as, if you like, butch Batavian counterparts to Ovid's *Heroides*, in which the 'heroes', whether unloved by their enemies' descendants or forgotten by their compatriots, give the inside, or at least the *other* side, of the story. Is it an accident that the very opening poem of the collection, Belle-Isle's, is billed as the portrait 'of a hero of France' ('Herois Galli')?

## Heroes and humanists

There is no space here for a detailed politico-historical commentary on the *Icones*, though a finer calibration of the views expressed by the narrators vis-à-vis those retailed in Heerkens's footnotes might well be instructive; as would a sorting of the various insights and speculations drawn from the poet's reported conversations with historical actors versus his use of published sources (the latter sometimes written by those very actors). The icon of Belle-Isle runs

---

[53] His *icunculae* of the kings of France ranged from just 30 to 40 verses, apart from the one on Louis XI, which exceeded 700 (*De valetudine literatorum* (1790), p. vii).

to over 38 pages. It opens with the dead man's memories of a vigorous and salubrious rural childhood and concludes with his pious acceptance of the early deaths of his wife and only son, the Duc de Guise, at the age of 26, and his deep gratitude to his son's wife, who tended to him kindly in his final years. In a tight, racy, but highly allusive, style, one that takes no prisoners in assuming a reader already well apprised of the main events and players, Belle-Isle records the highlights of his brilliant career from relative obscurity to favourite of Prince Eugene of Savoy, from confidante of Cardinal Fleury to involvement in, if not responsibility for, some of the major international conflicts of the day.[54]

Belle-Isle emerges from the pages of Heerkens's poem as a hawkish character, forever at pains to persuade the elderly and prevaricating Fleury of the dangers posed to France by its enemies, foreseeing the unravelling of the peace of Aix-la-Chapelle, advocating invasion of England to restore the Stuart prince, Edward. But he protests that he is no warmonger! He regrets especially that he has been held culpable for the outbreak of the War of the Austrian Succession. On the home stage, the grandson of Fouquet is understandably unhappy at being thought an 'ape of Colbert', a power behind the throne; he assures the reader that he was always consultative. He hated abuse of privilege but was not, as rumour has it, anti-noble. Among his self-acknowledged failings is a certain brusqueness and ingenuousness. In this regard he regrets he did not have his brother's talent for judging character.

The heart of the icon is, in fact, Belle-Isle's lament for the death of his younger brother, Louis-Charles-Armand Fouquet, himself a high-ranking soldier and diplomat. In 1747 the Chevalier de Belle-Isle, lieutenant general of France, engaged the Piedmontese in the disastrous Battle of the Assietta Pass, where he fell with some 5,000 French troops. Of a secret route discovered through the Alps, to Turin, our grieving narrator exclaims:

Quid mihi grataris? Miserandi causa doloris,
   Erepti fratris causa, reperta via est.
Sic, quod ad humanae sortis succedit honores,
   Poena fit, & lacrimae sunt tua vota tuae.
Nil jam de teneris, simul ut prope crevimus annis,

---

[54] Including his heroic retreat from the siege of Prague in 1742, which Heerkens compares favourably, in an interesting pair of footnotes, to Xenophon's retreat from Persia (*Icones*, pp. 14–15, and nn. 16–17).

> Tam carum in vita, quam mihi frater erat.
> Perpetuus comes in castris, & omnis in aulis,
> > Dulce latus nostrum, consiliumque fuit.

Why do you congratulate me? The reason the route was discovered was pitiful grief, the reason was the brother snatched away from me. Thus, the crowning laurels of human fortune become a punishment, and your wishes are your tears. Nothing in my life – already from childhood, since we grew up at almost the same time – was as dear to me as my brother. He was my constant and ever-present companion in the camps and in the courts; his company and his counsel were sweet to me. (pp. 23–4)

The ensuing set piece contrasting the characters of the Duke and the Chevalier may have been suggested to Heerkens by Plutarch's parallel lives, or even by the Sallustian pairing of Cato and Caesar. Heerkens's friend, Vonck, had devoted the best part of his inaugural oration to the Mannheim Academy of Sciences ('A Political–Historical Meditation on the Happy Mixture of Integrity and Prudence in History') to a discussion of that famous *synkrisis*.[55] It is worth quoting Belle-Isle's eulogy in full:

> Longe homines melius me simpliciore videbat,
> > Et quas quisque apte posset obire vices.
> Me falli candore & me probitate sinebam;
> > Justo & plus placuit quisque laboris amans.
> Ille laboris amans, hominumque attritior usu,
> > Norat ut aspectu, per tria verba virum.
> Multa dabat ratio, quod in illo saepe stupebam,
> > Et mens doctrinis pluribus aucta bonis.
> Nil nisi militiam, regnique negotia doctus,
> > Jam puer applicitus rebus, & actor eram.
> Rebus, & ille minus distractus honoribus, omne
> > Ingenium studiis, quae placuere, dedit.
> Litterulis Latiis imbutus, lector Horati,
> > Caesaris, & Taciti, duxque sagatus, erat.

---

[55] Vonck, *Meditatio politico-historica de felici integritatis ac prudentiae in historia temperamento* (Utrecht, 1764), pp. 11–27.

Utque suis junxit me linguae Academiae nostrae,⁵⁶
  Isque datus fratri justius esset honor;
Astronomus, caelumque tuens, spectator & acer
  Rerum naturae, Plinius alter erat.
Tamque a se studiis diversis, militis artem
  Junxit, & egregium quod facit esse ducem.
Cum data bina simul tam carum vulnera fratrem,
  Ante suumque mihi surripuere diem,
Non mihi sufficiens, nec belli rebus habebar.
  Pars deerat certe, maxima parsque mei!

He saw through men much better than I, who am simpler, and he saw what challenge each man was best fitted for; I allowed myself to be misled by frankness and honesty, and whoever was a hard worker pleased me more than they should. He was a lover of hard work, and more worn down through his dealings with men, so that he could judge someone at a glance or from three words. Much discernment gave him [this gift], which I often marvelled at in him, and a mind enriched with the fruits of wide learning. Already as a boy, I was informed about nothing but soldiering and diplomacy, applying myself to and involving myself in these things. He was less distracted by them and by honours, and devoted all his talents to the studies which delighted him. He was imbued in Latin letters, a reader of Horace, Caesar and Tacitus, and a sagacious leader. And when our Academy welcomed me as a member, it would have been fairer for that honour to have gone to my brother. He was an astronomer, and gazed at the heavens, and he was a keen observer of nature, a second Pliny! He added military science, and that of the formation of a good leader, to such a diverse range of studies. When those two wounds were dealt and carried off my dear brother before his time, I was considered unfit for myself, let alone for matters of war. To be sure, a part was missing, the best part of myself! (pp. 24–5)

But if Belle-Isle modestly defers here to his more learned younger brother, he was by no means an uncultured man (as his briefing Heerkens on the history of the French monarchs already bears out). Towards the end of this poem, he bemoans declining standards of education in France, and that he

---

⁵⁶ Heerkens was in fact present at Belle-Isle's elevation to the Académie française, as he informs us in a footnote (p. 25, n. 30).

himself had slackened in his humanist studies when young. In a fascinating footnote, Heerkens records the old soldier's disgust at a contemporary fashion for bringing young boys of 10, 7 or even 5 years, into mixed adult gatherings, where they were corrupted by flattery and diverted from all necessary discipline. At one time such young children would have been kept at home under tutors, and then sent to the colleges, and inured to hard work, and not admitted to the company of their parents' friends until they had attained the age of 18! Moreover, Belle-Isle 'reflected that the contempt for the ancient languages had begun in France when he was a youth, but that it was condemned by all the best parents; and when it gained strength, it was severely criticised by Louis XIV himself' (pp. 34–5, n. 41). An impassioned plea for the study of Latin letters is here put into the verse speaker's mouth (which Heerkens avers he had straight from Belle-Isle's). After all, even if it is not obviously useful to have learned these things, there is no harm in giving boys something to do! For, 'whoever has free time in his earliest youth is also corrupted; and a life devoted to hard work is helpful to himself and to his friends' ('Quisquis enim primo vacat, & corrumpitur, aevo: / Seque suosque juvat vita laboris amans', p. 35).

Captured by the perfidious English *en route* to Prussia to negotiate with Frederick the Great, Belle-Isle defends himself against the perception that he was trying to contract peace with his foes during his incarceration: 'While I was detained in London, and at leisure, I wrote, so that you might be instructed in the events of my life. I am believed to have undertaken peace negotiations in these lands; and then, that I was betrayed [to the enemy] through a pre-arranged trick' ('Detento Thamesis dum praestitit otia, scripsi, / Et res, & vitam cur docearis meam. / Credor, in his terris tractasse negotia pacis, / Indeque praestructo deditus esse dolo', p. 18).[57] This, reports Heerkens in a footnote, was English propaganda designed to give Frederick the impression that the French had won them over through Belle-Isle's cunning.[58] The theme

---

[57] France and Emperor Charles-Albert of Bavaria demanded the restitution of their ambassador, 'but nature almost, and good luck, had made the Englishman wild at heart, and he was deaf to all law' ('Sed natura fere, fortunaque fecerat Anglum / Mente ferocem, & jus surdus ad omne fuit', p. 18).
[58] In a note Heerkens records a parallel rumour that Camille Tallard (1652–1728), Marlborough's conquered adversary at Blenheim, had allowed himself to be captured so that he could seduce the English away from their Dutch allies and reconcile them with the French. The broken alliance, according to Heerkens's Belle-Isle, was, rather, a consequence of Marlborough's wife (Sarah Jennyns) falling out with Queen Anne.

of, as it were, sleeping with the enemy, recurs in Heerkens's icon of van Hoey, in the context of Dutch distrust of his deal-making with the French (p. 42). For his brilliant oratorical skills, candour and modesty, van Hoey, who had studied literature and jurisprudence at Leiden, had first come to the attention of pro-Republican Grand Pensionary of Holland, Simon van Slingelandt (1664–1736).[59] He is on the point of being dispatched to Denmark for his first diplomatic posting, but, in a passage which uncannily chimes with Heerkens's own hankering after warmer climes, van Hoey confesses: 'I feared making my home under a frozen sky. While I was being urged, though, France demands the wavering one, happy France, well suited to my temperament! And just as soon as I arrived, as soon as I was caught sight of, I was loved, and I was almost as pleasing to the French as a Frenchman' ('Sed timui, gelido ferre sub axe larem. / Dum tamen impellor, dubitantem Gallia poscit, / Conveniens animo Gallia laeta meo. / Protinus adveniens, simulac spectabar, amatus, / Tamque placens Gallis, quam prope Gallus, eram', p. 42).

The long conclusion to van Hoey's icon, after our hero has proved himself a patriot and a peacemaker and is recalled from France,[60] is given over to his blessed retirement in the countryside near The Hague. A footnote (p. 49, n. 16) compares van Hoey's career and final years to those of Cicero and, closer to home, to those of Dutch poet and politician, Jacob Cats: Cats had served twice as ambassador in England; both he and van Hoey were blessed with most pleasant personalities ('ingenii amoenissimi erat & optimi animi paritas'); they had both chosen to withdraw to the same place and at almost the same time of their lives. The comparison was proposed by Heerkens to van Hoey himself, to the latter's somewhat embarrassed delight. Even van Hoey's villa recalled Cats's, and his rustic dress.[61] It is difficult, however, not to read Heerkens's verse *ekphrasis* of van Hoey's villa, where the old man lives out the golden years of a

---

[59] Heerkens's note on Slingelandt is highly laudatory and perhaps an indication of pro-Patriot leanings at this date (p. 41, n. 3).
[60] 'I left my host country with moistened cheeks, the court which had seen me grown old; it was a harsh thing that I should lack my friends forever after, and in those years, to turn around the sails of my life' (p. 48).
[61] 'His villa was, like Cats's, set on many acres, and situated about three miles to the east of The Hague, bordering on its woodland. He used to live there, not only setting up his kitchen according to the French custom, but furnishing his own hearths with wood. He was commonly found by visitors strolling about, and dressed in the same toga you see Cats wearing in pictures of him in his country house, surrounded by his works' (p. 50, n. 17).

born-again Corycian gardener, as a sort of wish-fulfilment dream for his *own* retirement:

> Rure, memor luxus, sine multo vivere luxu,
> > Rure notos didici, frigora rure pati.
> Sed non rure homines, humanaque foedera fugit,
> > Apta sodilitiis, apta senecta jocis.
> Sive lares Batavus, seu viseret advena Gallus,
> > Comis amicitiae cultor, & hospes eram.
> Cumque ego Versaliis post tertia lustra carerem,
> > Saepe memor visa est aula relicta mei.
> Misit saepe mihi Rex & Regina salutem,
> > Tantus & invidiam non mihi fecit honor.
> Nec dedit invidiam Legatis obvia Gallis,
> > Semper & illorum plena cohorte domus,
> Partibus adversis mihi quondam carus, & aulae
> > Factus eram. Villam visit & illa meam.
> Sed plausus hominum, perituraque commoda jacto,
> > Sint mea propitii cum bona cuncta Dei.

Remembering luxury, I learned how to live in the country without many luxuries. I learned to suffer the hot winds and the cold of the country. But old age, suited to fellowship, suited to high spirits, did not flee mankind in the country, did not flee human company. Whether a Dutchman or a foreigner from France visited my hearth I was a cheerful cultivator of friendship and host. After I had been absent from Versailles for more than fifteen years the court often seemed to remember my departure. The King and Queen often sent me greetings, and so great an honour did not inspire envy. Nor did envy result from the fact that my home was open to French envoys; it always had its full complement of them. I became dear to those who were once my enemies, and to the court. Even *she* visited my villa.[62] But I boast about the applause of men, and of goods that will perish, since all these things are the gifts to me of a propitious God. (p. 51)

---

[62] 'Anna, daughter of George II, King of England ... as she was most interested in and frequented men outstanding for their generous spirit ('hominum bonitate animi insignium'), visited our van Hoey, accompanied by her children, on more than one occasion' (p. 51, n. 19).

Heerkens had entertained the fantasy of a cultured, country life, surrounded by likeminded friends, in poems to Tenhove and van Sijzen.[63] In the event, it seems, his most frequent visitors and faithful companions in the countryside would be of the feathered variety.

## From Black Sea fish to North Sea birds

While he was preparing to publish his politico-historical icons Heerkens was at work on a very different series of portraits, which he executed, as it were, *en plein air*. He had already begun publishing the occasional bird poem in the *Journal des sçavans* from the early 1770s, around the time of his reception into the Haarlem Maatschappij de Wetenschappen (1772).[64] In the preface to his *Aves Frisicae*,[65] Heerkens reminds us that, since childhood, he had diligently applied himself to the study of history, 'the so-called messenger of antiquity', but that when he had reached his early 40s he found himself 'torn, rather than drawn' away from that cherished pursuit. He seemed now to be condemned to inertia, 'since, in committing to Latin letters my judgements on famous men, and on events affecting the nation, the fruits of my historical research', he could be deemed an 'insufficiently quiet man' ('non satis quieti hominis', p. v). And so he retired to his country house under an Ovidian shingle – 'he who has

---

[63] *Italica* (1793), pp. 78–83, at pp. 82–3, and pp. 112–17, at pp. 116–17. In the poem to Tenhove, dated Groningen, 25 April 1762, Heerkens reminisces about Rome, the ruins of the Villa Madama and the gardens of Ovid; then imagines a country house 'full of antiquities, and books bought from all quarters' ('Plena domus priscis, ac partis undique libris'), passing the time throwing a frisbee, and cultivating something of a Calabrian vegetable garden for their mutual friend, Fagel: 'He will see ancient marbles inserted in the walls of the forecourt, as he did before in the rural homes of Latium' ('Vestibuli muris insertaque prisca videbit / Marmora, per Latii ruris ut ante domus'). In the poem to van Sijzen, Heerkens writes somewhat cryptically of 'our third [friend]' ('noster tertius'). We learn belatedly in a footnote that this is Dutch admiral-turned-farmer Hendrik Lijnslager (p. 116, n. 6). While Heerkens is miserable in Venice, our 'comrade is doing exceptionally well, and cleaves to your side, and our third contemplates your farm from the city of his homeland [sc. Utrecht]. Let him contemplate, and let him come to visit us one day in our settled abode!' ('Praestat idem, laterique tuo comes haeret, et agrum / Tertius e patria cogitat urbe tuum. / Cogitet, et stabili nos quondam sede revisat', p. 116). Here follows a reverie about the poet's estate, his beech trees and a pine-lined avenue which even Tuscan porches would envy.

[64] The Flushing scientific academy he joined in 1769 was decidedly Orange-flavoured, as is clear from the inaugural volume of the Society's proceedings: *Verhandelingen uitgegeven door het Zeeuwsch Genootschap der Wetenschappen te Vlissingen* (Middelburg, 1769), dedicated to 'Zyne Doorluchtigste Hoogheid Willem den Vyfden, Prins van Oranje en Nassau'. William V was the Society's Protector.

[65] Rotterdam, 1788. The title page gives this date; the preface is signed 1787, which Worp takes as the date of the edition. A review in *Ésprit des journaux* (translated into French from the one by William Cowper in the *Analytical Review* (September 1789), signed 'G. G.') adds a London reprinting by 'Hamilton' in 1789 (December 1789), pp. 217–23.

hidden well has lived well' ('bene qui latuit, bene vixit') – and informed his friends, not for the first time, that he was renouncing the literary life.

But secretly, Heerkens confesses, he contrived to smuggle some reading matter out to his country villa; and he gradually came to the realization that he still needed to *write*, not just to read. But write what? As he was more familiar with the history of the Augustan period than any other – so he claimed – he had divined 'the reasons why Ovid was exiled: and since [Ovid] had been dear to me ever since my adolescence, and more than any other ancient poet, a commentary on his exile was the first small work that recalled my inclinations to the pen' (pp. vi–vii).[66] In the course of this commentary, Heerkens justified Ovid's scant and small-fry final works with reference to the oppressive political climate under Tiberius: 'how, in the last years of his life, there was almost no topic left for his muse, so that he turned his talents to the depiction of fishes'.[67] While that natural-historical subject pleased Pliny well enough,[68] posterity would have preferred Ovid to finish the *Fasti*. But *they* did not please Tiberius. During the latter's reign, Ovid's muse was severely restricted; the writer so 'diligent before Pontus penned no more than one or two letters to powerful friends'. He feared to give offence to the *princeps* even by ingratiating himself, but 'with [a work on] the nature of fishes, and a description of their habits, he could expect to delight, or at least not to offend, a suspicious master, one who was reasonably learned and interested in fish, as I have shown in my commentary' (p. viii). Once again Heerkens, in self-imposed exile, models himself, in both life and literature, on his favourite poet:

> Therefore, just as I admired the prudence of the poet who was exiled for foolishness, and just as I admired his quiet spirit, and had already followed him in putting aside the study of history, I deemed him fit to be followed in the choice of an equivalent subject matter for my muse. (p. viii)[69]

In fact, while in the preface to the *Aves* he states that the avian theme is innocuous, and does not touch even obliquely on public affairs ('quae ex obliquo publica non tangeret'), Heerkens begins his poem on the 'Goldcrest'

---

[66] The original text of this commentary has proved impossible to trace. A large part of it is presumably reproduced in the footnotes to the third book of *De valetudine literatorum* (1790), pp. 177–207.

[67] Heerkens never seems to have doubted that the *Halieutica* were by Ovid.

[68] 'He had seen countless fishes in the Black Sea which were not known in any other waters, and for that reason, and on account of their special nature, worthy of being described' (p. vii).

[69] Cf. Heerkens's verse celebration of Ovid's fortitude and prudence in *De valetudine literatorum* (1790), Book 3, pp. 264–7.

with what might be read, by those with ears to hear, as quiet criticism of the House of Orange:

> Regulus in nostris avis exiguissima terris,
>   Sive per antiphrasin nomina regis habet,
> Sive joci causa minima est ita dicta volucris,
>   Seu populis, regum queis grave nomen erat:
> Libertatis amans, infestaque terra tyrannis,
>   Regis avi nomen Graecia prima dedit.

> The goldcrest, the smallest bird in our lands, whether it has the name of 'king' by antiphrasis, or whether the diminutive little bird has been called this for a joke, or by peoples on whom the name of king lies heavily: it was Greece, a land that loves liberty, a land hostile to tyrants, which first gave the bird the name of 'king'. (p. 115)

The same poem ends with an enigmatic coda pointing to a 'very well-known' local identity, who, like our bird, 'is in constant fear of the shadow of his reputation' ('Regulus est quidam nostrae notissimus urbis, / Umbram qui famae pertimet usque suae', p. 127). This individual, 'who thinks that I bear the name of Curillus, the name under which I mingle with the illustrious Arcadians, from [*those* . . .] satires, defames me for writing the history of our country, and says that I will injure the bright names of our citizens at court' ('Quique putans satyris me nomen habere Curilli, / Nomine quo celebres Arcades inter eo, / Historiam patriae scribentem infamat, & aulae / Laesurum dicit nomina clara virum', pp. 127–8). What history would that have been? The *Icones*? The continuation of 'Eppius Lucumon's' *Annales*? And why is Heerkens making a disingenuous show of hiding behind that now definitively exploded pseudonym of his youth?[70]

---

[70] 'And now he whispers that I and they [sc. the historical writings] are "Curillus" – as if a name bestowed in honour [sc. by the Arcadians] were a disgrace. But it could be turned into an accusation later if I touch on public matters. And those [future historical writings?] would be written for the Fatherland, not for me. The work has been set aside. And I have begun to describe birds. The magpie and the raven now, I think, love my song. And as the Lark I have sung draws your eyes, it seeks the high aether and sings an even sweeter tune than usual. And this bird hopes that you, Reader, will have better eyes than that goldcrest has for my Fatherland' ('Jamque susurrando me dixit & illa Curillum. / Probro esset tamquam nomen Honore datum. / Post tamen in culpam, si tangam publica, verti / Posset. Et haec Patriae, non mihi, scripta forent. / Sepositus labor est. Et aves describere caepi. / Pica meum & corvus jam puto carmen amant. / Utque oculos cantata trahat, petit aethera summum, / Dulcius & solito cantat Alauda melos. / Sperat & haec volucris melius tua Lector habere / Lumina, quam Patriae regulus ille meae', p. 128).

The 'Quail' ('Coturnix'), too, closes with an intriguing, anti-Georgic, *sphragis*, in which the poet calls on the martial spirits of Tyrtaeus and Alcaeus, 'you whose rites I once celebrated',[71] not to let him lose his nerve and refuse to fight for his country. He must not be lulled into rustic oblivion by love of the countryside, or of study. Ironically, given the allusion in the preceding poem to his Curillan persona, with its undertones of intergenerational conflict, Heerkens concludes here: 'since Phoebus' late laurels befit his white hairs, let Mars' [too] fall to the poet' (p. 153).

\* \* \*

Whatever the circumstances of their incubation, Heerkens's first peep of Frisian birds were, on the whole, successfully fledged; most, initially, in the *Journal des sçavans*. In the preface to his collected *Aves*, Heerkens quotes Ovid, who 'called birds the "consolation of the countryside". And as they seemed a delightful and innocent race in the woods to him, so they seemed to me, from my earliest childhood, to be the most happy of animals' (p. viii). The *Aves Frisicae* represent some of Heerkens's very best, simplest, most natural poetry. No trace here of the compressed, almost Tacitean, syntax of the *Icones*. The verse is limpid, often exuberant.[72] Heerkens's engrossed observation of the behaviour of his domestic quails, who entertain him in the depths of winter, marking the hours of the day with their punctual and varied songs, has something about it of Lucretius's ataraxic rapture in the proem to Book 2 of the *De rerum natura* and the bliss of his weather-free Epicurean gods: 'It is also pleasant to watch them preening their backs, and plunging their bodies in the dirt strewn for them. While you are doing this you do not feel cares, fear, anger or desire, nor that winter is striking your windows with rain' ('Est quoque jucundum, sua tergora quamque scabentem / Cernere, & adstratis mergentem corpus arenis. / Haec inter non cura subit, timor, ira, cupido / Nec sentis, quod bruma tuas ferit imbre fenestras', p. 138). But of course Heerkens's 'it is *also* pleasant' must recall Virgil's 'fortunate is

---

[71] The accompanying note mentions an edition of 'my lyric poems, which I had begun to print in Groningen'. These have disappeared without a trace.

[72] Thus the metre, word-play and onomatopoeic alliteration of the opening lines of the 'Swallow' wonderfully convey its flapping and soaring: 'Pene omni populo quae nuncia veris hirundo, / Pene omnes penna praepete vincit aves' ('The swallow which announces spring to almost every people conquers almost every bird with its swift wing', p. 49).

**Figure 5.1** *Alauda* – The Lark.
Source: Gerard Nicolaas Heerkens, *Aves Frisicae* (Rotterdam, 1788), title page. Heerken's personal copy. Courtesy of the University of Groningen Library.

he, *too*, who knows the gods of country', the rider to his famous tribute to Lucretius' 'happy is he who has been able to know the causes of things'.[73]

Though the metre of the *Aves* is mostly elegiac, the 'Quail' and 'Blackbird', two of the longest poems, are in hexameters.[74] The tracks of Virgil are in any case ubiquitous, which is not surprising given Heerkens's discussion in the preface of several Jesuit bird poems modelled on the *Georgics*.[75] Thus, in the opening poem, 'Lark', the flight and song of that bird is a seasonal sign for farmers and reapers; an old man, a very keen bird-catcher in the 'Magpie', invites comparison with Virgil's Corycian gardener (pp. 32–4) as he identifies individual birds from Heerkens's farm and his own but forbears from snaring them: 'They are my darlings, and yours; my art does not rage save in far-off fields' ('Mea gaudia, suntque tuorum, / Ars mea longinquis non nisi saevit agris', p. 33). The georgic mood is particularly marked in 'Goose', a domesticated bird that provides man with direct benefits – feathers and food – and requires special care and housing, like Virgil's bees.

But Heerkens's whimsical sentimentality, his eye for the diminutively pathetic, somehow reaches beyond Virgil into the territory of Marco Girolamo Vida's 'Silkworms' – a model certainly exploited by Heerkens's Jesuit precursors.[76]

---

[73] Virgil, *Georgics* 2. 493: 'fortunatus et ille, deos qui novit agrestis'; 2. 490: 'felix qui potuit rerum cognoscere causas'.

[74] A second series of 10 birds would also have seen two in hexameters, 'Gavia' ('Sea-mew') and 'Anas' ('Duck'), of approximately 700 verses apiece! They were to be joined by updated versions of several already published separately: 'Cornix' ('Crow') and 'Corvus' ('Raven') (published together in *Journal des sçavans* (July 1772), pp. 552–7; 'Turtur' ('Turtle-Dove', published in *Journal des sçavans* (March 1774), pp. 493–8); 'Stork' ('Ciconia', published in *Journal des sçavans* (January 1775), pp. 250–61); 'Passer' ('Sparrow', published in *Journal des sçavans* (January 1776), pp. 211–19); 'Fringilla' [*sic*] ('Chaffinch', *Journal des sçavans* (April 1779), pp. 219–25). Earlier versions of 'Alcedo' ('Kingfisher') and 'Perdix' ('Partridge') have eluded me. As for the 1788 poems, I have found: 'Alauda', 'Regulus' and 'Pica' (*Journal des sçavans* (May 1772), pp. 507–14); 'Anser' (*Journal des sçavans* (September 1773), pp. 518–22); 'Hirundo' (*Journal des sçavans* (May 1774), pp. 252–61); 'Turdus' (*Journal des sçavans* (July 1774), pp. 467–76); 'Merula' (*Journal des sçavans* (April 1776), pp. 514–20 (the poem is signed Rotterdam, 17 March 1776)). In the *Aves Frisicae*, Heerkens alludes to two previous versions of his 'Starling' (p. 181, n. 1) which I have not yet been able to locate.

[75] See Yasmin Haskell, *Loyola's Bees: Ideology and Industry in Jesuit Latin Didactic Poetry* (Oxford: Oxford University Press, 2003), chap. 1, esp. pp. 42–3, 64–9.

[76] *Bombyces* (Rome, 1527). Vida was a favourite with the Jesuits. His didactic poem on the art of poetry was prescribed for their Humanities class by Ledesma before 1575 (François de Dainville, *L'Education des jesuites: XVIe–XVIIIe siècles*, ed. Marie-Madeleine Compere (Paris: Editions de Minuit, 1978), p. 173); together with his 'Silkworms' and 'Chess', it makes up the first batch of poems in the second volume of François Oudin's largely Jesuit *Poemata didascalica*, 3 vols (Paris, 1749) (cf. Chapter 2, p. 71). This volume also contains two Jesuit avian georgics, including Jean Roze's *Aviarium*, one of those mentioned by Heerkens in his *Aves* preface (he may have owned the original edition of Bordeaux, 1700). On Vida's 'Silkworms', see further Yasmin Haskell, 'Work or Play? Latin "Recreational" Georgic Poetry of the Italian Renaissance', *Humanistica Lovaniensia* 48 (1999), pp. 132–59. From his verse letter to the Jesuit Ignatius Weitenauer, however, it would seem that Heerkens had some misgivings about Vida's poetic style (*Italica* (1793), pp. 229–37, at p. 232, and n. 4).

And while the goose has the virtue of consuming very little but growing nice and fat, yielding a delicious November roast, stuffed with apples, not to mention *fois gras*, fit for kings (pp. 88–9), the final pages of its poem exhort the reader to vegetarianism in earnest, almost frantic tones.[77] God has subjected animals to man and exalted our powers and intelligence, 'but a king who uses well the powers he is granted ensures that his whole dependent tribe is happy and safe. He does not demand his subjects' life, nor that of a guest, like the king of the Cannibals whom a savage world nourishes' ('Sed rex concessis bene viribus usus, ut omnis / Subdita sit felix salvaque turba, facit. / Non a subjectis animam, nec ab hospite poscit, / Rex ut Cannibalum, quem ferus orbis alit', p. 103). Nor should we delude ourselves, says the poet, that the consumption of gooseflesh strengthens the mind: 'Much is snatched from the mind whenever compassion is snatched away, since this one thing is joined to all its various gifts' ('Multum animo rapitur, quoties miseratio rapta est. / Juncta quod haec variis dotibus una bonis', p. 104). Heerkens's philosophical pleading cannot fail to put us in mind of Pythagoras's diatribe against meat-eating near the end of Ovid's *Metamorphoses*.[78]

We have already noted that Heerkens was a dog lover, but his feeling for his fellow creatures seems to have extended to more humble species as well. Thus he commemorated a poor frog dissected in anatomy class: 'Unlucky little creature, born from a sad swamp so that you might be torn apart by the slow hand of the physician! Heerkens gathers up your bones and your wretched entrails, and constructs a small tomb for you on the banks of the swamp. If you survive, and swampy souls live on after death, may your feeble shade feel this act of piety' ('Bestiola infelix, quae tristi nata palude es, / Ut Medici lentâ dilacerare manu. / Ossa tua Herquenius miserandaque colligit exta, / Et tibi parva, vadi margine, busta struit. / Si superes, vivantque animae

---

[77] But in other poems Heerkens will discuss the effects of a bird's diet on its palatability (e.g. 'Thrush', *Aves*, p. 196).

[78] Cf. *Italica* 1793, Book 1 (= *Iter Venetum*), pp. 12–14 and n. 14, where the travelling poet, en route to Italy, is invited to dinner by the Jesuits in Mainz and is advised by an elderly but hale German doctor to follow a simple and near-vegetarian diet in Italy. The 'Samian' (sc. Pythagorean) precepts would keep him safe from the noxious effects of the air in Lazio, spread by swarming insects. Heerkens believes this 'Nestor' to have been the son of Westphalian physician, Johann Heinrich Cohausen (1665–1750), although it is hard to see how his preceptor can have attained the age of 80, as Heerkens claims, by the time of the latter's Italian journey in 1759. On Cohausen senior's satire on the prolongation of life by inhaling the breath of young girls (!), see Anna Marie Roos, 'Johann Heinrich Cohausen (1665–1750), Salt Iatrochemistry, and Theories of Longevity in his Satire, *Hermippus Redivivus* (1742)', *Medical History* 51 (2007), pp. 181–200.

post fata palustres, / Sentiat officium tennuis umbra pium').⁷⁹ Throughout the *Aves*, Heerkens champions even the most vexatious of his feathered friends against human prejudice and bad press. He is stunned at the hypocrisy of Dutch naturalists Martinus Houttuyn (1720–98) and Cornelis Nozeman (1721–86)⁸⁰ for their unfriendly attitude to the magpie:

> They both teach methods of capturing it and killing it by steel or poison, as if no animal were more pernicious to us! It amazes me that men expert in natural history, and especially Nozeman, can have written this – he who warned me when I was busy with my description of the starling that I should try, through my verse, to defend that bird against the injustice of the [local] edicts. But I have always been of the opinion that most birds are very beneficial, and especially to our countrymen: for those who live in swampy territory, the air becomes pestilent because of flying insects when there is a hotter summer; and to them, frogs, toads, snails and shrew-mice are most unwelcome and inconvenient animals. Those same learned men report that all of these creatures are food for the magpie. How great are the benefits we receive from smaller fly- and worm-eating birds I will show in my verses when the occasion arises. But the matter would deserve a long commentary all to itself. It will be enough if I add that there are hardly any wiser legislators in nature. (p. 47, n. 16)

\* \* \*

The prose preface of the *Aves* opens with an avowal of the deep pleasure to be had from the study of Nature, a pleasure which is felt from the outset, but which intensifies over time, so that all other pursuits (and, significantly, humanistic ones) can easily be set aside. This almost religious affirmation of a vocation for natural history may have been calculated to help secure Heerkens membership of the Académie des sciences in Paris. An encouraging letter from the Comte de Buffon suggested that:

> Vous méritez autant que personne d'être correspondant de l'académie. M. De Montigny et M. De Malesherbes peuvent aisément vous procurer cet

---

⁷⁹ *De officio medici* (1752), p. 69.
⁸⁰ See M. Boeseman and W. de Ligny, *Martinus Houttuyn (1720-1798) and his Contributions to the Natural Sciences, with Emphasis on Zoology* (Leiden: National Museum of Natural History, 2004), chap. 5, for their collaboration on Nozeman's pioneering, illustrated *Nederlandsche Vogelen*, which was begun in 1770 and only completed in 1829. Though he criticizes him here, Heerkens knew and corresponded with Nozeman (e.g. 'Blackbird', *Aves*, p. 283, n. 17), and calls him 'a most dear man' in the preface (p. xxiii).

agrément; si j'étois à Paris je me joindrois à eux; mais je n'y retournerai que vers la fin de fevrier. (27 January 1777)[81]

Though ultimately unsuccessful in the attempt, Heerkens's ornithological poetry was taken seriously enough to merit citation and refutation in, for example, Buffon's *Oiseaux*.[82] The *Aves Frisicae* is indeed a work of genuine and quietly ambitious natural-historical pretensions.[83] Heerkens affirms that he has bought up the most authoritative ornithological tomes he could lay his hands on in Holland, and that he has also consulted with friends and local bird-catchers (pp. x–xi). Above all, he has trusted the evidence of his own eyes, and has exercised caution when relaying the testimony of others (p. xxi).

*Attention* (*attentio*), applied over a long period of time, and restricted to a sample of 20 birds, has taught him things that have occurred to no other naturalist (p. xii).[84] The migratory Heerkens sings, at last, the benefits of nesting! The quality of this attention was apparently inculcated in our tyro twitcher by Dutch laywer turned naturalist and engraver, Pierre Lyonnet (1708–89), to whom a 'single caterpillar has ensured eternal fame'.[85] Lyonnet had stressed that 'a man devoted to the study of nature must apply his mind only to a few

---

[81] See J. A. Worp, 'Lettres de Voltaire, de Buffon et de Malesherbes à G.-N. Heerkens, médecin et homme de lettres hollandais', *Revue d'Histoire littéraire de la France* 21 (1914), pp. 188–91, at p. 190. Malesherbes's letter relates to the same affair; the great man makes flattering noises but is not sure whether he will be in Paris when Heerkens's name is put forward (p. 190).

[82] Georges Louis Leclerc Buffon, *Histoire naturelle des oiseaux*, 10 vols (Paris, 1771–86). Indeed, in the above-cited letter, Buffon politely criticizes Heerkens for asserting in his 'Swallow' – which the French naturalist, in writing his own *Oiseaux*, has 'épluché peut être de trop près' – that all swallows hibernate. In fact none do. 'Il y a aussi quelque petite critique à faire sur l'article des Cicognes; ce ne sont pas des Cicognes mais des Ibis qui sont en Egypte et on les a mal à propòs pris les uns pour les autres' (pp. 189–90).

[83] Apart from its intrinsic interest for historians of science, Heerkens's *Aves Frisicae* has probable scientific value as a document of observed patterns of bird behaviour in the context of environmental change. With zoologist Hugh Jones of The University of Western Australia I hope to explore the work more thoroughly in this regard. Heerkens carefully notes, for example, the decline in certain bird populations and the resilience of others in the wake of some very cold winters in Groningen ('Blackbird', *Aves*, p. 250, and pp. 280–1, n. 13).

[84] In the conclusion of his 'Swallow', Heerkens states his project modestly: 'Et dare conor aves, per praedia nostra frequentes / Inque dies oculos quae tenuere meos. / Rure mihi labor hinc jucundus: & otia fallunt, / Cumque observantur, cumque canuntur, aves. / Perdita restituam, non est, ut carmina Macri. / Unde animum subeat spiritus ille meum! / Sed, licet haud plumas avium numeremus in alis, / Multaque sollicitus mensor omissa putet; / Quas dedimus, placuistis aves, & Hirundo priores / Cum deceat, tenuis fama sequatur opus' ('And I am trying to present the birds which are frequent on our farm, and which command my attention [lit. 'hold my eyes'] every day. Hence a pleasant country labour, and the birds cheat me of my leisure both when they are observed and when they are sung. It's not that I wish to restore the songs of Macer, whence his spirit might enter my mind! But, although we don't count feathers on the wings of our birds, and the scrupulous surveyor may reckon that much has been omitted, the birds we have presented have pleased us, and since the Swallow deserves to be among the first, may a slender fame attend my work', p. 67).

[85] Lyonnet, *Traité anatomique de la chenille qui ronge le bois de saule* (The Hague, 1760).

subjects if he wishes posterity to have regard to his discoveries' ('Swallow', p. 70, n. 3).[86] Summarizing his scientific findings in the preface, Heerkens concludes that: not only does the nature of birds vary according to their homeland ('pro earum patria') but they are, generally speaking, extremely diverse; very few birds migrate to remote places; their lives are longer than previously thought; their marriage bonds are either perpetual, or at least much more enduring than has been believed to date; and finally, they are both useful and almost necessary animals to the life and health of mankind (p. xii).[87]

In selecting subjects for his 1788 collection, the poet had first to decide whether to exhibit 'many birds, one by one ('sigillatim'), in a few verses, or a few, more thoroughly known, in many' (p. x). This choice is reminiscent of his binary treatment of historical human subjects, the laconic *Annales* versus the more discursive *Icones*. In the case of the *Aves* he opts for the latter, calculating that discussion of a few well-known birds will pique the interest of ornithologists and, moreover, 'attract those who miss any meaning/matter ('res') in poetry ('carmine') apart from its song ('cantum')'. Yet Heerkens realized that it would be futile to offer verses to 'this century, which is unfavourable to Latin letters', without first baiting them with 'unknown things'. Since even the great ornithologists were relatively ignorant about some of the species he was proposing to describe, he saw his chance – so he thought – to compel the French, 'despisers of, and almost destroyers of the most useful Latin language', to read his work (pp. x–xi). As to his writing Latin *poetry*, an anonymous, if apparently not hostile, reviewer in the 'Dutch Journal of Scholars' has deemed it 'rash and inappropriate' ('inconsideratum & inconcinnum') for him to write in verse rather than prose. Heerkens counters, reasonably enough, that 'it is inconsiderate to oblige someone who provides his services to the public vineyard, free of charge, to labour with his right hand rather than his left'

---

[86] Heerkens reports that Lyonnet showed him numerous letters from the great Reaumur, requesting information, and said that he had always written back: "'You honour me with your questions, my lord, but you apply your mind and eyes to too many things if you expect the necessary accuracy ('quam debeo fidem') from my feeble powers of perception ('ab exigua perspicitate')'" ('Swallow', *Aves*, p. 70, n. 3).

[87] Already in Italy Heerkens was alert to birds as barometers of public health. Cardinal Passionei had defended the salubriousness of the Roman air but the foreign doctor was troubled by the absence of birds in and around the City (*Notabilia*, Book 2, p. 143). 'Thus', as he put it in his 'Sparrow', 'in my opinion, nothing adorns the skies and indicates the health of a region so much as an abundance of birds, the ornament of the countryside' ('Nil mihi sic coelum exornat terramque salubrem / Praedicat, ac volucrum copia, ruris honor', *Journal des sçavans* (January 1776), p. 214). Cf. *Empedocles* (1798), Book 1, p. 66, and Book 4, p. 13.

(p. xii). This would suggest that the *Aves*, like the *Icones*, were published at the author's own expense.

Unsurprisingly, Heerkens would soon have egg on his face. The caustic reviewer of the *Aves* in the *Journal des sçavans* (June 1787) found it 'amusing' that our poet had boldly undertaken to teach the French a lesson by writing in Latin:

> He is right in one respect: [at least] the subject matter he treats should get them to read it – since he writes almost as badly in verse as he does in prose! The French, whom he accuses generally and most falsely of hating and destroying the Latin language, will always know enough of it to recognise how little acquaintance with it *he* has, and what distaste for it his prose and his verse are capable of inspiring. (pp. 443–4)

What sort of response did Heerkens expect? Perhaps he hoped to find willing French ears in the readers of a journal where, after all, many of his Latin birds had originally been launched. And the batch of avian georgics on which he digresses in his preface to the *Aves* were all, pointedly, by *French* Jesuits.[88]

With regard to his scientific 'bait', among the didactic poet's more controversial contentions is that swallows hibernate underwater.[89] He gives credit for this discovery to Olaus Magnus (1490–1557);[90] for the refinement that they behave in this way only in Arctic climes to Athanasius Kircher (1601–80), thanks to the Jesuit's extensive correspondence network; but the observation that the swallows' hiding places vary according to their varying environments Heerkens claims for himself. Moreover, in his 'Lark', Heerkens takes Buffon's distinguished collaborator Philippe Guéneau de Montbeillard

---

[88] 'And I shall show them to be of that most cultured nation which has not only won a deserved place in my heart through its kindness, but through its example has influenced our customs. In presenting these poets I should congratulate myself much more were it not necessary to add that they were almost the last of their race to write a Latin poem among the French' (p. xv). The poems here showcased are Jean-Antoine du Cerceau's *Gallinae* and Jacques Vanière's *Columbae*. Heerkens even contemplates a new edition of them, together with Jean Roze's *Aviarium* and Anne-Philippe d'Inville's *Aves* (he claims to have in his possession 'unpublished birds of d'Inville', a supplement to the Paris edition of 1691?). He proposes to round these out with a further 20 birds of his own, in 10, 12 or 15 verses. On the French Jesuit georgics, see my *Loyola's Bees*, pp. 60–9.

[89] Barry Baldwin, 'Johnson's conglobulating swallows', *Notes and Queries* (1994), pp. 199–206: 'I particularly wonder about the Latin poem *Hirundo* by Heerkens, blamed by Buffon as a prime propagator of the submersion theory [that swallows hibernate under water], as 'conglobulare' would be perfect for hexameters; but despite my best efforts, Heerkens remains a mystery to me' (p. 205). Unfortunately Heerkens's swallows do not, like Johnson's, *conglobulare*!

[90] Swedish Catholic bishop, Olaus Magnus, wrote copiously on Swedish folklore and history, as well as on the northern oceans and natural history.

(1720–85) gently to task for giving credence to unsubstantiated assertions by Johann Leonhard Frisch ('Frischius') (1666–1743)[91] and Caspar Schwenckfeld ('Sueveneldus') (1563–1609)[92] that larks living in colder regions reproduce only once or twice, that is, less frequently than their more southern cousins: 'and yet he lent a willing ear to this vain witness, he who has just now completed the celebrated birds of Buffon' ('Et tamen huic testi tam vano praebuit aures, / Buffoni celebres qui modo finit aves', p. 4).[93] Montbeillard's refusal to credit the poet's arguments simply because they are relayed in verse is a sore point prodded at already in the preface. Heerkens returns to it almost obsessively in his notes to the 'Swallow'.[94] And what, after all, is his claim of swallows emerging from a Norwegian lake to the bizarre behaviour of Polish foxes – capturing and enslaving their vanquished enemies, and obliging them to lie on their backs as living sleds for carting prey and straw! – as reported by Cardinal Melchior de Polignac in his celebrated scientific poem, *Anti-Lucretius*, Polignac 'who was misbelieved by nobody just because he wrote in verse' (p. xxi).[95]

Each bird poem is followed by a battery of disciplined and informative endnotes, designed, no doubt, to forestall any future peremptory dismissal of the contents of Heerkens's verse. Here the author largely refrains from his usual penchant for gossip and autobiography, and tests the assertions of natural history writers from, for example, Aristotle and Pliny, through Isidore of

---

[91] Sometime singer and German army interpreter, Frisch became headmaster of a high school in Berlin; Heerkens calls him 'Lipsiensis' and commends his beautifully coloured bird illustrations, which he began to publish in 1733 as *Vorstellung der Vögel Deutschlands und beyläufig auch einiger Fremden; nach ihren Eigenschaften beschrieben* (Berlin, [1733]–63).

[92] Not the famous Protestant reformer, but the physician who practised in Hirschberg. He wrote natural-historical works influenced by Ulisse Aldrovandi and Conrad Gesner, and was author of a regional fauna of Silesia: *Therio-Trophevm Silesiae: In qvo Animalium, hoc est Qvadrupedum, Reptilium, Avium, Piscium, Insectorum natura, vis & usus sex libris perstringuntur* (Liegnitz, 1603); the fourth volume is devoted to birds.

[93] Heerkens writes in the preface that he met 'Guenaldus' by chance in Paris, when they were both admiring the 'birds, beautifully depicted, in the king's museum of images'. The two men were unknown to one another, and Montbeillard asked Heerkens to send him news about the presence or absence in his homeland of thrushes, swallows and storks. Heerkens learned the name of his famous interlocutor from the gallery's custodian, and 'gave thanks that I had come to know by sight the illustrious ornithologist whom I had often read with so much pleasure'. He prudently affirms his enduring goodwill towards Montbeillard in the preface to *Aves*, which, he assures us, was composed after the text and notes (pp. xxii–xxiii).

[94] At p. 71, n. 5; p. 74, n. 7; p. 78, n. 16; and by implication, p. 82, n. 23 (Pliny has unembarrassed recourse to the works of poets Nicander and Aemilius Macer in writing his tenth book) and pp. 85–6, n. 32 (what a loss to lovers of natural history Macer's 'Ornithogonia' must be may be inferred from its use as a source by Ovid and especially by Pliny). Cf. Chapter 6, p. 214.

[95] Heerkens implies perhaps that he should have been!

Seville, Albert the Great,[96] Pietro de' Crescenzi (c. 1230/35–c. 1320),[97] Conrad Gesner (1516–65),[98] Pierre Belon (Belonius) (1517–64),[99] Ulisse Aldrovandi (1522–1605),[100] Johannes Coler (1566–1639),[101] Ole Borch (Borrichius) (1626–90),[102] Giovanni Pietro Olina (seventeeth century),[103] to Jacob Theodor Klein (1685–1759),[104] Giuseppe Zinanni (1692–1753),[105] Carl von Linné (1707–78), Arnoud Vosmaer (Vosmarius) (1720–99),[106] Mathurin-Jacques

---

[96] Heerkens is incensed at the superstitious cruelty advocated by Albert for roasting 'true' goldcrests: 'There are those who have plucked them alive, and put them on a spit so that the bird could turn it itself. I find it a monstrous thing, which a priest of so little feeling teaches his people in such savage writings' ('Sunt quoque, qui vivam depilavere, veruque / Induerant vivam, vertat ut ipsa veru. / Res odiosa mihi, tam nulla mente sacerdos, / Tam fera qui populum per sua scripta docet', p. 121). And yet this barbaric practice found its supporters even in Heerkens's own century and the previous, and what's worse, among churchmen: Kircher, Schott and 'Rhancincius' (= 'the Polish Gabriel Racincius', in 'Thrush', p. 233, n. 22?)' (p. 134, n. 8). Aldrovandi even recommended dousing the plucked live bird with salt in order to extract a medicine: 'He was a doctor, but one whom ornithology called away from the practice of his art. Ornithology was not able to call him away from writing frivolous and stupid things every now and again' (!).

[97] Bolognese lawyer and landowner who wrote the influential *Liber ruralium commodorum* ('Book of Rural Benefits'), which circulated widely in manuscript until published in Augsburg in 1471, the first printed modern text on the management of a country estate.

[98] Swiss naturalist and linguist, and father of zoology for his monumental *Historiae animalium* in 5 vols (Zürich, 1551–87).

[99] French physician, scientific traveller in Greece, Asia Minor and Egypt, and author of important natural-historical works; Heerkens refers to his 'excellent/trustworthy work' ('luculentum opus'), *L'Histoire de la nature des oyseaux* (Paris, 1555) (pp. 292–3, n. 39).

[100] On the Bolognese naturalist and collector of curiosities, Aldrovandi, see Paula Findlen, *Possessing Nature: Museums, Collecting, and Scientific Culture in Early Modern Italy* (Berkeley: University of California Press, 1994), passim (chap. 1 for his museum).

[101] German Protestant preacher and author of *Oeconomia ruralis et domestica* (1593–1602). Heerkens acknowledges that Coler 'taught [him] much about agriculture, and something about recognising birds' ('Swallow', *Aves*, p. 78, n. 14). Cf. Manfred P. Fleischer, 'The First German Agricultural Manuals', *Agricultural History* 33 (1981), pp. 1–15.

[102] Borch was a Danish physician and poet, professor of philology at the University of Copenhagen from 1660, and from 1666 of chemistry and botany. He was the author of a commentary on hibernating animals which Heerkens reports was not only read to the Danish Academy but to the nobles of the royal court, and published in 1714: 'but this published work, containing many things very worth knowing about birds, has gone so unnoticed by modern writers on ornithology that I seem to be the first to cite the evidence of this second Olaus [i.e. after Olaus Magnus] in my *Birds*' ('Starling', *Aves*, p. 185, n. 8).

[103] The sumptuously illustrated *Uccelliera* (Rome, 1622) of Giovanni Pietro Olina was commissioned by the Cavalier Cassiano dal Pozzo in the latter's expectation of being admitted to the Accademia dei Lincei, Italy's equivalent of the Académie des sciences. See Francesco Solinas, *L'Uccelliera: un libro di arte e di scienza nella Roma dei primi Lincei* (Florence: Olschki, 2000).

[104] Klein was director of the Danziger Naturforscher-Gesellschaft and an opponent of Linnaeus. He is described in a note to the 'Lark' as 'an attentive ('attentus') observer of birds, a concise writer and not one to follow idle talk' (p. 11, n. 8). We share Heerkens's exasperation when in a note to the 'Swallow' he relates how Klein collected evidence from a hundred local peasants to prove the submarine hibernation theory; that they laughed at him for asking them to repeat such obvious things to learned men: 'What impression, indeed, might those witnesses, and the whole Vandal mob, form of learned men who deny credence to Klein together with all his witnesses?' (p. 71, n. 4).

[105] Heerkens refers to Zinanni's pioneering work devoted exclusively to the nests and eggs of birds, *Delle uova e dei nidi degli uccelli* (Venice, 1737).

[106] As his entry in the list of fellows of the Zeeland science academy styles him: 'Member of the Imperial Academy ['Keizerlyke Academie', sc. the German 'Leopoldina'] and Correspondent of the

Brisson (1723–1806)[107] and Philip Fermin (1729–1813).[108] Among this august scientific company the recurring citation of Ovid is noteworthy. Ovid is adduced, for example, as witness to the superior quail-rearing abilities of the ancients, and is said to have 'persuaded himself, with a sufficiently scientific argument, that naturally plump birds would often age on that account, which fault of nature should be corrected in captive birds by having them engage in frequent battle' (p. 165, n. 18).

In the opening lines of his 'Turtle Dove', a piece published in the *Journal des sçavans* (March 1774) but not in the *Aves*, Heerkens lures the reader with a mischievous decoy: 'The fame and favour of the turtle dove, above all, teach us how useful it is to become known through friendly poems. Who does not believe that the bird is chaste? Who does not think it both amorous and an example of holy matrimony?' ('Quanta sit utilitas per amica poëmata nosci, / Turturis inprimis fama favorque docent. / Quis castam non credit avem? Quis amoribus aptam / Non putat, ut thalamis sit quoque norma piis?'). The poet proceeds to reveal the unedifying truth: this frisky and adulterous breed owes its undeserved reputation to the *poets*, and especially, it seems, to Italian Renaissance poets such as Pontano and Mantuan. But Ovid, naturally enough, knew the bird's character better, as Heerkens demonstrates by citing *Heroides* 15 and *Amores* 2. 6. And in the closing lines of his own poem, apologizing for its length, Heerkens claims that: 'Naso himself is quite often with me, setting his screech-owl before my eyes,[109] but the brevity of such a great man is inimitable!' ('Naso, strigem ante oculos ponens, mihi saepius ipse est, / Sed brevitas tanti non imitanda viri!', p. 498). Not only is the poet of the Black Sea fishes an excellent observer of nature, then, he possesses the gift of capturing and preserving for posterity his scientific prey in enviably clear and succinct verses.

---

Royal Academy of Sciences in Paris, Director of the Nature and Art Cabinet of the ... Prince of Orange and Nassau, in The Hague' (*Verhandelingen Uitgegeven door het Zeeuwsch Genootschap der Wetenschappen te Vlissingen*, Part 1 (Middelburg, 1769), p. xlv). Coincidentally, Vosmaer was a fan of Clara Feyoena van Sytzama's, and it was through his intercession that she was elected member of the prestigious Dutch literary society, 'Kunstliefde Spaart Geen Vlijt' ('Love of Art Spares no Pains'), founded in The Hague in 1772. Cf. Claudette Baar-de Weerd, *Vrouwen en genootschappen in Nederland en in ons omringende landen (1750–1810)* (Hildershum: Verloren, 2009), pp. 113–14.

[107] Brisson was a French naturalist (later natural philosopher), member of the Académie des sciences and author of *Ornithologie, ou, Méthode contenant la Division des Oiseaux en Ordres, Sections, Genres, Espèces et leur Variétés*, 6 vols (Paris, 1760).

[108] Fermin was a medical doctor and well-known writer on Suriname, where he lived for eight years.

[109] Cf. *Fasti* 6. 133–4.

## What's in a (Latin) name? The neologisms of Linnaeus

True to his word, Heerkens calibrates in his *Aves* the published opinions of the learned with those of local country folk and with his personal observations of birds, both in the wild and in captivity.[110] The learned are not infrequently found wanting in discrimination and even common sense: 'The end of March has provided me with the eggs of a bird which they deny can lay before the first of May' ('Martius extremus mihi praebuit ova volucris, / Ante dies Maii quam peperisse negant', 'Lark', p. 2). The accompanying note makes clear that 'they' are 'the writers on birds ... who copy one another', but are 'refuted by peasant boys' (p. 10, n. 5). However, Heerkens is usually rather circumspect in his criticism of ornithological authorities, whether in his verse text or the accompanying notes. Thus, in a note to verse 46 of his 'Magpie': 'I said that magpies raised young once a year, at least among our people, not because I believe they do so more frequently anywhere else, but so that I might seem to contradict Giuseppe Zinanni, an excellent observer, less harshly, who has written that they do it twice a year' (p. 42, n. 8).[111] He is especially tactful when challenging Montbeillard, regularly tagging the great man, *illustris* or *illustrissimus*.[112] He cannot, however, maintain his scientific composure, nor even the semblance of an enlightened *politesse*, in the face of Linnaeus's innovations in natural-historical nomenclature.

---

[110] Our veritable Dutch Dr Dolittle kept, for example, quail (p. 138), geese, possibly a lark (p. 9), a starling (pp. 176–7), a stork, and during a bitter winter tried unsuccessfully to revivify by his fire several frozen bullfinches (p. 123); but he loved his playful pet crossbill best of all (pp. 14–15). Heerkens's favourite bird in the wild seems to have been the heron, to which he devotes a long note in the 'Blackbird' (pp. 277–9, n. 10). It is among the most prudent, long-lived and blessed, 'a contemplative bird which ... amuses itself with its own mind, in solitude, like a human philosopher' (p. 279).

[111] Cf. a long note in the 'Quail' in which Heerkens sets forth his reasons why Italian quails should not migrate to Africa, then asks: 'Why did I make no mention of those arguments in my verses? I preferred to follow the common opinion established among common people with such obstinacy/persistence ('pertinacia') on the part of the most serious men, than to be overly provocative' (pp. 157–8, n. 5). In a later passage of verse from the same poem, he pleads: 'Let no-one believe that I wish to break wind at those who deserve fame, or that I am writing my birds to create marvels, and to attract attention with paradoxes. I vow that most of what I have written was known to the ancients, and that I have discovered few things: and that the quail hibernates is not a new discovery' ('Nequis me famam meritis oppedere velle, / Scribere neu quis aves, faciam ut miracula, credat, / Detineamque animos paradoxis. Cognita priscis / Pleraque me testor scripsisse, inventaque pauca: / Inventumque novum non est, sopita coturnix', p. 143).

[112] The 'most illustrious man was deceived' into believing that magpies migrate *en masse* for the winter from his observation of a few solitary couples in the fields of France in the month of March ('Magpie', *Aves*, p. 45, n. 13); 'It is therefore more likely [that redwings come to Burgundy from Lotharingia] than from the very far north, I say more likely lest I contradict the most illustrious Guéneau using less gentle words' ('Thrush', *Aves*, p. 233, n. 21); and, more boldly: 'See what a slight little argument seduces even the most illustrious writers [sc. Montbeillard] away from the truth!' ('Swallow', *Aves*, p. 83, n. 27).

In 'our Surinam', for example, there is a bird which, in spite of its bright colouring, Dutch colonists had no qualms about calling a 'magpie' on account of its distinctive movements. Fermin classified it a magpie on the basis of its observed behaviours. But Linnaeus, 'having measured and counted the feathers of its tail, called it by another name and transferred it to some genus or other – one that Brisson, however, judged not to be that of the magpie'. Heerkens sarcastically inquires whether those 'leaders in scientific battle ('antesignani physicorum') would have done a better service to those wishing to identify birds had they classified the magpie as belonging to the kind that hops or moves its tail? . . . I say nothing of the right which Linnaeus has arrogated to himself to give the bird a new name on the basis of such uncertain features ('signis tam incertis')' (p. 39, n. 3). But Heerkens's most extensive attack on Linnaeus comes in a note to the 'Blackbird', in which he rails not only against the Swede's arbitrary collocation of unrelated bird species but also of man, monkey and bat. Linnaeus's 'paradoxes' detract from the faith and respect invested in the learned; distract intelligent youth from their proper studies; and, most significantly, by substituting 'barbarous words'[113] for the traditional terms of Pliny and Aristotle, do irreparable harm to the memory.[114] Heerkens scoffs that 'he who teaches madness will find students more easily than he who teaches thirst – and he who taught thirst has found students!' On the other hand, 'we must not despair of the judgement of the human race'. To this end, he gives us, still in the footnote, a taster of his forthcoming poem on the 'Sea-mew' ('Gavia'):

> Ventura peritior aetas
> Surget, & huic opera partaeque per irrita famae
> Constituet pretium. Veterum mihi more sequenti
> Naturam, nec res ex tegmine, fortuitisque,
> Spectanti, ad dignas animo succedere spes est
> Notitias: tabulaque in parva ostendere magnas
> Si nequeo, stultas fugiam dare, garrula, quasque
> Prodat anus, pennasque coquo detraxerat alis.

---

[113] Linnaeus is deemed a 'barbarian' not because he is a Goth, but because he has been 'born without ears' and coined those 'new and most unharmonious ('dissonantissimae') terms' (p. 295, n. 42).
[114] Cf. Chapter 6, pp. 208–10.

A future, wiser, age will come, and will fix the price of this fame won through vain publications. For me, following Nature according to the custom of the ancients, and not inspecting matters only from the surface, or from accidents, there is hope for attaining to knowledge worth knowing. If I am unable to demonstrate great things on a small canvas I shall flee from retailing stupid ones such as a garrulous old woman spouts, and the feathers she had plucked from wings for the cook. (p. 295, n. 42)

The feather-plucking crone, presumably, is none other than Linnaeus himself. An even more *ad hominem* attack is reserved for Heerkens's old bête noire, d'Alembert, in the next note but one. A certain French writer, who has committed a grammatical, not to say taxonomic gaffe, in assigning 66 different thrushes to the *genus turdinum*,[115] will not be named and censured by Heerkens because he owes 'respect to a Frenchman who cares so much about foreigners that he has deigned, in this century, to write in Latin'. That man is moreover, a 'colleague of d'Alembert's in the Academy [sc. of Sciences]'. The culprit here is no doubt Brisson,[116] but the real target of Heerkens's sarcasm is d'Alembert himself:

*That* d'Alembert, a man of such great judgement, licensed only the explicators of scientific matters to write in Latin [sc. in the *Préface* to the *Encyclopédie*], but to write it any old way – lest, that is, anyone who was going to write plainly should waste their time. But that writer will waste his time who is scarcely understood, and understood with such difficulty that he is therefore rejected.[117] And if he is not rejected because he teaches matters of great moment, it seems impudent for a writer to produce barbarous and uncivilised words for posterity. Therefore d'Alembert could have permitted those who were going to write in Latin some diligence, especially the French, to whom writing an elegant Latin comes very easily, as is seen from the many polished writings redounding to the nation's glory. (pp. 296–7, n. 44)

Philological care goes along with the requisite attentiveness for reading the book of Nature. It demands a patience and humility that disposes us to recognize also the right sort of scientific detail. Moreover, a truly enlightened writing of the book of Nature must proceed from omnivorous reading. Despite first appearances, our huffy humanist's anxieties do not pertain merely to style,

---

[115] 'Seeing, indeed, a "Thrush-like" ('Turdinum') genus mentioned by him I did not recognise it at first. "Thrush-like" birds ('Aves *Turdines*') were unknown to me, and given so many innumerable kinds of them, I thought them to be very exotic'. This is surely disingenuous!
[116] See his *Ornithologie*, II, pp. 200–339, and pp. iv–vi of the *Table*.
[117] But Brisson had actually supplied Latin and *French* text, in parallel columns.

but go to the foreseen impoverishment and attrition of natural knowledge. Buffon/Montbeillard may have written in their chapter on the Swallow, 'il ne s'agit point ici de descriptions poétiques',[118] but Heerkens's use of Ovid and other literary sources – he quotes for example from Renaissance Latin poets Pietro Angèli da Barga (thrush-catching in Tuscany) and Jacob Micyllius (fighting falcons and magpies) – is not just belletristic. As he pillaged the poets in his *Notabilia* for clues to ancient life and customs, he extracts from the widest variety of learned sources whatever he thinks may be of value, even incidental value, to modern investigators of bird populations and behaviour. In short, natural history itself has a history, and part of that history is only recoverable from books – including books of Latin verse.

\* \* \*

In a note to his 'Magpie', Heerkens observes in dismay that the *Acta Eruditorum Harlemensium* (i.e. the proceedings of the national scientific academy, the Hollandsche Maatschappij der Wetenschappen) has recently published a *quaestio*, 'Why is the magpie not seen in Holland?' suggested by 'one of our ornithologists, Martinet'.[119] 'That a learned man could have even proposed the topic is remarkable', sneers Heerkens, 'but I am more amazed that it was included in the *Proceedings*. Might not those *Proceedings* deceive posterity, whom [perhaps] the sumptuous work of Nozeman will not reach, or whatever else the Dutch have dedicated to the subject of birds?' (p. 45, n. 12). Like so much history and literature, then, knowledge of the natural world – that is, the accumulated and coordinated testimony of alert observers – is subject to the capricious depredations of time. Heerkens laments, for example, that only the tiniest fraction of the ornithological writings of the Greeks has come down to us. Indeed, sometimes even the *survival* of books can be part of the problem – if they are the wrong books. Thus, in the first of his notes on the magpie, he reminds us that the *pica caudata* was not known in antiquity, but writers

---

[118] See the online edition of *Oiseaux* found in *Histoire Naturelle, générale et particulière, avec la description du cabinet du Roy* (1779), vols 16-24, XXI, p. 561, which can be consulted at the French Centre national de la recherche scientifique's 'L'Oeuvres de Georges-Louis Leclerc, Comte de Buffon (1707-1788)' website, <www.buffon.cnrs.fr/>.

[119] Presumably Jan Floris Martinet (1729-95), natural historian, reformed preacher and author of the much-translated (into French, German, English and Malay) *Katechismus der Natuur* (1777-9). The Haarlem proceedings were published between 1754 and 1793, and largely comprised prize-winning answers to questions set by fellows of the Society. Cf. J. A. Bierens de Haan, *De Hollandsche Maatschappij der Wetenschappen 1752-1952* (1952; repr. Haarlem, 1970), p. 279.

ever since have consistently attributed to that bird whatever they read in the ancients about the *pica glandaria*. Even when Renaissance naturalist, Ulisse Aldrovandi, noted the distinction in a late work, this widespread error was not reversed. It is less surprising, Heerkens suggests, that Aldrovandi's observation was not accepted – he was old, he was failing and his writings were voluminous and by no means universally read – than that 'men of great name' to whose attention the distinction had come both noted it and subsequently rejected it (sc. in their other works):

> But it should be observed at the same time that those men were polygraphs, and they didn't have time to read over/revise their writings ('revidenda scripta'). Meanwhile, those books that are published in beautiful type, and boast the accompaniment of beautiful figures, are a witness to posterity that nothing certain can be learned from the most esteemed writings; and they divert our eyes away from the less grand, little works that teach the truth. (p. 38)

Our birdwatcher of Borgercompagnie surely aspired to be counted in the latter category for his modest, unadorned *Aves*. He compares the composition of poetry while walking to the pleasures of fishing or hunting: 'He who brings home four or five verses, even if he hasn't caught anything, returns happy ... Things that are to be related in verse need to be considered and weighed; when care is hurrying us along, when we write unfettered by metre, we often do not think enough' (p. xiii). And in this humble, late offering Heerkens's eagle-eyed attention to detail has paid off in crisply delineated portraits of a sometimes exquisite naturalism, whether it be of his servant losing a shoe – the 'dear covering for his frozen foot' – down a hollow tree, and then extracting by chance a tangled clump of semi-conscious swallows, or the white goose waddling with its new chicks 'who, with the voice that displeases, nevertheless pleases you'.[120] And yet, there can be no last word in versified natural history. As is the case

---

[120] Sometimes, also, in vivid flights of imagination! Thus a sort of bird *bougonia* when swallows stir from their putative underwater hibernation, a natural wonder Heerkens confesses he has not witnessed first-hand: 'Norway recently marvelled in springtime as they rose, roused, from the lake, through all the fields. Some stood as if unconscious, drowsy, on the shore, and took in the breezes, like fish exiled from water. Others preened their wings, others again, almost revived, were seen to help their elderly companions with their little beaks' ('Surgentesque lacu Norvegia tempore verno / Mirata est totis excita nuper agris. / Pars quasi mentis inops, sopitaque litore stabat, / Captabatque auras, piscis ut exul aquis. / Scabere pars alas, pars altera pene refecta, / Rostello socios visa juvare senes', 'Swallow', *Aves*, p. 51).

with almost all his surviving works, Heerkens has left his tracks in print in earlier versions of many of these poems. Uniquely in the *Aves*, however, he has a scientific sanction for his revisions and additions, to which he is happy to confess in the preface: 'dies diem docet' ('we learn by experience'). In our final chapter we will find Heerkens oscillating between competing impulses to provisionality and closure in his medical didactic verse.

**Figure 5.2** Heerkens's epitaph for the trusty dog he adopted in Italy.
*Source:* Gravestone, 1758. Courtesy of the Groninger Museum

# 6

# Inscriptions and Prescriptions: The Art of Healing in Long and Short

## Enlightening the humanist doctor

> Quid faciat Medicum, qua vivere lege, quid aegris
> Debeat, utque bona se juvet arte, canam.
>
> *De officio medici*

In the preface to the first edition of his *Empedocles* (Groningen, 1783), his second collection of medical epigrams, Heerkens asserts not only that 'the good epigram requires verses that are consistently good', but that consistently good verses are required to a greater extent in the epigram than in any longer poem. To that extent the short epigram, he suggests, will not suffer the repetition of words which even the best elegiac poets of longer works have permitted themselves. Ironically, this 'flaw' is prominent in the programmatic poems, addressed to the reader, at the head of each of the *Empedocles*'s five books.[1] Such repetition and syntactical mirroring is, of course, a well-known feature of Ovid's elegiac didactic poetry.[2] And it is a conspicuous, even obtrusive, feature

---

[1] *Empedocles* (1783), 1, 1: 'Omnis enim medicina, omnis sapientia quondam / Scripta rudi fixo, nec nisi carmen erat. / Carmine dicta brevi meminisse licebat; & aevum, / Sit breve, venturum quod meminisse velis' (p. 2); 3, 1 (*ad Lectorem*): 'Non meus, Empedocles, frustra liber esse vocatus / Dicitur, Empedocles cui bene notus erit' (p. 58). References to this text throughout are to Book, then poem number.

[2] In just the first eight lines of the *Ars amatoria*, for example, note the repetitions/variations on *ars, lego, Automedon*.

of perhaps Heerkens's single most Ovidian poem, which appeared not long after his return from his medical studies in France: *De officio medici* (1752).[3]

'On the duties of the doctor', published in Groningen by Jacob Bolt, is a poem as much about human psychology as human bodies: 'Learn how to know men and the hidden paths of the human heart, learn what passions, hope and fear produce. There is nothing sweeter, nothing more useful to know!' ('Noscere disce homines & pectoris avia nostri, / Quos spes affectus disce timorque facit. / Dulcius, utilius scitu nihil!', p. 22). Medicine is an art, a truly *Ovidian* art, in this sparkling, mid-length, elegiac didactic poem. The erstwhile schoolboy satirist, now in his physical and literary prime, equipped with that freshly minted medical degree from Reims, offers the good citizens of Groningen a peace offering. Heerkens's *Ars amandi / Ars sanandi* is a poem which aims, I suspect, to heal both new diseases *and* old wounds. One can't help feeling that the solidarity Heerkens prescribes for the community of physicians (pp. 36–40) – they must not suffer the patient to complain in their presence about, or flaunt the advice of, their colleagues – is one he hopes to enjoy from the wider Republic of 'Frisian' Letters.[4]

The patient and his doctor(s) play the respective roles in the economy of this poem as the beloved and her lover(s) in Ovid's. Where Ovid bids us not to lie in wait for our rivals,[5] Heerkens pleads for friendship and harmony among learned physicians: 'What is more sacred than the practice of friendship? Virtue herself, seemly virtue, without you she lies grim and dejected; without you, my beautiful girlfriend will scrap in my bosom. Alas, how brief is our life, and it goes to waste, tormented by bitter disputes and alternating reproaches!' ('Usus amicitiae, quid sanctius? Ipsaque virtus / Ipsa decens virtus te sine torva

---

[3] To take just the repetition of words and phrases at the *beginning* of alternate lines or couplets, I have counted some 43 instances (in 86 lines) in a poem of 758 verses.
[4] Heerkens's exhortation, 'Come easy mind, well-adjusted; modesty, a desire to please, fitting, obliging attentiveness!' ('Mens facilis, concinna! Modestia, cura placendi, / Commoda sedulitas officiosa veni!', p. 40) may be primarily intended for a Dutch audience. At any rate, the poet imagines himself in dialogue with a gruff Batavian doctor, who scoffs at French *politesse* ('What are you cawing, French scum, demented little pastry?'; 'Quid cornicaris faex Gallica, crostule [sic] demens') and defends his right to speak his mind: 'The flatterer is foul; let the tongue which is born free enjoy being bold' ('Turpis adulator. Proavorum vivito more; / Lingua licenter amet, libera nata, loqui', p. 41). But Heerkens, in *propria persona*, prays for a life free from quarrels, and that 'the gods may grant that I die grateful for the gift of this life, and not complaining; he who has lived badly, dies complaining' ('Di faciant, vitae moriar pro munere gratus, / Non querulus: querulus, qui male vixit, abit', p. 41).
[5] *Ars. am.* 2. 595–6.

jacet. / Te sine suavities dulci neque constet amori, / Te sine pulcra meo pugnet Amica sinu. / Heu mihi quam brevis est, & acerbis litibus aetas / Alternisque perit exagitata probris!', p. 40). Ovid calls it a profanation of the mysteries to divulge the names of our sexual conquests;[6] in the interests of professional solidarity, Heerkens urges us to follow the example of the wise Italians who decreed that medical consultations should not be made public (p. 42).[7] Had that good law been in force more widely, 'the sacred rites of Phoebus would not have been mocked by the wit of Molière, and would have been attacked more sparingly by disgraceful jokes' ('Nec Moleri salibus delusa sacraria Phoebi, / Risorumve probris parcius acta forent', p. 42).

Although at one point the poet threatens to write a satire against an ungrateful and querulous former patient, the new, enlightened Dr Heerkens stays his pen: 'Sing, throw down your rod, Muse, let no frown mar this work of mine!' ('Cane, projice virgam / Musa, nec huic operi ruga sit ulla meo', p. 38). And already on the first page of his poem he is eschewing religious controversy. It is not the doctor's place to 'attack the dying man with harsh words, there is no need to recite the scourges of an avenging God' ('Non opus est saevis morientem incessere verbis, / Non opus ulturi flagra referre Dei', p. 17). Our liberal Catholic counsels against attempting deathbed conversions: 'Whether the sick man follows a different rite, as happens, whether it's the one Rome teaches, or yours, Luther – don't impose the sad scruples of Amesius[8] or

---

[6] Ars. am. 2. 601–4: 'Quis Cereris ritus ausit vulgare profanis, / Magna Threicia sacra reperta Samo? / Exigua est virtus praestare silentia rebus: / At contra gravis est culpa tacenda loqui!' Note that Heerkens may also have these lines in mind when advising us not to make open promises to our patients: 'Granted that you will be no Hippocrates without the gift of the gab, I'd prefer you to follow *Harpocrates* [god of Silence], and Dr Tight-Lippius ... Whatever you promise, be brief, so that you may be less clear. You can speak certain things clearly, but *really* certain things. Nebulous oracles always err. If Jupiter himself were making promises from the Tripod, he would be cautious' ('Si non Hippocrates nisi linguae munere fias, / Maluero Harpocratem, SWYGHUSIUMQUE sequi / ... Quid quid promittas, brevis esto: obscurior ut sis. / Certa potes clare sed bene certa loqui. / Nubila semper errant oracula: Jupiter ipse / Si quid promisit Tripode, cautus erat', p. 35).
[7] Nor to discuss, or air our differences with our colleagues in front of the patient: 'Therefore, when there is need for advice, avoid quarrelsome spats, nor allow the house of the sick to hear squabbles. When the gloomy house is tottering with tears and sobs, when the patient entreats you for help with broken eyes – cruel doctors, those dwellings see you in conflict, and earnest debates over nothing! For what is the dispute about? Whether your or his herb should be administered, when they both have the same value' ('Ergo ubi consiliis opus est, rixosa cavete / Jurgia, nec lites audiat aegra domus. / Cum lachrymis domus & singultu moesta fatiscit, / Effractisque oculis cum rogat aeger opem; / Crudeles Medici! vos disceptare, gravesque / De nihilo rixas pallida tecta vident. / Ambigitur quid enim? Tua detur, an illius herba, / Sint omni quamvis utilitate pares', p. 39).
[8] William Ames (1576–1633), Heerkens tells us in the accompanying note, was a 'celebrated theologian and professor at Franeker at the beginning of the last century; he was a most ferocious disputant on the discrepancies between religions, first going into battle, in many long volumes, against the Synod of Dordrecht, then against the Lutherans and Arminians, and Bellarmine', n. (a).

talk about changing religion' ('Si sacris, ut fit, diversis utitur aeger / Seu quae Roma docet, sive Luthere, tuis. / Noli Amesii scrupulos obtrudere tristes / Neu de mutanda Relligione loqui', p. 17). The theme of oppressive religion, couched in almost Lucretian terms as 'gloomy superstition', is reprised twice in the poem. The second time, it is again the learned physician who is exhorted to indulge his patient, not to remove from him all hope like 'those whom merciless Religion, austere and grave, Religion, without pity, impels and drives' ('Sic quos Relligio inclemens austera gravisque, / Relligio veniae nescia trudit agit', p. 43). Earlier, Heerkens had warned against the damage done by overzealous schoolmasters – and he speaks from personal experience:

> Maesta superstitio quid procreet; ex misero ex me
>     Discite: robusto corpore natus eram.
> Indole laetus ad haec, ut cui jam pectore Phoebus,
>     Ut qui jam Clariae semina mentis habet.
> Sed puerum duri pervertit acerba magistri
>     Relligio, ante oculos semper Avernus erat.
> Crimen erat risus! minimo percepta voluptas,
>     Ceu dapibus: linguae gaudia! crimen erant.
> Crimen & impubi, scelus aspexisse puellam!
>     Et scelus heu! Stygiis quod lueretur aquis.
> Nil igitur misero mihi nil fecisse videbar
>     Quam peccasse. omnis vita scelesta fuit.

What gloomy superstition spawns, learn from me, from miserable me! I was born with good health. I was blessed with talent, too, as one whom Phoebus already possessed, as one who held the seeds of a Clarian mind. But the bitter religion of a harsh master ruined the boy, and Avernus was always before my eyes. Laughter was a crime. The least perceived pleasure, whether in meals, or the joys of language – they were a crime. And it was a crime, and a sin, for a prepubescent boy to have looked upon a girl! And it was a sin, alas, that would be paid for in the river Styx! (p. 29)

The Jesuit alumnus replays a warning here aired already in his *De valetudine literatorum* (at least, in the complete version first published in 1790). It was a local medical doctor, Eutropius Eiding, engaged by his concerned father, who helped the young Heerkens overcome these irrational pricks of conscience: 'When at last my mind was purged with hellebore, I lived again: SUPERSTITION WAS CONQUERED BY THE POUTICES OF EIDING!' ('Dum tandem Helleboro mens expurgata, revixi: PULTIBUS EIDINII VICTA SUPERSTITIO!').[9]

This tribute to the almost Epicurean Eiding is followed by a passage in which an almost Christ-like Galen summons his flock – in language still freighted with Lucretius:[10]

> Me, me, qui vitio mentis quocunque tenentur,
>   Queis timor, anxietas, livor & ira nocet,
> Quos gravis Ambitio, quos improbus ardor habendi,
>   Quos veneri intentos saeva libido coquit.
> Me me conveniant, docto monet ore Galenus,
>   Parete & melior me duce quisquis erit.

All those who are gripped by a disorder of the mind, whom fear, anxiety, envy and anger afflict; whom heavy Ambition, the unholy desire for possessions, whom wild lust burns in their quest for sex ... let them come [to me], counsels Galen of learned speech, obey! And he who follows me, me, will improve!

But in the *De officio medici* a more stringent Lucretian moral medicine competes with, and is ultimately overpowered by, a milder Ovidian one: 'I do not use harsh warnings, nor bitter laws; from our art comes a gentler, surer benefit. I will give you the drugs to remove the burning of Venus, and

---

[9] 'The prefect of the Westphalian college had inspired me as a young boy to take for qualms of conscience, and for real and very serious sins against chastity, those things that should not be considered qualms of conscience or the shadows of sin. And since those things afflicted my mind for almost a whole year, and to such an extent that I dared not raise my eyes, when I returned to my father during the vacation and seemed not sufficiently to heed his advice, I was entrusted to a physician [= Eutropius Eiding] whom I knew to be greatly respected by my father: and by that man's clear arguments, together with strong words, I was restored within a week or two to a rational perspective on my doubts, and I was sent back to school – but into the care of a wiser director of conscience' (*De valetudine literatorum* (1790), p. 151, n. 23); in the original text the narrative is in the third person. But in the dedicatory elegy to the *De officio medici*, to Cardinal Querini, Heerkens remembers fondly the superior of his Meppen college: 'Dear, kind Immendorf, sweetest Rector of morals, Father more loveable than reverend' ('Care immendorfi, Rector suavissime morum, / Comis, amabilior quam reverende Pater!', 'Elegia', p. 5).

[10] Cf. Lucretius's attacks on ambition, avarice and romantic love in Books 3 and 4 of the *De rerum natura*.

of avarice' ('Non gravibus monitis, nec amaris legibus utor; / Lenius a nostra certius arte bonum. / Pharmaca queis Veneris, queis tollitur aestus avari, / Pharmaca quo livor quo cadat ira, dabo', p. 30). We might here compare Ovid's 'softly softly' didactic approach in the *Remedia amoris*: 'I do not bid you break off your affair mid-course; the laws of my regime are not so draconian' ('Non ego te iubeo medias abrumpere curas: / Non sunt imperii tam fera iussa mei'); 'And can anyone call my precepts harsh?' ('Et quisquam praecepta potest mea dura vocare?').[11]

Heerkens advises the physician to ingratiate himself with the patient: 'Start from the winds, be angry with the winds and the breeze if the wind and breeze do not favour your patient' ('Incipe de ventis, ventisque irascere & aurae / Si minus aegroto ventus & aura favent', p. 14). Like Ovid's lover, he must make show to mirror his target's personal preferences: 'Thus if you prescribe and praise what the sick man hates, even if he condemns it unjustly, you will be a fool. Don't be churlish! Find fault with what he blames; the honest victor likes to dissimulate, to give way' ('Sic si praescribas laudesque, quod oderit aeger / Quodque vel immerito damnet, ineptus eris, / Ne sis morosus, reprehende quod arguit ille: / Dissimulare probus, cedere victor amat', p. 20).[12] When a patient is abusive, or neglects his medicine, or condemns it for not acting more quickly, the doctor must 'put up with and excuse this' ('Perfer & excusa'), as 'impatience is the companion of all disease, and is rarely gentler than the illness itself' (p. 36). The Christian charity required by Heerkens of the diplomatic doctor recalls Ovid's advice in the *Ars amatoria* to the hopeful lover, who must be patient and obsequious in order to win his girl: 'If she isn't very nice or responsive to your amorous advances, put up with this and stick it out: later she will be kind' ('Si nec blanda satis, nec erit tibi comis amanti, / Perfer et obdura: postmodo mitis erit').[13]

The admonition to call a doctor before it is too late, however, approaches Ovid's advice in the *Remedia amoris* to prevent and resist the disease of love before it takes hold: 'That which you could have averted in the beginning with a little art, the greater part of men pays for with fever and death' ('Quid quid

---

[11] *Rem. am.* 495–6; 523.
[12] Cf. *Ars. am.* 2. 199–200: 'If she blames, you too blame! Whatever she approves, you approve! Say what she says and deny what she denies! ('Arguet, arguito; quicquid probat illa, probate; / Quod dicet, dicas; quod negat illa, neges').
[13] *Ars. am.* 2. 177–8; Cf. *Am.* 3. 11. 7; *Trist.* 5. 11. 7.

principio minima diverteris arte, / Plurima pars hominum morte febrique luit', p. 27). Cf. Ovid: 'Resist beginnings. The medicine is prepared too late when the malady has become entrenched' ('Principiis obsta; sero medicina paratur, / Cum mala per longas convaluere moras').[14] Like Ovidian lovesickness, the diseases of Heerkens's patients lurk undetected: 'Health is often hidden. A harmful illness lies deep in the inmost marrow, concealing its poison; the unfortunate man has drawn it into his body with long abuse – and he would have it depart in instant flight' ('Abdita saepe salus. Latet altis ima medullis / Dissimulans virus pestis iniqua suum. / Hanc longo infelix contraxit corpus abusu, / Hanc subita jubeat quisquis abire fuga', p. 27). The important task of taking the patient's case history is somehow reminiscent of Ovid's (ultimately Lucretian) recommendation in *Remedia amoris* to pry – up to a point – into the beloved's blemishes and off-putting sexual behaviour: 'You must ask how he has misbehaved, how the patient has lived. Did he deserve this punishment for a crime? You must inquire frequently. Though he blushes, and he keeps it close to his chest, you must still inquire. I want you to know all' ('Quaerendum est, quid peccarit, qui vixerit aeger, / Demeruitne luem crimine? saepe roges. / Ora rubor licet ora notet, pectusque coarctet, / Quaerendum tamen est, Omnia disce velim', p. 28).[15]

The 'all' which our poet-doctor enjoins us to extract from the reluctant patient includes, pointedly, details of his sex life. Heerkens's note relays the advice of 'the most sage Baglivi', who exhorted doctors treating new clients always to suspect and raise the possibility of venereal disease; and Heerkens reproduces *ad loc*, one of the epigrams from his Leiden *Xenia* to that effect. Contrary to the fears he expressed in a letter to Vonck,[16] then, it would seem that Heerkens had little cause to worry about Cardinal Querini objecting to his frankness on this sensitive subject. Then again, our Ovidian bachelor, with delicious and surely deliberate irony, does caution his patients against the immoderate use of sex – dangerous, apparently, not just for scholars![17] Like Ovid's omnipresent preceptor of love, Heerkens's dutiful doctor is to be admitted not only to his patient's dining room, but even to the bedroom:

---

[14] *Rem. am.* 90–1.
[15] Cf. *Rem. Am.* vv. 417–40.
[16] Cf. Chapter 3, p. 117.
[17] Cf. *De valetudine literatorum* (1749), pp. 10–12; and (1790), Book 2, p. 126, and n. 96.

> Hortor ut arcescas medicum tibi, corpore sano,
>   Prandiaque et festis convivia longa diebus,
> Atque intemperias et tua vina regat.
>   Tum noctes confide illi, Thalamique labores,
> Aptaque dilitiis tempora disce tuis.
>   Sed cave, ne Nupta corruptus forte petaci
> Tot tibi praescribat, quot roget illa, vices.
>   Rides! Hocque in re potes o! potes arte carere,
> Auxilio, clamas, non opus esse? Cave,
>   Plurima pars hominum, temere dum vivitur, errat.

I encourage you to summon the doctor to you when you are well, that he may direct your lunches and dinners; that he may direct your long holiday parties and keep your excesses and carousing in check. Then, entrust your nights to him, the labours of the bedroom, and learn the appropriate times for your lovemaking. But beware, lest perhaps he is corrupted by a wanton bride, and prescribe for you as many sessions as *she* demands! You laugh! Oh, you exclaim, you can do without art in that regard, you have no need of help? Beware! The greater part of men, living immoderately, go astray. (p. 26)

The playful counterpoint with Ovid's didactic poetry is more or less constant, and more or less marked throughout *De officio medici*. The ship of human difference is governed by 'Typhis' in both Ovid and Heerkens; in the *Ars amatoria* it is the poet who plays the role of helmsman–master of love, while in *De officio medici* it is the addressee, the humanist physician.[18] Heerkens quotes directly from the *Ars amatoria* when he describes the variety of human temperaments: 'Pectoribus mores tot sunt, quot in orbe figurae!'[19] And he illustrates the theme of diversity of tastes with a keen eye for Ovidian hyperbole: 'Cicero was less harsh on Verres than Erasmus on the gifts of the Rhine, the scale-bearing foes [sc. fish]!' Invoking the Virgilian didactic topos *vidi ego* ('I have seen') with mock solemnity, Heerkens avows:

---

[18] 'But although countless deaths are threatened in the waves, you will fly, Typhis, safely through the reefs and through the deep' ('Sed licet innumerae minitentur in aequore mortes, / Tutus per scopulos per vada Typhi volas', p. 22).
[19] *Ars. am.* 1. 759.

Vidi poma, pyri qui detestantur odorem,
  Vidi, qui fugerent ut mala monstra, rosam.
Vestphalus ut sagas quae nocte bovilia mulgent,
  Vestphalus ut pernis noxia spectra pavet:
Utque Atrei infelix frater, cum viscera nati
  Gustaret, mensâ figit, & obstupuit!
Sic leporum ugit ille dapes, sic alter odorem
  Quem facit accensis Caffea nota fabis.
Caseus huic horror, qui si foret omnibus horror,
  Morborum minus hic, & minus esset opum.

I have seen those who detest apples and the smell of a pear; I have seen those who would flee a rose like a dreadful monster; like the Westphalian who fears witches that milk cows at night, like the Westphalian who fears ghosts harmful to their legs of ham;[20] and as the unhappy brother of Atreus, when he tasted the flesh of his son, fled from the table and was struck dumb! And so that one flees a banquet of hares, and so another the odour produced by a famous coffee with its roasting beans; this one has a horror of cheese – which horror, if it were common to all, would mean less disease over here [sc. in the United Provinces], and less wealth. (p. 21)

Heerkens uses pagan machinery in true Ovidian style, domesticating and deflating mythological examples, and inflating the claims for his own art ('Wretched Eurydice wouldn't have died if I had come to her aid!'; 'Non misera Euridice, me subveniente, perisset!', p. 19). And it is surely no accident that, in rounding off a digression on his visit to the observatory of Paris, he references Ovid's famous digression on Cephalus and Procris.[21] Praising the health-giving air of that city, Heerkens exclaims: 'Such a breeze, oh such a breeze, wretched Cephalus, you were coaxing from the heat when Procris was about to die by your dart! But let us return to our journey . . .' ('Talem aestu Cephale ah talem miserande vocabas, / Cum moritura tuo cuspide Procris erat. / Sed revocemus

---

[20] Cf. *Aves Frisicae* where Heerkens suggests that superstitious fear of the owl's cry was not endemic to former citizens of the Groningen countryside residing in the north, west and east, but was introduced to the southern part of the province by immigrant Westphalians and other German peoples ('Blackbird' ('Merula'), p. 279, n. 12).
[21] *Ars. am.* 3. 685–746.

iter...', p. 23). Ovid's epyllion had ended with a similar self-exhortation: 'Sed repetamus opus'.[22]

Heerkens maintains a mild, conciliatory and light-hearted temper throughout his poem in all but one respect: his intolerance for self-congratulatory, 'barbaric' science. Abraham Munting (1626–83), professor of medicine in Groningen, wrote much on botany and on the 'British herb',[23] and published a great fat tome ('magnum quadratum volumen') in the eighty-first year of the previous century. Our poet excoriates him in a footnote for writing only 'briefly about the powers of the plant, amply about the means by which he had discovered it and of the Glory which discoverers of plants have won for themselves from the ancients; but he discourses *most* amply on the siege of the city of Groningen, on the etymology of the districts of Frisia, on the harshness and excellence of our language, which he writes that Adam used, the "ancient ancestor of the human race"!' (p. 19, n. (e)). If that weren't enough, Munting rambles on about the islands of the farthest ocean in such hideous prose that he himself admits that 'he has imitated the barbarous words of the vulgar botanists ('Herbariorumque Trivialium')'. According to Heerkens, no learned physician should risk praising this 'British herb' in front of his patient: 'If the sick man sees you making a false judgement will he be happy to entrust his body to your judgement?' ('Judicii peccata tui si viderit aeger, / Judicione tuo credere corpus amet?', p. 20). Note that the faulty judgement referred to here is one of literary taste as much as of scientific judgement, and in any case assumes a learned patient.[24]

Later in the poem, Heerkens inveighs against the 'botanical madness' of Linnaeus and his followers in suddenly strident tones (anticipating his snide remarks in the *Aves Frisicae*):

Montes & scopulos peragrant, camposque nivalis
    Lapponiae, & styga jam forte LENAEE petis!
Ut referas plantam, proprio quam nomine dones!
    Ut dicas: foliis quot, quibus illa viret.
Sed bona cui morbo? Non dicitur. Herba LENAEI

---

[22] *Ars. am.* 3.747.
[23] Possibly the 'Muntingia calabura', native to Jamaica, a genus of the *Polyandria monogynia* class and order, producing small, edible fruits.
[24] This is clear from the sequel to his curious outburst: Heerkens relates how he had once received advice on his poetry from a learned Frenchman, who, though a man of good taste, made the mistake of mixing in with his admonitions praise of a tasteless writer (p. 20).

> Noxia forte, Arti sicut & ipse nocet.
> Induit injussus nova nomina cuilibet herbae,
> Nomina prô ipso barbariora viro!
> Cognita quae fuerat, tituloque superba celebri,
> Planta Dioscoridis nobilitata libris:
> Nomine plebeio, seu quò magè laederet aures,
> Nomine barbarico dedecoranda fuit.

They wander mountains and cliffs, and you, Linnaeus, seek out the snowy fields of Lapland, and now perhaps the Styx, so that you may bring back a plant to which you can give your own name; and so that you may report the leaves, and how many there are, with which it grows! But what disease is it good for? It isn't said. The Linnaean plant may be poisonous, just as he is poisonous for our Art. Unbidden, he endows whatever plant he pleases with new names, names more barbarous than the man himself! The plant which was known, and boasted a famous title, and was ennobled in the books of Dioscorides, is to be denigrated with a plebeian name, or – to afflict the ears all the more – a barbarian one! (p. 31)

As he did in Munting's case, Heerkens takes issue with knowledge that is 'useless' inasmuch as it has no direct bearing on human happiness.[25] There is, perhaps, something of Horace's *nil admirari*[26] in that charge, but Heerkens's criticism is angrier: both Munting and Linnaeus are arraigned for being, as it were, on the side of Babel, for crimes against language and clarity; and also,

---

[25] He grudgingly concedes that the Linnaean approach 'may perhaps conceal something useful, but the totality of any one work cannot please' ('Credo aliquid novitas tegat utile forte Lenaei, / Sed cuivis operis summa placere nequit', p. 32). And of course the Ovidian Heerkens is rather fascinated by the idea of the loves of the plants and even polygamy: 'Let the *Singenesya* marry her *Cryptogamos*. Marry *Moneciae*, and you, *Polyandria*, also marry – though you are a plant not content with one man!' ('Nubat Cryptogamo Singenesya suo. / Nubite Moneciae, Polyandria tu quoque nube, / Non contenta uno sis licet herba viro!', pp. 32-3).

[26] 'Nil admirari prope res est una, Numici, / solaque quae possit facere et servare beatum. / hunc solem et stellas et decedentia certis / tempora momentis sunt qui formidine nulla / imbuti spectent' ('To admire nothing, Numicius, is the one thing that can make you and keep you happy. Such are they who look on this sun, and the stars, and the seasons passing at certain times, untainted by any fear', *Epist*. 1. 6. 1-5). Heerkens approaches an Horatian tone even more nearly, though, in his observations on the Paris observatory: 'Let others count stars and the circuits of the revolving heavens, and mark the rate [lit. 'foot'] at which the remote constellations run. Ah, I envy you nothing, Cassini, look to the limits of the universe – the earth, little as it is, is big enough for me!' ('Astra alii numerent, coelique volubilis orbes, / Et pede quo currant dissita signa, notent. / Invideo nihil ah CASSINI perspice mundi / Limina, terra mihi quantula cunque satis!', p. 23). Cf. Horace, *Carm*. 1. 28. 1-6 on the futility of Archytus's mathematical and astronomical speculations.

and for throwing out perfectly good, *reasonable* ancient science in favour of preposterous, modern intellectual presumption. Thus, in addition to his offences against humanist medicine, Heerkens has an axe to grind with Linnaeus's contention that man went about on all fours before he walked on two feet. The passage is strongly redolent of his diatribe against Rousseau in the *De valetudine literatorum*.[27] And Heerkens despairs of worthy men who have, as it were, gone over to the dark side:

> This man [Linnaeus] is venerated and his art praised by men who are not fauns, who are famous and distinguished: van Royen, the Jussieu brothers, Gronovius and Artedi (alas, now drowned in the waters of Amsterdam!). Others celebrate him, no doubt, because some little plant or root or stalk was named after them. Ambition, and a zeal for fame, gave this quadrupedal Swede cunning and talent. But let not empty honour, let not the Faun's munificence move you, celebrated men of great name! Laurels, and the Cytherean myrtle, should crown your locks, van Royen – not the vain *Rojana*. (p. 32)

That our poet should name his former medical professor, botanist and didactic poet, Adriaan van Royen, in the company of those who have preferred cheap fame to genuine glory may be playful irreverence – that would certainly not be out of character for the younger Heerkens – or, on a more suspicious reading, is it a clue that van Royen was one of the mysterious Leiden critics who prevented the long version of the *De valetudine literatorum* from going to print in 1749?[28] Be that as it may, Heerkens conflates in his *De officio medici* a turning away from (Latin) humanism with a turning away from medical utility – both *qua* the Ovidian moral medicine he promotes above all in this poem, and as the cumulative learning of the profession he would painstakingly assemble in his *Empedocles*. None of this obliges us to see Heerkens as a scientific reactionary, however. If anything, he is a true son of the scientific revolution, suspicious of the Baconian idols of marketplace and theatre. In the *Empedocles* he challenges,

---

[27] Cf. Chapter 2, pp. 89–91
[28] Against this view, perhaps, is Heerkens's acknowledgement of van Royen's precedence as a medical poet in the 1749 edition of the *De valetudine litteratorum*: 'Nor do we lack an example for our labours: Look at van Royen! He was for a long time our Apollo in Leiden' ('Nec caret exemplo quod molior: aspice (b) Rojum. / Ille diu Leidae noster Apollo fuit', p. 3). However, the prodigal son may have been erring on the side of caution at the time of his Batavian homecoming.

where necessary, or at least supplements with the lessons of his own experience, the voices of time-hallowed learned medicine.

## Empedocles in Epigrams

It will be remembered that, in the *Notabilia*, Heerkens had evinced a passion for collecting inscriptions, of which a bumper crop ('segetem'), we were told, might be harvested in Rome.[29] While he had shared with us some modern inscriptions for their novelty and titillation value,[30] he scrutinized the ancient ones, especially, with an eye to their didactic–historical utility. Thus he chided Fontenelle for seeing 'no value in the inscriptions in the Columbarium [tomb of the servants of Livia Augustus] save in their paradigmatic Latinity.'[31] But don't they also show something of the customs of antiquity, something of the Roman economy? Something of the luxury and magnificence of those times?' (*Notabilia*, Book 2, p. 178). From the small and apparently insignificant, then, important historical, social or indeed scientific insights may be gleaned. This is the same omnivorous eye for detail that alighted on Ovid's Polyphemus in the *Metamorphoses* as evidence of the decline of Calabrian agriculture from ancient times;[32] the same eye which ranged over the peat fields of the Groningen Omlandia with loving and patient attention.

If, however, we expect to find in the preface to Heerkens's *Empedocles* (1783) a précis of the modern Dutch physician's views on older traditions and new

---

[29] *Notabilia*, Book 2, p. 124. In Venice, too, there are many notable and magnificent epitaphs to be collected from the city's churches, but Heerkens muses wryly that it is sufficient there for someone merely to have possessed wealth to be commemorated, not to have done something memorable with it.

[30] *Notabilia*, Book 2, p. 128. In Ferrara, Ariosto's Latin tomb inscription has been relocated. Heerkens is concerned that his soul will wander about on Judgement Day anxiously looking for its body. Raphael's picture of his girlfriend in the Barberini palace shows her 'pointing with one hand to her lower belly, as it were, wearing on this hand [sc. arm] a bracelet in which there are these letters: Raphael of Urbino's. The inscription is so clear and brief that you can see that not much diligence or effort is required in collecting them' (ibid.).

[31] Discovered in 1726 and described and illustrated by Antonio Francesco Gori a year later.

[32] See *Notabilia*, Book 1, pp. 42–3, on Ovid's inclusion of milk products ('lacticinia'), and omission of olives and olive oil, from the gifts of the Calabrian Polyphemus to Galatea, and indeed from Pythagoras's speech in Book 15 of the *Metamorphoses*. Both speakers might have mentioned that food in error 'had Ovid not been so careful of the truth and so expert in the period' ('nisi Ovidius veri admodum studiosus, et peritissimus saeculi fuisset'). Today, reckons Heerkens, even a well-born Calabrian farmer would find it difficult to provide milk products from his estates: 'But let's return to Rome, where it would assuredly be desirable for many Polyphemuses to be brought back from the dead around the city. Then the [modern] Romans would have milk products, they would have much cheaper butter than that which is transported to them on ships from Ireland, or from our shores.'

trends in medical science, and his place within them – something along the lines, perhaps, of his preface to the *Aves Frisicae* – we shall be disappointed. Heerkens gives us, instead, an almost adventitious dissertation on the literary proprieties of the epigram. He muses on the relative importance of prosody, facility/fluency, wisdom and wit in compositions of this genre, concluding that a humorous punchline is not essential to it, and not even brevity. In so saying he attacks what he deems the nonsense spouted by the writers of the *Encyclopédie*, who legislate against epigrams longer than eight verses, ignoring the evidence, for example, of the Greek Anthology:

> They will see Martial, not without scorn, objecting to the fussy lover of brevity, this distich: "Disce, quod ignoras: Marsi doctique Pedonis / Saepe duplex unum pagina tractat opus" ['Learn what you don't know. A work of learned Marsus and Pedo often took up a double-sided page']. But who is that Marsus? Who is Pedo? Who is the Gaetulicus praised by Martial in another place? They were the three most noted Roman writers of epigram after Catullus, or rather, the only ones. (*Empedocles* (1783), p. vi)

Most of the remainder, indeed bulk, of Heerkens's preface (pp. vi–xxiii) is given over to a scholarly excursion designed to restore to the Republic of Letters these unjustly neglected epigrammatic poets. Our moderate Catholic author is stunned by the hypocrisy of the Jesuit François Vavasseur (1605–81), who wrote a huge tome on the epigram in which he peremptorily dismissed the Romans Marsus, Pedo and Gaetulicus because they had produced only 'erotic trifles'. But 'the life of a priest, which [Vavasseur] followed, does not oblige one to disagree with oneself. He who so many times deemed Catullus and Martial fit for reading, who writes about them on almost every page, what right does he have to rejoice that less obscene poets have perished while those two survive?' (p. vi).

Be that as it may, in his *first* collection of medical epigrams, which was published in Leiden by Elie Luzac in 1748 and dedicated to his philosopher-friend, Nicolaus Engelhard, Heerkens had confined himself, in the main, to distichs and tetrastichs.[33] Those *Xenia Physico-Medica* ('Parting Medical–Philosophical

---

[33] From the preface of the expanded 1798 second edition of his *Empedocles*, in seven books, it would appear that Heerkens composed two *centuriae* of medical precepts while at Leiden, the second dictated to him (sc. for versification) by a group of Scots and Irish physicians he had befriended there. They would be dedicated to 'the very famous and cultivated old man, Hamilton', a Scot, and were directed to the concerns of the elderly. Heerkens implies that this second *centuria* was published, but only the first collection is in fact extant (pp. iii–iv).

Gifts/Poems') were composed on the sly and on the side, when the disgraced young satirist was supposed to be concentrating on his medical studies.[34] They were cobbled together to substitute for an abandoned Latin translation of Louis Racine's *Religion* that Heerkens had originally earmarked for dedication to his Groningen mentor. The *Xenia* were, of course, composed before Heerkens's first trip to Paris, where the encouragement of Fontenelle and friends must have planted the seed of a much more ambitious collection of verse precepts on hygiene.[35] That seed would only begin to germinate and pullulate in Italy, some eleven years later.

\* \* \*

The *Empedocles* (1783), as its title already suggests, takes itself much more seriously than Heerkens's earlier *Xenia*. The long opening poem of the first book, 'To the Reader', justifies the enterprise of versifying medical precepts by appeal to Hippocrates's excerpting oracular remedies from votive tablets displayed in the temples of Aesculapius. Indeed, each of Heerkens's five books is launched with a more or less programmatic poem 'To the Reader'. The second of these runs to 62 lines, and informs us that its book has followed its predecessor after some 30 years; that it was compiled while the poet was convalescing with a foot injury. While Heerkens admits that the work progressed in a rather desultory fashion there is a hint of Lucretius's *avia Pieridum*, betraying a more ambitious vision, in his reflection: 'It was pleasing/ useful to have studied the doctors during the passionate years [of my youth]; from them the more trackless age of life was [made] more cautious' ('*Juverat ardentes medicis studuisse per annos: / Avia pars vitae cautior inde fuit*', p. 26,

---

[34] 'I didn't become so insensible to [poetry] that a few little verses didn't occur to me, from time to time, in which secretly ('furtim') I expressed the opinions of Hippocrates and others' (p. 4).

[35] This is revealed in the preface to the second edition of the *Empedocles* (1798). Heerkens had been advised that François-Joachim de Pierre de Bernis (a celebrated French epigrammatist and favourite of Madame Pompadour) was about to join the royal household. Discovering that Bernis suffered from a stomach complaint, Heerkens saw his chance and presented the learned gentleman with a copy of his *Xenia*, including a new dedicatory tetrastich. The next day, Bernis arranged for Heerkens to show off his impromptu poetic talents in front of Fontenelle and his guests, and to show up d'Alembert into the bargain. The latter had been putting it about that Heerkens's elegy in praise of the Westphalian Jesuits, which was doing the rounds in Paris to much applause, had been dictated to him by his former teachers. By the end of Fontenelle's party, Heerkens had 'won the favour of not a few of those present, and appeals that I continue to write and devote myself to this enterprise. But I could not hope to compile sufficient aphorisms – and as my poem on the Health of the Learned, already underway, and continually in my hands, excused me from that task then, so too later did so many arguments levelled against my maligned Muse when I was back in my homeland' (1798, p. vii).

my emphasis).³⁶ The *ad Lectorem* of Book 4 (50 lines) announces that formerly, according to Horace, poets were licensed to draw their subject matter from philosophy, but now this path is barred to them: 'When you write serious things, they don't seem serious, and the Muse who has spoken them, as I have seen, is not believed' ('Seria cum scribis, non seria scripta videntur, / Musaque quae, vidi, dixerit, orba fide est', p. 91). Heerkens had 'seen', of course, when he published his poem on the swallow, and claimed to have discovered that it hibernated along the banks of the Ems: 'Someone had assessed this judgement, presented in song; he said that there was nothing more to object to than that it was presented in song. Does the truth, therefore, cease to be the truth in song, and is no reason persuasive when it is set in metre?' ('Penderat hanc aliquis rationem, carmine dictam; / Carmine quod dicta est, nil magis obstat, ait. / Verum igitur, verum per carmina desinit esse, / Nec ratio numeris ulla ligata movet?', p. 92). And as for the present project, does Hippocrates cease to be trustworthy when he is put into verse by Nicander? Heerkens climbs onto his old hobbyhorse about the 'paradoxes' of the French,³⁷ who have denied that Latin poems can be composed in modern times: 'but that true things cannot be related in poems, that is an invention of your genius, Montbeillard. He who presents his case in song, disproves it' ('Sed quod carminibus narrari vera nequirent, / Pectoris inventum est Montbeliarde tui. / Carmine qui dicit rationem, expendit et illam', p. 92).

The opening poem of Heerkens's third book gives the rationale for the title of the work as a whole: 'It will not be said that my book is called "Empedocles" in vain by those who know Empedocles' ('Non meus, Empedocles, frustra liber esse vocatus / Dicitur, Empedocles cui bene notus erit'). In the twenty-odd lines that follow, Heerkens supplies a potted biography of the philosopher-poet who 'expounded in verse what he saw, and whatever was published in ancient times was always seasoned with verse' ('Versibus exposuit, quae vidit; et edita priscis / Temporibus, versu condita semper erant'). Empedocles 'wrote so harmoniously ('numerosus') about natural philosophy and medicine ('de Physica'), that he surpassed all who followed and preceded him. His writings were preserved long, and for more than a thousand years, but were lost from

---

³⁶ Cf. Lucretius, *De rerum natura* 1. 926–7: 'avia Pieridum peragro loca nullius ante / trita solo' ('I range through the trackless haunts of the Muses never before touched by human foot').
³⁷ Or at least, of the *philosophes*. Cf. Chapter 2, pp. 90, 98 of Rousseau, and Chapter 5, p. 194.

sight by the uncultured race that [then] arose' ('Sed sic de Physica scripsit numerosus, ut omnes / Vicerit asseclas, quique fuere prius. / Conservata diu scripta, et mille amplius annis, / Perdidit ex oculis gens rudis orta suis'). While Empedocles's ancient legacy has been buried, 'one thing is known: whatever excellent discoveries were made by the old man were not articulated save in the briefest verse' ('Unum illud scitur, senis optima quaeque reperta / Non nisi versiculo dicta fuisse brevi'). This is a rather curious claim, of course, as Empedocles is principally remembered for his long hexameter didactic poems using Homeric diction (*Physics* and *Purifications*); as such, he was a model for Lucretius's six-book cosmological epic! Yet Heerkens concludes by asking the reader to judge whether 'I seem to have captured ('comprehendere') my subject in a few words; and acute ones' ('Resque meas videor paucis comprehendere verbis, / Argutisne? tuo, Lector, ab ore sciam', p. 59).[38]

If we return to the prose preface, we can see that the author has already there attempted to stitch together something of a philosopher's cloak for the epigrammatic poet. While conceding that humour and wit are an ornament to the epigram, he argues forcefully that they are not its defining features:

> A greater endowment is harmony ('numerus'), *a truth worthy of being known is greater*, one content to be told in well-fashioned verses. Laughter is often not to be wrenched out of people, but a sensible truth, expressed in harmonious verses, in some way compels a favourable judgement from its readers. A joke or witticism, unless it is really felicitous, is an arbitrary thing. But reason, and a memorable and sensible thing, once heard, moves the minds of all, by the will of nature – just as that which is true and just, memorable or pitiable, can be known and felt by everyone. (p. iii, my emphasis)

Well, 'known and felt' at least by everyone able to read Heerkens's Latin.

Heerkens maintains, moreover, that the ability to appreciate a joke varies from country to country. The reason for this variation is, it seems, as much

---

[38] The fifth and final poem 'To the Reader' is shorter and sweeter. The poet reflects that he was once noted and notorious in his hometown; now he is not only unknown to his compatriots, he is addressed by them as a foreigner. The thought is reminiscent of the well-known finale to *Tristia* 3. 14, where Ovid laments he is losing his language. Heerkens's star flickers briefly again, though, when he and his maidservant are bitten by a dog reputed to be rabid: 'And lo, forthwith, just as when I was a boy writing poems, my name is on everyone's lips, of the high and the low; and he whom the Groningeners know from the deaths of the living, they point out, now, because his puppy is ill-humoured' ('Protinus ecce, puer tanquam cum carmina scripsi / Ordinibus cunctis nomen in ore meum est; / Quemque Groningates viventum a funere norint, / Designant, catulus, nunc quia tristis erat', p. 121).

physiological as cultural: 'Those whom the nature of their climate and country has endowed with dull senses ('crassos sensus') find the most felicitous humorist silly' (ibid.). When he was in Paris and frequented the epigrammatist and comic dramatist, Alexis Piron (1689–1773), the Dutchman had observed that the latter's witticisms were sure to raise a laugh among the French, but not necessarily among foreigners. Fontenelle's jokes were even more subtle ('adeo tenuibus delicatisque'), going over the heads even of some Parisians. Our reformed satirist now skates, momentarily, on more dangerous ice: 'Had he [Fontenelle] dwelt among a people very well known to me [sc. the Frisians who hadn't appreciated the satires of 'Curillus'] his witticisms would have all fallen on deaf ears' (ibid.).

Not that an ear for harmonious *verse* is given to everyone either. And the talent for consistently producing poems which happily combine meaning with harmonious verses ('feliciter junctis verbis numerosos admodum versus facere', p. iv) is, according to Heerkens, to be found only in Virgil among the Romans, Ariosto among the Italians, and Boileau and Racine among the French. That said, *Ovid*, in his view, was blessed with an equally rare talent, that of an 'inimitable facility/fluency', which led him to boast, with probable justice, that he was the most read of all his contemporaries, preferred even to Virgil: 'I have said that the musical ('numerosum') gift has fallen to a few Greeks, Italians and Frenchmen; but I will not say that there exists, in those languages, a writer with a facility on a par with Ovid's. But if there are any, I confess I do not know them' (ibid.). Is Heerkens implying, then, that Ovid, rather than, say, Martial, should be our principal model for the modern Latin epigram? Not in so many words, but the criterion of utility already hinted at in this preface suggests that the best precepts on hygiene are, by definition, those which are most easily digested by their target audience, hence smoothly Ovidian. To what extent does Heerkens himself live up to the standard he implicitly sets for himself, in this preface, of facility and utility?

\* \* \*

Whatever Heerkens's literary ambitions for his *Empedocles*, when it came to the second, expanded, edition, considerations of comprehensiveness, if not compendiousness, seem to have overtaken those of poetic pleasure. Not only has the work doubled in size,[39] the number and range of medical

---

[39] It has 310 pages compared to 152 in the first edition. Book 1 comprises 176 poems; Book 2, 211; Book 3, 266; Book 4, 293; Book 5, 308; Book 6, 304; and Book 7, 305.

authorities represented has also boomed (over 60, for example, in the first book alone).[40] As for contemporary 'field leaders', Heerkens versifies several pronouncements from the mouth ('ab ore') of Albrecht von Haller (1708–77). Haller, for example, is the source of an anecdote illustrating the importance of setting the child on a good diet from his earliest years, from which he will not deviate later in life. An African boy raised among sheep eats nothing but sheep's greens ('ovium ... olus'); and fame has it that such a boy, removed from his native land and transported to Switzerland, lived 200 years (6, 202). Heerkens must have visited Haller – the Swiss prodigy was a physician, anatomist, botanist, as well as German and Latin poet – on his return journey from Italy.[41]

It was in Italy, in Padua, that Heerkens's garden of medical epigrams came into flower, under the solicitous eye of Giambattista Morgagni.[42] Fellow senior citizens of Padua, antiquarian and professor of physics, the marquis Giovanni Poleni (c. 1683–1761), and Giovanni Antonio Volpi (1686–1766), professor of philosophy, and later of Greek and Latin literature, also had their two verses' worth. Heerkens would endear himself to Poleni, who despaired of the state of Dutch astronomy – where were the Tycho Brahes and Heveliuses? – by quoting from Ovid's *Fasti* and blaming the weather.[43] He bore a letter of introduction from no less stellar a scientific personage than Jean-Jacques

---

[40] His sources range from the ancients (Homer, Pythagoras, Empedocles, Hippocrates, Aristotle, Cicero, Pliny, Dioscorides, Moschion, Galen, Celsus, Aetius etc.), through Arab, Byzantine and Latin medieval writers (Avicenna, Alexander of Tralles, Paul of Aegina, Rhazes, Arnaud de Villeneuve etc.), to Renaissance and early modern physicians (Michele Savanorola, Jason van der Velde, Marsilio Cagnati, Girolamo Mercuriale, Girolamo Cardano, Leonello dei Vittori da Faenza, Giovanni Bruerino Campeggi, Giovanni Benedetto Sinibaldi, Levinus Lemnius, Pieter van Foreest, Laurent Joubert, Antoine Mizauld, Georg Riedlin, Caspar Bartholin, Vobiscus Fortunatus Plemp etc.), celebrity nearer contemporaries such as Giorgio Baglivi (1668–1707), Bernardino Ramazzini (1633–1714), Hermann Boerhaave (1668–1738), Friedrich Hoffmann (1660–1742) and Gerard van Swieten (1700–22), and even single issues of seventeenth- and eighteenth-century learned journals (especially the *Acta Lipsiensium* [sc. *Acta eruditorum*, Leipzig] and of the Academia Nova Curiosorum [= Leopoldina]).

[41] Thus 'from Haller's mouth, Lausanne 1760': 'Domestic life in the mountains is not lazy, and toughens you up; and this [mountain] mob is the only one in the Swiss world that grows old' ('Haud pigra montanis, et vita domestica durat: / Unumque Helvetico vulgus in orbe senet', 1798, 2, 59.)

[42] In the preface to the 1798 edition, Heerkens reports that, despite the encouragement of his Parisian friends, he intermitted his writing of medical epigrams until he met Morgagni in Padua during his Italian journey. The work's first tetrastichs, and more than 60 dispersed throughout, were composed 'in his presence' ('coram illo'), and 'demonstrate the usefulness of his attention' ('curae quidem huius utilitatem ostendere', p. vii).

[43] *Italica* (1793), pp. 91–2: 'Praetereaque animis tantum felicibus, astra / Nasonem, et Superûm supposuisse domus'; and in the accompanying n. 15: 'Indicare hic ea, quae fastorum libro 1, versibusque 297, 298, et versibus 305 et 306 Ovidius dixit, satis apparet.'

d'Ortous de Mairan (1678–1771), but it was when he let drop his admiration for the didactic poetry of Jesuit Carlo Noceti (1694–1759), who had rendered Mairan's meteorological theories into Latin hexameters, that he really won Volpi's heart. Volpi, a Latin poet of some note, showed the young Dutchman his impressive library of modern Latin poets and became his literary mentor and promoter in Italy.[44] But the *Empedocles* itself was blessed, if not commissioned, by the venerable and lovable professor Morgagni himself.[45] The octogenerian physician was also the poet's most ventriloquized source, at least in the 1798 edition.[46] It might be more accurate to say that Heerkens was Morgagni's mouthpiece. This at least is suggested by the elaborated account of the work's genesis in the *Italica* (1793), in Heerkens's second elegiac letter to Tenhove. When he was down on his luck in Venice, and hoping, in order to get noticed, to publish the poetic account of his journey there, Heerkens had sought in Morgagni a learned pair of eyes to look over a draft of the *Iter Venetum*.[47] Together with a letter of introduction, he had sent the learned physician a complimentary copy of his Leiden *Xenia*. Morgagni, an elegant Latin stylist in his own right, was delighted and distracted by those renditions of the aphorisms of Hippocrates 'and a few oracles [sc. pronouncements] by more modern doctors, encapsulated in the briefest and clearest verse of which I was capable'. He made Heerkens an offer too good to refuse: if he would only persevere in that most useful genre of poetry, Morgagni would relieve him of the burden of finding and selecting, 'among the immense works of

---

[44] As Heerkens notes in his second elegiac letter to Tenhove (*Italica* (1793), pp. 84–96, at p. 92, n. 16), Volpi had won fame for his *Carmina*, published in Padua in 1725, and his commentary on Latin satire, published in 1744.

[45] The second epigram of the first book, 'Giambattista Morgagni, from his mouth', exhorts Heerkens to help 'many to grow old' by relaying 'in a few verses', the 'signs and prospects of a reasonably easy old age' ('Signa, satis facilis spemque ostentare senectae ... / Dic ea, de paucis recitabere versibus, et quod / Pluris erit, multis posse senere, dabis' (1798), p. 1). It follows a poem purporting to render a letter from a certain 'Villanovan' to Petrarch, from a manuscript in the library at Padua, proposing a supplement to the School of Salernum. (Of course this cannot have been the famous thirteenth-century physician, Arnaud de Villeneuve.)

[46] Suffice it to note Heerkens's rendition of the opinion of the renowned author of *De sedibus et causis morborum per anatomen indagatis* on the compassion we must show to monstrous births, who often live much longer than expected through the grace of God: 'The lives of the able-bodied, who throw away their lives through impulsiveness and wrong decisions, are often less healthy, and shorter!' ('Aegrior, et brevior vegetorum est plurima, vitam / Impete praecipitans per male suasa suam!', 1, 35). Other precepts of Morgagni are more mundane, such as that warning against the abuse of roasted fowl (1, 114).

[47] It was Volpi, in the end, on whom Heerkens foisted a draft of his *Iter Venetum*. The older philologist became rather too invested in the project: 'The critic friend observes the work from close up, like the author, and it deceives him so many times, like the young girl's figure!' ('Censor amicus opus prope spectat, ut author: eumque / Fallit opus toties! Quam sua forma nurum', p. 95).

the physicians, the most salubrious opinions, and those most necessary to know'.[48]

The contents of the third book of the 1798 *Empedocles* seem to have been especially dear to the old man's heart. It is devoted to the doctrine of insensible perspiration as developed by a much-maligned former Chair of Medicine at Padua, Santorio Santorio (1561–1636).[49] Via Heerkens's pen, Morgagni's hero receives an almost too enthusiastic endorsement from his contemporary Swiss colleague, Haller: 'The Italian Santorio has added more to the medical art than all the centuries that followed the old man of Cos [sc. Hippocrates]' ('Plus Italus medicae Sanctorius addidit arti, / Quam tot post Coum saecla secuta senem', 3, 263). 'And so his short work' – derived from experiments weighing the body pre- and post-food, urination and evacuation – 'which someone could read in an hour, achieves the same renown as Galen's, whom, I think, no-one has read twice' ('Per breve sic et opus, quod perlegat hora, Galeni, / Haud quem ullus legit bis, puto, nomen habet').[50] We are left wondering how much of Heerkens's *Empedocles* is, in fact, of his own selection, if not invention. By the time he was ready to continue his journey south, and had bidden Morgagni his final farewell, the poet claims to have versified 'more than a hundred' aphorisms furnished him by his medical muse. But the first edition of the *Empedocles*, published in Groningen only a quarter century later, was enlarged by 'not a few other [aphorisms] discovered/invented by me, but less skilfully sorted' ('adjunctis haud paucis aliis a me inventis, sed minus dextrè discretis').[51] And we can probably safely infer from the nearly 2,000 epigrams featured in the 1798 edition, that, no matter how generous a hand Morgagni had in the work's birth and infancy, the *Empedocles* was substantially Heerkens's own creation.[52]

---

[48] *Italica* (1798), pp. 84–96, at pp. 90–1, and n. 12.
[49] The second epigram of the third book, 'Morgagni ad Authorem', enjoins: 'Go on, then, write the aphorisms of Santorio that will make this well-known [sc. how passions, climate and food affect healthy perspiration], or at least, let your Muse grant that they be read. You should count it less of a boon that you are recited on account of a few distichs, but that these can give help to many is a great one' ('Sanctori, fac ergo, aphorismos, id bene sciri, / Vel mage qui faciant, det tua musa legi. / Pauca, bonum minus est, ob disticha quod reciteris, / Grande sed haec multos posse juvare, putes', p. 72).
[50] Heerkens must be referring to Santorio's *De statica medicina* (Venice, 1614), which lent itself well to versification, being already presented in numbered (prose) aphorisms.
[51] *Italica* (1793), p. 90, n. 12.
[52] In the letter to Tenhove, Heerkens looks forward to publishing the second edition of the *Empedocles* soon, 'mindful of the words'/'remembering the dicta' of Morgagni ('Morganji dictorum memor'). I don't think we need assume that Heerkens is referring to physical notes, but it is clear that Morgagni's spirit continues to preside, in some sense, over the work.

Curiously, that hand was not even acknowledged in the first edition, neither in the preface nor in the attribution of precepts. The first edition is also more typical of our author in incorporating a greater number of rather digressive footnotes.

Heerkens's epigrams make for fascinating reading, not least because they provide, one assumes, a revealing cross-section of the beliefs and concerns of the contemporary Dutch doctor: Hippocrates that bitter earwax portends long life (1, 22); Boerhaave on Dutch colonial cities which are being founded in the same sorts of insalubrious locations as at home (1, 26); Matthaeus Martinus citing salt as a cause for melancholy (1, 127); Sinibaldi on passions, especially anger, causing barrenness in women (2, 157); the same, on the higher rate of conception among small women than large – because their husbands' members penetrate more deeply (2, 170), but then, in the following epigram, Massaria on the infertility of men with overly long penises (2, 171); Mizauld, on a woman who retained the skeleton of a foetus in her uterus for 12 years and still managed to service her farmer husband (2, 178); Mercuriale relaying Empedocles's observation on the ill-effects of the south wind on pregnant women (1, 73), and Richard Lassels, an English traveller in Italy, on windy locations causing madness (4, 4); Levinus Lemnius noting that old men sire particularly beautiful daughters, in early spring (6, 74). Very occasionally we encounter a precept that chimes with twenty-first-century opinion, such as the following public health warning from Friedrich Hoffmann: 'Drinking too much beer is harmful, and, when combined with tobacco smoking, how many deaths it has caused in my country!' ('Plurima pota nocet cervisia, cumque tabaci / Fumo juncta, meo quot facit orbe neces!', 4, 231).

The *Empedocles* is, however, no book of medical marvels and monsters. Heerkens is at pains to display the appropriate levels of professional scepticism and conservatism. In response to the April 1721 issue of the Leipzig *Acta eruditorum*, on the German who loves to eat eels, the 'Helens of the dining-table', Heerkens mocks at the inference that the consumption of long-lived creatures can somehow ensure our own longevity (2, 126).[53] Nor should we blithely heed the Scot, 'Homius', and allow ourselves an ample and high-meat diet: medical advice should always be

---

[53] Presumably the *Acta Eruditorum* (Leipzig) but I have not found the article to which Heerkens refers. Is it perhaps the September review of Richard Bradley's *Philosophical Account of the Works of Nature*?

appropriate to the nationality or environment of the patient (1, 75).[54] The author is amazed that sugar is so highly prized by the modern French, even though its ill-effects were known already by the dietary writer, Bruerino: 'and as young man, I would marvel at its abuse among the doctors of the people, man, so little heeded were the precepts handed down! We must plead, therefore, that it should be lawful to be teachable, or else the flighty mind will not hold onto any precepts' ('Hujus et, in medicis populi, mirarer abusum / Vir juvenisque, adeo sunt data scita nihil! / Orandum est igitur, fas ut sit posse doceri, / Scita secusque animus non tenet ulla levis', 1, 124). In France, it seems, it is forbidden to forbid! Heerkens takes exception to 'Marsiglio Cagnati, on Health', who has denied that the consumption of six or seven different foods is more burdensome on the stomach than that of an equal quantity of two: 'You would think it impossible to deny, even though it's a doctor's prerogative, but Cagnati, in that book which teaches many things, denies it. But since doctors derive their fame from expounding paradoxes, it is useful, when such things are brought out in the open, to learn their value' ('Idque negare, licet medici esse, haud posse putaris, / Cagnatus libro, multa docente, negat. / Sed, quia dat medicis, paradoxa exponere, famam, / Talibus à visis discere pensa, juvat', 2, 132). And our cautious author even calls the great Ramazzini to account, when the latter overrules Hippocrates's advice that the wet-nurse and pregnant mother should avoid intercourse: 'Let's grant you convince us that the precept is doubtful: the ancient doctor's pronouncement will be laughed at – and so will the modern' ('Perficeres, demus, scitum id dubitabile credi, / Risa vetus medici, voxque recentis erit', 6, 86).[55]

In the definitive 1798 edition – but not, interestingly, in the first – the opinions of more than one author, from different periods, are often combined in a single poem, to which Heerkens sometimes also adds his own voice: 'Ramazzini, and the poet, Lotichius, on the adverse health effects on Lombard peasants of eating cheese' (4, 154); 'Galen, Bartholin and the Author' on the religious proscription of meals combining sea and land creatures, and the general decline of health after Luther overruled Jewish dietary laws – except

---

[54] Cf. *De valetudine literatorum* (1790), pp. 82–3, and nn. 41–2 on the Scottish physician, Francis Home (1719–1813), student in Leiden in 1742–8, later professor of *materia medica* at Edinburgh, and author of an influential *Principia Medicinae* (1758).

[55] Cf. the reported opinion of van Swieten: 'Infrequent sex for the wet-nurse is harmful, frequent is very bad. It burns up the milk in the breasts and makes it extremely noxious' ('Rara venus nutricis obest, deterrima crebra est: / Lac cremat in mammis, pernocuumque facit', 6, 58).

in Denmark, where, though not Catholic, the populace is even more austere in forgoing meat four times a week (2, 120); on the dangers of passive smoking in enclosed spaces, gleaned by the author from 'cultivated Frenchmen' (2, 36); to Zacuto's finding that women become ferocious and mad in the heat, the author's personal observation of women lying in the streets in Naples, foaming at the mouth (2, 159); confirming van Swieten's observation that, in 'our country', evening *pruritus* caused by worms is rare in children but is a frequent affliction of rich and elderly men – nevertheless, when he was 'not [yet?] a doctor' ('haud medico'), Heerkens saw a 10-year-old girl cured of worms by eating purslane (6, 280); on more dangerous parasites, the opinion of 'N. Mead [sic], an English doctor, and the Author', on the plague being presaged by swarming midges (4, 15),[56] and the 'Author to Girolamo Mercuriale', on their absence, due to smoke or vapour, after an earthquake in Ferrara, which preserved that city from the plague (4, 18).[57]

While Heerkens's misgivings about midges are hardly the result of original epidemiological research,[58] several of his epigrams do offer evidence of the calibration of traditional teaching with first-hand observations made, for example, during his travels. Thus a poem claiming: 'The goddess of health could be believed to prescribe the entire diet of the Italians, were it not that cheese is used, and so frequently. And that pleasing, and now inveterate, poison is added to rice, and this daily [rice] is eaten before every meal. A great part of the people thus suffers from liver complaints: and that sharp food may be the first

---

[56] 'Mead, an Englishman, saw that they were a noxious race, and that the lungs conceived the plague from inhaling them' ('Toxiferum hos vidit genus esse Meadius Anglus, / His et inhalatis pectus habere luem'). Heerkens in fact means the physician, Richard Mead (1673–1754), author of *A Short Discourse Concerning Pestilential Contagion, and the Method to be Used to Prevent it* (London, 1720). Cf. *Notabilia*, Book 3, p. 34, on Mead's implication of these pests in the Great Plague of Marseilles of 1720, and Heerkens's understanding 'through a reasonably certain tradition' that a plague in Groningen in 1664 was known in advance by a 'very fine dark blue cloud' entering its homes (3, 34).

[57] '"The Author to [A. T.] Petronius, on "the food of the Romans [and on preserving health = *De victu Romanorum et de sanitate tuenda* (Rome, 1581)]"', on infestations in the Pontine Marshes (1, 74).

[58] He does, however, devote some pages to such insects in the *Notabilia*: 'How much these flying insects [= fireflies] differ from those which are seen in our regions I experienced when making a night-time journey through the Pontine Marshes. I marvelled at all the air close to the land blazing as if with little sparks, and learned from the coach driver that these were *lucciole*. This is what the Italians today call this kind of fly; the ancients, according to Pliny, called them *cicindelae*, the Greeks *lampyres* and *pigolampides*' (Book 3, pp. 32–4, at p. 33). Cf. *Italica* (1793), Book 1, p. 13 (= *Iter Venetum*), on a good diet being protective against the corrupting effects of 'small flying insects'; and in the third letter to van Lynden, where Heerkens puns on *invisi culices* ('unseen/hated midges'), and points out that the pestiferous ones he observed on his return journey from Naples were precisely those 'only seen at night', namely the *luxiolae/cicindulae* [sic] (p. 122, and n. 8).

to inflame it' ('Omnem Italis victum, nisi caseus esset in usu, / Tamque frequens, credi posset Hygeia dare: / Inditur idque placens, vetus et jam virus, oryzae: / Haecque diurna omnem sumitur ante dapem. / Multaque pars gentis jecoris sic noxia morbo est: / Idque cremet princeps, acer et ille cibus', 1, 92).[59] His Italian experiences also prompt our Catholic author to worry about excessive consumption of fish during the ecclesiastical fast (1, 90); and he attributes high rates of death by dropsy among his own compatriots to a fish diet.[60]

A handful of findings 'of the Author' provide more personal insights. In the sixth book, dedicated to diseases of childhood, Heerkens reveals:

Quo quis erat valde puerile exterritus aevo,
   Cum vano afficitur post seniorque metu:
Ne caderem e scala, patrio puer ore monebar,
   Esse esse in fatis decidere inde meis.
Seria et id dictum quadrimo voce, pavorem
   Nunc stanti in scala vel breviore facit.

The vain fear with which one is greatly affected as a boy is the one that affects you in later life: I was warned by my father not to fall down stairs. It is, since then, it is my destiny to fall. And that thing, said in a serious voice to a four-year-old, creates fear for me now when I am standing even on low stairs. (6, 236)

Among longer narrative pieces of interest is the case history of a short mystery illness that befell the author after taking a morning cup of coffee, on 3 July 1762. His physicians attributed it to imperfectly washed strawberries consumed the night before, but Heerkens himself is convinced that the poison entered his body through a stowaway spider in the – for him – unwonted beverage. Another longish poem tells the intriguing story of a homeless, leprous girl he had encountered abroad, and apparently fed and nursed back to health, 'on account of her [Ovidian] fatherland, Sulmona' ('A me cumque cibum leprosa

---

[59] There are several caveats against cheese consumption in Book 1, notable among which is the observation of Heerkens's compatriot, the famous microscopist, Swammerdam: 'All cheese has worms, and if they were visible they would strike fear into those for whom cheese is an established food' ('Caseus omnis habet vermes, visique pavorem / Incuterent, quibus est caseus esca vetus', 1, 94)!

[60] 'Piscivoros nimium, plerumque hydrope perisse, / Plus aliâ ostendit patria terra mihi. / Hocque cibo piscator abusus, hydropicus ut fit, / Aque aqueo juvenis frigore saepe perit' (2, 134).

ibi virgo rogasset, / Sulmonem ob patriam visa et alenda fuit', 6, 150). Ovid himself proves a source of medical wisdom in a poem, 'the Author to Zacuto on a treatment indicated by Ovid in the *Fasti*'. Smearing thick mud over the sting of an African bee alleviates the pain and prevents swelling: 'and this remedy, not well known, was indicated by a very ancient author, who has not won the respect he deserves even though he has been read continuously' ('Hancque ostendit opem male notam pervetus author, / Haud meritus, legitur quamlibet usque, fidem', 5, 138).

As for the literary value of Heerkens's epigrams, the Baconian tetrastich with which the sixth book opens, stands out for its delicacy of sentiment:

> Vere vides ut jam folia aestu a principe sylvis
>   Decidere, et pueris vix data vita perit.
> Villicus haud caveat foliis, sed cura parentum
>   Haud soboli invigilans, quod misereris, habet.

> In spring, as you already see early summer's leaves falling from the trees, the life which has scarcely been given to young boys also fails. The overseer may not care about leaves, but the oversight of parents not watching over their offspring will give you cause for regret.

And sometimes, to be sure, the carefully crafted syntax of a poem serves to clarify its content, sharpening it for the memory: 'The hypochondriac, shunning all company, at the time of plague alone – and at no other – should be imitated by every man' ('Nullum hypochondriacus socians sibi, tempore pestis / Uno, et non alio, cuique imitandus homo est', 4, 57). It would be difficult, however, to claim that Heerkens's 1798 *Empedoclea* consistently or even generally combine the *dulce* with the *utile*. No witty punchline, metrical grace, nor even Ovidian 'facility' can redeem scores of terse, if not tortuous, two- and four-liners on the colour, odour and buoyancy of faeces, the loudness of farts, flatulence after sex, disorders of menstruation and testicular tumours caused by the retention of sperm. Moreover, the long, proemial poems have all but disappeared from the heads of the seven books of the 1798 collection. In this, Heerkens's last published work, the elderly doctor seems to have bowed to the Apollo of learned medicine before the Apollo of poetry. And one has the impression that, in spite of Morgagni's programmatic hope that the poet will make good the omissions of 'the Muse of Salernum ... to indicate the signs and give hope for a reasonably easy old age' (1, 2),[61] what the *Empedocles* really captures is Heerkens thinking aloud to himself as a university-trained physician rather than his best poetic efforts as a public health popularizer to enlighten the general reader. He is taking, and putting in order, a lifetime's worth of medical notes.

Heerkens has, in effect, assembled a compendium of the classical medical tradition; a *vade mecum* for the modern practitioner, to substitute for, or perhaps to orient to, the massive library of case histories, *consilia*, *observationes* and the like which a (very) late humanist physician might be expected to command – which Heerkens himself commanded. Eminent citizens of the Republic of Letters – Alsted, Comenius, Bayle and Leibniz – had voiced an anxiety about the proliferation of books, of 'information overload', already in the seventeenth century.[62] Heerkens's *Empedocles* is not arranged in the form of a commonplace book or dictionary; its entries are not ordered alphabetically, for example, by author.[63] Nevertheless, it may be seen to fulfil, in its own idiosyncratic way, some of the mnemo-didactic promises of a work such as Ephraim Chambers's *Cyclopedia*: that of 'learned abridgment' in the context of an ever-growing archive of scientific knowledge, of refreshing the memory of already skilled readers, and perhaps of piquing and directing the future study of neophyte physicians.[64]

The solemn, oracular prescriptions of the *Empedocles* are indeed a world away from the spunky, witty and sociable Ovidian persona of Heerkens's youth, but the final poem in the collection proves that the author is still identifying, in his autumn years, with the most autobiographical of the Roman poets. It begins:

> Consulat ut senibus senior, sua forte det aetas,
>
> > Conato id scitis quae sibi parta videt.

---

[61] Cf. the opening epigram of the seventh and final book, 'of the Author', announcing that 'this book is a teaching note/memorandum ['nota'], and had to be written so that I would have the salubrious doctrine for my old age before my eyes. It will also allow those who do not wish to read so many medical books to be well, and to grow old with me, and by an easy regime' ('Nota docens liber hic, scribendus eratque, senectae / Esset ut ante oculos dogma salubre meae. / Totque cui haud medicos lubuit legisse, valere, / Per curam et facilem consenuisse dabit').

[62] See Richard Yeo, 'A Solution to the Multitude of Books: Ephraim Chambers's *Cyclopedia* (1728) as "the Best Book in the Universe"', *Journal of the History of Ideas* 64 (2003), pp. 61–72; and in the same issue, Ann Blair, 'Reading Strategies for Coping with Information Overload in the Early Modern Period', pp. 11–28.

[63] Only the first edition, in fact, has a simple alphabetical index of topics (pp. xxvi–viii).

[64] Cf. Yeo, 'A Solution', pp. 68–8, 71.

Nam juvenis studui medicis, ut, qui artis ab horum
  Subsidio vitae jungere posset opes.
Et mihi tres fratres vidi, totidemque sorores,
  Arsque, inopem ob nuptam, culta necesse foret,
Bis juveni accessa, et vivo patre, Gallia, vitae
  Secius ostendit, quod placuitque, genus.
Altera enim, ac medici sors dura, spoponderat auctas,
  Accepta, et vitae suppeditasset opes.
Sed quia se modico tuita, et vario orbe, ducumque
  Ante ora, et curis sors sine dulcis erat,
Non lecta de sorte queror, studia et dedit illa,
  Cara omni à vita, sint ut amata seni . . .

Perhaps his age will permit an older man to counsel older men; someone who has tested what is in his maxims, which he sees he has garnered for himself. For, as a young man, I studied the doctors, as one who, with the aid of their art, might add a living to a life. And I saw [the arrival] of three brothers, and as many sisters, and the art must needs be cultivated because of a lack of dowries. I saw France twice as a young man, while my father was alive, and it showed me a different way of life, and one that was pleasing. For it was different from the harsh lot of a doctor, and had I embraced it, promised increased wealth, more than sufficient for my life.[65] But since a condition sustained by a moderate income was sweet, and one of travel and exchange with leading men, and one without cares, I do not complain about my choice of career, and it allowed those studies that have been dear [to me] all my life to be loved by an old man.

---

[65] Does he mean that an opportunity for ongoing employment presented itself in Paris?

# Conclusion: Notes from the Margins

## Seize and freeze, or dilate and dilute?

From his earliest, cheeky, occasional poems through to the riotous monster of the revised *De valetudine literatorum*, with all its accretions and interpolations, Gerard Nicolaas Heerkens oscillated between a desire to capture and distil his life, times and intellectual passions in emblematic Latin verse, and one to embellish and put down for the record everything that might ever be said about them – sometimes at the risk of irrelevance. As we saw in our fifth chapter, Heerkens is explicit about making such a choice in the preface to the *Aves Frisicae*. His usual metre, the elegiac, was modular, and thus lent itself well to his bipolar talents. Sometimes, notably in the *Empedocles*, Heerkens is a writer drawn to the concision of prescription, to the cryptic doctor's note. Sometimes, as in the *De valetudine literatorum* and *Icones*, the poet's telegraphic verse text is underpinned by long, elucidatory footnotes, narrative, discursive and not always to the point. But in the *Aves*, for example, the poems are allowed to speak for themselves; the endnotes function more as a flourish of scientific tail-feathers. Throughout his oeuvre, Heerkens exhibits a naturalist's or physician's eye for the minor but revealing detail – a detail that often only emerges, however, from an abundance, if not superfluity, of information.[1] His asides and digressions, his distractions, are the 'sauce' which,

---

[1] Heerkens's delightful character sketch in the *De valetudine literatorum* (1790) of the writer Prosper Jolyot de Crébillon exemplifies his habit of alighting on a small but memorable fragment of received opinion, only to refute it: 'Crébillon used a mild tobacco, one which he said the Turks used, and King Stanislaus. Nevertheless he realised it was bad for him and wished that he had not become dependent on it through use. Lavocatus [= the abbé Jean-Baptiste Ladvocat (1709–65)] writes that he took up the habit so that he could tolerate the odour of his dogs, thirty of which he was always surrounded by. But the dogs did not smell, and the author only ever counted twenty that approached the old man frequently. They were kept for the best part of the day in a very large vestibule, and were taken out at set hours by a young servant, and in the presence of their master were so obedient to the rod that he then carried that they never caused him, nor anyone else, any annoyance. He said he took in the first one or two as a gift from Saint-Évremond (whom, as a young man he often visited in London, as French secretary (? 'legato Galliae a secretis')), and that from those the family had grown, because to those born at home he had first granted life and sustenance, then his heart' (Book 3, pp. 168–9, n. 40).

as the unsympathetic Chardon-la-Rochette well puts it, is often 'worth more than the fish'.[2]

We have also observed, in the *Italica* and *Notabilia*, a somewhat tautological verse/prose reversibility; and through almost all of Heerkens's verse and prose, texts and paratexts, a tendency to recycle, to repetition verging on redundancy, especially of elements of autobiography. In making a life study out of his own literary life – and not just in that much revisited trope of exile – Heerkens resembles the writer he loved best: Ovid. He is the physician–poet forever writing his own case history, even as he takes the pulse of the eighteenth-century Republic of Letters. Heerkens's relationship with the Roman poet he had cleaved to since early childhood is one of fierce affection and loyalty, and, true to Ovid's injunction in the *Ars amatoria* to mirror the beloved's interests and preferences, of a sedulous openness to any and every opportunity for serendipitous self-identification. In his literary production, though, Heerkens does not attempt anything as obvious as an 'Ovid by numbers', consciously shadowing the target corpus as his own poetic career unfolds.[3] Moreover, Ovid for Heerkens is not so much the teller of tales or the titillating tutor in love as a learned, truthful, and above all *industrious*, writer, with eclectic passions, like his own – for antiquarianism, natural history, psychology and medicine, biography, autobiography and travel. Ovid, in short, is a friend, who anticipates Heerkens's own capacity both for memorable compression and for polymathic curiosity and literary exuberance.

## Letters to the dead ... and to the nearly dead

Worp's final assessment of Heerkens's literary achievement is, on balance, fair enough. Our eighteenth-century Dutch Ovid did not subject himself

---

[2] Chardon-la-Rochette observed of the footnotes to the *Icones*: 'les notes de ce cinquième portrait, où il décrit les ruines d'Herculanum, de Stabia, de Pompeia, et leur découverte dans le siécle dernier, ainsi que celles qui accompagnent les quatre portraits précédens, sont curieuses; et l'on peut faire ici, sans scrupule, l'application de notre proverbe: "La sauce vaut mieux que le poisson"', 'Anecdotes littéraires sur Heerkens recueillies par Chardon-la-Rochette', *Magasin Encyclopédique* an. 9, vol. 5 (1804), pp. 75–98, at p. 84.

[3] In the Jesuit Laurent Le Brun's *Ovidius Christianus* (appended to his *Virgilius Christianus* (Paris, 1661)), the *Heroides* are transformed into pastoral epistles from New France, the *Metamorphoses* into conversions of penitents, and the *Tristia* into pious lamentations.

sufficiently to the *limae labor*, a charge brought against him already by his friend, the Jansenist poet, Louis Racine. His Latin prose is convoluted and sometimes confounding. His verse can be frustratingly obscure. But Heerkens was nothing if not a compulsive communicator, a conspiratorial anecdotalist, a self-inventor extraordinaire. Thus, while his writing contains plenty of incidental detail to sustain our attention as historians of classical scholarship or of the Enlightenment, it remains primarily compelling for preserving the moving image of a late humanist life, an eighteenth-century Latinate subjectivity constructed, on the go, out of the traces of ancient and early modern literary lives.

Ovid's is only the most significant of a number of virtual friendships Heerkens sustained with classical Latin poets and historians (notably Juvenal, Horace, Statius, Livy and Suetonius). These fulfilled a similar, though not identical, function within his vocational and emotional economy as the solemn relationships contracted by Renaissance readers such as Petrarch and Machiavelli with *their* ancients.[4] Like the Renaissance humanists, Heerkens is in daily dialogue with the dead; and like them, he is still speaking to his ancients in their own language, Latin. He solicits their opinions; he defends them against their modern detractors; he scrutinizes their personal lives; he even visits some of them, in spirit at least, in the ruins of their Roman homes. Heerkens's ancients, in turn, embed him in both horizontal and vertical matrices of intellectual and emotional community (by now, perforce, deeper and more ramified than those inhabited by the Italian humanists); they are a source of consolation against his present-day mistakes and misfortunes; and, most importantly, they provide him with the stuff out of which he weaves a literary life, if not a livelihood.

To these, as it were, foundational friendships, we may add a looser layer of Latin *recentiores*, extending from Einhard in the ninth century through to the Groningen humanists (Agricola, Emmius, Alting, Gansfort), from poets Petrus Lotichius to Lieven de Meyere, S. J., to the Bavarian Jesuits commemorated in the *Iter Venetum*.[5] But the Latin-writing Heerkens never turned his back on

---

[4] On Renaissance 'conversations' with ancient writers, cf. Anthony Grafton, *Commerce with the Classics: Ancient Books and Renaissance Readers* (Ann Arbor: University of Michigan Press, 1997).

[5] *Italica* (1793), Book 1, pp. 44–8. In Munich, he strolls through Jesuit 'halls full of statues of learned men, and crammed with twice ten thousand books'; among them is 'treasure denied to my homeland'.

the Dutch vernacular classics. He felt it his patriotic and even personal duty to introduce and promote on the international literary stage Catholic poet and playwright, Joost van den Vondel (1587–1689), through whose translation of the *Metamorphoses* he may have first encountered Ovid, and Calvinist poet, moralist and emblematist, Jacob Cats (1577–1660). There is, in short, a non-trivial sense in which Heerkens's ancient and early modern interlocutors were as alive for him as contemporary writers such as Fontenelle and Voltaire, Passionei and Morgagni.

But does Heerkens himself then not verge on the madness of the bibliomane he caricatures in his Horatian satire entitled, 'in which the vain loquacity of a certain silly lover of the Muses about the pomp and furniture of his library is described'?[6] In the expanded version of this piece in his *Marii Curilli Groningensis Satyrae* (Groningen, 1758), the learned poet could almost be talking about himself when he writes of a certain reborn Damasippus[7] living among his books as among 'so many peaceful and faithful friends' ('tot placidos tot fidos inter amicos'), friends who do not give him the grief of a quarrelsome wife demanding children:

> Quae mala cunque dies fastidia nubilus affert,
>
> Et circumspicere & tacite hos perpendere, multum
>
> Delectat, crede, atque animum solatur egenum.
>
> Nunc his assideo, nunc ambulo propter, & unum
>
> Atque alium tango, nunc ordinis altera pranso
>
> Gratia si placuit, veteres sejungo sodales,
>
> Constituoque novos. Nunc dulci motus amore
>
> Oscula saepe dedi melioribus, & mihi longo
>
> Tempore jam notis: nam quo praeceptor, eodem
>
> Affectu cultuque liber dignissimus. illos
>
> Quod doceant, venerere, hos, quod docuere docentque.
>
> Sunt equidem angustae mentes, queis copia major

---

[6] 'Satyra in quâ inepti cujusdam Philomusi de librorum pompâ et apparatu, vana describitur loquacitas'. The date of the pamphlet (TEMPO #1087) is given as 1737 (when Heerkens would have been 11 years of age); the updated version in the *Marii Curilli Satyrae* (#4) reports that it was actually published in Groningen in 1746.

[7] Cf. Horace, *Sat.* 2. 3; and Cicero, *Ad Att.* 12. 29, 33: *Ad fam.* 7. 23.

Librorum officere, & discentem onerare videtur;

Sensa quis illa tamen probet? Abjectissima sensa.

Rebus in utlibus non peccat copia; num quis

Si magis est opulentus, opum quoque nesciat usum?

Whatever each cloudy day brings in the way of troubles, believe me, it brings me great pleasure to survey and silently to examine my books, and it soothes the poor soul. Now I sit next to them; now I walk by them and touch this one and that; now, after breakfast, if another charming arrangement takes my fancy, I separate old companions and introduce them to new. Now, moved by sweet love, I have often given kisses to my favourites, and those known to me the longest: for a book is most worthy of the same affection and respect as a teacher. You will venerate these ones for what they may teach you, those, because they have taught and are still teaching. There are, to be sure, narrow minds to whom it seems that a great quantity of books is harmful and burdensome to the learner. Who will approve that opinion? It is worthless! Quantity in useful things is not a fault! For what rich man does not know the use of his riches? (1758, p. 27)

Note, however, that the bibliomane's books are put on show, arranged, rearranged – in a word, fetishized. One suspects that they are hardly if ever read. Heerkens's book-lover aspires to be a citizen of the Republic of Letters, is desperate to impress the scholarly satirist, but he has no taste or discrimination when it comes to the written contents of his trophy tomes. In his *De valetudine literatorum*, Heerkens gave explicit advice on the dangers and benefits, physical and moral, of the life of letters. In the present satire, apparently inspired by the example of a recently deceased local collector,[8] he reveals by default what he considered to be a healthy relationship with books. Heerkens's friends are not his books *per se* – it is true, of course, that he amassed an enormous personal collection – but their *authors*, both living and dead, known so intimately as to be internalized, represented and to some extent incarnated in the living poet. Heerkens's is a sociable and embodied learning that demanded to be performed, in print and in person: 'How great is Menage among the learned!

---

[8] Namely one 'Entrupius [*sic*], who died in 1746, and when this Satire was first published, his library, ample and well-furnished, to be sure, was about to give rise to a famous auction in Groningen, but this Satire made it more famous and profitable for his heirs' (*Marii Curilli Satyrae* (1758), p. 33, n. 25).

And he confesses that he learned more from company than from his books' ('Quantus apud doctos Menagius! Isque fatetur, / Se plus convictu, quam didicisse libris', pp. 41–2, and n. 60).

Probably the most important network of living Latin writers with which Heerkens engaged was that of the Society of Jesus. From the German-speaking lands through France and Italy, the marginal Dutch Catholic received encouragement and practical support from and was active within an extensive and largely still flourishing *Jesuit* Republic of Latin letters. This cultural network overlapped in part with those of the various contemporary learned academies in which our author also had varying degrees of involvement (such as the Kurpfälzische Akademie der Wissenschaften in Mannheim; the Arcadians in Rome; the Académie des Inscriptions et Belles-Lettres in Paris). As the century wore on, it is true, the Jesuits were increasingly on the nose in certain quarters of enlightened Paris and Rome. But if Cardinal Bernis agitated for the suppression of the order, he was, as we saw in Chapter 2, among the earliest champions in Paris of Heerkens's efforts in that quintessentially Jesuit genre of Latin didactic poetry. Confirmed Jesuit-haters Louis Racine and Domenico Passionei never questioned their Dutch friend's choice of literary language.

The ever-spreading Latin tentacles of the Society of Jesus were, of course, the object of d'Alembert's vociferous and triumphalist disdain.[9] One can only imagine the contempt and suspicions they will have aroused in Protestant Groningen by the second half of the century. In the eighteenth century, even Latin-schooled Dutch writers were beginning to turn their backs on the classical language as a literary medium.[10] While Latin remained the *sine qua non* of university education in the United Provinces, Heerkens did not envisage a glorious future for himself writing praises and paraphrases of doctoral dissertations.[11] From his earliest years he yearned to be part of the

---

[9] But see Dan Edelstein, 'Humanism, *l'Esprit Philosophique*, and the *Encyclopédie*', *Republics of Letters: A Journal for the Study of Knowledge, Politics, and the Arts* 1.1 (2009), available online at <http://rofl.stanford.edu/node/27>, on d'Alembert's enthusiasm (and of the *philosophes* in general) for an updated style of erudition.

[10] Cf. Joost Kloek and Wijnand Mijnhardt, *1800: Blueprints for a National Community, Dutch Culture in a European Perspective* 2 (Assen: Van Gorcum & Palgrave Macmillan, 2004), pp. 105, 249, 396.

[11] A passage in the expanded second satire, 'Andreades's letter to Curillus', makes this clear (*Marii Curilli Satyrae*, p. 10). What will Curillus sing about if he does not renounce poetry? 'Should I then, if the Academy has decreed that a handsome book with wide margins be published by a boy doctor, sing with justice about rainwater, logs or walls, and congratulate the author as if he had done a service to the human race?' ('Ergo, si librum speciosum & margine lata, / A puero doctore Academia jusserit edi, / De stillicidiis, de tignis, parietumque / Jure canam, & genus humanum ut si demeruisset, / Gratuler auctori!').

international action: to use Latin verse to bring Tomi to Rome, and Rome to Tomi.

This brings us, finally, to another potential Latinate network, or cluster of networks, in which we might reasonably have expected the enlightened Dr Heerkens to operate – one which, after all, theoretically legitimized his moonlighting as poet, moralist, antiquarian and naturalist – namely, the international community of humanist physicians. But if it was a professor of medicine, Adriaan van Royen, who first set him on the path of Latin didactic poetry, and if he dedicated the first edition of his *De valetudine literatorum* to Groningen professor of medicine, Jakob Hendrik Croeser, and rendered into Latin verse precepts 'from the mouth' of such internationally renowned medical scientists as Haller and Morgagni, Heerkens's extant dealings with contemporary physicians, Latin-writing or not, were surprisingly limited. His primary Latin correspondent, Vonck, was a lawyer, as indeed were several other members of their literary confraternity. Godevard Johannes van Persyn, for example, wrote a Latin didactic poem on Roman law ('De fatis iurisprudentiae Romanae carmen') in honour of their mutual friend, Joachim Johannes Schwartz, on the occasion of the latter's accession to the Chair of Law at Groningen in 1752.[12] Though himself a J. U. D., Heerkens never seems to have been drawn to legal subjects for poetry.

## What's so enlightened about the Latin Enlightenment?

Heerkens's library of some 5,000 books included a considerable number of works by rational–theological, unitarian, anticlerical, heretical, deistic, sceptical, Epicurean and even atheist, writers, including Tindal,[13] Herbert of Cherbury, Sozzini, Campanella, Johann Crell, La Mothe Le Vayer, Toland, d'Holbach, Fréret, Werenfels, Sarpi, Isaac La Peyrère, Sextus Empiricus, Borelli, Cardano, Bayle, Gisbertus Cuper, Spinoza, Voltaire, Rousseau, Montesquieu,

---

[12] See Appendix to J. J. Schwartz, *Sermo academicus. De Finibus Critices in libris veteris prudentiae regundis* (Groningen, 1752), pp. 3–12; a poem by Vonck can be found at pp. 1–2. A 1752 letter from Persyn to Heerkens, congratulating him on his *De officio medici*, and announcing the imminent publication of his legal poem, is held in the Groninger Archives (460 Familie De Marees van Swinderen 453).

[13] A rare work in English.

Voltaire and Condorcet.[14] True, these constitute only a small fraction of the whole, which comprises an impressive collection of medical texts, naturally enough, and also of history, chronology, the Roman classics, neo-Latin poetry, lexicography, literary history, travel and geography. Nevertheless, it is clear that, at the very least, Heerkens's was no pious Jesuit *Biblioteca Selecta*, but the library of a clued-up and aspirational eighteenth-century intellectual.

What Heerkens read and what he wrote, of course, are two different matters. But if his expressed social and political views are not to be counted among the most original or progressive (or consistent) of the century, the foregoing chapters have shown him to have possessed a genuinely cosmopolitan and critical spirit. Heerkens was especially wary of claims to intellectual and moral supremacy whether in his own countrymen or in the culturally ascendant French. In matters of religion he could both praise and criticize the providers of the Jesuit education who had equipped him with the tools of his literary trade, but also with the darker religious scruples that plagued him as an adolescent. He would not be pressured by his beloved Cardinal Querini into excising from his *De valetudine literatorum* verses highly critical of Pope Paul II, the nemesis of Renaissance humanist, Pomponio Leto.[15] As a medical student abroad, Heerkens hobnobbed with the *philosophes* and maintained a mild, non-partisan Christian faith, which he seems sincerely to have believed was good for his health. He was a lifelong acolyte of the Wolffian Nicolaus Engelhard, and, probably through his publisher, Elie Luzac, came to know and endorse the philosophy of Berlin-based Huguenot author, Johann Heinrich Samuel Formey (1711–97), also a Wolffian. Heerkens was promiscuous in dedicating his own works to poets and politicians, Patriots and Stadtholders, professors and princes of the Roman Church.

Nested within Heerkens's heterogeneous circle of friends and acquaintances are key clusters of Latin writers or at least willing readers of modern Latin: Jesuits, of course; antiquarians, unsurprisingly; but also vernacular *littérateurs* such as Fontenelle, Louis Racine, Jean-Jacques le Franc, Crébillon, and, at one time, Voltaire; the cardinals Bernis, Querini and Passionei; lawyers, politicians, military men such as Vonck, Belle-Isle, van Hoey, Buonamici, Tanucci; and

---

[14] My thanks to Giovanni Tarantino for his advice on the significance of these items in Heerkens's library.

[15] *De valetudine literatorum* (1790), Book 1, pp. 71–2, n. 27: 'Although I revere the memory of the most learned Cardinal, the truth of history is dearer to me.'

professional philosophers and scientists such as Engelhard, Croeser, Nollet, Morgagni and Poleni. We are bound to ask: to what extent could a *Latin* voice be raised and heard on the stage of the *Lumières* as a voice for Enlightenment? If so, was it necessarily a voice from the wings? In Heerkens's case I think we must answer both questions in the affirmative. It is, paradoxically, the increasing marginality of Latin in France from the second half of the eighteenth century that affords him a unique position from which to critique the moral follies and cultural blind-spots of *both* the French and the Dutch – and to triangulate them in the *Notabilia*, for example, with a happy mean represented by the still largely Latin-writing intelligentsia of modern Italy. In his *Satyra de moribus Parhisiorum et Frisiae* ('Satire on the Customs of the Parisians and of Frisia', Groningen, 1750) the poet, reluctantly returned from France, rehearses a sort of dialogue with himself about the pros and cons of each country and its citizens – and cleverly sits on the Latin fence. Latin allows Heerkens to speak more freely, in certain quarters, than he might have in the vernacular. In a word, it allows him to speak stereophonically.

We should also bear in mind that Heerkens's use of Latin will have meant subtly different things to his Dutch, French and Italian, audiences. Latin was far from being a neutral and expedient 'international' language, as, for example, is scientific English today. Kloek and Mijnhardt point out of the use of French in the Netherlands at this time:

> The replacement of Latin by French as the lingua franca in [the Republic of Letters] coincided with a wave of French expansionism that was unprecedented in Europe. Many intellectuals in Germany, Britain and in the Netherlands therefore came to look on the French language as a Trojan horse with which France sought to achieve its imperialist goals, and the *res publica* concept visibly paled under the imperialist cloud.[16]

I would like to suggest that Heerkens used *Latin* as something of a Trojan horse to smuggle French (and for that matter, Italian) high-cultural medicine into a not wholly receptive Dutch citizen body.[17] But if the older *philosophes* regarded our Dutch Latin poet, mid-century, with an attitude of bemused and benign

---

[16] Kloek and Mijnhardt, *1800: Blueprints*, p. 195.
[17] See, for example in *De valetudine literatorum*; *Satyra de moribus*; *Satyra ad C. V. Vonck*; *Icones*. He was of course preaching to the semi-converted by writing in Latin; presumably he was not addressing the same 'modest crowd' he attempted to 'instruct' at the time of his abortive outing as a Dutch journalist.

paternalism, an older Heerkens will use Latin in a more confrontational way, notably in his *Aves Frisicae*, where Latin verse is laced with scientific birdlime in the (misjudged) attempt to compel the chauvinistic French to read it!

In recalling the learned of all European nations to their common humanistic homeland, Heerkens does not so much advocate a return to the ancients as, perhaps, a sort of updated and pan-European version of early eighteenth-century Dutch literary eclecticism.[18] While he evinces in his writings many identifiably Enlightenment values – belief in human progress, in the pursuit of worldly happiness, the eradication of superstition, cultural relativism – Heerkens hesitates to throw the Latin baby out with the bathwater. This is because, as he knew well from his cultural- and natural-historical researches, philology and scholarship were disciplines that could act as a brake on the arrogance and caprice of contemporary intellectual celebrity. They compelled patience and attention. In the same way, the composition of Latin verse allowed for the slow and proper digestion of both the old and the new, and the extraction of the literary and scientific nutrition necessary for the continued health and growth of the Republic of Letters.

## Bringing Ovid in from the cold

Unfortunately, as attested by the later eighteenth-century pages of the *Journal des sçavans* – the venue where Heerkens published many of his shorter pieces over some 30 years – the French Republic of Letters seems to have found Latin verse increasingly difficult to metabolise with the waning of the *ancien régime*. Heerkens's are often the only offerings. And even if he cannot be dubbed the *last*

---

[18] Kloek and Mijnhardt's characterization is again germane: 'feelings of unease about the Republic's civilization being in jeopardy sparked a revival of interest in the Dutch linguistic, literary and historical heritage, in which the crucial importance of Latin as the language of literature and of scholarly communication was emphasized. The prevailing mood is well illustrated by the attitude adopted by Dutch academics and writers in the international *querelle des anciens et des modernes*. This debate centered on the question of whether contemporary authors were preferable to those of classical antiquity. Erudite commentators in the Republic thought the question itself ill-conceived. In their country, the classics and the moderns were not viewed as opposite poles; on the contrary, the classics were ranked alongside Hooft, Vondel, and the Dutch neo-Latin poets as equally essential to Dutch cultural identity. Since the French arguments in favor of the moderns also amounted to a panegyric on contemporary French literature, many Dutch intellectuals saw the *querelle* as yet another attempt by the French to cover Dutch culture with a French gloss' (*1800: Blueprints*, p. 99).

of the Latin poet-doctors,[19] there is a note of melancholy in his transcription, in the conclusion of his preface to *De valetudine literatorum*, so fraught with reminiscences of a lost Parisian spring, of what he appears to have taken at face value for Ovid's last will and testament. We are informed that these epigrammatic verses, relayed to him by the scholar–soldier, Castruccio Buonamici, from a 'reasonably old Beneventan codex', were 'written about/inscribed on' (? 'factos in') a cypress tree which was before [Ovid's] eyes when he was lying on his death bed ('lecto mortuali jacenti')':[20]

> Arbor, inutilibus quae surgis ad aethera ramis,
> > Surgere sic saltem quae videare mihi,
> Unde meos annos, Superi si cuncta gubernant,
> > Sanctorum vincis, tot celebrumque virum?
> Spes senis est Samii, spes vita ea longa Platonis,
> > Spe nihil, et tantum, sorte beata, vides.
> Sim, quod eram, videamque rogis evanidus, orbis,
> > Quem veneror, dominum, sors erit, hora, Dei.

Tree, growing up to heaven with useless branches – at least that is how you seem to me to grow – if the Gods are in control, wherefore do you surpass my years, and those of so many holy and celebrated men? There is the hope of the old man of Samos [sc. Pythagoras], the long life of Plato gives hope. You see nothing with hope, and just so much, blessed in your fate! Let me be what I was, and as I pass away on the funeral pyre, let me see the lord of the world, whom I venerate; that hour will be a God's lot.

As Heerkens himself concedes, the inclusion of these verses was 'perhaps not necessary'; nor, for that matter, was that of the ten icons on his relatives, the Canters, with which he pads out the supernumerary pages of his effectively self-published volume. But they nicely exemplify the lure of the lapidary for our author, his instincts to bear witness and to *inscribe*, even as he was ever more resigned to the transience of his and his friends' cultural currency, and aware that his Latin literary monuments were fast falling into shadow. The

---

[19] For other contenders, see Dirk Sacré, 'An Imitator of Fracastorius' *Syphilis*: Gadso Coopmans (1746–1810) and his *Varis*', *Humanistica Lovaniensia* 45 (1996), pp. 520–38; and Brescian Habsburg poet, Wilhelm Menis, whose Lucretian *Hygea* was published in Zadar in 1847.

[20] Cf. *Tristia* 3. 3. 59–64.

most outstanding instance of Heerkens's compulsion to set the record straight, that of cramming an historical essay on Ovid's exile into the footnotes near the end of his *De valetudine literatorum*, was, no doubt, artistically ill-advised. On one level it is a bid for the author's own scholarly redemption after the mortification of his 'Tereus'; but it is also a final gesture of piety and solidarity with Ovid, Heerkens's paradigmatic man of letters, and for all times and ages. In his commentary Heerkens vents his spleen against the hated Augustus and admires the courage, prudence and equanimity of a poet who was, as he reminds us elsewhere, prescribed for boys in the Jesuit classroom,[21] but who was still capable of offering consolation and inspiration to a lonely old man.

---

[21] See his letter to the Jesuit Ignatius Weitenauer: 'Your school presents Ovid before the others, and well teaches epic, born before the elegy, after it. Choose some musical verses from Ovid, as there is much music in not a few of his: mixing these in with others, tell the boy to judge, by ear, however many verses he would approve or not for their music' ('Vestra schola ante alios Nasonem ostendit, / eposque / Ante elegos natum, post bene, credo, docet. / Versiculos aliquot lege de Nasone canoros, / Ut canor haud paucis plurimus ejus inest: / Hos miscens aliis, puerum dignosse jubeto / Aure minus quoquot plusque canore probet', *Italica* (1793), p. 234).

# Appendix

## Published Works of Gerard Nicolaas Heerkens

*Key*

Worp: Jacob Adolf Worp, 'Gerard Nicolaas Heerkens', in *Groningsche Volksalmanak voor het jaar 1899* (1898), 1–51.

Van Alphen: University of Groningen Library, The Van Alphen Collection, Dutch Pamphlets, 1542–1853, #1013–#1037A. (See Gregorius van Alphen, *Catalogus der pamfletten van de bibliotheek der Rijksuniversiteit te Groningen 1542–1853 (niet voorkomende in de catalogi van Broekema, Knuttel, Petit, Van Someren, Tiele en Van der Wulp)* (Groningen: J. B. Wolters, 1944); the collection is available digitally via subscription at 'The Early Modern Pamphlets Online' (TEMPO), <http://tempo.idcpublishers.info/>.)

√ noted but not seen by Worp; seen by Haskell

+ not noted by Worp; noted or seen by Haskell

† not seen by Haskell

Please note: I do not list here first printings in learned journals of pieces subsequently published separately.

---

| | |
|---|---|
| 1726 | Heerkens born 8 July, at Kleinemeer, to Anna Maria Meijknecht and Eppo Joannes Ignatius Heerkens |
| 1738 | Sent to study with the Jesuits at Meppen |
| 1743 | Returns to Kleinemeer |
| 1744 | Commences legal studies at University of Groningen; Jean Barbeyrac, professor of public law, dies |

| | | |
|---|---|---|
| 1746 | 23 January: wedding of Hermann Wolthers and Louise Christina Conring | *Elegia ad Magistratum Groninganum ut restituantur Academiae Professores* by 'Palladophilos', sc. Heerkens (= Van Alphen #1012) |
| | | Heerkens contributes to the Wolthers–Conring *Bruilofts-Gezangen* (Groningen: Gesina Elama), pp. 16–20 (= Van Alphen #1032) |
| | Clara Feyoena van Sytzama's *Bellingeweerder Uitspanningen* published (Groningen: Jurjen Spandaw) | Heerkens contributes to the *Bellingeweerder Uitspanningen* (pp. 50–4) |
| | Groningen literary quarrel (May–June) | Exchange of Latin and Dutch pamphlets, beginning with *Carmen Curilli cum Musis valediceret, et ad graviora studia animum appelleret* (= Van Alphen #1013–#1037A) |
| | | *Democritus Groninganus: Sermo 1* (1746?) (= Van Alphen #1085) |
| | | *Satyra in qua, inepti cujusdam Phylomusi de librorum pompa, et apparatu, vana describitur loquacitas* (Groningen: Febens, misdated '1737') (= Van Alphen #1087) |
| 1746/7 | Heerkens transfers to Leiden; enrols at Leiden University 21 August 1747 | |
| 1747 | | *Egberti Wiardii, Medici, Tumulus. Seu justa funebria, quae amantissimi praeceptoris memoriae persolvit G. Nic. Heerkens* (Groningen: Typis Cornelii Barlinckhof, Civitatis Typographi Ordinarii) (= Van Alphen #1089) + |
| | | *Elegia in Exequias Pauli Lamanni, Consultissimi, Amplissmique [sic] Urbis Groningae Consulis* (Groningen: Jacob Bolt) (= Van Alphen #1093) + |
| | | *Elegia ad Principem Auriacum . . . dedicata P. R. de Iddekinge Urbis Groningae Consuli* (Groningen: Typis Cornelii Barlinckhof) (= Van Alphen #1957A) + |
| | | *Pro Patria. Elegia. Post Praelium Lafeldense. / Elegia. Post Bergae Excidium* (Leiden: apud Petrum van der Aa) (= Van Alphen #1039) + |

| | | |
|---|---|---|
| 1748 | Justus Conring dies; Heerkens goes to Paris in the autumn | *Panegyris, de laudibus Gulielmi principis arausii . . . Reipublicae Belgii gubernatoris* (Leiden: Jean Luzac) (= Van Alphen #1101) + |
| | | *Elegia de duobus cometis pacis adventum celebrantibus* (Leiden: Elie Luzac, Jr.) (= Van Alphen #1098) + |
| | | *Xenia Physico-Medica: Accedunt quaedam Epigrammata* (Leiden: Elie Luzac) |
| | | *Frisii Poetae Elegia De adventu suo in Galliam* (Paris: typis Valleyrii) √ |
| | | Disputation on the abuse of tea, apparently defended before the Paris medical faculty (Worp, p. 14) † |
| 1749 | In autumn leaves Paris for Reims; takes doctorate in medicine on 11 September | *De valetudine litteratorum* (Leiden: apud Joannem Luzac, 1749; the same work Reims: Typis Academiae, 1749) |
| 1750 | | *Satyra de moribus Frisiae et Parhisiorum* (Groningen: Jacob Sypkes) |
| 1751 | Earliest extant letter to Vonck | 'Epistola ad Hermannum fratrem' (poem) (in *Journal des sçavans* (October), pp. 282–6) + |
| | | *Publii Curilli Satyra ad Corn. Valerium Vonck* (Groningen: Jacob Sypkes) + |
| 1752 | In the winter commences work on icons of kings of France (Worp, p. 17) | *De Officio Medici Poema* (Groningen: Jacob Bolt, 1752); verse letters to Jean-Jacques le Franc and Jacob de Bunting follow, and a iambic by le Franc |
| 1753 | | *Sermo de laudibus Ignorantiae ad. Jac. Beugel; Ictum, Sermo de Obliviis ad Luc. Hammingium; Epistola ad Fred. De Weiler Legationi Batavae apud Aulam Regis Christianissimi à Secretis, &c.* (reviewed and excerpted in *Journal des sçavans* (August), pp. 200–2) +† |
| 1754 | | *Quaestiones Medicae Parisinae* (Groningen: Jacob Bolt) |

| | | |
|---|---|---|
| 1755 | | *Eginharti de vita Caroli Magni commentarius. Cum annotationibus Ger. Nicolai Heerkens* (Groningen: Jacob Bolt) |
| 1756 | Mother dies | |
| 1757 | Appointed editor of *Opregte Groninger Courant* and *De Groninger Patriot* | 'Elegia pro Poetis' (in *Journal des sçavans* (May), p. 499) +† |
| 1758 | Father dies | *Marii Curilli Groningensis Satyrae* (Groningen: Jacob Bolt) |
| | | 'Phaleuques de Monsieur Heerkens, sur le Mariage de Mrs. Schwardz & Van Douveren ...' (in *Journal des sçavans* (June), pp. 174–5) + |
| 1759 | Commences journey to Italy in September | *Seditiosae insolentiae per noctem Groningae, intra 22 et vigesimum tertium Februarii diem commissae detestatio* (Groningen: Jacob Sypkes) † |
| | | 'Sisinnio suo' (on Heerkens's near-poisoning after drinking from a copper vessel) (in *Bibliothèque des Sciences et des Beaux-Arts* (Jan/Feb/March), pp. 239–40) + |
| 1760 | Commences homeward journey in September | *Iter Venetum ad Illustrissimum Virum, Comitem Ottonem Fred. de Lynden Dominum in Voorst...* (Venice: Jo. Baptistae Pasquali, 1760) |
| | | Unauthorized abridged version (Utrecht: Henry Spruit, 1760) + † |
| 1762 | | Ger. Nicolai Herquenii Arcad. Socii, et Acad. Reg. Paris. Liter. Et Antiq. Legati, *Italicorum liber unus* (Groningen: Jacob Bolt) |
| 1764 | | 'Portraits de quelques Peintres Hollandois par M. Heerkens, de Clenemur': 'Petrus van Laar', 'Joannes Stenius', 'David Tenierus', 'Joannes Breugel' (elegiac poems in *Journal des sçavans* (December), pp. 464–7) + |

| | | |
|---|---|---|
| 1765 | Engelhard dies | 'Memoriae Nicolai Engelhardi ... Elegia' (in *Journal des sçavans* (August), pp. 262–4) + |
| | | Gerardi Heerkens Clenemerii, Arcad. Roman. Et Corton. Socii, Acad. Reg. Paris. Liter. Et Antiq. Legati *Notabilia libri II* (Groningen: Henry Vechner) |
| 1767 | | *Anni Rustici Januarius* (Groningen) † (a ghost?) The poem is printed in full in the *Nova acta eruditorum* (May), 1766/7, pp. 234–40) + |
| 1768 | Vonck dies | 'Januarius' (in *Journal des sçavans* (January), pp. 304–8] + |
| | | 'Februarius' (in *Journal des sçavans* (May), pp. 561–6) + |
| | | 'Phillidis Catellae Epitaphium' and 'Phillis Catella, de genere mortis suae' (in *Journal des sçavans* (October), p. 286) + |
| | | 'Martius' (in *Journal des sçavans* (October), pp. 281–6) + |
| 1769 | Founding of the Zeeuws Genootschap der Wetenschapen | 'Aprilis' (in *Journal des sçavans* (March 1771), pp. 256–64) + |
| 1770 | | Gerardi Heerkens Arcadum Romanor. Acad. Corton. Et Societ. Vlissing Socii, Acad. Reg. Paris. Liter. Et Antiq. Legati *Notabilia libri III. et IV.* (Groningen: Henry Vechner) |
| | | 'Portraits de quelques Peintres Hollandois': 'Cornelius Polenburg', 'Didericus et Gualherus Crabet', 'Paulus et Mathaeus Bril', 'Janus Torrentius', 'Jacobus Ruisdaal', 'Joannes Stradanus'; and 'Inscriptio Villae Palesteinae Joannis Osy, Civis Roterodamensis' (elegiac poems in *Journal des sçavans* (January), pp. 241–7) + |
| 1772 | | 'Cornix et Corvus' (in *Journal des sçavans* (July), pp. 552–7) + |
| 1774 | | 'Turtur' (in *Journal des sçavans* (March), pp. 493–8) + |

| | | |
|---|---|---|
| 1775 | | 'Ciconia' (in *Journal des sçavans* (January), pp. 250–61) + |
| 1776 | | *Eppii Lucumonis Annalium Foederati Belgii Liber Primus, ab origine tumultuum ad usque inducias historiam foederati Belgii comprehendens* (Rotterdam: Iuxta exemplar Venetum Typis Jacobi Bronkhorstii) √ |
| | | 'Passer' and 'Lectori Avium Suarum' (in *Journal des sçavans* (January), pp. 211–23) + |
| 1778 | | 'In Obitum Petri Burmanni Secundi' (in P. Burmanni Secundi, *Carminum Appendix* (Leiden, 1779), pp. 53–4) + |
| 1779 | | 'Fringilla' [*sic*] (in *Journal des sçavans* (April), pp. 219–25) + |
| 1780 | | 'Epitaphium Catellae' (in *Journal des sçavans* (October), p. 259) +† |
| 1781 | | 'Elegia de Aquâ Plantis Saluberrimâ' (in *Journal des sçavans* (May), pp. 496–502) + |
| 1783 | Sends copy of *Empedocles* to Ignatius Weitenauer, who repays him with MS of the 'Tereus' | Ger. Nicolai Heerkens complurium Academiarum Socii, *Empedocles libri quinque* (Groningen: Henry Vechner) |
| | | *In obitum nobilissimi consultissimi fidelissimi viri Lucae Hammink Domini in Lellens, Jurisconsulti, et juratorum magistratus socii. Elegia.* (Groningen: Vechner) (= Van Alphen #1527) |
| 1784 | Adam Widder dies, described by Heerkens in his one-page epitaph as a Leibnizian, and 'a friend for 40 years' | *Piae Memoriae Doctissimi Celeberrimi Animique Dotibus Egregii Viri F. Adami Widder Heidelbergensis In Acad. Groning. Prof. Publ.* (n. l.) + |
| 1787 | | Ger. Nicolai Heerkens Groningani, academiarum complurium socii, *Icones* (Utrecht: apud Bartholomeum Wild, Bibliopolam; the same edition Paris: apud B. Dusaulchoi, Bibliopolam) |

| | |
|---|---|
| 1788 | *Aves Frisicae* (Rotterdam: C. R. Hake) (Worp dates to 1787) |
| 1790 | Ger. Nicolai Heerkens complurium academiarum socii, *De valetudine literatorum libri iii* (Groningen: Vechner's Widow) |
| 1791 | *Johanni van Hoorn, nobilissimo, doctissimo, amplissimo viro ... threnus exsequialis* (Groningen: Jacob Bolt) √ |
| 1793 | Ger. Nicolai Heerkens complurium academiarum socii, *Italicorum libri iii* (Groningen: Vechner's Widow) |
| 1797 | *Icon Joannis Sibenii Trip* (Groningen: Vechner's Widow) |
| 1798 | Ger. Nicolai Heerkens complurium academiarum socii, *Empedocles. Sive Physicorum Epigrammatum libri septem* (Groningae: Vechner's Widow) |
| 1801 | Heerkens dies aged 75 |

# Bibliography

For Heerkens's published works please consult the Appendix.

## Manuscript sources

*Alkmaar Regional Archives*
  17.3.11/ 608 Album Amicorum van Arnoldus Kulenkamp, 1741–52.

*Biblioteca Civica Queriniana (Brescia, Italy)*
  Carteggi Queriniani: MS E.IV.8 cc. 25r–26v.

*Groninger Archives (Groningen, The Netherlands)*
  465/112 – Familie Trip, epitaph for Lucas Trip, after 1783.
  460/453 – Familie De Marees van Swinderen, letter to Heerkens by Persyn, 1752.

*Historisch Centrum Overijssel (Zwolle, The Netherlands)*
  1493/64 – Familie Heerkens, letter from Heerkens to parents, c. 1748.
  1493/75 – Familie Heerkens, autograph of 'Frisii Poetae Elegia ..', 1748.

*Houghton Library, Harvard University*
  *69M-91 – Racine to Heerkens, 8 March 1750.

*Koninklijke Bibliotheek (National Library of the Netherlands, The Hague)*

74 B2 – two letters from H. van Wijn to Heerkens, 30 April 1791 and 18 November 1791?

74 D9 – two letters from Heerkens to C. Saxe, 6 March 1787 and undated.

78 J1 – 'Album Amicorum G. van Doeveren', c. 1753.

132 G40 – 'Album Amicorum E. P. van Visvliet', c. 1762.

393 D16 – *Curilli Juvenilia*, convolute of printed poems with MS notes by Heerkens (middle of the eighteenth century).

767 B15 – convolute of printed poems (middle of the eighteenth century).

*Museum Meermanno-Westreenianum (The Hague, The Netherlands)*

S 128 IV / 401/13–14 – letter from G. N. Heerkens to P. B. van Damme.

S 95:16 / 242/265–/573 – six letters from G. N. Heerkens to Johan Meerman (1773–96).

*Tresoar: Fries Historisch en Letterkundig Centrum (Leeuwarden, The Netherlands)*

A 1330 – 'Vita Petri Lotichii' by Heerkens, bound with author's copy of *Poëmata Petri Lotichii Secundi Solitariensis* (Leipzig, 1580), 2nd half of eighteenth century.

*University of Groningen Library*

uklu RACINE – Racine to Heerkens, 8 September 1750, 1 October 1750 and 15 November 1750.

## Printed primary literature

Bakker, Pieter Huisinga, *Poëzy*, 3 vols, Amsterdam, 1773–90.

Barthélemy, Jean-Jacques, *Voyage du jeune Anacharsis en Grèce dans le milieu du IVe siècle*, Paris, 1788.

Bartholin, Thomas, *De peregrinatione medica*, Copenhagen: 1674.

Bèze, Theodore, *Icones, id est verae imagines virorum doctrina simul et pietate illustrium ... quibus adiectae sunt nonnullae picturae quas Emblemata vocant*, Geneva, 1580.

Bianchi, Giovanni, *De conchis minus notis liber*, 1739; 2nd edn, 1760.

Brisson, Mathurin-Jacques, *Ornithologie, ou Méthode contenant la Division des Oiseaux en Ordres, Sections, Genres, Espèces et leur Variétés*, Paris, 1760.

Brucker, Jacobus, *Historia critica Philosophiae*, 5 vols, Leipzig, 1733–63.
Buffon, Georges Louis Leclerc, *Histoire naturelle des oiseaux*, 10 vols, Paris, 1771–86.
Buonamici, Castrucci, *De rebus ad Velitras gestis Commentarius ad Trojanum Aquavivum Aragonium S. R. E. Principem Cardinalem*, ed. Cornelius Valerius Vonck, Amsterdam, 1748.
—, *Commentariorum libri tres de Bello Italico*, Leiden, 1750 and 1751.
Capmartin de Chaupy, Bertrand, *Découverte de la maison de campagne d'Horace*, 3 vols, Rome, 1767–9.
*Catalogus bibliothecae: quam reliquit Gerardus Nicolaus Heerkens*, Groningen, 1805.
Coler, Johannes, *Oeconomia ruralis et domestica*, Wittemberg, 1593–1605.
Corneille, Pierre, *Othon*, [Frankfurt?], 1664.
Correr, Gregorio, *Progne*, ed. and trans. Gary Grund, *Humanist Tragedies*, Cambridge, MA, 2011, pp. 110–87.
Crinito, Pietro, *De poetis Latinis*, Florence, 1505.
D'Alembert, Jean le Rond, *Œuvres de d'Alembert*, 5 vols, Paris, 1821–2.
De' Crescenzi, Pietro, *Liber ruralium commodorum*, Augsburg, 1471.
Duclos, Charles Pinot, *Considérations sur les moeurs de ce siècle*, 1751.
Egnazio, Giovanni Battista, *De Caesaribus*, Venice, 1519.
Eschinardi, Francesco, S. J., *Descrizione di Roma e dell'agro romano*, Rome, 1750.
Falete, Girolamo, *De bello Sicambrico libri IV; praemissa est epistola Cornelii Valerii Vonck ad virum illustrem Janum de Back*, Nijmegen, 1749.
Ferrari, Guido, S. J., *De politica arte oratio . . . nunc primum edita curante Cornelio Valerio Vonck*, Nijmegen, 1750.
Frisch, Johann Leonhard, *Vorstellung der Vögel Deutschlandes und beyläufig auch einiger Fremden; nach ihren Eigenschaften beschrieben*, Berlin, [1733]–63.
Gerdil, Giacinto Sigismondo, *Réflexions sur la théorie & la pratique de l'éducation contre les principes de M. Rousseau*, Turin, 1763.
Gesner, Conrad, *Historiae animalium*, 5 vols, Zurich, 1551–87.
Hoeufft, Jacob Hendrik, *Parnassus Latino-Belgicus: sive plerique e poëtis Belgii Latinis epigrammate atque adnotatione illustrati*, Amsterdam; Breda, 1819.
Home, Francis, *Principia Medicinae*, Edinburgh, 1758.
Hondius, Hendrick, the Elder, *Pictorum aliquot celebrium, præcipué Germaniæ Inferioris, effigies*, The Hague, 1610.
Jourdan, Antoine-Jacques-Louis, *Dictionnaire des sciences médicales*, Paris, 1820–5.
Klotz, Christian Adolph, 'Elogium Cornelii Valerii Vonckii', *Acta Litteraria* 6 (1771), pp. 54–67.
Lampsonius, Dominicus, *Pictorum aliquot celebrium Germaniae inferioris effigies*, Antwerp, 1572.
Landívar, Rafael, S. J., *Rusticatio Mexicana*, Bologna, 1782.
La Sante, Gilles Anne Xavier de, S. J., *Ferrum*, Nyon, 1707.

— (ed.), *Musae rhetorices*, Paris, 1732.

Le Brun, Laurent, S. J., *Ovidius Christianus*, in his *Virgilius Christianus*, Paris, 1661.

Le Franc, Jean-Jacques, *Didon*, Paris, 1734.

—, *Lumières voilées: Oeuvres choisies d'un magistrat chrétien du XVIIIe siècle*, ed. Theodore E. D. Braun and Guillaume Robichez, Saint-Etienne: Publications de l'Université de Saint-Etienne, 2007.

—, *Poésies sacrées et philosophiques, tirées des livres saints . . . Nouvelle édition, considérablement augmentée [suivie de l'Examen des poésies sacrées, du marquis de Mirabeau]*, 1734; new edn Paris, 1763.

Lévesque de Pouilly, Louis-Jean, *Théorie des sentimens agréables Ou, a près avoir indiqué les règles que la Nature suit dans la distribution du plaisir, on établit les principes de la theologie naturelle & ceux de la philosophie morale*, Geneva, 1747.

Lipsius, Justus, *Politica*, ed. Jan Waszink, Assen: Van Gorcum, 2004.

Martinet, Jan Floris, *Katechismus der Natuur*, Amsterdam, 1777–9.

Menis, Wilhelm, *Hygea de arte bene diuque vivendi liber primus*, Zadar, 1847.

Meurs, Johannes van, *Icones, elogia ac vitæ professorum Lugdunensium apud Batavos*, Leiden, 1613.

Misson, Maximilien, *Nouveau Voyage d'Italie*, The Hague, 1702.

Noceti, Carlo, S. J., *Iris*, Venice, 1729.

—, *Aurora borealis*, Rome, 1747.

Olina, Giovanni Pietro, *Uccelliera, overo, Discorso della natura e proprietà di diversi uccelli*, Rome, 1622.

Oudin, François, S. J., *Poemata didascalica*, 3 vols, Paris, 1749.

Platner, I. Z., *De morbis ex immunditiis*, Leipzig, 1731.

Polignac, Melchior de, *Anti-Lucretius sive de Deo et Natura*, Paris, 1747.

Racine, Louis, *La Religion*, Paris, 1742.

Reusner, Nicolaus, *Icones sive imagines viuae, literis claris virorum, Italiae, Graeciae, Germaniae, Galliae, Angliae, Ungariae*, Basel, 1589.

Sannazaro, Jacopo, *Latin Poetry*, trans. Michael C. J. Putnam, Cambridge, MA: Harvard University Press, 2009.

Santorio, Santorio, *De statica medicina*, Venice, 1614.

Schwenckfeld, Caspar, *Therio-Trophevm Silesiae: In qvo Animalium, hoc est Qvadrupedum, Reptilium, Avium, Piscium, Insectorum natura, vis & usus sex libris perstringuntur*, Liegnitz, 1603.

Sytzama, Clara Feyoena van, *Bellingeweerder Uitspanningen . . . Benevens een voorrede en aanhangsel, betreffende het doorlugtigste huis van Orange en Nassau*, Groningen, 1746.

Trip, Lucas, *De Bescheiden Hekeldichter*, 1746.

—, *Tydwinst in ledige uuren, of Proeven van stigtelyken aandagt, door M. L. 2e en verbeterde druk*, 1764; Leiden, 1774.

The Van Alphen Collection, Dutch Pamphlets, 1542–1853, #1013–#1037A (catalogued in Gregorius van Alphen, Catalogus der pamfletten van de bibliotheek der Rijksuniversiteit te Groningen 1542–1853) (niet voorkomende in de catalogi van Broekema, Knuttel, Petit, Van Someren, Tiele en Van der Wulp), Groningen: J. B. Wolters, 1944.

Van Royen, Adriaan, *Carmen elegiacum de Amoribus et Connubiis Plantarum*, Leiden, 1732.

*Verhandelingen uitgegeven door het Zeeuwsch Genootschap der Wetenschappen te Vlissingen*, Middelburg, 1769.

Vida, Marco Girolamo, *Bombyces*, Rome, 1527.

Vonck, Cornelis Walraven, *Meditatio politico-historica de felici integritatis ac prudentiae in historia temperamento*, Utrecht, 1764.

Wieling, Abraham, *Mercurii Stygii Iter Subterraneum sive Adriani Hardy Somnium, et alia cum commentariis perpetuis*, Oneiropoli, [s. a.].

Zinanni, Giuseppe, *Delle uova e dei nidi degli uccelli*, Venice, 1737.

Zwinger, Theodor, *Icones aliquot clarorum virorum Germaniae, Angliae, Galliae, Ungariae. Cum elogis*, Basel, 1589.

## Secondary literature

Agnati, Ulrico, *Per la storia romana di Urbino e Pesaro*, Rome: L'Erma di Brettschneider, 1999.

Akkerman, Fokke, Gerda C. Huisman and A. J. Vanderjagt (eds), *Wessel Gansfort (1419–1489) and Northern Humanism*, Leiden: Brill, 1993.

Allen, Christopher, 'Boileau's Art poétique Latinized', in Yasmin Haskell and Juanita Feros Ruys (eds), *Latinity and Alterity in the Early Modern Period*, Tempe, AZ: ACMRS, 2010, pp. 79–96.

Ammann-Bubenik, Johannes, 'Kaierserien und Habsburgergenealogien – eine poetische Gattung', in Manuel Baumbach (ed.), *Tradita et inventa: Beiträge zur Rezeption der Antike*, Heidelberg: C. Winter, 2000, pp. 73–89.

Anema, Seerp, *Een vergeten dichteres uit de achttiende eeuw* (Clara Feyona van Sytzama), Amsterdam: P. N. van Kampen, 1921.

Baar-de Weerd, Claudette, *Vrouwen en genootschappen in Nederland en in ons omringende landen (1750–1810)*, Hildershum: Verloren, 2009.

Baldwin, Barry, 'Johnson's Conglobulating Swallows', *Notes and Queries* (1994), pp. 199–206.

Barber, B. R. and J. Forman, 'Introduction to Jean-Jacques Rousseau's "Preface to Narcisse"', *Political Theory* 6 (1978), pp. 537–42.

Berkel, Klaas van, 'Science in the Service of the Enlightenment: 1700-1795', in Klaas van Berkel, Albert van Helden and Lodewijk Palm (eds), *A History of Science in the Netherlands: Survey, Themes and Reference*, Leiden: Brill, 1999, pp. 68-94.

Berrigan, J. R. and G. Tournoy, 'Gregorii Correri Venetae Tragoedia cui titulus Progne: A Critical Edition and Translation', *Humanistica Lovaniensia* 29 (1980), pp. 13-99.

Bertucci, Paola, *Viaggio nel paese delle meraviglie: scienza e curiosità nell'Italia del Settecento*, Turin: Bollati Boringhieri, 2007.

Bierens de Haan, J. A., *De Hollandsche Maatschappij der Wetenschappen 1752-1952*, 1952; repr. Haarlem: H.D. Tjeenk Willink, 1970.

Bireley, Robert, *The Counter-Reformation Prince: Anti-Macchiavellianism or Catholic Statecraft in Early Modern Europe*, Chapel Hill: University of North Carolina Press, 1990.

Blair, Ann, 'Reading Strategies for Coping with Information Overload in the Early Modern Period', *Journal of the History of Ideas* 64 (2003), pp. 11-28.

Boeseman, M. and W. de Ligny, *Martinus Houttuyn (1720-1798) and his Contributions to the Natural Sciences, with Emphasis on Zoology*, Leiden: National Museum of Natural History, 2004.

Bots, Hans and Françoise Waquet, *La République des Lettres*, Paris: Belin, 1997.

Brockliss, Laurence, 'Medical Education and Centres of Excellence in Eighteenth-Century Europe: Towards an Identification', in Ole Peter Grell, Andrew Cunningham and Jon Arrizabalaga (eds), *Centres of Medical Excellence? Medical Travel and Education in Europe: 1500-1789*, Aldershot: Ashgate, 2010, pp. 17-46.

Bruinvis, C. W., 'Album van Arnoldus Kulenkamp. De dichteres Clara Feyoena van Sytzama', *De navorscher* 54 (1904), pp. 389-94.

Burke, Peter, 'Tacitism, Scepticism, and Reason of State', in J. H. Burns (ed.), *The Cambridge History of Political Thought 1450-1700*, Cambridge: Cambridge University Press, 1991, pp. 479-98.

—, *Languages and Communities in Early Modern Europe*, Cambridge: Cambridge University Press, 2004.

—, 'Translations into Latin in Early Modern Europe', in Peter Burke and Ronnie Hsia (eds), *Cultural Translation in Early Modern Europe*, Cambridge: Cambridge University Press, 2007, pp. 65-80.

Bury, Emmanuel (ed.), *Tous vos gens à Latin: Le latin, langue savante, langue mondaine (XIVe-XVIIe siècles)*, Geneva: Droz, 2005.

Campanelli, Maurizio, 'Settecento Latino I', *L'Ellisse. Studi storici di letteratura italiana* 2 (2007), pp. 99-133.

—, 'Settecento Latino II', *L'Ellisse. Studi storici di letteratura italiana* 3 (2008), pp. 85-110.

—, 'Theories and Polemics on Language', in M. Wyatt (ed.), *The Cambridge Companion Guide to the Italian Renaissance*, Cambridge: Cambridge University Press, forthcoming.

—, 'Una satira sull'architettura tra Piranesi e Winckelmann', *Atti e Memorie dell'Arcadia*, n.s. 1 (forthcoming).

Catana, Leo, 'The Concept "System of Philosophy": The Case of Jacob Brucker's Historiography of Philosophy', *History and Theory* 44 (2005), pp. 72–90.

Chardon-la-Rochette, Simon, 'Anecdotes littéraires sur Heerkens recueillies par Chardon-la-Rochette', *Magasin Encyclopédique* an. 9, vol. 5 (1804), pp. 75–98.

Dainville, François de, S. J., *L'Education des jesuites: XVIe–XVIIIe siècles*, ed. Marie-Madeleine Compere, Paris: Editions de Minuit, 1978.

Daston, Lorraine, 'The Ideal and the Reality of the Republic of Letter in the Enlightenment', *Science in Context* 4 (1991), pp. 367–86.

Dibon, Paul and Françoise Waquet, *Johannes Fredericus Gronovius: pèlerin de la République des Lettres: recherches sur le voyage savant au XVIIè siècle*, Geneva: Droz, 1984.

Edelstein, Dan, 'Humanism, l'Esprit Philosophique, and the Encyclopédie', *Republics of Letters: A Journal for the Study of Knowledge, Politics, and the Arts* 1.1 (2009), available online at <http://rofl.stanford.edu/node/27>.

Eijnatten, Joris van, *Liberty and Concord in the United Provinces: Religious Toleration and the Public in the Eighteenth-Century Netherlands*, Leiden: Brill, 2003.

Findlen, Paula, *Possessing Nature: Museums, Collecting, and Scientific Culture in Early Modern Italy*, Berkeley: University of California Press, 1994.

Fischer, K.-D., 'Medici poetae de sanitate conservanda', *Vox Latina* 42 (fasc. 94) (1988), pp. 472–85.

Fleischer, Manfred P., 'The First German Agricultural Manuals', *Agricultural History* 33 (1981), pp. 1–15.

Ford, Philip, 'Claude Quillet's Callipaedia (1655): Eugenics Treatise or Pregnancy Manual?' in Yasmin Haskell and Philip Hardie (eds), *Poets and Teachers: Latin Didactic Poetry and the Didactic Authority of Latin Poet from the Renaissance to the Present*, Bari: Levante Editori, 1999, pp. 125–39.

Frijhoff, Willem and Marijke Spies (eds), *Dutch Culture in a European Perspective: 1650, Hard-Won Unity*, Houndmills: Palgrave Macmillan, 2004.

Frischer, Bernard D. and Iain Gordon Brown, *Allan Ramsay and the Search for Horace's Villa*, Aldershot: Ashgate, 2001.

Fucilla, J. G., 'An Italian Letter by Voltaire', *Modern Language Notes* (1955), pp. 424–6.

Goldgar, Ann, *Impolite Learning: Conduct and Community in the Republic of Letters, 1680–1750*, New Haven: Yale University Press, 1995.

Grafton, Anthony, *Commerce with the Classics: Ancient Books and Renaissance Readers*, Ann Arbor: University of Michigan Press, 1997.

—, *Bring out Your Dead: The Past as Revelation*, Cambridge, MA: Harvard University Press, 2002.

Graziosi, Elisabetta, 'Revisiting Arcadia: Women and Academies in Eighteenth Century Italy', in Paula Findlen, Wendy Wassyng Roworth and Catherine M. Sama (eds), *Italy's Eighteenth Century: Gender and Culture in the Age of the Grand Tour*, Stanford: Stanford University Press, 2009, pp. 103–24.

Haskell, Yasmin, 'Work or Play? Latin "Recreational" Georgic Poetry of the Italian Renaissance', *Humanistica Lovaniensia* 48 (1999), pp. 132–59.

—, *Loyola's Bees: Ideology and Industry in Jesuit Latin Didactic Poetry*, Oxford: Oxford University Press, 2003.

—, 'A Dutch Doctor's Observations on the Health of Scholars Young and Old: Gerard Nicolaas Heerkens' *De valetudine litteratorum* (Leiden and Reims, 1749; Groningen 1790)', in Maria Berggren and Christer Henriksén (eds), *Miraculum eruditionis: Neo-Latin Studies in Honour of Hans Helander*, Uppsala: Uppsala Universitet, 2007, pp. 151–65.

— (ed.), *Diseases of the Imagination and Imaginary Disease in the Early Modern Period*, Turnhout: Brepols, 2012.

—, 'Physician, heal thyself! Emotions and the Health of the Learned in Samuel Auguste André David Tissot (1728–1797) and Gerard Nicolaas Heerkens (1728–1801)', in Henry Martyn Lloyd (ed.), 'The Discourse of Sensibility: The Knowing Body in the Enlightenment', Special Issue of *Studies in History and Philosophy of Science* (forthcoming).

Haskell, Yasmin and Susan Broomhall (eds), 'Humanism and Medicine in the Early Modern Era', special issue of *Intellectual History Review* 18.1 (2008).

Heeres, J. E., 'Stad en lande tijdens het erfstadhouderschap van Willem IV', *Bijdragen voor Vaderlandsche Geschiedenis en Oudheidkunde* 3.4 (1888), pp. 252–344.

Heilbron, John, *Electricity in the Seventeenth and Eighteenth Centuries: A Study of Early Modern Physics*, rev. edn, Mineola, NY: Dover, 1999.

Helander, Hans, *Neo-Latin Literature in Sweden in the Period 1620–1720: Stylistics, Vocabulary & Characteristic Ideas*, Uppsala: Uppsala Universitet, 2004.

Hoitsema, C., *De Drukkersgeslachten Sipkes-Hoitsema en de Groninger Courant*, Groningen: Verenigde Drukkerijen Hoitsema, 1953.

Hutter, Peter, *Germanische Stammväter und römisch-deutsches Kaisertum*, Hildesheim; New York: Olms, 2000.

Israel, Jonathan I., *Radical Enlightenment: Philosophy and the Making of Modernity 1650–1750*, Oxford: Oxford University Press, 2002.

—, *Enlightenment Contested: Philosophy, Modernity, and the Emancipation of Man 1670–1752*, Oxford: Oxford University Press, 2006.

Jeu, Annelies de, *'t Spoor der dichteressen': Netwerken en publicatiemogelijkheden van schrijvende vrouwen in de Republiek (1600–1750)*, Hilversum: Verloren, 2000.

Kloek, Joost and Wijnand Mijnhardt, *1800: Blueprints for a National Community*, Dutch Culture in a European Perspective, 2, Assen: Van Gorcum and Palgrave Macmillan, 2004.

Knoeff, Rina, 'Herman Boerhaave at Leiden: Communis Europae praeceptor', in Ole Peter Grell, Andrew Cunningham and Jon Arrizabalaga (eds), *Centres of Medical Excellence? Medical Travel and Education in Europe: 1500-1789*, Aldershot: Ashgate, 2010, pp. 269-86.

Laureys, Marc, 'History and Poetry in Philippus Meyerus's Humanist Latin Portraits of the Prophet Mohammed and the Ottoman Rulers (1594)', in Yasmin Haskell and Juanita Feros Ruys (eds), *Latinity and Alterity in the Early Modern Period*, Turnhout: Brepols; Tempe, AZ: ACMRS, 2010, pp. 273-300.

Laveissière, Sylvain (ed.), *Un peintre français dans l'Italie des Lumières*, Milan: Silvana Editoriale, 2012.

Lehner, Ulrich, 'What is Catholic Enlightenment?', *History Compass* 8 (2010), pp. 166-78.

Lehner, Ulrich L. and Michael Printy (eds), *A Companion to the Catholic Enlightenment in Europe*, Leiden: Brill, 2010.

Lugli, Giuseppe, *Horace's Sabine Farm*, trans. G. Bagnani, Rome: Luciano Morpurgo, 1930.

Martels, Z. R. W. M. von, 'Augerius Gislenius Busbequius. Leven en werk van de keizerlijke gezant aan het hof van Süleyman de Grote: Een biografische, literaire, en historische studie met editie van onuitgegeven teksten', Unpublished dissertation, University of Groningen, 1989.

—, 'The Colouring Effect of Attic Style and Stoicism in Busbequius's Turkish Letters', in Martels (ed.), *Travel Fact and Travel Fiction: Studies on Fiction, Literary Tradition, Scholarly Discovery and Observation in Travel Writing*, Leiden: Brill, 1994, pp. 140-57.

Michaud, Louis-Gabriel, *Biographie universelle ancienne et moderne*, new edn, 85 vols, Paris, 1857.

Miller, Peter, *Peiresc's Europe: Learning and Virtue in the Seventeenth Century*, New Haven: Yale University Press, 2000.

Moltzer, H. E. (ed.), *Hareniana: Brieven van W. en O. Z. Van Haren*, Groningen: J. B. Wolters, 1876.

Myers, Esther, 'Irish Students in the Netherlands', *Archivum Hibernicum* 59 (2005), pp. 66-78.

Nardo, Dante, 'Scienza e filologia nel primo settecento padovano: gli studi classici di G.B. Morgagni, G. Poleni, G. Pontedera, L. Targa', *Quaderni per la storia dell'Università di Padova* 14 (1981), pp. 1-40.

Natali, Giulio, *Il Settecento*, 2 vols, 6th edn, Milan: Vallardi, 1964.

Oosterkamp, Klaus, 'Sneldicht ter gelegenheid van het huwelijk van Clara Feyoena van Sytzama barones van Bellingeweer etc. etc. met de heer Van Raesfelt, heer van Heemse, Den Alerdinck etc. etc.', *Info Bulletin Winsum* 12.3 (2007), pp. 21-4.

Pantin, Isabelle, 'Latin et langues vernaculaires dans la littérature scientifique européenne au début de l'époque moderne (1550-1635)', in R. Chartier and P. Corsi (eds), *Sciences et langues en Europe*, Paris: E.H.E.S.S., 1996, pp. 43-58.

—, 'The Role of Translations in European Scientific Exchanges (XVIth-XVIIth Centuries)', in Peter Burke and Ronnie Hsia (eds), *Cultural Translation in Early Modern Europe*, Cambridge: Cambridge University Press, 2007, pp. 163-79.

Pelc, Milan, *Illustrium imagines: Das Porträtbuch der Renaissance*, Leiden: Brill, 2002.

Pomata, Gianna and Nancy Siraisi (eds), *Historia: Empiricism and Erudition in Early Modern Europe*, Cambridge, MA: MIT Press, 2005.

Porter, Roy and Mikuláš Teich, *The Enlightenment in National Context*, Cambridge: Cambridge University Press, 1981.

Powers, John C., *Herman Boerhaave and the Pedagogical Reform of Eighteenth-Century Chemistry*, Bloomington: Indiana University Press, 2001.

Price Zimmermann, T. C., *Paolo Giovio: The Historian and the Crisis of Sixteenth-Century Italy*, Princeton: University of Princeton Press, 1995.

—, 'Paolo Giovio and the Rhetoric of Individuality', in Thomas Mayer and Daniel R. Woolf (eds), *The Rhetorics of Life-Writing in Early Modern Europe: Forms of Biography from Cassandra Fedele to Louis XIV*, Ann Arbor: Michigan University Press, 1995, pp. 39-62.

Rave, Paul O., 'Paolo Giovio und die Bildnisvitenbücher des Humanismus', *Jahrbuch der Berliner Museen* 1 (1959), pp. 119-54.

Robertson, John, *The Case for the Enlightenment: Scotland and Naples 1680-1760*, Cambridge: Cambridge University Press, 2003.

Rogge, Y. H., 'Cornelis Walraven Vonck', *Oud Holland* 17 (1899), pp. 95-119.

Sacré, Dirk, 'An Imitator of Fracastorius's Syphilis: Gadso Coopmans (1746-1810) and his *Varis*', *Humanistica Lovaniensia* 45 (1996), pp. 520-38.

Salandin, G. A. and A. Pancino, *Il 'teatro' di filosofia sperimentale di Giovanni Poleni*, Trieste: Lint, 1987.

Schotel, G. D. J., *De Academie te Leiden in de 16e, 17e en 18e Eeuw*, Haarlem: Kruseman & Tjeenk Willink, 1875.

Schuurman, Paul, *Ideas, Mental Faculties, and Method: The Logic of Ideas of Descartes and Locke and its Reception in the Dutch Republic, 1630-1750*, Leiden: Brill, 2004.

Siraisi, Nancy G., *History, Medicine, and the Traditions of Renaissance Learning*, Ann Arbor: University of Michigan Press, 2007.

Solinas, Francesco, *L'Uccelliera: un libro di arte e di scienza nella Roma dei primi Lincei*, Florence: Olschki, 2000.

Soll, Jacob, *Publishing the Prince: History, Reading, and the Birth of Political Criticism*, Ann Arbor: University of Michigan Press, 2005.

Sorkin, David, *The Religious Enlightenment: Protestants, Jews, and Catholics from London to Vienna*, Princeton: Princeton University Press, 2008.

'Sotheby and Co., notice of sale', *Cahiers Raciniens* 21 (1969), 8 November 1966, pp. 78–9.

Stancati, Claudia, '"Mais j'en écrirai en latin" Latin as an "Epilanguage" in Descartes' Philosophy', in Pascale Hummel (ed.), *Epilanguages: Beyond Idioms and Languages*, Paris: Philologicum, 2009, pp. 52–69.

Tammeling, B. P., *De Krant Bekeken. De Geschiedenis van de Dagbladen in Groningen en Drenthe*, Groningen: Noorden, 1988.

Taylor, Jean Gelman, *The Social World of Batavia: European and Eurasian in Dutch Asia*, Madison: University of Wisconsin Press, 1983.

Tersteeg, Jacques, 'Clara Feyoena's dichterkring te Bellingeweer', *Info Bulletin Winsum* (Historische Vereniging Winsum-Obergum) 12.3 (2007), pp. 11–20.

Thibault, John C., *The Mystery of Ovid's Exile*, Berkeley: University of California Press, 1964.

Tsakiropoulou-Summers, T., '*Tantum potuit suadere libido*: Religion and Pleasure in Polignac's *Anti-Lucretius*', *Eighteenth-Century Thought* 2 (2004), pp. 165–205.

Tuck, Richard, *Philosophy and Government 1572–1651*, Cambridge: Cambridge University Press, 1993.

Van Gemert, Lia, José van Aelst, Hermina Joldersma and Olga Van Marion (eds), *Womens Writing from the Low Countries 1200–1875: A Bilingual Anthology*, Amsterdam: Amsterdam University Press, 2011.

Velema, Wyger R. E., *Enlightenment and Conservatism in the Dutch Republic: The Political Thought of Elie Luzac (1721–1796)*, Assen and Maastricht: Van Gorcum, 1993.

—, *Republicans: Essays on Eighteenth-Century Dutch Political Thought*, Leiden: Brill, 2007.

Venturi, Franco, *Settecento Riformatore. III, La prima crisi dell'Antico Regime (1768–1776)*, Turin: Einaudi, 1979.

Vercruysse, Jeroom, *Voltaire et la Hollande*, Geneva: Institut et Musée Voltaire, 1966.

Vila, Anne, *Enlightenment and Pathology: Sensibility in the Literature and Medicine of Eighteenth-Century France*, Baltimore: Johns Hopkins University Press, 1998.

Visser, A. S. Q., 'From the Republic of Letters to the Olympus: The Rise and Fall of Medical Humanism in 67 Portraits', in Jan Frans van Dijkhuizen (ed.), *Living in Posterity: Essays in Honour of Bart Westerweel*, Hilvershum: Verloren, 2004.

Vliet, Pieter van der, *Onno Zwier van Haren (1713–1779): Staatsman en Dichter*, Hilversum: Verloren, 1996.

Waquet, Françoise, *Le modèle français et l'Italie savante: Conscience de soi et perception de l'autre dans la République des lettres (1660-1750)*, Rome: École Française de Rome, 1989.

Wielema, Michiel R., 'Nicolaus Engelhard (1696-1765). De Leibniz-Wolffiaanse metafysica in Groningen', in H. Krop, J. A. van Ruler and A. J. Vanderjagt (eds), *Zeer kundige professoren: beoefening van de filosofie in Groningen van 1614 tot 1996*, Hilversum: Verloren, 1997, pp. 149-61.

Worp, J. A., 'Gerard Nicolaas Heerkens', *Groningsche Volksalmanak voor het jaar 1899* (1898), pp. 1-51.

—, 'Lettres de Voltaire, de Buffon et de Malesherbes à G.-N. Heerkens, médecin et homme de lettres hollandais', *Revue d'histoire littéraire de la France* 21 (1914), pp. 188-91.

Yeo, Richard, 'A Solution to the Multitude of Books: Ephraim Chambers's *Cyclopedia* (1728) as "the Best Book in the Universe"', *Journal of the History of Ideas* 64 (2003), pp. 61-72.

# Online resources

Annual Report of the Huygens Institute (2005), available at <www.huygensinstituut.knaw.nl/wp-content/bestanden/Jaarverslag2005ned.pdf>.

*The Catholic Encyclopedia*, New York: Robert Appleton Company, 1907; 2009, available online at <www.newadvent.org/cathen/02519b.htm>.

Centre national de la recherche scientifique (France), 'L'Oeuvres de Georges-Louis Leclerc, Comte de Buffon (1707-1788)', available at <www.buffon.cnrs.fr/>.

Courtauld Institute, 'Picturing the Netherlandish Canon', available at <www.courtauld.org.uk/netherlandishcanon/>.

Croatiae auctores Latini (CroALa), Collectio electronica, available at <www.ffzg.unizg.hr/klafil/croala/>.

*Digitaal Vrouwenlexicon van Nederland*, available at <www.historici.nl/Onderzoek/Projecten/DVN>.

*Digitale Bibliotheek voor de Nederlandse Letteren* (DBNL), available at <www.dbnl.org/index.php>.

*Dizionario Biografico degli Italiani*, available at <www.treccani.it/biografie/>.

Edelstein, Daniel, 'The Super-Enlightenment', Stanford University Libraries, available at <http://collections.stanford.edu/supere/>.

Groningen Regional Archives, 'De dichtende burgemeester Lucas Trip', available at <www.groningerarchieven.nl/historie/stadsverhalen/taal-en-literatuur/de-dichtende-burgemeester-lucas-trip>.

Institut de France, Académie des Inscriptions et Belles-Lettres, available at <www.aibl.fr/>.
Molhuysen, P. C. and P. J. Blok, *Nieuw Nederlandsch Biografisch Woordenboek*, Leiden, 1911–37, available at <www.dbnl.org/tekst/molh003nieu00_01/>.
Oxford, Bodleian Library, description of collection MSS D'Orville 1–618, available at <www.bodley.ox.ac.uk/dept/scwmss/wmss/online/1500-1900/dorvilleCLD/dorvilleCLD.html>.
Tempo: Early Modern Pamphlets Online (including the Van Alphen collection), available by subscription at <http://tempo.idcpublishers.info/>.
Van der Aa, A. J., *Biographisch woordenboek der Nederlanden*, Haarlem, 1852–78, available at <www.dbnl.org/tekst/aa__001biog00_01>.

# Index

Académie des Inscriptions et Belles-Lettres (*als* Academy of Inscriptions and Belles Lettres) 27, 30, 165, 232
   secretary of 149, 165
Académie des sciences (Paris) 29, 186
Académie française 109n. 10, 155, 176n. 56
Academy of the Arcadians (Rome) (*als* Accademia degli Arcadi), Arcadians 21, 20n. 67, 45, 64, 116, 136, 181, 232
*Acta Eruditorum* (Leipzig) 217n. 40, 220
*Acta Eruditorum Harlemensium* 196
*Acta Lipsiensium see Acta Eruditorum* (Leipzig)
Agricola, Rudolph 16, 32, 40n. 27, 83
air,
   health-giving 141, 188n. 87, 207
   noxious 122n. 44, 124, 185n. 78, 186
Albani, Alessandro (cardinal) 20, 156n. 5
Alberthoma, Albert 62
Aldrovandi, Ulisse 190n. 92, 191, 197
Alps 17, 40, 61, 84n. 58, 120n. 43, 173
Alting, Gerhard 40, 58, 62, 66, 119n. 39
   in pamphlet war 42n. 33, 43–6, 48, 50–2, 53–7, 58–61, 103
Alting, Menso 32, 84
Alting, Willem Arnold 43n. 36, 76n. 20
Ames, William 201n. 8
Anacharsis 160
ancients 128, 135n. 11, 137, 149, 151–2, 156n. 4, 192, 193n. 111, 195, 197, 208, 222n. 58, 236
   versus moderns 4, 36, 39–65
   virtual friendships with 32, 229
'Andreades' *see* Conring, Justus
Angèli da Barga, Pietro 196
animals 186, 188
   GNH's feeling for 185
   *see also* birds; dogs; vegetarianism
antiquarianism 17, 20, 33, 77, 79, 82, 126, 130, 135n. 11, 138, 151, 156, 166, 217, 240

Apollo, as figure in pamphlet war 40–60, 64, 210n. 28, 224
Arcadians *see* Academy of the Arcadians
Ariosto, Ludovico 216
   Latin tomb inscription 211n. 30
   Titian portrait of 150, 153
Aristippus 143–4
Aristotle 83n. 47, 190, 194, 217n. 40
Augustus 48, 59, 64, 149, 211, 238
autobiography, GNH 6, 11, 35, 108, 119, 131–3, 162, 172, 225, 228 *see also* biography
*Aves Frisicae* 29, 151, 156n. 4, 179, 182, 183, 184n. 74, 187, 212, 227, 236

Baglivi, Giorgio 97n. 88, 205, 217n. 40
Bakker, Pieter Huizinga (pamphlet war) 43, 47, 50, 61–2
Bandini, Angelo Maria 25
Barclay, John, ashes of 153
Bayle, Pierre 160, 225, 233
beaux ésprits 79
Belle-Isle, Duc de *see* Charles-Louis-Auguste Fouquet
Belon, Pierre (*als* Belonius) 191
Benedict XIV (pope) 12, 133, 137, 155
Benedictines 22n. 70
Bentley, Richard 84, 115n. 29
Bergantini, Giampietro 72, 73n. 11
Berthier, Guillaume-Françoise, S. J. 72, 73n. 10, 82–3
Berverwijk, Jan van 81n. 40
Beucker, Ignatius, S. J. 15
Bianchi, Giovanni 19
*Bibliothèque des sciences et de beaux arts see* Hague Journal, The
biography, biographies 81n. 20, 100, 123n. 42, 166–8, 171–2 *see also* Icones; 'Life of Charlemagne'
birds 180–9, 194–6
   GNH on nature of 188, 192
   as indicators of health 186, 188n. 87

underwater hibernation 189–90, 214
  writers on 190–3
  *see also* Aves Frisicae
Boerhaave, Hermann 102, 217n. 40, 220
Boileau-Despréaux, Nicolas 4, 39, 53,
  62–3, 216
Boindin, Nicolas 88
Bolhuis, Michiel van (pamphlet war) 44–7,
  50, 55, 58, 61–2
Borch, Ole (*als* Borrichius) 191
Bornman, Hendrik G. 107
Boscovich, Bartolommeo (*als* Bara) S. J. 20
Brisson, Mathurin-Jacques 192, 194–5
Brucker, Jacobus 16
buildings 132–7, 142–3n. 29, 150 *see also*
  monuments; ruins
Buffon, Georges-Louis Leclerc 29, 186–7,
  189–90, 196
Bunting, Jacob de 11
Buonamici, Castruccio (count) 12, 21n.
  69, 22, 107–8, 119n. 39, 133, 138–9,
  144, 156, 237
Burman, Peter, Jr 84, 105, 112n. 25,
  119n. 39
Burmania, Geertruida Foek van 33
Busbequius 132

Cagnati, Marsilio 217n. 40, 221
Camerana, Giulio Vittorio Incisa di 19
  GNH's elegy to 118n. 37, 119n. 39, 121–3
Canter family, GNH's writing on 12n. 37,
  29n. 91, 237
Canter, Johan Andreas 118, 119n. 39,
  168n. 39
Capmartin de Chaupy, Bertrand 136
Cappellen tot den Pol, Joan Derk van
  der 13, 162n. 18
Capua 23, 130n. 3, 150
  GNH travels through 21–2, 124n. 48,
  126n. 53
Carafa, Giovanni (duke of Noja) 123–4n. 47
Cardano, Girolamo 217n. 40, 233
Caserta, palace at 23, 126n. 51
*castrati* 150
catacombs, visit to 147
Catholicism,
  GNH's 32, 37, 45, 48, 50, 53, 65, 69, 133,
  201, 223
  popular/associated with superstition 60,
  89, 144, 146, 171n. 50

Cats, Jacob 80n. 36, 83, 88n. 66, 100–1, 177,
  230
Catullus 6, 55, 115n. 29, 212
Celsus 60, 217n. 40
Chais, Charles 121
Chardon-la-Rochette, Simon 165,
  166n. 31, 228
children 147, 222
  theories on raising 91, 93, 176
Cicero 18n. 58, 82n. 45, 112, 138n. 19, 177,
  206, 217n. 40 *see also* Lagomarsini,
  Girolamo
Clement Augustus (elector) 15
Clermont de Tonnerre, Gaspard 162n. 21
climate, effects on character 140–2, 216
  *see also* health
Cohausen, Johann Heinrich 185n. 78
Coler, Johannes 191
Cologne 15, 111
Comédie française 8, 90, 101n. 93,
  157n. 8
Conring, Andries 35
Conring, Justus (*als* Joost) 35–7, 39n. 24,
  46, 64–5, 95
  in pamphlet war (as 'Andreades') 38n. 17,
  39, 42–5, 47–51, 53–64, 232n. 11
Conring, Louise Christina 37 *see also*
  Wolthers-Conring wedding
Contucci, Archangelo Contuccio, S. J. 20,
  73n. 11, 151
Cordara, Giulio Cesare, S. J. 20, 110n. 15,
  118, 138–9, 156n. 5
Cornaro, Alvise 104
Crébillon, Prosper Jolyot de 8, 9, 75,
  227n. 1, 234
Croeser, Jakob Hendrik 80, 233, 235
*cultus* 99, 100, 143
'Curillus' (= GNH) 6, 37, 39–64, 114, 117,
  181, 216, 232n. 11
Cuspinianus, Johannes 2, 169

d'Alembert, Jean le Rond 9n. 25, 78, 82n.
  45, 232
  attacks Latin 3n. 6, 4, 9n. 27, 86
  and GNH 27, 85–9, 91, 148–9, 195,
  231n. 35
Damasippus 61n. 80, 230
de' Crescenzi, Pietro 191
*De Groninger Patriot* 13
de Hossche, Sidron, S. J. 83

de la Croix, Charles Eugène Gabriel (marquis de Castries) 161
de Meyere, Lieven, S. J. 229
de Montgon, Charles Alexandre 128n. 56
*De officio medici*,
  dedication to Querini of 6n. 13, 11, 112, *113*, 114, 203n. 9
  Ovidian influences found in 200-6, 210
*De valetudine literatorum* 71, 74n. 12, 77-9, 84, 92, 95, *96*, 104, 167, 210, 227
  autobiographical preface 7, 9-10, 27, 31, 77n. 24, 237
  *see also* autobiography, GNH
*Dictionnaire des sciences médicales* 73
diet GNH's writings on 93, 151, 217, 220-3
  *see also* vegetarianism, health
Dioscorides 209, 217n. 40
dogs,
  anecdotes about 215n. 38, 227n. 1
  epitaphs for 21n. 69, 133
  GNH's pet 21
d'Olivet, Pierre-Joseph Thoulier 8, 71-3
d'Orville, Jacques Philippe, elegies of 112
  correspondence of 107n. 5
Driessen, Jan Pieter 62
Duclos, Charles Pinot 78-9
Dutch language 47, 63-4, 83-4
Dutch Patriot Revolt 77, 162

education,
  corruption by bad 101
  declining standards in France 175
  GNH's Jesuit 6, 60, 65, 89, 202, 234, 238
  Latin 91, 232
  overambitious parents 36, 91-2
  *see also* learning
Egnazio, Giovan Battista 168
Eiding, Eutropius 203
Einhard 160, 229 *see also* 'Life of Charlemagne'
electricity, in Latin verse 72, 73n. 11
Emmius, Ubbo 32, 229
Empedocles 215, 217n. 40, 220
*Empedocles* (GNH's) 29, 165, 213-14, 216, 218-20, 225, 227
  in preface to 3n. 7, 9n. 25, 12n. 38, 29n. 91, 31, 89n. 67, 169n. 47, 199, 210-12

*Encyclopédie* 4, 9n. 27, 78n. 29, 195, 212
Engelhard, Nicolaus 7, 39, 110, 112n. 23, 212, 234
  GNH's letters to 118n. 37, 119n. 39, 123n. 47, 127n. 54, 135n. 11, 138, 139n. 24
Enlightenment,
  French 72, 78
  Latin 1, 4, 233-6
  views/values of 5, 99, 236
epigram(s),
  GNH on genre of 212, 215-16, 224
  medical, GNH encouraged to write 7, 9n. 26, 19, 29, 72, 217n. 45, 219
  revealing beliefs of contemporary doctors 220-2
  *see also* inscriptions; *Empedocles*; *Xenia physico-medica*
Erasmus, Desiderius 58, 138, 140, 141n. 26, 206
'Erasmus Secundus' (= GNH) 39n. 24, 52, 64
érudits 79, 90, 94
Eugene of Savoy (prince) 12, 115, 157n. 5, 174
exile, trope of 11, 15, 20, 31, 68, 117, 121, 128, 180, 228 *see also* Ovid

Facciolati, Giacomo, GNH searches for 17
Fagel, François 26, 131, 179n. 63
  GNH's letters to 118n. 37, 119n. 39, 130n. 4, 147n. 36
Fermin, Philip 192, 194
Ferney, Voltaire's chateaux at 27, 88
Ferracino, Bartolommeo, GNH makes contact with 19
Ferrari, Guido, S.J. 12, 107, 115-16, 156
fish 180, 206, 223
Flavio, Biondo 21, 130
Fleury, André-Hercule de (cardinal) 128n. 56, 162n. 21, 173
Florence 25, 129
Flushing Scientific Academy *see* Zeeuwsch Genootschap der Wetenschappen
Fockens, Joannes Lucaszoon (pamphlet war) 42n. 33, 53n. 60, 58, 61n. 78, 61n. 81
Fontenelle, Bernard Le Bovier de 20, 72, 81, 104, 149-50, 211, 213, 216

Formey, Johann Heinrich Samuel 234
Fouquet, Charles-Louis-Auguste (Duc de Belle-Isle) 12, 27, 90, 161
 GNH's icon of 162, 164, 172–6
 in *De valetudine literatorum* 101n. 94, 161
Fouquet, Louis-Charles-Armand 173
Fouquet, Nicolas 161
Fracastoro, Girolamo 83n. 46
friendship, friendships 127, 178, 200
 GNH's 19–20, 88, 108, 116–17, 123, 229, 234
Friesland *see* Frisia
Frisch, Johann Leonhard (*als* Frischius) 190
Frisia 44, 64, 208
 cultural climate of 11, 31, 40, 59, 63, 67, 216
 exile to 68, 117
 poets of (in pamphlet war) 32, 42, 45–6, 50, 54, 56
Fulvio, Andrea 166

Galen 42, 102, 203, 217n. 40, 219, 221
Gansfort, Wessel Harmensz 84, 229
Genoa 25–6, 120–1, 131, 152
Gerdil, Giacinto Sigismondo 27
Gesner, Conrad 190n. 92, 191
Giovio, Paolo 166–7, 171
Gori, Antonio Francesco 211n. 31
Goths 98, 144, 145n. 31
Grand Tour 11, 117, 119–20, 131, 146, 151n. 43, 155, 159
Greek Anthology 108n. 8, 172, 212
Groningen 1n. 1, 11
 beer industry of 80
 and GNH 6, 27, 37, 39n. 21, 57, 69, 84n. 58, 105, 200
 humanists of 32, 154, 229
 and pamphlet war 49, 64–7, 89, 103
 political tensions in 35
 as Tomi 31, 123
 *see also* Frisia
Grotius, Hugo 2–3, 108n. 8, 138, 151, 168n. 40

Hague, The 27–8, 111, 119, 162n. 21, 177
Hague Journal, The 24n. 75, 119, 121
Haller, Albrecht von 217, 219, 233
Hamilton, Ezechial 7, 212n. 33
Haren, Onno Zwier van 28, 108–9
Haren, Willem van 8n. 23, 83n. 49, 118

health,
 and diet 82n. 43, 93, 94n. 85, 220–2
 and excessive study 84, 91–5, 97–8
 and insects 222
 of learned men *see De valetudine literatorum*
 *see also* climate; scholars
Heerkens, Eppo Johannes Ignatius 6, 9, 12, 36, 74n. 14
Heinsius, Antonius 163, 164n. 24, 172
Hélian, Louis 147
Hemsterhuis, Meinard 39n. 22, 40, 43–6, 49, 57–8, 62, 107n. 5
Herculaneum 22, 29, 127, 133
Hessus, Helius Eobanus 100, 16n. 37
Hippocrates 97, 201n. 6, 213–14, 217–21
historiography 12, 114, 141n. 27, 157, 161, 169
history 157, 159–60, 170–1, 180–1
 GNH's passion for 155–6, 179
 recoverable only from books 196
 writing *see* historiography
 *see also* natural history
Hoey, Abraham van 12, 162, 164, 178n. 62, 234
 GNH's icon of 177
 letter to 162n. 21
Hoffmann, Friedrich 217n. 40, 220
Hollandsche Maatschappij der Wetenschappen 196
Home, Francis 221n. 54
Hope, Henry 75
Horace, Horatian 40, 46, 50, 55, 62, 84, 120, 124, 135–6, 175, 209, 214
 d'Alembert's scorn for 148–9
 Sabine farm of 21, 136
 style 48, 58, 209n. 26, 230
Houttuyn, Martinus 186
Huusman, Roelof *see* Agricola, Rudolph
hypochondria 224 *see also* madness; melancholy

*Icones* 30, 161–72
 GNH's political views in 13, 165
inscriptions 24, 28, 94, 126n. 51, 130n. 3, 137, 149–53, 166–7, 211
insects *see* health
Iperen, Josua van (*als* 'Eripanus', in pamphlet war) 28, 48–50, 58, 61, 62n. 84, 64, 119n. 39

*Italica* 14–15, 24n. 75, 28, 109n. 14, 118–19, 126–7, 139, 162, 218
Italy, Italians 22, 52, 115–16, 118, 131, 139
  *see also* Rome
*Iter Venetum* 25, 27, 118–20, 218

Jesuits 8, 9, 12, 15, 16, 20, 21, 29, 43n. 45, 50n. 56, 59, 71–3, 82, 83, 101, 108n. 8, 112, 118, 130n. 3, 133, 138, 139n. 22, 145–6, 166n. 30, 184, 185n. 78, 189, 202, 212, 218, 228n. 3, 229, 232
  enemies of 20, 137, 23
  GNH's elegy in honour of 9, 89, 213n. 35
  *see also* education
Jordan, Charles-Etienne 18
*Journal de sçavans* 115, 179, 182, 236
*Journal de Trévoux* 9, 10n. 28, 14n. 43, 72, 74, 82
journalism, GNH's Dutch-language 13, 31
journeys, GNH's *see* travel
Juvenal 46, 50, 54–5, 59, 61, 79, 135

Keysler, Johann Georg 119n. 40, 130n. 3, 132–3, 147
Kircher, Athanasius, S.J. 20, 130n. 3, 189, 191n. 96
Kleinemeer 6
Kleinemeerian, GNH the 135, 152
Kulenkamp, Arnoldus 34
  *album amicorum* of 36n. 9, 36n. 10, 40n. 26, 48
Kurpfälzische Akademie der Wissenschaften 232

La Vallette, Antoine 137n. 17
Ladvocat, Jean-Baptiste 227n. 1
Lagomarsini, Girolamo, S.J. (editor of Cicero) 20, 73n. 11, 138
Lambertini, Prospero Lorenzo, (pope) *see* Benedict XIV
Lami, Giovanni 25
Lampsonius, Dominicus 169n. 41
Latin, language 1–4, 11–12, 78–80, 232
  GNH's hopes for 3n. 7
  GNH's tirade on decline of 85–8
  versus French 3, 27, 85, 188–9, 195
*lazzaroni* 22, 145 *see also* Naples
Le Beau, Charles 149

Le Brun, Laurent, S. J. 228n. 3
Le Camus, Antoine 98
Le Franc, Jean-Jacques (marquis de Pompignan) 8, 12n. 36, 120, 162, 234
  and the Académie française 8n. 20, 155
  and Einhard edition 155–8, 160
  GNH's letters to 4, 12, 28, 72
learning 90, 92–4
  not injurious to health 97–9
  *see also* education, pedantry, scholars
Leiden,
  GNH at university in 6–7, 212n. 33
  professors of 75–6
Lemnius, Levinus 217n. 40, 220
library, libraries 6, 17, 25, 30, 94, 147n. 37, 153
  of 'bibliomane' 230–1
  of GNH 158n. 9, 233–4
  of Passionei 20, 163
  visited by GNH 15, 16, 90, 218
'Life of Charlemagne' 12, 155, 159
  *see also* Einhard
Lijnslager, Hendrik 179n. 63
Linière, François 80n. 35
Linnaeus, Carl 191
  GNH's contempt for 193–5, 208–10
  and van Royen 7, 75n. 15
Lipsius, Justus 3, 110n. 15, 124
Livy 21, 134, 141, 158
Lorraine, Charles de, GNH dines with 28, 81n. 41
Lotichius, Petrus, Secundus 16, 112, 119n. 39, 221, 229
Lotichius, Philip 107
Lucretius 182, 184, 203, 213, 215
Luzac, Elie (publisher) 7, 14, 115n. 31, 212, 234
Luzac, Johan (printer) 75
Lynden, Otto Frederick van (count) 15, 28, 107–8, 139
  GNH sojourns with 117
  GNH's letters/poems to 19, 21, 118, 119n. 39, 120n. 43, 123, 126, 129–30, 135n. 13, 138, 148, 222n. 58
Lyonnet, Pierre 187–8

madness 89, 220 *see also* hypochondria; melancholy
Magnus, Olaus 189, 191n. 102

Mairan, Jean-Jacques d'Ortous de  218
Malesherbes, Guillaume-Chrétien de
    Lamoignon de  29, 186–7
Mannheim Academy of Sciences  174, 232
marriage,
    Clara Feyoena van Sytzama's to Isaak
        Reinder  35
    GNH's avoidance of  32, 111
Martinet, Jan Floris  196
Maurits, J. Jac.  118n. 36, 119n. 39
Maurus, Rabanus  160
Mazzocchi, Antonio  22
Mazzolari, Giuseppe Maria, S.J.  72,
    73n. 11
Mead, Richard  222n. 56
medals  30n. 95, 94, 108n. 8, 112, 167
medicine,
    GNH's sources for  217n. 40
    GNH's vocation in  5–6
    injurious to health  97
    Ovidian  200, 203, 210
    patron of *see* Apollo
Meerman, Gerard  19n. 62, 109, 119n. 39
Meerman, Johan  14, 109, 121, 152
    GNH's correspondence with  30n. 95,
        31n. 96, 107n. 5, 109n. 14, 110n. 15,
        162n. 18
melancholy  94, 220
mentors, GNH's  7, 39n. 25, 51, 80, 88,
    97n. 88, 110, 213, 218 *see also*
    teachers
Meppen, Jesuit college of  6, 15, 203n. 9
Mercuriale, Girolamo  217n. 40, 220, 222
Meyerus, Antonius  169
Meyerus, Philippus  169
Micyllius, Jacob  84n. 60
    GNH quotes from  196
Misson, Maximilien  132–3, 147
Mizauld, Antoine  217n. 40, 220
Molinari, Giovanni Carlo  155
Montbeillard, Philippe Guéneau de  189–90,
    193, 196, 214
Montesquieu  141, 159, 233
Monte Testaccio  20n. 67, 135
Montfaucon, Bernard de  130, 144
monuments  5, 18, 126n. 51, 132
    to Groningen humanists  154
    modern Romans' respect for  140–1, 153
Morelli, Jacopo  30
Morelli, Maria Maddalena  139

Morgagni, Giambattista (Giovanni
    Battista)  17, 19, 29, 75n. 15, 138,
    93n. 83, 217–19, 225, 230, 233, 235
mosaics, GNH's references to  22, 150
Munich  16, 120, 229n. 5
Munting, Abraham  208–9
museums  20, 21n. 69, 73n. 10
    Kircherianum, GNH's observations
        in  133, 151
    Paolo Giovio's in Como  166–7

Naples  22
    people of (Neapolitans)  123n. 47,
        138–9, 141–3, 145, 148
Nassau, dynasty,
    GNH's political alignment  13, 165
    stadtholder(s) of,
        GNH's dedications to  10n. 28, 14, 234
        GNH's icon of  164
        patronage of GNH  28
    supporters of (Orange party)  35
natural history, historians  72, 80, 151, 186,
    196–7
    GNH's sources for  190–2
Neapolitans *see* Naples, people of
Nijmegen gymnasium  107
Noceti, Carlo, S. J.  73, 116, 118, 218
Nollet, Jean-Antoine  8, 72, 235
*Notabilia*  18–25, 129–34, 147, 149–52,
    211, 228
    GNH's sources for  130
Nozeman, Cornelis  186, 196

Offerhaus, Leonard  112, 171n. 52
Olina, Giovanni Pietro  191
Olivieri-Giordani, Annibale degli
    Abbati  19
*Opregte Groninger Courant*  13
Orange party *see* Nassau, dynasty; *see also*
    Regent party
Oudendorp, Frans van  112, 114
Oudin, François, S. J.  71n. 2, 184n. 76
Ovid,
    *Ars amatoria*  170, 199n. 2, 204, 206,
        228
    exile of  30, 56, 59, 67–8, 76, 84n. 60, 96,
        157n. 7, 180, 238
    *Fasti*  170n. 48, 180, 217, 224
    GNH's elegy to ghost of (pamphlet
        war)  55–6

GNH's identification with 11, 31, 46–7, 51, 123, 206, 228, 238
GNH visit to gardens of 163, 179n. 63
*Halieutica* 181n. 67
*Heroides* 172, 192
  as historical and natural-historical source 182, 192, 205–6, 211n. 32, 224
*Metamorphoses* 185, 211, 230
  as model for modern epigram 216
*Tristia* 11, 15, 25, 84n. 60, 125, 215n. 38

Padua 17, 19, 24n. 75, 120, 217
painters, paintings,
  Dutch/Flemish 152, 168
  as historical sources 80n. 36
  in GNH's collection 28n. 85
Palais de Justice 6n. 14, 8
Papal States, poverty/ squalor of 22, 24, 118, 140
Paris, GNH in 7–9, 27–9, 71–2, 74, 90, 149, 216
Passionei, Fontenelle Domenico Silvio 20–1, 137–9, 163–4, 172, 188n. 87, 230, 232, 234
patients 97, 161n. 16, 200–1, 203–5, 208, 221
Patriots (Dutch) 13–14, 162n. 18, 177n. 59
  *see also* Dutch Patriot Revolt
Paul II (pope) 234
Pécheux, Laurent 21, 150
pedantry 84–5, 109, 114–15, 133, 161
Peiresc, Nicolas-Claude Fabri de 77
perspiration 93n. 83, 94, 219 *see also* Santorio, Santorio
Persyn, Godevard Johannes van 233
Pesaro 19
*philosophes* 4, 79, 89–91, 214, 234–5
physicians,
  GNH pleads for friendship among 200
  humanist 2, 4n. 8, 5, 9, 13, 15, 16, 18n. 58, 19, 71, 72n. 7, 79, 80, 83n. 46, 97n. 88, 100, 112n. 75, 138, 141, 151, 156, 167, 206, 208, 217, 218, 225, 233
  and intemperate study 92, 94, 97, 99–100
  views/practices of 85, 89–90, 103, 185, 211–12
  *see also* patients
Pierre de Bernis, François-Joachim de (cardinal) 8–9, 213n. 35

Pindus, Mount 7, 42, 44–6, 48–50, 54, 59–60, 64, 68, 77n. 24, 92, 114, 115n. 29
Piron, Alexis 8, 216
Pisa 25
Pliny 83n. 47, 124n. 48, 175, 180, 190, 194, 217n. 40, 222n. 58
Plutarch, Plutarchan 160, 171, 174
*Poemata didascalica* 71, 73, 184n. 76
poetry,
  didactic 2, 7, 7n. 17, 10, 11, 62, 70, 71–3, 74, 83, 116n. 32, 169–70, 184, 189, 198, 199–200, 204, 206, 210, 215, 218, 232, 233
  elegiac 5, 7, 7n. 17, 11, 15, 26, 35, 37n. 15, 46, 48n. 48, 52n. 59, 56, 57, 70, 71, 110n. 17, 112n. 25, 118, 120n. 4, 162n. 21, 169, 184, 199–200, 218, 218n. 44, 227, 242, 243 *see also* epigram(s)
  GNH's friends' advice on 108n. 8, 115n. 31, 119, 208n. 24
  Latin, contemporary distaste for 9n. 24, 62, 188
  satirical 3n. 6, 4n. 8, 5, 6, 10, 20, 20n. 67, 23n. 74, 27n. 83, 37–70, 81n. 42, 88n. 65, 110n. 15, 112n. 23, 114–6, 117n. 35, 181, 201, 216, 230–1, 232n. 11, 235
  as subject/figure of pamphlet war 39–55, 57–62, 232n. 11
Poleni, Giovanni 17, 217, 235
Polignac, Melchior de (cardinal) 86n. 63, 87, 190
*politesse* 99, 109n. 13, 153, 193, 200n. 4
  *see also* cultus
Pompeii 29 *see also* Herculaneum
Pontine Marshes 21, 123, 135, 222n. 57, 222n. 58
Poot, Hubertus 41, 83, 84
Pope, the 19n. 65, 24n. 76, 59, 111, 133, 138, 163 *see also* Benedict XIV; Paul II
Procope (café), 8, 74, 85n. 61, 90, 91
Propertius 46, 115n. 29
'Pylignus' (= GNH) 34
Pythagoras 185, 211n. 32, 217n. 40, 237

Querini, Angelo Maria (cardinal) 11n. 35, 18, 107–8, 115–17, 155, 205, 234
  correspondents of 108n. 8
  GNH's verse dedication to 6n. 13, 11, 156n. 5, 203n. 9

Racine, Louis 8, 9, 20, 115, 216, 229, 232, 234
　GNH advised to translate poem of 7n. 17, 213
　GNH's correspondence with 8n. 21, 110
Ramazzini, Bernardino 217n. 40, 221
Regent party 35–7 *see also* Nassau, dynasty
Reims, medical degree conferred on GNH in 10, 75, 80n. 34, 102, 200
Republic of (Latin) Letters 29–30, 40n. 28, 77–9, 80n. 33, 91, 108, 152, 161, 200, 212, 228, 235–6
　citizens of 225, 231–2
Rimini 31
Rome 19–21, 24, 73, 123, 128, 136–7
　ancient civilisation praised 148–50, 157–9, 211
　contemporary 125, 128, 132, 136–7, 140–1, 145
　GNH's writing on 98, 128, 140–1, 179n. 63
　*see also* ruins
Rousseau, Jean-Jacques 89–90, 93n. 81, 233
　GNH's outburst against 85, 91, 98, 100–1, 210
Royen, Adriaan van 7, 71, 75n. 15, 210, 233
Roze, Jean, S.J., *Aviarum* of 184n. 76, 189n. 88
ruins 17, 21, 128, 135, 144, 145n. 31, 163, 179n. 63, 229

Sabinus, George 169
Sambucus, Joannes (*als* János Zsámboky) 2, 167
Santorio, Santorio 93n. 83, 219
Sarbiewski, Kasimir, S.J. (*als* Sarbievius) 15, 17
Savastano, Francesco Eulalio, S.J. 72
Saxe, Christophe 109n. 12
Scaliger, Joseph, ghost of 82–3, 163n. 23, 168
scholars,
　diseases/health of 76n. 20, 80–1, 92–4, 123n. 46
　emotions of 95
　sex and 73, 205
　*see also* De valetudine literatorum
Schwartz, Francis Xavier, S.J. 16
Schwartz, Joachim Johannes 110, 233

Schwenckfeld, Caspar (*als* Sueveneldus) 190
Scriverius, Petrus 83
sensitivity 99–100, 216
Sharp, Samuel, GNH's censure of 148, 151
Siena 24, 25
Sijzen, Roelof Bernhard van, GNH's elegiac letters to 10n. 32, 18, 118n. 36, 118n. 37, 119n. 39, 120n. 41, 121, 179
Sinibaldi, Giovanni Benedetto 217n. 40, 220
Sipkes, Jacob 13
Slingelandt, Simon van 177
smoking 80, 83n. 51, 220, 222
　Crébillon 227n. 1
Society of Jesus *see* Jesuits
stadtholders *see* Nassau, dynasty
Steege, Jacob (*als* Jacobus) van der 3n. 7, 13, 31n. 98, 162n. 18
Suetonius 111, 160, 229
superstition 60, 89, 144–6, 202–3, 236
Swieten, Gerard van 217n. 40, 221n. 56, 222
Swinderen, Wicher van 43, 46, 62
Sytzama, Clara Feyoena van 33, *34*, 35–8, 192n. 106
　GNH's elegy for 67–8
　literary circle of 33, 37, 48, 58, 63n. 89
　references to in pamphlet war 44, 62n. 85
Sytzama, Pico Galenus van 33, 35
Sytzama, Pier Willem van 33, 36

Tacitus 98, 157, 175
Tanucci, Bernardo 119n. 39, 138–9, 234
Tasso, Torquato 153
teachers, GNH's 7, 9, 15, 71, 75–6, 80, 84n. 59, 110n. 15, 213n. 35, 234
Tenhove, Nicolaas, GNH's elegiac letters to 19n. 62, 118n. 37, 119n. 39, 121, 162n. 18, 179, 218, 219n. 52
Tibullus 41, 46, 144
Tissot, Samuel Auguste André David 91–5, 97–8, 101
tobacco *see* smoking
travel,
　boat 17, 21, 25
　coach 8, 15, 17, 21, 23–4, 120–21, 125, 131, 140n. 25, 149

GNH's Italian journey 15–26, 28, 118n. 36, 123, 127n. 54, 222n. 58
GNH's 'Venetian journey' *see Iter Venetum*
writing about/travelogues 14n. 46, 133–4, 150, 152
  *see also* Grand Tour
Trip, Lucas 37–8, 39n. 21, 40, 44
  in pamphlet war 45–7, 49–50, 53, 55–8, 61–4, 66
Trissino, Parmenio, GNH received by 17

Utrecht 188n. 36, 179n. 63
  Peace of 163

Varius, Lucius 30, 165
vegetarianism 93n. 78, 185
Velius, Caspar Ursinus 169
Venice 11, 18–19, 109, 122–3, 147, 179n. 63, 218
Verona 17, 21, 120
Vida, Marco Girolamo 184
Villeneuve, Arnaud de 90, 100, 217n. 40, 218n. 45
Villeneuve, Claude-Alexandre de (comte de Vence) 118n. 37, 119n. 39, 168n. 42
Virgil 30, 135n. 11, 182, 184, 206, 216
Volpi, Giovanni Antonio (*als* Gianantonio) 19, 217–18
Voltaire, François-Marie Arouet 8–9, 27, 74–5, 79, 83, 88–9, 148, 157, 159
  anti-Latin sentiments of 12, 87
  GNH's observations on 81–2
von Linné, Carl *see* Linnaeus
Vonck, Cornelis Walraven 10, 27n. 3, 105, 106, 107–19, 139n. 20, 174, 233
  GNH's letters to 12, 13, 28, 156, 205
  GNH's Satire to 27n. 83, 42n. 31

Vondel, Joost van den 39, 83, 169, 230, 236n. 18
Vosmaer, Arnoud (*als* Vosmarius) 191–2

War of the Austrian Succession 8n. 23, 12, 161, 173
Weitenauer, Ignatius, S. J. 119n. 39, 166n. 30, 184n. 76, 238n. 21
Wijn, Hendrik van 109n. 12
Willem IV (prince of Orange) 13, 112
Willem V (prince of Orange) 14, 28
Wolbers, Joannes (in pamphlet war) 40–1, 46, 48, 57–8, 62
  love poetry of 52, 54
Wolthers, Hermann 37
Wolthers-Conring *Bruilofts-Gezangen* 37n. 15, 43n. 36, 44n. 41, 48n. 49, 58n. 71, 61n. 78, 65, 69
Wolthers-Conring wedding 37, 38, 40, 41, 67
women,
  GNH's opinions/observations of 20, 24–6, 81, 130, 144, 150
  GNH's poems for 81
  GNH's relationships with 15, 26–8, 111, 126
  learned 25, 81, 130, 139
  medical beliefs relating to 220–2
Worp, J. A. 6n. 12, 7n. 18, 8n. 21, 21n. 69, 25n. 78, 27, 28n. 86, 28n. 88, 30, 42n. 33, 110n. 16, 161n. 15, 162n. 18, 179n. 65, 228

*Xenia physico-medica* 7, 71, 88, 205, 212–13, 218

Zeeuwsch Genootschape der Wetenschappen 28, 151, 153, 179n. 64
Zinanni, Giuseppe 191, 193

Lightning Source UK Ltd.
Milton Keynes UK
UKOW05f0239200914

238872UK00001B/41/P

9 781472 587503